HISTORY

OF THE

ANTI-CORN-LAW LEAGUE

HISTORY

OF THE

ANTI-CORN-LAW LEAGUE

BY

ARCHIBALD PRENTICE

SECOND EDITION

WITH A NEW INTRODUCTION BY

W. H. CHALONER

IN TWO VOLUMES

VOLUME II

REPRINTS OF ECONOMIC CLASSICS

Augustus M. Kelley, Bookseller
New York, 1968

Published by
FRANK CASS AND COMPANY LIMITED
67 Great Russell Street, London WC1

Published in the U.S.A. by A. M. Kelley,
24 East 22nd Street, New York, U.S.A.

First edition   1853
Second edition   1968

SBN 7146 1352 5

Library of Congress Catalog Card No. 68—21422

Printed in Great Britain

HF
2043
P8
1968
V.2

HISTORY

OF THE

ANTI-CORN-LAW LEAGUE.

BY

ARCHIBALD PRENTICE,

ONE OF ITS EXECUTIVE COUNCIL,

AUTHOR OF

" HISTORICAL SKETCHES OF MANCHESTER;" "A TOUR IN THE UNITED

STATES," &C.

VOL. II.

LONDON:

W. & F. G. CASH, BISHOPSGATE STREET.

1853.

CONTENTS.

CHAPTER I.

CHAPTER II.

CHAPTER III.

CHAPTER IV.

CHAPTER V.

CHAPTER VI.

CHAPTER VII.

CHAPTER VIII.

CHAPTER IX.

CHAPTER X.

CHAPTER XI.

CHAPTER XII.

CHAPTER XIII.

CHAPTER XXII.

CHAPTER XXIII.

CHAPTER XXIV.

HISTORY

OF

THE ANTI-CORN-LAW LEAGUE.

CHAPTER I.

OPENING OF THE FREE TRADE HALL.

The beginning of 1843 saw workmen busily engaged in erecting the Free Trade Hall, which, intended to stand for two or three years, by which time it was supposed the Corn Law would be repealed, remained standing, often used, until 1853, when the defeat of the Derby-Disraeli ministry, and the avowal in both houses of Parliament, that the principles of free trade were fully recognized there, gave assurance that agitation on the question was no longer necessary. It had been determined that the weekly meetings of the League should be continued at Manchester until they could be held with greater national effect in Exeter Hall or in one of the great metropolitan theatres, and on the 5th January the Corn Exchange meetings were resumed. The Rev. Dr. Hewlett, of Coventry, who was the first speaker, declared that he felt it his bounden duty to oppose every enactment that interfered with the communication of the Giver of all good to all mankind. The Hon. C. P. Villiers, who was most enthusiastically received, followed, and ably vindicated the constitution and proceedings of the League from the charges brought against them by the monopolists, who were now following the very

course which they professed to condemn so strongly. He
met and confuted many of the fallacies by which the
monopoly was defended, and expressed his hope of the
success of a movement which, considered in all its bearings,
in its ultimate consequences, and the peaceful relations
which it was calculated to establish between men in different climes and countries, would be seen to be admirably
designed to spread the spirit of Christianity, and to diffuse
the blessings of plenty all over the earth.   Mr. Mark
Philips, Mr. Cobden, and Mr. John Brooks followed, and
the unanimous thanks of the meeting were voted to Mr.
Hewlett and Mr. Villiers.   On the Wednesday of the same
week, a tea party of the working classes, 700 in number,
was held in Bolton, addressed by Mr. Brotherton, Mr.
Brooks, Dr. Bowring, Mr. Bright, and Mr. Moore, at
which a great number of working men came forward and
added their mites to the rapidly increasing League fund,
intended to furnish the means, at the rate of a thousand
pounds a week, for twelve months, of instructing the people
in the doctrines of free trade.

The London *Times* had not yet discovered that the
League was a GREAT FACT.   The monied interests had not
yet spoken out; and meetings of manufacturers in a room
which held only some fifteen hundred persons were held
to be indicative of no great amount of public opinion.
That influential journal—influential when it joined any
movement which had gained strength without its aid, and
was likely to be triumphant in spite of its opposition—had
found that the revenue for the quarter ending 5th Jan.
1843, as compared with the corresponding quarter of the
preceding year, had decreased no less than £940,062,
occasioned mainly by diminished consumption of articles
used by the industrial classes of the community, and
it said: "It seems to us very clear, whatever our free
trade friends may say, that any alteration which may be
made in the Corn Laws ought not to be made irrespective

of financial considerations. We cannot at these times afford to throw away a revenue." The "best possible public instructor" did not see, or, more probably would not see, until the monied interest of London saw, that the nation could not "afford" to sustain a monopoly which had diminished the revenue at the rate of a million sterling in three months. As not one single quarter of wheat could be imported at a shilling duty, without first raising by one shilling the price of every quarter in the home market, it was clear to everybody but a legislator, or a leading journalist, that a million taken for revenue could not be had without putting at least five millions into the pockets of the landowners, and diminishing, by so much, the consumption of other articles contributing to that revenue. In the very same paper which contained this argument against the repeal of the Corn Laws was a statement that flour was 30 per cent. dearer in London than in Paris.

On Thursday, 12th January, another meeting was held in Manchester, at which Mr. Wilson stated, that on the previous Thursday there had been a tea party at Accrington, attended by Dr. Bowring, and Mr. Rawson ; one at Colne, on Friday, attended by Mr. Bright, and Mr. Moore ; one on Monday, at Todmorden, attended by Mr. Bright, and Mr. Moore ; two on Friday, at Lancaster, one hall being too small to hold all who congregated ; and one on Wednesday, at Preston, attended by Mr. Brooks, and Mr. Moore, and by Sir Hesketh Fleetwood, and Sir George Strickland, the members for the borough. Mr. Wilson noticed the rapid progress of the £50,000 fund. "The work of distributing tracts may now be said to be commenced in earnest. I made inquiries before coming here, to learn what had been issued during the present year, and the reply was, between *six and seven tons weight*. I inquired how many had been issued during the last three days, and found that the number amounted to three quarters of a million

publications." The secretary then read a long list of subscriptions from every part of the country, and reports of
the labours of the lecturers. The Rev. W. Thornton, of
Stockport, addressed the meeting, and gave a distressing
account of the state of the borough, and Mr. John Brooks in
a business-like way, showed the mischief done to trade by
the coffee monopoly. The Rev. J. W. Massie in the course
of a speech of considerable length, and great eloquence, said:

" Because of the position that was taken by my brethren in Manchester, as well as myself, various assaults have been made upon our
character, and various stratagems have been used to affect the interests
and reputation of those who were the most prominent on that occasion.
I do confess, however, that there never was an event in my own humble
life, nor a circumstance in my history, as far as I now review it, that I
could look upon with such perfect confidence and satisfaction, as the
event that identified me with the movement of the Anti-Corn-Law
League for the abolition of the Corn Laws. (Applause.) The very
attacks which have been made, where my poor unworthy name has been
singled out in that volumious article in the *Quarterly Review*, where I
stood as the only ' *Reverend* ' as they call me,—as the only ' learned,'
as they sneeringly address me—and as the only something else, as they
say when referring to the violent language which I am said to have
used,—those are to me a distinction of more value than if the
Quarterly Review had sent me a pound for every page, and crowned my
head and name with laurels and titles. (Applause.) I do think it is
with the greatest propriety that the ministers of religion come forward,
when there are such statements to be made as Mr. Thornton has made
this evening, coming from Stockport. (Hear, hear.) I do think if the
ministers of religion remain silent, whilst they in their official capacity
are called to witness the things which he describes himself as having
witnessed, they belie their profession, they dishonour their Christianity,
they do injury to religion, and they are not worthy of the name of
Christians."

The meeting was then addressed by Mr. Hudson, of
Sabden, who said that a number of block printers in that
neighbourhood, out of employment, had been for several
weeks breaking stones for the highway, preferring the
hard labour and small pay in that employment, to relief
from the parish funds.

The erection of the Free Trade Hall was now nearly completed, but there was no relaxation in the process of instruction, although the space in the Corn Exchange was inadequate to hold the crowds which pressed for admittance. Another meeting was held there January 19th. Mr. Wilson said :—" At Glasgow, on Wednesday week, upwards of 2000 persons assembled at the greatest banquet ever recollected to have been held in that city. On that occasion Mr. Fox Maule one of the members of the late government which had proposed an 8s. fixed duty, publicly avowed his opinion in favour of total and unconditional repeal. At Edinburgh a large and influential meeting was held on Friday, when upwards of £600 was subscribed' to the League Fund. At Leith, on Saturday, a meeting was held, and since then other meetings have been held at Perth, Dundee, Stirling, and Dunfermline; and yesterday a second banquet was taking place at Glasgow I mentioned at last meeting that the town councils of Glasgow, Edinburgh, and Dundee, had decided on presenting the freedom of their respective cities to Mr. Cobden, and we learn that Stirling has determined to follow the example." Mr. Wilson also stated that 70 bales of tracts had been sent out that week, weighing about four tons, and 50 more bales were ready to be sent out. The speakers of the evening were Mr. J. L. Ricardo, M.P., and Mr. Villiers' colleague in the representation of Wolverhampton, Mr. Thomas Thornely, and Mr. R. R. Moore, Mr. Brotherton, and Mr. W. Rawson.

There needed not the attendance of members of Parliament to attract audiences in the Corn Exchange. Another crowded meeting was held there on Friday, January 27th. Mr. Wilson stated that since they last met, there had been meetings at Hawick, York, Newcastle-upon-Tyne, Ashton-under-Lyne, Skipton, Doncaster, Oldham, Bristol, Barnsley, Taunton, and Wakefield; that at Ashton £1,000 had been subscribed, at Doncaster £100, at Oldham £150; and that the sum then raised at Edinburgh was £1,000, while the subscription had commenced at Glasgow by ten gentlemen putting down their names for £100 each. A long list of subscriptions, in smaller sums, was read by Mr. Hickin, the secretary, after which Mr. Ben. Pearson addressed the meeting. He was followed by Mr. Bright, who gave the following account of the movement in Scotland :—

" I was not present at the first banquet that was given in Glasgow ; but I have heard, and you have heard, accounts of the excellent manner in which it passed off, and of the influence it was likely to have, and we have heard something of the influence it has had upon the people of Scotland. At that meeting, the Hon. Fox Maule, who is heir, I believe, to one of the largest landed properties in Scotland, came forward, and boldly avowed himself in favour of the principles of the League. (Applause.) From that meeting the deputation proceeded to Edinburgh; and the Edinburgh meeting was one of very great importance. Upon that platform were not less than twenty-nine ministers of religion who are living in that city (applause); and I believe it may be taken as a rule that those twenty-nine ministers of religion represented the opinions of at least twenty-nine congregations of the Christian people in that city. (Applause.) And some ministers of religion are of a sort, I will not say that religion may be proud of, but, at any rate, that the people may be proud of. (Applause.) They are not of a class who are to be made the tools or the instruments of any ministry or of any party. (Applause.) I believe they have taken up this question in the conscientious belief that it is one nearly allied to the duties of the office which they have assumed. They believe that the Corn Law is a law operating constantly, incessantly, and most powerfully, to destroy the labours which they are engaged in bringing to perfection amongst their people ; and therefore they came forward, unanimously almost, throughout Scotland, to raise their voice against the longer continuance of this law. I would say of these men as was said of some preachers of the olden times,—

> ' No servile doctrines such as power approves,
> They to the poor and broken-hearted taught:
> With truths which tyrants hate and conscience loves,
> They winged and barbed the arrows of their thought;
> Sin in high places was the mark they sought.'

(Loud applause.) I may mention that among the subscriptions given in Edinburgh was one, and it was entirely unsolicited, from the mother of a late secretary, or under secretary, for Ireland, a gentleman who is known, and probably will be known for ages, for one single sentence that passed from his lips: he said—' Property has its duties as well as its rights.' (Applause.) And the mother of that Mr. Drummond sent £5 down to the League Fund in Edinburgh; thus testifying her opinion, and showing that she coincided in the view that her son has expressed. (Applause.) And you may rely upon it, when you find a man of high and noble sentiments taking a high and excellent part, if you ask who was his mother, you will find that he had a high-minded and excellent mother. (Applause.) We had a meeting at Dumfermline; a meeting composed almost entirely of weavers; and there was a most unanimous opinion there expressed in condemnation of this law. We went to Leith also, and there we found an enthusiastic reception from many who have hitherto been scarcely convinced that our course was wise or our object just. We went from thence to Kirkaldy; but on the way, after crossing the Forth from Edinburgh, on our landing the whole population turned out to meet us, with a band of music, as if they had intended that we should make a sort of triumphant entry into their county. (Hear, and applause.) There, at Kirkaldy, we found a meeting of 1,500 persons assembled—in fact, containing almost the entire adult population of the place; such a meeting, I dare say, as has been rarely seen there. (Applause.) We were received by Colonel Fergusson, who is a large landed proprietor, and by Mr. Fergus, a large manufacturer and landed proprietor also; and the meeting was most cheering and enthusiastic. We passed on to Dundee the same night, where 2,000 people were assembled, and a large number of them ladies. Among the landed proprietors on the platform were Sir John Ogilvie, Mr. Carnegie, of Craigie; Mr. Kinloch, of Kinloch, and others; and it was stated to us that more than one-half of the landed property of Forfarshire was in the hands of men who were total and immediate repealers of the Corn Law. (Applause.) We went on to the royal burgh of Perth: there was no time to get up a meeting; there had been not more, I suppose, than an hour's notice; but the council chamber was filled with the Lord Provost, the council, and some 200 or 300 of the inhabitants. We had the opportunity of addressing them shortly, and the municipal honours were conferred upon Richard Cobden. (Cheers.) We proceeded on to Stirling, to a meeting the same evening; and it was held in a room so long that it was necessary to have a platform at each end, and a chairman and deputy chairman, and part of the speakers spoke from one end, and part from the other end. (Applause.) And I believe that one-seventh of the whole population, men, women, and children, of the city of Stirling, were assembled in that room. There was a great number of farmers, and many large landed proprietors. Mr. Murray, of Polmaise, was in the chair; and he and many others expressed themselves in favour of total and immediate repeal. From Stirling we went to Glasgow, to a meeting of the 'Young Men's Free Trade Association;' and a more magnificent meeting I think I scarcely ever beheld. And it was a meeting of a kind which they have not often had in Scotland ; it was a tea-party, and there was a great number of ladies present; and it was said by many that that meeting would be found more influential in its effect upon the people of Glasgow, than was the meeting of the week previous. From Glasgow we came to Hawick, in Roxburghshire : there, in a very small town, near 500 people were assembled at a tea-party and meeting. The Hon. John Elliott, who is brother to Lord Minto, and also brother-in-law to Lord John Russell, was there, and he expressed himself in favour of total repeal. (Loud applause.) From Hawick we came to Newcastle-upon-Tyne ; and there we had, I have no doubt, the largest meeting ever held there upon the question of free trade. It was a tea-party too, though somewhat unusual on this subject, and a great many ladies were present; and whether I refer to the meeting, or to those on the platform, it was the opinion of all that there never had been assembled, to their knowledge, in any room in Newcastle, upon any political question, a body of individuals who were so likely to influence the opinions of the town and neighbourhood."

Mr. Bright's speech communicated to the meeting much of his high determination and hope of ultimate and not distant triumph. He was followed by the Rev. E. H. Nolan, and Mr. Norton, of Lincoln. At the conclusion, Mr. Bright said he deeply regretted to learn that Mr. Cobden, who had just returned from Bristol, had lost his youngest child during his absence from home.

The Free Trade Hall was now finished—ready for a series of meetings for nearly four years, unparalleled in the history of any country, for numbers, unity of purpose, determination, enthusiasm, and that constant hope of success which was founded in a deep conviction of the justice of the cause for which all this agitation and all this long course of public instruction was required. The description of the Hall is thus given in the *Manchester Times* of January 31st. :

" The site of the Hall is St. Peter's Field ; and it is bounded on two of its sides by Peter-street and Windmill-street, the front and principal entrances being from South-street. The back of the building abuts upon the New

Connection Methodist Chapel. It is sufficient to say of the exterior that it is a substantial brick erection, built by Messrs. Bowden and Edwards, a series of arches running along the walls to give strength to them, and beauty to their appearance at the same time. The dimensions are 135 feet by 105 feet. The height of the walls is 27 feet. The roof is in three compartments, running lengthwise of the building, and the central compartment, which is somewhat loftier than the outer ones, being supported by massive iron columns in the interior. The outer compartments of the roof also rest principally upon these columns, so as to throw as little as possible of a lateral pressure upon the walls. The roof, although of slate, is extremely light for a building of such dimensions, and the use of plaster having been dispensed with in the construction of a ceiling (for which thin laths, covered with paper, are substituted), it will be seen how absurd were the reports spread by interested parties against the safety of the structure. To secure greater comfort and convenience to company set down for admission at the principal entrances, a spacious awning, extending the whole length of the front of the Hall has been thrown across South-street, and internal communications have thus been secured with the Wellington Hotel, which having been for some time unoccupied, the committee have engaged for the sake of the conveniences it was found capable of supplying, in the shape of ante-rooms and places of meeting for the committees and stewards having the management of the meetings and banquets.

"Entering the hall from the awning in South-street, just described, the visitor is struck with the extent of space which bursts upon the eye—of which an examination of the exterior of the building affords a very inadequate idea —as well as with the magnificence of the place generally. But at the opposite end is a daïs which commands a better view of the whole, and there we will go and take our stand

S. U. Libraries

for a moment, while we proceed with the description. This daïs is of three different elevations, running the whole width of the building, the front, or lower one being about two feet above the floor of the hall, and ten feet wide, and the second and third ones, behind it, have each a rise of about two feet six inches, and about half the width of the first. Taking our stand upon the uppermost then, we command a view of the entire space within the building, giving an area of fourteen thousand one hundred and seventy-five square feet. Among the first objects which attract the eye are the three galleries, which extend along the two sides, and across the farther end of the hall—the entrances to them being from the large room of the Wellington Hotel, by means of covered ways across South-street. They are light and elegant in structure, being only about seven feet in depth, with two rows of seats extending along the front, and an aisle at the back. The front is covered with drapery, having the appearance of a deep crimson velvet, with a rich ornamental design printed on it in gold (by Messrs. J. and C. Yates, of Charlotte-street), representing a sheaf of wheat, labelled with the little magic word 'FREE,' encircled by a wreath of olive leaves—the emblem of peace and plenty—from which branches out an elegant scroll to fill up the compartments. A line of massive columns support each of these galleries, which have been draperied to represent white marble: the order of architecture being the Grecian Doric. The ceiling of the building is divided into three compartments, corresponding with the roof, as we have before described it, being hung with a light blue marble paper. The two lines of lofty columns running down the entire length of the hall, on either side of the central compartment, and which are fourteen in number, have a fine effect. They are after the Ionic order of architecture, the drapery being intended to represent white marble, and they are encircled with wreaths of artificial leaves and flowers, which have an elegant and pleasing effect. The walls of the hall are papered, the colour being a good representation of grained oak, and the cornice which surmounts it is of crimson. The mode of lighting the hall is generally admired. There are in all sixteen gas burners—six along the centre of each of the outer compartments of the ceiling, and four along the inner one. They have been constructed by Messrs. Bradford and Son, on a new principle, and are styled, *par excellence*, 'the League Lights.' They consist of a novel arrangement of flat flames, so as to throw out an immense body of light, the four centre ones having each thirty six jets of gas and the others eighteen jets. The effect of these immense bodies of flame, however, is softened by shades made of silk rendered transparent, conveying a good representation of ground glass, but they are richly painted, and the design is altogether very elegant. Grids in the sides of the floor of the hall admit the cold air underneath the gas lights, thus carrying off at the same time any unpleasant effluvia from the gas. Among other ornaments and decorations of the hall we have omitted to name the number of small, elegant silk banners disposed along the front of the galleries and other parts of the room, bearing short and appropriate mottoes to the occasion. In place of a cornice along either side of the central compartment, stretching from one end of the room to the other, were festoons of a rich deep crimson, with ends pendant, which gave a beautiful finish to the embellishments. A large and splendid transparency will also be placed over the dais, behind the chairman, on which is expressed in bold and legible characters, in one word, all that is sought for in this grand movement, on which the eyes of the whole kingdom are concentrated : and that word is—' JUSTICE.' "

Amongst the persons who answered invitations to the opening meeting, were, the late Earl of Derby, who regretted an infirmity which made it impossible for him to attend; Lord John Russell, who, "with his opinions" could not attend; Lord Kinnaird, who wrote at some length, and expressed his hope that Sir Robert Peel would see the policy and the justice of carrying out free-trade principles; the Earl of Ducie, who regretted his inability to be present, and expressed his best wishes for the success of the agitation; the Marquis of Westminister, who expressed his good wishes for the complete success of the League in its arduous conflict with monopoly; the Earl of Clarendon, who regretted his inability to attend, and highly commended the prize essays, especially the one written by Mr. W. Rathbone Greg; the Earl of Carlisle, who expressed his convictions that greater changes than had been made was necessary for the well-being of all classes of society; from the Earl of Radnor, who regretted that he could not attend; from the Earl of Listowel, who expressed his conviction that the day was not far remote when all restrictions on the food of the people would be removed; Lord Nugent, who noticed with pleasure the conversions that was going on amongst those who had been supporters of the Corn Laws; Lord Charles Fitzroy, who congratulated the cause on the powerful speech of Mr. Cobden, at Glasgow; Mr. G. Poulett Scrope, brother to the late Poulett Thompson, Lord Sydenham, who expressed his admiration of the zeal, ability, and devotion, of the leading members of the League; and a number of members of parliament, who would be prevented attending by other engagements.

The following deputies had arrived at the time of the opening of the preliminary meeting, on the 30th January.

Accrington .... Messrs. W. Dixon, E. Bowker, R. Smith, and J. Grimshaw.
Bolton .... Mr. C. J. Darbishire.
Bury .... Mr. John Walker.
Batley .... Messrs. John Burnley and C. R. Greenwood.
Bristol........ Messrs. S. P. Jackson, and Frederick Wills.
Carlisle ...... Messrs. J. P. Dixon, R. Ferguson, and — Steel.
Colebrookdale.. Mr. Abraham Darby.

Dundee ......Messrs. Edward Baxter and J. G. Baxter.

Edinburgh ....Mr. William Dunlop.

Glasgow ......Messrs. W. Graham, W. Laing, J. S. Reid, and James Drummond.

Huddersfield ..Messrs. William Brooke, J. Boothroyd, Bernard Buxton, George Crossland, W. Edwards, David Haigh, C. H. Jones, Thomas Mallinson, F. Schwann, W. Willans, and William Cawthra.

Halifax ......Messrs. Edward Ackroyd and W. Morris.

Holmfirth ....Mr. George Robinson.

Halshaw Moor..Mr. Thomas Barnes.

Hyde ....Messrs John Hibbert. J. Thornely, J. Pownall, and H. Hibbert.

Knutsford ....Mr. J. Long.

Leeds ....Messrs. E. Birchall, Saml. Birchall, and E. Birchall.

Liverpool ....Messrs. Lawrence Heyworth, C. Holland, R. Sheil, J. T. Truck, J. B. Cooke, John Finch, jun., James Harvey, and E. C. Rawlins, jun., and along with them were Edward Holland, Esq., High Sheriff, Worcestershire.

Lincoln ......Messrs. John Norton and William Parry.

Lancaster ....Messrs. W. and G. Jackson.

Middleton ....Messrs. E. K. Brown, J. Hughes, J. Jones, T. Mallalieu, J. Rushton, and Geoffrey Smith.

Macclesfield ..Messrs. Alex. Carruthers and J. Howe.

Mansfield ....Messrs. Hollins, Isaac Heywood, and Wm. Hollins.

Nantwich ....Messrs. Philip and Thomas Barker.

Oldham ......Messrs. John Ascroft, J. Brierley, jun., P. Brierley, John Bentley, J. Chadwick, J. Gillam, Thomas Gartside, J. S. Hague, A. Milne, H. Nelson, J. Potter, J. Platt, J. Riley, S. Riley, Alex. Taylor, and John Riley.

Preston ......Mr. S. Jones.

Queenshead ..Messrs. M. Stocks and Thomas Kenworthy.

Rochdale......Messrs. Thomas Booth and John Hoyle.

Stalybridge....Messrs. George Benson, H. Boothroyd, and J. Spencer.

Stockport ....Messrs. Ald. Baker, H. Barlow, D. C. Bagshaw, H. Coppock, G. Chapman, E. Dooley, J. D. Fernley, Ald. Hollins, J. Higginbottam, H. Hunt, B. Hodgson, G. Henshall, C. Hudson, J. Littlewood, J. Little, J. Livesey, J. Longson, P. E. Marsland,

Stockport ......J. J. Moody, — M'Clure, W. Nelstrop, Alfred
            Orrell (mayor), J. Ogden, W. R. Potts, W. J.
            Priestnall, F. Stewart, G. Smith, H. W Sefton, T.
            Tym, Ald. Wilkinson, G. and S. Wilkinson, T.
            Waterhouse, B. Walmsley, G. Wood, W. William-
            son, John Hampson.
Settle ....Mr. James Thompson.
Stroud ....Mr. J. H. S. Lewis.
Sunderland....Mr. Thomas Robinson.
Varley Iron Works, Monmouthshire..Mr. Morris Jones.
Wigan ....Mr. E. Evans.
Warrington....Messrs. P. Rylands, J. Crossfield, — Eskrigge,
            M'Minn, and Millner.
Walsall ......Mr. S. Cox.

The following are the names of the ministers of religion
who had accepted the invitation, the greater number of
whom attended :—

Aspland R. B., Dukinfield
Ackworth J., F.A., P.P., Horton
    College, Bradford
Archer —, Hillsboro' Hall, Bles-
    sington
Atkin T., Glossop
Atkinson C., Leeds
Baker Charles, Stockport
Blair James, Dumferline
Borland J. W., Wheat Park, Lanark
Bonner W. H., Bilston
Buckingham T. P., Thornslye, near
    Stourbridge
Bryan J. H., Stalybridge
Buckley James, Penistone
Bramwell John, Stainland, near
    Halifax
Brooks James, Hyde
Burns R., D.D., Paisley
Bishop F., Warrington
Balfour A., Tyldesley Banks, near
    Leigh
Burfelt J., Salisbury
Bagguly William, Manchester

Baird Archibald, Paisley
Bowen Samuel, Macclesfield
Bycott T., Barnsley
Colston J., Styal, near Wilmslow
Cockin T., Holmfirth
Currie W., Lockwood
Cairns R. R., Paisley
Carbutt F., Leeds
Cummins J., Leeds
Deakin T., Stand
Davies J. T., Tintwistle
Dowson H., Bradford
Dean James, Topsham, near Exeter
Davies J., St. Bridge
Dobbin James, Annan
Dawson James, Dudley
Dawson T., Bacup
Dyson J., Halshaw Moor
Davies Joseph, Manchester
Dean H., Colne
Edwards James, Brighton
Edmonds J., St Helens
Ewing Alexander, Halifax
Ely J., Leeds

Edwards E., Hatherlow
Fletcher Joseph, Hanley
Fox Joseph, Leeds
Gill Thomas, Burnley
Galloway J. C., West Bromwich
Guthrie J., Kendal
Gilbert T., Nottingham
Gwyther James, Manchester
Giles J. E., Leeds
Giles J. E., jun., Hulme
Garner James, Dunham
Gadsby William, Manchester
Gilchrist Mr., Clitheroe
Harrison J., Stockport
Hudston John, Ashton
Healey Samuel, Hazel Grove
Harbottle Joseph, Accrington
Harvey Mr., Glasgow
Hawkes E., Kendal
Howarth F., Bury
Hearne D., Manchester
Harrison J., Heywood
Hoyle Giles, Manchester
Jackson W. E., Heywood
Jones Thomas, Bryn, Llewelyn, North Wales
Jones Morris, Varteg Iron Works
Jones Edward, Colne
Kennedy James, Bury
King Dr., Glasgow
Kershaw J., Rochdale
Lord Thomas, Oldham
Linwood William, Mansfield
Marshall William, Wigan
Massie J. W., Manchester
Morris R., Burton
Morris G., Stretford
Massie Robert, Newton
Nolan E. H., Manchester
Owens Owen, Holywell
Pottinger Thomas, Bradford
Parson B., Stroud
Pickles John, Wrinewall

Rogers Thomas, Prescot
Roaf W., Wigan
Rhodes H. G., Fullwood, Shiffnall
Rogers W., Dudley
Rugland John, Hindley
Richardson James
Robberds J. G., Chorlton-upon-Medlock
Roseman William, Bury
Ridley J. W., Stockport
Robinson G., Bury
Stowell W. H., Rotherham College
Shepherd J. B., Bury
Spencer Thomas, Hinton, near Bath
Shuttleworth W., Manchester
Sevier C. T., Warrington
Simpson J. P., Preston
Slater R., Preston
Smith T. N., Denton
Smith W., Stockport
Skinner F., Blackburn
Sayce S., Wrexham
Steward A., Barnet
Stokes W., West Bromwich
Strettles J. B., Salford
Spencer —, Ashton-in-Mackerfield
Stephens —, Todmorden
Saxton G. P., Hulme
Smith T., St. Bridge
Thorburn W. R., M.A., Hall Fold, near Rochdale
Turner W., near Wigan
Tunstall J., Liverpool
Thornton J., Stockport
Tyler W., Prince's-Spitalfields
Todd Simpson, Bacup
Thompson C., Manchester
Vardey W., Newcastle
Whitworth C., Chorlton-upon-Medlock
Wade Arthur Savage, D.D., London
White John, Northowram
Watts H., Shrewsbury

Wynn J., Burnley
Wright J., Stockport
Wells G. H., Gorton
Wheelden John, Manchester
Williamson J., Horton-in-Craven

Williamson W., Barnoldswick
Wickstead C., Leeds
Wright J., Coseley, near Bilston
Waddington T., Stockport

A preliminary meeting was held on the 30th January, in the Town Hall, Mr. R. H. Greg, in the chair. The meeting was addressed by the chairman, Mr. J. Bright, Mr. P. H. Taylor, of London, and the Rev. J. W. Massie, and committees were appointed—one to consider the effects of the Corn Law on agriculture, one to consider their effects on commerce and manufactures, and another to consider their effects on the physical. moral, and political condition of the people.

CHAPTER II.

THE GREAT GATHERING.

The great gathering took place in the new Free Trade Hall on the evening of the 30th January, Mr. Mark Philips, the senior member for the borough, in the chair. The meeting was probably the most magnificent ever seen within doors. The Hall, with the single exception of the great feudal structure at Westminster, the largest in the kingdom, was not merely filled but crammed in every part. Well might Dr. Bowring exclaim that he was *awe-struck* by the sight of the vast assemblage; and well might he who saw the Manchester Anti-Corn-Law Association when only seven persons met to commence the righteous agitation, rejoice to witness the presence of more than as many thousands, all evidencing their enthusiasm in the cause, and well might he prognosticate its speedy triumph. Mr. George Wilson read the following list of contributions towards the £50,000 fund:

	£	s.	D.		£	s.	D.
Ayr (N. B.)	20	0	0	Bowriefauld, Forfar	3	0	0
Alnwick	15	0	0	Battley, Yorkshire	31	4	6
Abergele	5	0	0	Berwick-upon-Tweed	5	10	0
Accrington	420	0	0	Backbarrow	1	0	0
Auchterarder	4	0	0	Bishops Stortford	5	7	0
Annan	10	0	0	Bilston	110	0	0
Arbroath	78	0	0	Belper	69	0	0
Ashton-under-Lyne	1000	0	0	Bolton	936	0	0
Blackburn	600	0	0	Belfast	160	0	0

	£	s.	D.
Burslem	50	0	0
Bridport	55	0	0
Barnard Castle	40	0	0
Bury	928	9	9
Bridgnorth	30	0	0
Burnley	700	0	0
Birmingham	500	0	0
Bath	50	0	0
Beddington Corner	20	0	0
Bacup	500	0	0
Barnoldswick	3	11	2
Brighouse	50	0	0
Beverley	8	11	0
Bristol	1000	0	0
Bow, Bromley, and Oldford	5	6	9
Bradford	600	0	0
Cockermouth	35	0	0
Cheltenham	25	0	0
Coventry	91	9	10
Carlisle	311	0	0
Chorley	50	0	0
Cupar, Provost of	10	0	0
Clifton, near Bristol	13	11	6
Clitheroe	150	0	0
Congleton	40	0	0
Colne	150	0	0
Colebrookdale	129	0	0
Cirencester	2	0	0
Chapel-en-le-Frith	10	0	0
Cleckheaton	40	0	0
Carmarthen	10	0	0
Dunstable	12	19	0
Darlington	180	0	0
Darlaston	13	5	11
Devizes	21	1	6
Dunfermline (N. B.)	16	10	0
Dumbarton	12	0	0
Dudley	51	0	0
Derby	450	0	0
Dundee	500	0	0
Doncaster	75	0	0

	£	s.	D
Denton	30	0	0
Driffield	10	0	0
Davenport	5	11	5
Dunbar (N. B.)	8	0	0
Dronfield	1	16	6
Edenfield	5	0	0
Exeter	5	16	6
Edinburgh (N. B.)	1000	0	0
Eccles and Patricroft	60	0	0
Frodsham	10	0	0
Forfar	30	0	0
Fordingbridge	11	12	0
Greenock (N. B.)	50	0	0
Glastonbury	6	0	0
Great Torrington	5	0	0
Glossop	50	0	0
Gloucester	25	9	0
Glasgow	2500	0	0
Gasbro'	3	0	0
Holmfirth	171	19	8
Hawick (N. B.)	50	0	0
Hamilton (N. B.)	10	0	0
Hudderfield	1805	11	7
Horton-in-Craven	8	8	0
Hereford	8	10	0
Heckmondwike, York	40	0	0
Holywell, N. Wales	57	0	0
Halifax	1010	2	6
Hebden Bridge	280	0	0
Haslingden	120	0	0
Hyde Operatives	60	0	0
Heywood	70	0	0
Halshaw Moor	260	0	0
Honiton	7	10	0
Hammersmith	20	0	0
Hazel Grove	8	12	6
Ilkeston	35	0	0
Idle	16	0	0
Kelso (N. B.)	50	0	0
Kendal	190	0	0
Kilmarnock (N. B.)	25	0	0
Kirkaldy (N. B.)	125	0	0

	£	s.	d.		£	s.	d.
Kerriemuir	10	3	4	Poole	9	12	6
Knaresborough	11	0	0	Prescott	7	0	0
Llanfyllin, N. Wales..	1	1	0	Paisley	38	0	0
Lincoln	8	9	9	Pately Bridge	20	9	5
Liverpool	2200	0	0	Penrith	2	0	0
Linlithgow	9	0	0	Plymouth	10	0	0
Langholme (N. B.) ..	7	0	0	Queen's Head	14	0	0
Leighton Buzzard ..	8	0	0	Ross	14	0	0
Lancaster	89	0	0	Rochdale	2200	0	0
Leigh	50	0	0	Stratfford, Essex	13	0	0
Lane End, Potteries	3	0	0	Swansea	30	0	0
Leicester	500	0	0	Stirling (N. B.)	70	5	0
Leeds	1500	0	0	Settle	16	16	6
Luddenden Foot	36	11	6	Sunderland	95	8	6
Loughborough	36	0	0	Swaffham	12	6	10
Lymington	12	0	0	Stockport	508	0	0
Leek	15	0	0	Sandbach	10	0	0
Lees	20	0	0	Saddleworth	234	4	0
Montrose (N. B.)	7	17	6	Sabden	19	2	7
Maidstone, Kent	7	0	0	Shepton Mallett	15	0	0
Macclesfield	28	0	0	Sudbury	14	7	0
Maybole (N. B.)	3	10	0	Stourbridge	70	0	0
Madeley	105	0	0	Slateford	5	0	0
Marsden	10	0	0	Scarbro'	5	0	0
Manchester	7000	0	0	Skipton	200	0	0
Newport	3	0	0	Stroud	75	0	0
Newcastle-under-Lyne	50	0	0	Sheffield	800	0	0
Newtownwards, Ireland	6	6	0	Stockton-on-Tees	5	4	0
Northwich	30	0	0	Swaddincote	32	10	6
Nottingham	850	0	0	Stalybridge (sundries)	4	13	7
Nantwich	80	0	0	Styal	3	0	10
Norwich	52	0	0	Stalybridge	400	0	0
Northampton	12	0	0	Taunton	10	0	0
Ottley	94	7	6	Thetford	1	2	6
Over Darwen	4	13	6	Truro, Cornwall	6	0	0
Oldham	500	0	0	Thornton	5	0	0
Ossett.	35	0	0	Tiverton, Devon	15	0	0
Old Meldrum	4	12	0	Todmorden	405	9	1
Perth	20	0	0	Thomaby	3	10	0
Preston	450	0	0	Tavistock	17	5	0
Peniston	7	10	0	West Bromwich	50	0	0
Padiham	70	0	0	Winnell's Hill	5	0	0

	£	s.	D.		£	s.	D.
Wilton	2	10	0	Warrington	460	0	0
Watford, Herts	6	0	0	Wigan	350	0	0
Workmen of T. Ashton	19	12	6	Whitehaven	50	0	0
Wootton-under-Edge...	50	0	0	Worcester	50	0	0
Wrexham	11	5	0	Warminster	3	10	0
Wolverhampton	150	0	0	Wellington	4	0	0
Ware, Hertz	1	0	0	York	40	0	0

These subscriptions, the chairman said, amounted to £40,460. Mr. Taylor, of London, said that there would be a liberal contribution there, if members of the League would direct the applications. The meeting was addressed by Mr. John Brooks, who said that there should be not only a fund of £50,000, but an annual fund to that amount until the victory was gained ; Mr. John Bright, who spoke with great energy and spirit; Mr. R. R. Moore, the Rev. Mr. Parsons, of Ebley, the Rev. Mr. Massie, and Colonel Thompson, and before the close of the meeting it was announced that the sum subscribed was £42,000. The amount of money contributed, on a very few months' notice, was of itself a proof of extraordinary organization and extraordinary zeal—of zeal not to be tired out by years of never hopeless, but always discouraging struggle—of organization which promised final and not distant success. The Council of the League was laughed to scorn when it came boldly forward and called upon the public to aid its efforts by subscribing the sum of £50,000. The press, in the interest of the monopolists, raised a shout of derision, and characterised the claim as if it had proceeded either from madmen or from knaves, who knew that it would not be responded to, and who had made it only to give momentary alarm to their antagonists. But the result proved that the Council was right in its estimate of public opinion and feeling. A noble and generous response had been given to the call. Localities not then experiencing, in their full extent, the mischievous operation of the Corn Law, and others reduced by its withering influence almost to ruin ; great and little hamlets; manufacturing towns and agricultural villages ; places, the existence of which, and their very names, were unknown to the League ; places from whence little was expected but whence much had come— all united, and hence it was that the sum of £42,000, independently of the London collections, had already been subscribed, and that the greater part of this splendid protest against oppression was already in the hands of the treasurer. *The remainder was forthcoming.* The money had yet to do its work ; not like the funds of the Carlton Club in brutalizing the electors—not to purchase a man's birthright for a mess of pottage, but to send printed INSTRUCTION into the house of every voter throughout the kingdom, These silent missionaries, the tracts, would silently work their way. They would speak truths to the sight, and truths that would prevail. The lecturer's voice could not be heard in every village ; but the tracts, suited to every capacity, would reach *every house where* an elector lived. Wherever five pounds had been raised, and a hundred bundles of tracts distributed amongst scattered voters, there was an organization which would have a powerful effect in every election contest. Everywhere were there organized anti-corn-law associations—everywhere registered members of the League. Even in the smallest boroughs the candidate would find total repealers exercising their moral influence; and no county candidate could go into a village without finding men thoroughly qualified to discuss the question, and determined to enunciate the doctrines of free trade, regardless of all local intimidation. The organization that could raise £50,000 could do more.

On the morning of Tuesday, February 1st, a meeting of deputies was held in the Town Hall, to consider the effects of the Corn Laws on the agricultural classes, the chair being occupied by Mr. R. H. Greg, who might have been described as an extensive landowner, had he not been a more extensive cotton spinner and manufacturer. The meeting was addressed by him, by Mr. Milner Gibson, a Suffolk landowner, by Mr. Walker, of Longford, Mr. John Toll, of Berkshire, Mr. Chadwick, of Arksey, near Doncaster, Mr. Charles Sheriff, a Gloucestershire farmer, Col. Thompson, and others. It was shown that the agriculture of a great part of England, in spite of all the protection heaped upon it, was in the most wretched condition; that a great majority of the tenants-at-will were without capital or skill; little better in condition than common labourers; that the labourers received miserable wages, and that the workhouses were filled with persons of that class; that diminished consumption had caused reduction of prices; and that poor's rates were rapidly increasing in agricultural parishes, not only from the demands of their own unemployed poor, but from the return of labourers who had ceased to find employment in manufacturing towns. This was contrasted with the state of things in Scotland, where long leases and *corn-rents* gave encouragement to the employment of capital and enterprise, and where men of education could sustain a more highly respectable station than had yet been attained by the generality of English farmers.

Another meeting of deputies was held on Wednesday, Mr. H. Ashworth in the chair, to consider the effects of the Corn Laws on manufacture and commerce. The speakers were Mr. Thomas Bazley; Mr. P. A. Taylor, of London; Mr. W. H. Greg, author of one of the prize essays, now known as a frequent contributor to the Edinburgh Review; his brother, Mr. R. H. Greg; Mr. T. Plint, of Leeds; Mr. Taunton, of Coventry; Mr. Scholefield, M.P., of Birmingham; Mr. E. Baxter, of Dundee; Mr. Duncan Maclaren, now Lord Provost of Edinburgh, and others. Deeply affecting details were given not only of continued, but of continually increasing, distress.

A dinner or banquet took place in the Free Trade Hall in the evening, at which 3,800 persons sat down. The chair was occupied by Mr. Mark Philips and the assemblage was addressed by him, by Mr. T. M. Gibson, Col. Thompson, Sir De Lacy Evans, Daniel O'Connell, Dr. Bowring, Mr. W. Aldam, Mr. J. Bright, and the Rev. J. E. Giles. The proceedings were interesting in a high degree; but we are hastening on to the more apparently though not more really important movement in the metropolis, requiring a due proportion of notice.

On Thursday, a meeting of ministers of religion was held in the Town Hall to consider the bearing of the Corn Laws upon the physical, moral, and religious condition of the people. There were about three hundred ministers present. The Rev. Dr. Burns occupied the chair, and near him were the Revs. Thos. Spencer, of Bath; William Mc.Kerrow; J. E. Giles, of Leeds; J. Ackworth, of Bradford; B. Aspland, Dukinfield; J. Bakewell; C. Baker, Stockport; J. Burfit and J. Gilbert, Nottingham; Mr. Skinner, Blackburn; Mr. Dean, Devonshire; H. Baird, Paisley; Dr. Beard; J. Bramhall, Stainland; R. Cairns, Paisley; H. Dawson, Bradford; R. Fletcher; J. W. Gilchrist, Galway; Dr. King, Glasgow; G. Nolan; J. W. Massie; and G. Scholes, Leeds. The proceedings were akin to those which had taken place at the great conference of ministers held in the previous year.

A second banquet was held in the Free Trade Hall in the evening, addressed by Mr. John Brooks, the chairman; Mr. Torrens Mc.Cullagh; Rev. T. Spencer; Mr. H. E. Wright, of Philadelphia; Mr. James Wilson, now in the whig administration; Mr. John Bright; Rev. J. W. Massie; and Col. Thompson. Another meeting of deputies was held on Friday morning, and another banquet on Friday evening, at which between 7,000 and 8,000 persons were present. At its conclusion, Mr. George Wilson, who occupied the chair, said: " This evening will terminate the great gatherings of the week. In every respect they have been such as the most sanguine anticipations of our

friends could by any possibility have desired. Whether
we regard them in point of numbers, in point of wealth,
of station, or of influence, we can fairly point to them as
surpassing anything of the kind ever seen in this country
on this or any other public subject." In the course of the
proceedings the resolutions passed at the meeting of
delegates in the morning, were submitted to the meeting,
and when that pledging the League never to rest satisfied
till they had accomplished the object for which they were
banded together, was submitted, it was loudly cheered,
the whole company rising from their seats, and waving
hats and handkerchiefs.

Before the invasion of the metropolis by the forces of
the League, it may be well to give the impression produced on the mind of a foreigner by the operations carried
on in its offices in Manchester. They have thus been
described by J. G. Kohl, in his "Ireland, Scotland, and
England":

"Manchester is the centre of the Anti-Corn-Law, as
Birmingham is of the Universal-Suffrage, agitation. At
Manchester are held the general meetings of the Anti-
Corn-Law League, and here it is that the committee of the
League constantly sits. The kindness of a friend procured
me admission to the great establishment of the League at
Manchester, where I had the satisfaction of seeing and
hearing much that surprised and interested me. George
Wilson and other well-known leaders of the League, who
were assembled in the committee-room, received me as a
stranger, with much kindness and hospitality, readily
answering all my questions, and making me acquainted
with the details of their operations. I could not help asking myself whether in Germany, men, who attacked, with
such talent and energy, the fundamental laws of the state,
would not have been long ago shut up in some gloomy
prison as conspirators and traitors, instead of being permitted to carry on their operations thus freely and boldly

in the broad light of day ; and, secondly, whether in Germany, such men would ever have ventured to admit a stranger into all their secrets with such frank and open cordiality.

" I was astonished to observe how the Leaguers, all private persons, mostly merchants, manufacturers, and men of letters, conducted political business, like statesmen and ministers. A talent for public business seems an innate faculty in the English. Whilst I was in the committee-room immense numbers of letters were brought in, opened, read, and answered, without a moment's delay. These letters, pouring in from all parts of the United Kingdom, were of the most various contents, some trivial, some important, but all connected with the objects of the party. Some brought news of the movements of eminent Leaguers or of their opponents, for the eye of the League is ever fixed upon the doings both of friend and enemy. Others contained pecuniary contributions, from well-wishers of the cause ; for each of whom the president immediately dictated an appropriate letter of thanks. Other letters related anecdotes, showing the progress of the cause, and the gradual defection of the farmers, the most resolute supporters of Peel.

" The League has now, by means of local associations in all parts of the kingdom, extended its operation and influence over the whole country, and attained an astonishing national importance. Its festivals, Anti-Corn-Law bazaars, Anti-Corn-Law banquets, and others of like nature, appear like great national anniversaries. Besides the acknowledged members of the League, there are numbers of important men who work with them and for them in secret. Every person who contributes £50 to the League fund has a seat and a voice in their council. They have committees of working men for the more thorough dissemination of their doctrines among the lower classes, and committees of ladies to procure the co-operation of women.

They have lecturers, who are perpetually traversing the
country to fan the flames of agitation in the minds of the
people. These lecturers, who sometimes earn as much as
£600 a year, often hold conferences and disputations with
lecturers of the opposite party, and not unfrequently drive
them in disgrace from the field. It is also the business of
the travelling lecturers, to keep a vigilant watch on every
movement of the enemy, and acquaint the League with
every circumstance likely to affect its interests. The
Leaguers write direct letters to the Queen, the Duke of
Wellington, Sir Robert Peel, and other distinguished
people, to whom, as well as to the foreign ambassadors,
they send copies of those journals containing the most
faithful accounts of their proceedings. Sometimes they
send personal deputations to distinguished opponents, in
order to tell them disagreeable truths to their faces. Nor
do the Leaguers neglect the potent instrumentality of that
hundred-armed Briareus, the press. Not only do they
spread their opinions through the medium of those
journals favourable to them; they issue many periodicals
of their own, which are exclusively devoted to the interests
of the League. These contain, of course, full reports of
all meetings, proceedings, and lectures against the Corn
Laws; extracts from Anti-Corn-Law publications, repeating for the thousandth time that monopoly is contrary to
the order of nature, and that the League seeks only to
restore the just order of Providence; original articles
headed ' Signs of the Times,' 'Anti-Corn-Law Agitation
in London,' ' Progress of the Good Work,' &c., &c.; and
last not least, poems entitled 'Lays of the League,' advocating in various ways the cause of free trade, and
satirising their opponents generally with more lengthiness
than wit. Nor does the Anti-Corn-Law party omit to avail
itself of the agency of those cheap little pamphlets called
' Tracts,' which are such favourite party weapons in
England. With these tiny dissertations, seldom costing

more than twopence or threepence, and generally written by some well-known Anti-Corn-Law leader, such as Cobden and Sturge, the League are perpetually attacking the public, as with a bombardment of small shot. I saw three or four dozen of such publications announced at the same time by one bookseller, Mr. Gadsby. Still tinier weapons, however, are the Anti-Corn-Law wafers, consisting of short mottoes, couplets, and aphorisms of every class, grave and gay, serious and satirical, witty and unmeaning; but all bearing on the one point of monopoly and free trade. These are sometimes taken from the Bible, sometimes from the works of celebrated writers and orators, sometimes from the speeches and publications of the Leaguers themselves, and sometimes are produced by the inventive ingenuity of the editor. Eighteen sheets of these wafers are sold in a pretty cover for one shilling, and each sheet contains forty mottoes. Astonishing indeed is the profuse expenditure of labour, ingenuity, wit, and talent, and likewise of stupidity, folly, and dullness, with which, in this wonderful England, the smallest party operations are carried on! Even in children's books, do both the Leaguers and Anti-Leaguers carry on their warfare, thus early sowing the seeds of party spirit in the minds of future generations.

"All the publications of the League are not only written, but printed, bound, and published, at the League Rooms, in Market-street, Manchester. I went through the various rooms where these operations were carried on, until I came at last·to the great League Depôt, where books, pamphlets, letters, newspapers, speeches, reports, tracts, and wafers, were all piled in neat packets of every possible size and appearance, like the packets of muslin and calico, in the great warehouses of Manchester. Beyond this was a refreshment room, in which tea was offered us by several ladies, with whom we engaged in conversation for a little while.

"I cannot join the sanguine expectations of the Leaguers, that Sir Robert Peel will be the last English minister who will venture to uphold monopoly. It is well known how long such struggles generally last, and how very frequently, when the longed-for prize appears on the point of being attained, it is suddenly snatched away from that oft deluded Tantalus—the people. The immediate aim of the Leaguers is the abolition of the Corn Laws, but they do not propose to stop at the attainment of this object. They will then turn the same weapons which brought down the Corn Laws, against all other trade monopolies and custom-house regulations, first in England and then in other countries, until at length all commercial restrictions between different nations, shall be totally done away with, and trade rejoice in the golden sunshine of freedom all over the world. A tempting object, but alas! a long and doubtful road."

M. Kohl is more liberal to the lecturers than the League was. There was none of their number with a salary at all approaching £600 a year. The most efficient of the remunerated assistants laboured for less pay than they might have had in other avocations, and so far might be considered as contributors towards the funds of the League. It may easily be conceived, that arrangements for so many meetings, at so many places, the great amount of correspondence, the superintendence of so large an amount of subscriptions, the distribution of so many tracts, involved great labour, and a great division and sub-division of labour. The executive committee met daily, and often twice a day. The rooms were occupied from early in the morning until late at night, by various other committees, each in its own department of business. These committees had their sub-committees, all labouring as earnestly and as continuously as if ample fortune and world-wide fame would be their reward; all working gratuitously, and without the consciousness of their names ever being mentioned out of the scene of their labours. Amongst these were a few whom Mr. John Brooks designated the " stokers," as resembling a class of railway labourers, unnoticed and unknown, but from whose work a race horse speed is obtained—Mr. S. P. Robinson, Mr. Wm. Macartney, Mr. Wm. Mc. Call, Mr. E. J. Royle, and others—ready at all times to put their hands to any thing that would forward the movement. At most of the great manufacturing and commercial towns, each with popular dependencies, there was a similar division and sub-division of labour, voluntarily and eagerly tendered, and continuously bestowed. Great, therefore, as was the business done which money could do, it was comparatively insignificant when compared with what was done by volunteered and gratuitous agency.

It is not to be supposed that a committee, or board, or council, directing the expenditure of £50,000 a year, was without the torment of incessant application for employment and pay. There were plenty of persons who thought that they could at once serve their country and themselves. Abundant offers there were from men who believed that respectively as orators, or writers, or canvassers, or tract distributors, they could greatly advance the cause of free trade, and thus legitimately put some small portion of the thousand pounds a week into their own proper pockets. Nor were there wanting members of the general body, subscribing pretty liberally, and giving their own labour freely, who thought that their recommendations of serviceable men ought to meet with favourable consideration. There were some annoyances of that sort certainly, vexatious enough occasionally, but there was the ready answer to all, that so abundant was the gratuitous service, that there was no necessity for an extensive paid staff. From a few obscure places there came hints that a little assistance to a struggling newspaper, advocating, under unfavourable circumstances, free-trade doctrines, would be beneficial; but they were modestly made, and in no instance was the disposition not to understand the hint, followed by any cessation of zeal on the part of the applicants.

Parliament was opened on Thursday, 2nd February There was not much in the Queen's speech to encourage the free traders. Her Majesty regretted the " diminished receipts from some of the ordinary sources of revenue ; and feared that it must in part be attributed to the reduced consumption of many articles, caused by that depression of the manufacturing industry of the country which has so long prevailed, and which her Majesty had so deeply lamented." There was no indication either in the speech or in the short debate, of any measure to remove that depression which had so long prevailed and was so much lamented.

In the debate in the Commons, on the address, February 3rd, Mr. Villiers asked whether Sir Robert Peel had meant, in his speech of the previous evening, to declare himself against all change in the Corn Law. Sir Robert said that protection had hitherto been the rule, and that rule would be observed if ever there should be any change. This declaration of the minister gave considerable alarm to the agriculturists ; but, on consideration, they felt that his hold on office depended on their support ; and that, notwithstanding his refusal to bind himself irrevocably to their monopoly, he was bound fast enough by their will.

On the following Thursday, Lord Stanhope moved in the Lords for a committee to 'consider the condition of the productive classes, whose distress he attributed to the new tariff, the Corn Law, and machinery ! Lord Brougham ridiculed the arguments of Lord Stanhope, and then blamed the conduct of the Anti-Corn-Law League as injurious to a good cause, and expressed himself as indignantly against strong language as if he never, during his long and previously useful public life, had used any himself. On the division there were only 29 votes, of which 25 were against the motion.

On Monday, February 13th, 'Lord Howick's motion for
a committee to enquire into the distress of the country,
gave rise to a debate, which dragged its slow length over
four nights. His lordship's speech was upon the whole
effective, although he had the disadvantage of being known
as favouring a sort of half-way house measure of relief, between the whig eight shilling duty and a total repeal of the
Corn Law. Of this disadvantage Mr. Gladstone, a clever
debater, was not slow to avail himself. His lordship had
said, that Sir Robert Peel halted between two opinions.
"But," said Mr. Gladstone, "the noble lord halts between
two opinions, and instead of being prepared boldly to
apply his principles of freedom to trade, and to say what
he would do for the country, he declares that he would
not venture to determine to what degree restrictions should
be maintained. What, then became of the whole speech of
the noble lord? It was an able speech, but its object was
to show the mischief of restrictions on commerce, and the
evil tendency of the system of protection; and while he was
reproaching his right hon. friend because he maintained a
certain portion of restriction, the noble lord himself
appeared to be ready likewise to maintain a portion of
restrictions." Mr. Gladstone's admissions were those of
a free trader. He said: "He would make an admission
to the noble lord—that if a change in the Corn Law
were to take place, and if that change were to procure
an increased importation of foreign corn, and if that
importation of foreign corn were to be paid for in British
manufactures, he thought it would be taking a most short
and false view of the interests of British agriculture to
view that importation of foreign corn as so much displacement of British agricultural commerce. Why, the first
effect would be that it might reduce prices, but undoubtedly
*it would give a demand for the labour of those now unemployed,
and thereby create a new class of producers, and raise the
wages of those who had now low wages,* and thereby enable

them *to consume more largely.* More wheat, he doubted not, was consumed in a state of comfort than in a state of poverty; and even if more wheat were not consumed, the amount of wheat was increased by foreign importation, no doubt there would be a further increase of and demand for other articles of agricultural commerce. He had not the least hesitation in declaring that that admission might save a great deal of time in that house; it was a proposition that could not be disputed."

Yet, with such admissions, alarming as they were to the agricultural interest, Mr. Gladstone and his colleagues refused to give that encouragement to trade which would follow an explicit avowal that they intended to *act* on the principles of free trade. Mr. Labouchere made a smart speech but not a very effective one; for while he said he wanted a permanent measure, it was known that he was for a fixed duty which would possess no more permanency than the sliding scale. Mr. Ferrand made a speech, full, as usual, of abuse of the mill-owners; in which, in reference to the last general election, he said: "The great contest between the two parties had been between the rival principles of free trade and restriction. This had been the question expressly brought before the electors of Yorkshire by Lord Morpeth: the hand writing was said to be on the wall, and it was for the electors of England to read it for or against protection. Thus it was that Sir Robert Peel obtained office—pledged to protect the best interests of the country; but what he had done? He had attacked those interests by undermining them through the principles of free trade. The measures of the right hon. baronet had given a great shock to the great interests of the country; and it was the duty of those who had pledged themselves in the most solemn manner to their constituents, to stand firm to their promises." After the blows of Mr. Ferrand's flail had been impartially administered to both ministers and free traders, the debate was adjourned.

Mr. Ewart opened the second night's debate in an able and honest speech, full of proofs of the downward progress of trade, the consequences of our refusal to receive in exchange for our goods the produce of other countries. Mr. Liddell followed, and attributed the distress to over-production, in a country where one half of the people were in rags! Lord Worsley complained that ministers called the present Corn Law a "temporary" measure, and thus kept the farmer in uncertainty and alarm. Mr. Knight abused the League; the best argument, perhaps, that he had to offer. Mr. Ward gave a frightful account of the state of Sheffield. "There had been no building mania there, for only 300 houses were in course of building in 1837, but at the present moment there were no less than 3,400 houses untenanted, and a gentleman in whom he (Mr. Ward) had the most perfect confidence, wrote to him, 'I have considerable property in houses, and I have not a single tenant who is not in arrears of rent, some for two, others for three half years ; and this is the general condition of the town.' Another gentleman, whose letter he had that day received, stated, 'The affairs of the town are getting worse and worse ; the distress is intense and increasing.' The amount which had been raised for the relief of the poor was in 1839 £26,000, in 1840 £35,000, in 1841 £52,000, in 1842 and this year it would be at least £64,000." Mr. Disraeli said that if time were given for the operation of natural causes, trade would certainly revive ! Mr. Ross was rather behind the fair in proposing an 8s. duty, diminishing one shilling a year till the trade in corn was free. Mr. B. Hope attributed the distress to over-population and over production; and with this philosophical conclusion the debate for the night terminated.

Dr. Bowring commenced the third night's debate with a most distressing account of the state of Bolton. Mr. J. Wortley complained bitterly that the hon. member for Bolton had spoken of gentlemen on the ministerial side of

the house "as if they were anxious only for the continuance of their luxuries, and were totally insensible to the sufferings of the poor." Mr. Wallace showed that trade on the Clyde was not more prosperous than it was in Bolton or Sheffield. Mr. Escott made a curious substitution of effect for cause. He asked: "How is it that the distress has increased since the price of provisions fell?" The price of provisions had fallen because of diminished consumption, the consequence and effect of the distress. Mr. C. Wood spoiled a good speech by an argument in favour of a "reasonable" fixed duty, which laid him open to the sarcasms of Sir James Graham, who followed, and with whose address the debate for the night terminated. The agriculturists did not like the following passage in his address :—
" They were accustomed in that house to bandy about all sorts of criminations and recriminations respecting free-trade principles ; as to who were the authors of them, and as to those by whom they had only been adopted. After all, however, it was ridiculous to make such points the subject matter of such disputes. By most men these principles were now acknowledged to be the principles of common sense, and the outline of these principles was now disputed but by few. The time had long gone by when this country could exist solely as an agricultural country. We were now a commercial people. As long as Great Britain remained, as she now was, the mistress of the seas, she must be the emporium of the commerce of the world ; and he felt perfectly satisfied that agricultural prosperity in this country, if deprived of the support of manufacturing prosperity, could not and would not long exist. He would even go further than this. He would say that with the increasing population of this country—increasing as it did at the rate of somewhere about 220,000 per annum—it was indispensably necessary that there should be a progressive extension of commerce, and that none were more deeply interested in securing such exten-

sion than the landed interest of England. There was an increasing population; that increasing population must be employed; it could only be employed by payment of wages; wages could only be paid out of profits, and profits were dependent on demand. He held these to be *the principles of every man of common sense.*" They certainly were the principles of common sense and common justice, and *therefore* Sir James Graham and his colleagues declined to act upon them. " Common sense was off and up the Cowgate," until some other day.

The fourth night's debate was commenced by Mr. Peter Borthwick (once of Dalkeith), who rather ungraciously said that he could not give his unqualified approbation of her Majesty's ministers, but generously added they were better than their predecessors. Sir C. Napier followed, and made a speech which excited much laughter, and in which he recommended the League to make a compromise with the monopolists! Mr. Cochrane attributed the distress to speculation and agitation, but admitted that a total repeal of the Corn Law would be better than the present uncertainty. Mr. Villiers made a short speech, in which he demolished some of the fallacies advanced on the other side of the house. He said, "he could not condescend to answer the cavils and attacks that had been brought against the Anti-Corn-Law League. He thought that the Anti-Corn-Law League was well occupied in diffusing political truth. They were doing in their vocation what the religious societies were doing for religion; what the scientific societies were doing for agriculture. They could not put down the League but by doing justice, and with nothing short of that would it be satisfied." Lord Sandon, the representative of commercial Liverpool, "was perfectly convinced that we should sacrifice more by opening up our agriculture to a competition with every new soil than we could possibly gain by the speculative projects of those who contended for such a course!" Mr. Muntz, with his one idea, of

course attributed the distress to the want of paper money.
Sir John Hanmer declared in favour of a moderate fixed
duty, and at the same time protested against the "fallacy
of protection!" Mr. P. M. Stewart, Mr. Colquhoun, Mr.
F. Baring, and Mr. Goulburn followed, and at a late hour
Sir A. L. Hay moved the adjournment of the debate. It
was believed that Sir Robert Peel was waiting to reply to
Cobden, and that Cobden was waiting to reply to Peel, and
men looked eagerly forward to the encounter. In the
mean time the Council of the League had transferred its
sittings to London, had resolved on having weekly meetings at the Crown and Anchor, and its lecturers were
attending many meetings in the metropolis and its suburbs.
There was nothing in the debate, so far, notwithstanding
some important admissions, to give any hope that the
agitation would not be long and arduous.

CHAPTER III.

FEAR OF ASSASSINATION.

A short time before this memorable debate a melancholy
event occurred which had considerably shaken the equa-
nimity of the premier. It is thus described by Miss
Martineau, in her "Thirty Year's Peace":—"While all
was gloomiest, in January, 1843, an event happened which
might almost justify any increase of panic. Sir R. Peel's
private secretary, Mr. Edward Drummond, was shot in the
street, and died of the wound. It was at first supposed he
was mistaken for the premier; and, in a season such as
this, which was manifestly unsettling weak wits, it was
some time before Sir R. Peel was considered safe. Two
policemen in plain clothes followed him in the streets;
and the newspapers, which were all aware of the fact, considerately forbore (all but one) to notice the fact. •Mr.
Drummond's murderer, however, was proved a lunatic, and
lodged for life in an asylum. Yet, there was mischief in
the occurrence. Drunken men were heard to threaten the
Queen and the Minister; and infirm brains began to work
in that direction, as we see by the police reports of the time.

"Something worse than the 'fears of the brave' were
'the follies of the wise.' Grave statesmen, honourable
gentlemen, benevolent Christians, began to conceive of
conduct in their adversaries, and to utter imputations,
which could never have come into their heads at an ordinary time. The Anti-Corn-Law League had not had time
to win the respect and command the deference which it
was soon to enjoy: but it was known to be organized and

led by men of station, character, and substance—men of
enlarged education, and of that virtuous and decorous
conduct which distinguishes the middle class of England.
Yet it was believed—believed by men of education, by men
in parliament, by men in attendance on the government—
that the Anti-Corn-Law League sanctioned assassination,
and did not object to carry its aims by means of it. This
is, perhaps, the strongest manifestation of the tribulation
of the time. In the midst of it a strange and mournful
scene took place in the House of Commons—a scene which
would willingly be forgotten, but that the Spirit of History
must forget nothing which indicates or affects the course
of events. Sir R. Peel was ill, harassed with public anxi-
eties, and deeply wounded in his private feelings, by the
murder of his secretary, who was also his intimate friend.
Mr. Cobden was then little known—at least, by his opponents. He was known as the chief man of the League ;
and the League was believed to patronize assassination ! "
    The fifth night's debate was opened by Mr. Mark
Philips, who refuted heavy charges made by Mr. Ferrand
against the humanity of manufacturers. He was followed
by the other member for Manchester, Mr. Gibson, who
thoroughly refuted Sir James Graham's assertion as to the
increase of factories. Lord Ellesmere was the only speaker
on the ministerial side who suggested a remedy for the
distress. It was, the voluntary dissolution of the League !
The debate, as between whigs and tories on Corn Law repeal, was in substance this. The party *out* asked, " Why
don't you do it? " The party *in* retorted, " Why did'nt
you do it? " Mr. Cobden's speech, for which Sir Robert
Peel had waited till near midnight, was thus characterized
by the *Morning Post*, a paper not prone to compliment any
member of the League :—

    " Mr. Cobden approved himself not forgetful of the tone and temper
which suit the purpose of Anti-Corn-Law agitators out of doors. He
hurled at the heads of country gentlemen the same taunts and charges

which he has repeated, times without number, out of doors. He told them that they were not agriculturists, but merely rent-owners. He told them that the Corn Laws were not to protect farmers and labourers but to raise rents. These statements may be condemned, as we are disposed most gravely to condemn them; they may be described as untrue; they may be referred to malice as their source; but they are straightforward. They are uttered in the presence of country gentlemen, who constitute, numerically, the largest party in the house; and the utterer, by consequence, exposes himself to prompt retaliation of the most crushing kind. Mr. Cobden charged Mr. George Bankes and the other Dorsetshire landowners, with pauperising and brutalising their labourers. He defied any landowner to prove that the Corn Laws could by possibility protect labourers or farmers. He charged Sir Edward Knatchbull with having claimed the continuance of the Corn Laws as necessary to the maintenance of an aristocracy. He reminded Lord Stanley of the admission which had fallen from that noble lord, to the effect, that Corn Laws raised rents, but did not raise wages! *No man answered these charges of Mr. Cobden. No man attempted to answer them.* Sir Robert Peel's speech, whatever might be its merits, contained no defence of the Corn Laws on those general grounds on which Mr. Cobden assailed them. No; Sir Robert Peel avowed himself a *free trader* as decidedly as Mr. Cobden; but the right hon. baronet appealed to existing interests, as rendering caution in dealing with the Corn Laws indispensable. 'Mr. Huskisson was a free trader,' urged Sir Robert, 'but he was no friend to immediate and precipitate repeal. Adam Smith, the theoretical free trader, approved himself no less anxious, than the practical statesman, to proceed with the utmost caution in the application of free-trade principles.' These statements may be exceedingly sound, or they may be the reverse; *but, assuredly, these statements contain no reply to the arguments of Mr. Cobden.* If country gentlemen be really ashamed to utter one word in favour of protective principles, if they were willing to listen in silence to the furious assaults of their opponents, and if the defence to which they trust, amounts merely to a qualified admission of the truth of the principles and statements in which their opponents trust, then let country gentlemen cease to wonder at the progress made by the Anti-Corn-Law League. 'Heaven,' says the proverb, 'helps those who help themselves.' In this world, assuredly, those who will *not* help themselves will find few friends."

"No man answered Mr. Cobden," and "no man attempted to answer him." "Sir Robert Peel's speech contained no defence of the Corn Law on those general grounds on

which Mr. Cobden assailed them." These were truths,
and the acknowledgment was from an organ of the monopolists which had been notorious for bitter denunciations
of the free traders. Yes, no man answered Mr. Cobden's
charges, and no man, not even Peel himself, *attempted* to
answer them. The country gentlemen felt that they were
unanswerable. Peel felt that they were unanswerable. But
he saw that the squires were cowering under the withering
sarcasm, and scared out of the arena of debate, by the
straightforward statements and forcible arguments of the
honest and fearless representative of free-trade principles;
he saw that, under such circumstances, a victory gained by
mere numbers, while all the fair stand-up fighting was on
the other side, would be a virtual defeat; and the necessity
of diverting the current of opinion into another channel.
He knew the house he had to deal with. He raised a new
dispute to draw attention from that which had gone against
him; or, as was expressed in the *Manchester Guardian*, a
paper not apt to be unfavourable to him, he created a noise
and a smoke, that his retreat might be concealed in the
confusion. Mr. Cobden had more than once, without a
single cry of "order," asserted the responsibility of the
premier. No one perceived anything unparliamentary in
his language. Not a single angry "hear" indicated that any
one believed that the word *responsibility* was used in any
other than its parliamentary import. At the conclusion of
Mr. Cobden's speech, Sir Robert Peel and Mr. Bankes
rose together; and strong proof was then given that the
house was totally unconscious of any breach of parliamentary conventionalities, for loud cries arose of " Bankes,"
" Bankes," that gentleman being expected to reply to the
statements as to the condition of his own agricultural constituents; but the Prime Minister, by violent gesticula-
tions, by striking an empty box before him with furious
violence, and by a countenance which indicated extreme
agitation, succeeded in obtaining the ear of the house, and

then, for the first time, was the turn given to Mr. Cobden's language that he had invoked the hand of the ASSASSAIN against Sir Robert Peel.

"Sir Robert Peel said: Sir, the honourable gentleman has stated here very emphatically, what he has more than once stated at the Conference of the Anti-Corn-Law League, that he holds me individually— (these words which were pronounced with much solemnity of manner, were followed by a loud cheer from the ministerial benches, of a very peculiar and emphatic kind. It lasted a considerable time, and while it continued, and for some time afterwards, the House presented an appearance of extreme excitement, the members in the galleries standing up, and many of those below whispering eagerly to each other)—individually responsible for the distress and suffering of the country; that he holds me personally responsible. (Renewed cheering of the same character.) Be the consequences of those insinuations what they may —(cheering renewed, with great vehemence)—never will I be influenced by menaces—(continued cheering)—to adopt a course which I consider —(the rest of the sentence was lost in renewed shouts from the ministerial benches).

"Mr. Cobden rose and said: I did not say that I held the right hon. gentleman personally responsible. (Shouts from the ministerial benches of 'yes, yes; you did, you did;' mingled with cries of 'order,' and 'chair.') I have said that I hold the right honourable gentleman responsible by virtue of his office—(renewed shouts from the same quarter, cries of 'no, no,' and confusion)—as the whole context of what I said was sufficient to explain. (Renewed cries of 'no, no,' from the ministerial benches.)"

"When Sir Robert," says the *Morning Chronicle*, "in the opening of his speech, in a manner peculiarly his own, gave the signal for this new light, then, and not till then, the sense so obtained burst forth with a frantic yell which would better have befitted a company of savages, who first saw and scented their victim, than a grave and dignified assembly, insulted by conduct deemed deserving of condemnation. For all this disorder, and for all the discredit which it is calculated to bring on the House of Commons, Sir Robert Peel is responsible. Mr. Cobden, as will be seen by the report, rose instantly, and disavowed having used the word 'personal.' Sir Robert Peel, from his seat fiercely replied, 'You did, you did.' The public well know, which no member of the House of Commons should ever forget, that what a member in explanation states to have been his words and meaning, is, by the acknowledged rule of the House, to be so taken and admitted. We have here the first minister of the crown, in his place in parliament, violating one of its plainest and most undisputed rules, and doing this with a coarseness of manner at which sober-minded Englishmen of all parties must feel shame. Sir Robert Peel, after his fierce and twice-repeated contradiction of Mr. Cobden, immediately says, 'I will not overstate any thing; therefore I will not say that I AM CERTAIN the honourable gentleman used the word *personally*.' Why, then, '*if not certain*,' why did he before, in such a tone of confidence, twice deny Mr. Cobden's disclaimer?"

Many persons thought that Mr. Cobden had no occasion to disclaim the use of the word "personal," even if he had used it. The responsibility of an administration is declared by the constitution; and as there can be no collective responsibility that is not shared individually, individual punishment, one way or other, must involve personal punishment. If the individual minister be beheaded, he personally suffers; if he be imprisoned, he personally suffers; if he be degraded, he personally suffers. There is an immense amount of SHAM in parliamentary language. If a member says that a minister is wicked and profligate, satisfaction is given by an explanation that the terms were applied to him not as a man but as a minister! Mr. Roebuck, in the passing of the Income Tax, had denounced Sir Robert Peel in language more personal and inflammatory than any which has been falsely attributed to Mr. Cobden. "The right honourable baronet," said he, "is the author and propounder of this measure. He sums up the whole cabinet in his person. The Conservatives without him are nothing. *He is the party. Upon his head, if he passes it, the whole responsibility will rest with undivided,*

with peculiar, and intense weight." We have likewise to remember against Mr. Roebuck, when taunting the House of
Commons for its dislike of physical force chartism, his
famous definition of moral force—*that it is only the fear of
physical force.* Why was no notice taken of this language
at the time? Simply because Mr. Roebuck was not Mr.
Cobden. Sir Robert Peel had not been beaten by the
lawyer as he was beaten by the "Manchester Manufacturer."

Mr. Roebuck thought that the League leader had been
put down. Taking advantage of the feeling of the House,
he rose to complain that Mr. Cobden had threatened to
send the League to his electors of Bath; and the three
hundred men who, with all manner of savage cries and
yells, had welcomed Peel's interpretation of responsibility
to his country, renewed their cries and yells of indignation
against Mr. Cobden for reminding Mr. Roebuck of his
responsibility to his constituents. What if Mr. Cobden
had. told him, jocularly and in private, that the League
would visit his constituents? Why should not every
member be told, publicly, and from the house tops, that
his backslidings would be exposed to the voters who send
him to parliament? It is the business of every man, to
the extent of his means and influence, to instruct constituents upon every question affecting their own and the
nation's interests. It was the especial business of the
League so to instruct the constituencies, throughout the
kingdom, that they might be enabled to make a right
choice of representatives when elections occurred, and to
judge correctly of the conduct of those who represented or
misrepresented them.

In giving a description of this unhappy scene, I have
expressed what I felt when I read the newspaper reports at
the time. I have regarded Peel as the partizan, not as
the statesman which he afterwards became. He was then
but a leader led. His better nature afterwards emancipated
him from a thraldom which he could not but feel as deeply

degrading. He rose to command where he had been accustomed to obey. He made such compensation for a long
support of oppression as his conscience dictated and his
judgment approved. The historian has to do with both
phases of his political life, and is not, because he afterwards
rose to the highest position both as a man and as a legislator, to pass without strong condemnation the error which
inflicted so many sufferings on the people. Perhaps the
yelling and the howling of his faction, when they thought
that an enemy had been put under their feet, may have
contributed to rouse the nobler attributes of his character.
He must have been deeply ashamed of such support, and
ashamed that to ensure it he must avail himself of the
tricks of the party politician, rather than aspire to the
statesman-like dignity which subsequently placed him high
amongst the highest men who had graced the annals of
English history. Soon after this lamentable scene in the
House of Commons observant men thought they could discover symptoms of change in the premier, leading them to
conclude that he was impatient of his slavery to a faction,
and others began to think of the possibility of his becoming
a corn-law repealer, if he could but see his way of com-
manding a majority. There were many saying, as Poulett
Thomson said on his way to the government of Canada,
" Peel could do it if he had the courage." On the division
the numbers were, for the motion, 191; against it, 306.

There were those also who thought that it would be true
conservatism to destroy the source of great mischiefs.
Amongst them was Thomas Carlyle, who, in his "Past and
Present" said: " O, my Conservative friends, who still
specially name, and struggle to approve yourselves ' Conservative,' would to heaven I could persuade you of this
world-old fact, than which Fate is not surer; That Truth
and Justice alone are *capable* of being 'conserved' and preserved! The thing which is unjust, which is *not* according
to God's Law, will you, on a God's Universe, try to conserve

that? It is old, say you? Yes, and the hotter haste ought *you*, of all others, to be in to let it grow no older! If but the faintest whisper in your hearts intimate to you that it is not fair,—hasten, for the sake of Conservatism itself, to probe it vigorously, to cast it forth at once, and for ever, if guilty. How will or can you preserve *it*? The thing is not fair? 'Impossible,' a thousandfold is marked on that. And ye call yourselves Conservatives, Aristocracies. Ought not honour and nobleness of mind, if they had departed from all the earth elsewhere, to find their last refuge with you? Ye unfortunate!

"The bough that is dead shall be cut away, for the sake of the tree itself. Old? yes, it is too old. Many a weary winter has it swung and creaked there, and knawed and fretted, with its dead wood, the organ in substance and still living fibre of this good tree; many a long summer has its ugly naked brown defaced the fair green umbrage; every day it has done mischief, and that only: off with it, for the tree's sake, if for nothing more; let the Conservatism that would preserve, cut *it* away. Did no wood forester apprise you that a dead bough, with its dead root striking there is extraneous, poisonous; is as a dead iron spike, some horrid rust ploughshare driven into the living substance;—nay, is far worse; for in every windstorm ('commercial crisis' or the like), it frets and creaks, jolts itself to and fro, and cannot be quiet as your dead iron spike would! If I were the Conservative Party of England (which is another bold figure of speech), I would not for a hundred thousand pounds an hour allow those Corn Laws to continue. All Potosi and Golconda put together would not purchase my assent to them. Do you count what treasuries of bitter indignation they are laying up for you in every just English heart? Do you know what questions, not as Corn-prices and Sliding scales alone, they are *forcing* every reflective Englishman to ask himself? Questions insoluble or hitherto unsolved; deeper than any of our Logic-

plummets hitherto will sound, questions deep enough,—
which it were better we did not name, even in thought.
You are forcing us to think of them. The utterance of them
is begun; and where will it be ended think you? When
now millions of one's brother-men sit in workhouses, and
five millions, as is insolently said, 'rejoice in potatoes' there
are various things that must be begun, let them end where
they can."

Mr. Cobden was not put down, not weakened, not lessened in public estimation; strengthened and encouraged
rather. The League deputies were in London, and the
first of their renewed metropolitan meetings was held in
the Crown and Anchor on the Wednesday after the melancholy scene in the House of Commons. Mr. Hamer
Stansfield, of Leeds, was called to the chair, and expressed
his warm indignation against the attempt to affix a stigma
on the name of Richard Cobden. Mr. Cobden's reception
was with rapturous cheers which lasted for several minutes.
After expressing his astonishment that he, a member of
the Peace Society before he was known as a politician, and
who conscientiously believed that it was worse than useless
to take human life even for murder, should be accused of
instigating to assassination, he went on calmly but forcibly
to represent the duty of London joining in the peaceful
and peace-preserving agitation. He was followed by Mr.
Bright, still described as of Rochdale, whose powerful
speech was interrupted by an announcement that a meeting
had been formed in the body of the house, formed of the
crowds which could not gain admission to the hall. A
deputation having been appointed to address the additional
assemblage, Mr. Bright resumed his speech, and claimed
for the League the credit of having preserved the peace in
an alarming state of affairs in the previous year, and said
that to such outbreaks the country would always be liable
so long as the Corn Laws existed, but that if they were
repealed there would not need to be maintained a soldier

in Lancashire or in Yorkshire. The meeting was subsequently addressed by Colonel Thompson, who said that argument was sadly wanting, when charges of instigating to assassination were resorted to ; and by Mr. Hume, who hailed Sir Robert Peel as a new convert to free trade, who would show his principles if he were not overborne by the aristocracy.

On the following evening nearly ten thousand persons congregated in the Free Trade Hall, at Manchester, to testify their unabated attachment to the cause of free trade and its distinguished advocate. Mr. Wilson, the chairman, after giving an account of the scene in the House of Commons, and reading some of the calumnies in the *Times*, the *Morning Herald*, and the *Standard*, said :—

For four years, under many a trying calumny and under the greatest provocations, we have never deviated from pursuing the object for which this League was established ; we have never, during that period, turned aside to refute the thousand-and-one misrepresentations, to call them by the mildest name, by which we have been beset; and if we depart from that rule, on the present occasion, it is on account of the attack being one of the grossest, one of the vilest, one of the most painful that could be heaped upon us. In the name then, of all who are included, collectively, or individually, in this accusation, I deny all alliance with, and approbation and knowledge of, any agent or means, other than those that are peaceful, moral, and in accordance with the principles of the British constitution, for the accomplishment of our object. (Great and prolonged cheering.) In the name of the ladies, (Great cheering,) the occupants of those galleries, (Immense cheering, the whole of the vast assemblage in the body of the hall waving their hats,) who have graced our meetings on many a previous occasion, and who are included in that base attack,—I deny it. (Deafening cheers.) In the name of the thousands of working men who stand before me in this hall, and who are included in that base attack,—I deny it. (Cheers.) In the name of the gentlemen who stand around me on this platform, who countenance our proceedings, who are identified with them, and who are included in this attack,—I deny it. (Renewed cheering.) In the name of the great body of merchants, manufacturers, traders, and others in this and in different parts of the country, identified with us, and who are included in this attack,—I deny it. (Continued cheering.) In the name of the mayors, magistrates, preservers of the peace, and members of both houses of the legislature, who have contributed to our funds, and who have also sanctioned our proceedings, and are included in the attack,—I deny it. (Prolonged cheering.) And, lastly, in the name of two thousand ministers of religion, (Loud and reiterated cheering,) who have left their sacred calling that they might lend their aid in obtaining bread for the hungry, and clothing for the naked, and who are included in the attack, —I deny it. (Renewed cheers.) And, finally, I hurl back the calumny upon whoever may choose to utter it, as a most atrocious, most wilful, most audacious falsehood. (Loud and long-continued cheering.) The hall, during this emphatic repudiation of the charges against the League, presented a most extraordinary scene of excitement, and it was not till the expiration of some moments after the chairman had taken his seat that it subsided.

The meeting was then addressed by Mr. Henry Ashworth, of Bolton, Mr. Thomas Bazley, Sir Thomas Potter, Mr. Benjamin Pearson, Mr. Alderman Callender, Mr. Jno. Bright, and others, and the following address was carried unanimously :—

"TO RICHARD COBDEN, ESQ., M.P.

" We, the undersigned, your fellow-townsmen, inhabitants of the boroughs of Manchester and Salford, desire to express our deep sense of the invaluable service which, during your residence amongst us, you have rendered to this town, and to the interests of our country.

" We more especially regard your untiring labours in the sacred cause of freedom of industry, as entitling you to the gratitude and confidence of all classes of the population of this empire; and we have rejoiced to witness the appreciation of your exertions recently manifested by the people and the municipalities of Scotland.

" Elected by the honest suffrages of the people of Stockport, we feel that you have been equally the representative of the dearest rights and interests of all your countrymen; and in tendering you our hearty support, we do it in the full conviction that we are but giving expression to the sentiments of millions whose voice is too rarely heard in the legislature of this empire.

" We have seen with indignation the attempts made by the monopolists, and their organs of the press, to heap slanders upon the man who has been so powerfully instrumental in denouncing the injustice of that legislation which has brought this once flourishing country to the verge of ruin; and we can understand that the distinguished position in which you are placed, is well calculated to excite the hostility of all who believe themselves interested in the continuance of the wrong which you have done so much to expose.

" Fortified by the approbation of your own conscience, and by that of a vast portion of your fellow countrymen, who have watched your career with intense and increasing interest, you can well afford to despise the assaults and calumnies with which the abettors of monopoly seek to turn you from the prosecution of the great work to which you have so nobly devoted yourself.

" We bid you go on. Your country and mankind call upon you not to falter in your course. The truths you promulgate and defend are established in the hearts of millions, and from those hearts the fervent prayer arises, that He who is the dispenser of mercies may prosper you in your arduous labours, and dispose the hearts of the rulers of this land to relieve the dire distress which is desolating thousands of homes. May they early and completely adopt those principles which can alone restore comfort and prosperity to the people of our beloved and much suffering country ! "

On the first of March, another meeting, the last there, was held at the Crown and Anchor, at which it was stated that since December 136 meetings had been held in London, and that the amount of subscriptions there had been £22,000 ; the latter a proof that the monied classes were beginning to take an increased interest in the subject. The meeting was addressed by Mr. Villiers, Mr. R. R. Moore, Sir De Lacy Evans ; and Mr. Cobden took part in the proceedings. Again speakers had to be detached to address the crowds which filled the large committee-rooms, the wide and long lobby, and the staircase. The chairman announced that the use of Exeter Hall had been applied for, but refused. On the following evening, at Rochdale, two meetings also arose out of one, the overflowing of the Theatre having filled the spacious Assembly Room. Mr. Bright addressed the one for an hour while I addressed the other, and then we changed places for another hour. There was no other remedy in London, Exeter Hall being refused, and no central site for the erection of a metropolitan Free Trade Hall being to be found, than resorting to Drury Lane Theatre, which was engaged for one night a week during the season of Lent. The meetings throughout the country, immediately following the attack in parliament on Cobden and the League, were so numerous that some pages of this volume would be filled with even the names of the places where they were held. When fit place of utterance was found in London, the movement might truly be called National, and its history, from that period, can be found in the London press, and more especially in the *League* weekly newspaper, which, in the course of the summer, took the place of the small fortnightly *Anti-Corn-Law Circular*. I am therefore hereafter released from much of the detail which I felt to be necessary in giving an account of the origin of the League, and its progress in the provinces.

CHAPTER IV.

DRURY LANE MEETINGS.

On the evening of Wednesday, March 15th, the first meeting of the League was held in Drury-Lane Theatre. Never, in the palmiest days of the legitimate drama, had pit, boxes, and gallery been so filled. The youthful chairman, George Wilson, was received with enthusiastic cheers, and Mr. Ewart, M.P., had a similar reception. Cobden's incontrovertible argument went home to the heads and hearts of that immense metropolitan audience. He concluded his speech by saying :—

"He could hardly describe the anguish of heart which he felt at finding that the men who were imposing the horrible system of monopoly upon the bread of the people, had actually succeeded in using as instruments for the maintenance of that law the class which suffered most severely from its operation ; and that they had hired men from that class to play the part of the bread-taxers in the present great conflict. He felt deep anguish at finding that those poor men had been made use of by designing parties who should have known better than to have employed them. The members of the Anti-Corn-Law League had been assailed as a body who wanted to injure the working class. Why, if the repealing the Corn Law were to benefit any class, it could only be by benefitting that class through the working class. (Hear, hear.) He took it for granted that whatever amount of corn they might bring into this country, the middle class and the upper class would not eat one ounce more bread than they did now. (Hear.) Who, then, were to consume the extra quantity? The working men, they who now, to the number of five millions, according to Dr. Marsham, were 'rejoicing in potatoes.' (Hear.) The working men must consume the corn. They would be set to work to pay for that corn with the produce of their wages. They went to the shopkeeper; the shopkeeper was enriched by the custom of the labourer. The shopkeeper went to the wholesale dealer; each shopkeeper went to the neighbouring shopkeeper, and they again enriched each other. The wholesale dealer went to the manufacturer; the manufacturer could only supply the demands of the wholesale dealer by setting to work more operatives. Such was the beautiful order in which Divine Providence regulated this world. There was a circle of continuous links, which could not be injured in any one point, but it would, like electricity, pervade the whole chain. (Great cheering.) Now, he had said that the working class, the shopkeeper, the merchant, the manufacturer, and the farmer, were interested in this question. But there was another class, which fancied itself secure, which was more deeply interested in the question than any other—and that was the landed aristocracy. (Hear, hear.) They called them (the Anti-Corn-Law League) their enemies. If they knew their position, they would call them their friends and their saviours. (Hear, hear.) For let them but continue this war with the people, let it only be continued on that most odious ground the bread monopoly, and not all the virtuous patriotism of your Radnors, your Kinnairds, your Clanricardes, and your Ducies, would save the landed aristocracy from the fate which it would inevitably bring upon them. Why, what were the ominous symptoms now? The town population arrayed against them, their own farmers and farm-labourers dropping from their side. They came up to London in the present session of parliament, after spending a troubled and uneasy autumn with their tenants and their labourers. The landlords dared not face their tenants during their last recess. (Hear, hear.) When they did get up dinners, they skulked into large towns like Devonport or Plymouth. They came up to London, knowing that they had left disaffected dependents at home; and what did they find in this metropolis? Why, this mighty metropolis, including its most fashionable quarters, putting itself at the head of the Anti-Corn-Law League. Let them go on, and in a short time they would find themselves like the French nobility previous to the revolution—an isolated, helpless, powerless class—a class that in their own inherent qualities, in their intellectual and moral powers, were inferior to any other classes of society. (Great cheering.) Their greatness and their power consisted in the favourable opinion of their fellow-citizens. They not only clung to feudal abuses, but they actually tried to put a restraint upon the supply of food for the people. They were warring against the progression of the age. They fancied that the system which still existed here was necessary; that their feudal system was necessary to the existence of the community. Why, their feudal system had gone in France, it had gone in Germany; in America it had never existed. The question now was, whether the feudal system in this country was to flourish beside an advancing and progressive manufacturing and commercial community? There were manufacturing and commercial communities in other countries, where feudalism did not exist. They would exist here by the side of feudalism, if feudalism would allow them, but if not by the side of feudalism, feudalism would not be permitted to stop the progress of civilization; if not by the side of it, then the manufacturing and commercial interests would flourish upon the ruins of feudalism. (Cheers.) He had only to ask every class that loved justice, that loved humanity, that wished well, not only to the physical, but to the moral, the intellectual, and the religious well-being of their countrymen, to take home with them the sentiments which they had heard that night, to lay them to heart, examine them carefully; and if, after examining the question, they fe't convinced of the enormity of the iniquity of which they complained, then they would indeed be accountable if they did not do all that they cou d, according to the talents which God had committed to them, to abolish this most monstrous evil."

John Bright, described as of Rochdale, not long to need a local designation, followed Cobden, with as accurate a knowledge of his subject, more passionate vehemence, and perhaps occasionally with more immediate power. After describing, with great effect, the pauperized condition of the country, and earnestly warning that great audience that London would not long remain exempt from the general wretchedness, he said:

"There was no institution of this country—the monarchy, aristocracy, the church, or any other whatever—of which he would not say, 'Attach it to the Corn Law, and I will predict its fate.' (Cheers.) In this country everything which he held dear was contained. In countries not far off, they had seen institutions shaken to their foundation by dire calamities. They had seen crowns and hierarchies shaken to the dust; they had seen ranks, and orders, and parties overthrown; but there was one party which survived all this, and that party was, the people. (Great cheering.) Whatever convulsion might happen in this country, whatever orders might be overthrown, the people would survive. (Renewed cheers.)

> 'There's yet on earth a far auguster thing,
> Small though it be, than parliament, or king.'

(Cheers.) A writer of great ability and reputation had said of Sir

Robert Peel that ' he was like a god, but his feet were made of clay.'
(Cheers and a laugh.) Did Sir Robert Peel know the source from
which he had sprung? Did he know all that he owed to that industry
which was oppressed, and trampled, and crushed by these laws?
(Cheers.) But it had been well said by the late Lord Stowell, that
' ambition breaks the ties of blood, and forgets the obligations of
gratitude.' (Cheers.) He would now ask the meeting what was their
duty? What was the duty of all their countrymen? He would tell
them that the question which they had to decide was, Whether this was
their country or the country of the monopolists? (Cheers.) Were they
mere sojourners in the land—mere lodgers—existing in this island, by
the sufferance of the monopolists and the owners of the soil? (Cheers.)
Were the people to sweat at the forge, and to toil in the mill, and were
they not to eat? (Hear, hear.) The monopolists said 'Yes.' (Cheers.)
For three weeks past he had attended meetings in the provinces—some
not less numerous than the present, and certainly none less enthusiastic.
(Cheers.) The provinces had spoken out, and they had acted as well
as spoken. (Cheers.) The Council of the League had asked for £50,000
to carry out this great cause, and they got it. (Loud cheers.) They
applied it to the purpose for which it was intended, and they had
effected to a great extent that purpose. (Cheers.) The hon. member
for Dorsetshire was astonished at their progress (cheers and laughter);
for he found their quiet, but powerful, tracts penetrating into the re-
motest corners of his estate. (Loud cheers.) There was still a great
deal to be done which could not be done without more money. He
would assure the people of London that they had more to do than
coming to the weekly meetings of the League. There were persons assembled not far from there that were at that moment thinking what was
doing in Drury Lane, though unfortunately they seldom thought of their
fellow-creatures (cheers); but in the provinces they were also thinking
what was doing in Drury Lane (cheers); but much as there was doing
still much remained to be done. If the men who were there, believed
that the country was ruined unless this law were repealed—believed that
the League was the best means of effecting the repeal of those laws, he
asked every such man, and every such woman too—(a laugh)—to give
something in aid of the great cause. (Cheers.) There were pages in
the history of the country to which every one of them might turn with
pride; but if they hesitated to assist in this great cause, he would call
upon them to tear every page of pride from the history of the country,
and to take care that no future historian should write the history of the
age in which they lived. (Cheers.) He had long looked to this city—
he had long looked to this very building—he had said, ' When can we
have a meeting in Drury Lane, and cram it full? (Cheers.) If we do,

we shall be near the attainment of our object.' They (the people of London) were the centre of a great empire, the fate of which was trembling in the balance, and which had long been struggling even to faintness with this great iniquity. (Loud cheers.) The provinces, without which they could not exist, and from which they drew all their wealth—all their sustenance—had done that which was the duty of the people of London. He spoke in the name of the numerous meetings which he had attended throughout the country, and he called on them to raise their voices to the legislature, and to co-operate with those meetings until that blessed and happy day should arrive, when this monopoly should be overthrown, and the blessings which God had provided for the whole of his people, should be enjoyed by all. (Immense cheering.)"

The enthusiasm of that crowded meeting must have been very galling to those, who, while professing to be free traders, held aloof from the movement, on the excuse that some of its leading men were imprudent and indiscreet. At a great meeting held at Stroud in that week, Earl Ducie showed that he was not to be held back by any such unhealthy or assumed fastidiousness. He said : "I am prepared to give my humble support to the exertions of the Anti-Corn-Law League. Although I do not agree with all that is said, and all that is done, by some of the individual members, I do agree with the conduct of the League itself, and *I do come here to identify myself with the League as a body. I come here ready to identify myself with every act of that body as a body ; and as long as they so act, I will defend their cause.* It may be asked why I as a farmer, am for the repeal of the Corn Laws, and what good the repeal would do to the farming interest ? I will meet this question by asking another. What good has the farmers received from the existence of the Corn Laws ? If their existence for twenty-seven years had done the farmer good—of course the farmer is now doing well, of course he is now very rich, his affairs are very prosperous ! But, gentlemen, I know the farmer will say he is not doing well ; he has been toiling early and late, enjoying all the advantages of protection, and yet he is neither rich nor prosperous.

Gentlemen, things cannot go on well while men are seeking
to confront the bounty of Providence, running counter to
the will of Providence, and restricting the interchange of
that bounty which the wise Giver of all good has dispensed
to all, by taxing the necessaries of life." Lord Ducie's
adhesion to all the acts of the League must have been
gall and wormwood to the splenetic and restless Lord
Brougham, who had endeavoured to throw discredit on the
body by a virulent attack upon some of its members.

Another great meeting was held, March 22nd, in Drury
Lane Theatre, boxes, pit, and gallery again crammed;
ladies taking as deep an interest in the proceedings as the
enrolled members of the League. The speakers were
Mr. G. Wilson; Mr. Villiers, M.P.; Mr. Leader, M.P.;
Mr. Christie, M.P.; and Mr. R. R. Moore. London was
beginning to be moved effectively. Hitherto it had been
behind the provinces, and its apparent apathy, notwithstanding the labours of an active anti-corn-law association,
had contributed to the impression that the enactments of
the landowners and of other equally selfish monopolists,
each aiding and supporting the other, were safe from all
the assaults directed against them from other parts of the
kingdom. It was a great object to have the metropolis
actively co-operating.

The enthusiastic meetings held in Drury Lane Theatre
had led me to believe that London was thoroughly roused
against landlord-law; but a few days' inquiry there, previous to the third meeting, with more than usual opportu-
nities of ascertaining the state of public opinion, dispelled
the illusion. It was, in truth, a hasty judgment to conclude
that a city equal in population, and enormously exceeding
in wealth, many kingdoms which have borne a great name
in history, was to be moved as a little town whose adult
inhabitants could all be congregated in one building, to be
instructed and moved to the protection of their own
interest. It was true that there was a newspaper press,

conducted with great ability, in which the best arguments
on both sides of any public question were certain to be
found; and it was true that the citizens were great newspaper readers and great talkers upon what appears in the
journals. But the London press had only recently commenced to discuss the corn-law question with any degree
of earnestness; and where there is no earnestness there
can be no force. Besides, as a newspaper reader, the
genuine Londoner, in the very abundance of his opportu-
nities, is more apt to glance slightly over than to look
closely into conflicting arguments; and thus the knowledge acquired is superficial, although the show of looking
at both sides, and the belief that he has thoroughly
inquired, makes your citizen exceedingly satisfied with his
own conclusions. Thus were found a great number of
persons who, knowing nothing of the real bearings of the
Corn Law, imagined that they were thoroughly acquainted
with the subject; and professed free traders were heard to
defend a fixed duty with as much vehemence as if they
really had hold of a principle.

Having seen what these meetings had to encounter, and
what the League had to overcome, I went to the Theatre
in Drury Lane on Wednesday, with my curiosity much
excited to know how far the arguments were understood
and appreciated by an audience not entirely coming together to inquire, but in some degree to be amused. The
spectacle fully equalled, and indeed greatly exceeded, my
expectations. The pit, the four tiers of boxes, and the
large gallery were literally crammed. As a mere *sight* it
was splendid; but to me, who had seen the rise of the
League, from a little meeting in a room over the stables
of the York Hotel, in Manchester, it possessed a great
additional interest. *There*, before me, was proof, at all
events, that the proceedings of the free traders had roused
a spirit either of inquiry or curiosity; that they were now
fully before the public; that they had now vindicated their

claim to be *heard*. *There* was the greatest assembly that could be brought together under one roof in the great metropolis of the world, *ready to hear*. My curiosity was roused, almost painfully roused, to ascertain in what spirit and with what intelligence they heard ; whether the excitement that might arise was from argument and a sense of justice, or merely from the gratification to the ear from impassioned oratory.

The first speaker introduced by the chairman was Mr. James Wilson. I knew that he was closely argumentative, relying more upon statistical figures than on figures of speech, and trusting more to facts and reasonings than to rhetorical flourishes. He was just the man to test the previously-acquired knowledge of the audience. If they listened with interest to plain statements, and appreciated a plainly-put point, then they had come to learn and not to be excited by flashes of oratory. And so it proved. They not only listened with deep interest to an address which lasted three quarters of an hour, but repeatedly applauded with enthusiasm when a telling argument was uttered. In his plain business-like way, Mr. Wilson demolished Lord Monteagle's fallacy about a fixed duty of 5s. being paid, not by the British consumer, but by the foreign grower of wheat, and went on with a number of statistical proofs of the injury inflicted by "protection," not only without wearying his audience, but manifestly to their high gratification. A memorial had appeared in the early part of the week, in which the great merchants, bankers, and traders of London had prayed that an efficient system of colonization might be established. I was afraid that the London people might be drawn from the real chase to the false trail ; but the portion of them before me soon showed that they were not thus to be deceived, for the moment Mr. Wilson distantly alluded to a wholesale emigration, there was an intense burst of indignant feeling. In short, I was convinced that it was not mere excitement that was sought at these meetings, but information ; and that there had been much previous thinking amongst the audience, so readily 'did they apprehend an argument, a point, and even a distant allusion.

Mr. W. J. Fox followed, whose pen had done good service to free trade. I had not seen him before, and was struck with his appearance. His stature was of the lowest, and instead of being thin and wiry as most actively-intellectual little men are, he had both a full round body, and a full round countenance, such as might betoken a sluggish temperament, were not that belied by the expression of his mouth and eyes. The singularity of his appearance was heightened by a thick mass of black hair which floated on his broad shoulders. He commenced his address, and, at once, the rich deep tones of his voice hushed the whole audience into the deepest attention. So beautifully articulated was every syllable, that his stage whisper might have been heard at the farthest extremity of the gallery. The matter was good—nay excellent; abounding with neatly-pointed epigram, cutting sarcasm, withering denunciation, and argument condensed and urged with laconic force. Nothing could be finer ; nothing told better than his proof of the truth of the free trade doctrines, that nothing *new* could be advanced on their side—truth not abounding in novelty—but additional evidences, everywhere furnished, of the pernicious consequences of the Corn Law. The speech read well ; but the reader could have no conception of its effect as delivered, with a beauty of elocution, which Macready, on those same boards, might have envied. The effect, when he called on his hearers to bind themselves in a solemn league never to cease their labours till the Corn Laws were destroyed, was electrical—thousands starting on their feet, with arms extended, as if ready to swear extinction to monopoly.

I confess that I thought it ill-judged, when, after a speech of such spirit-stirring effect, Mr. Gisborne took his turn in his usual course of genial jocosity. It seemed profanation to raise a laugh out of the deep-toned feeling that had been induced. There was another contrast in the appearance of the two men. Instead of the short unmoving figure, breathing forth solemn but sweet and thrilling tones, there was before us a tall slender gentleman, moving here and there along the stage, now bending over the table as if he would jump into the pit, and now with his hands on his haunches addressing the galleries, waving his arms about like a windmill, and uttering joke after joke, with as much enjoyment to his auditors as to himself. But Gisborne was capable of more than a joke, and if he raised a laugh, he showed that he could also furnish some good materials for thinking. His speech was on the whole exceedingly good and effective.

Richard Cobden came, last not least, and had a reception which justified what I had heard said before, that he was the most popular man in London. I acknowledge that I was somewhat disappointed. I had heard him speak, over and over again, with more effect. I was jealous of his reputation, and grudged that he should utter one sentence without evident effect. But from him I turned to the audience, and soon perceived that they had formed a just appreciation of the man. There was not that strained attention which was seen when Mr. Fox and Mr. Gisborne addressed them, and when every one seemed prepared for a burst of enthusiasm or a burst of laughter; but there was the quiet listening silence, expective not of excitement but of sound instruction,—the manifestly-expressed faith that there was something well worth hearing and well worth waiting for. And on reflection I thought the more of the intelligence of the audience for this—the more of the rapidly-maturing public opinion of London. It seemed to say : " Here is a man who does not strain after effect—does not divest an argument of one thread of sequence for effect—goes plainly on to instruct, not to excite—and is content to rest an argument on its own intrinsic value without artificial adornment." And in this faith of his hearers Cobden has his strength. He gets out all he has to say, and all he means to say. He convinces as he goes along, and with a simplicity and plainness which seem to render conviction irresistible. And thus are his hearers prepared for those occasional bursts of fervour which no man with Cobden's ideality and earnestness can keep pent up in his own bosom. His denunciation of the wickedness of transporting the best part of our population to find that food which their labour would bring home to them but for selfish laws, was given with all the power of a righteous indignation; and his affecting picture of emigrants leaving their native land was in the finest tone of sympathy for the sufferings of his fellow-creatures. On the one occasion and the other, the loudly expressed indignation, and the starting tear, convinced me that the great and brilliant audience was moved by a strong sense of justice, and a deeply-felt benevolence. Taking this meeting as representative of London, I concluded that public opinion and sentiment were vigorous and healthful.

For two days before the next meeting I had been much occupied in the splendid region created by the Marquis of Westminster to the west of the Queen's Palace, and in the more ancient but stately and aristocratic squares and streets in the northern part of the great West End. What a contrast there was to the squalor and wretchedness of Spitalfields and Wapping! Everywhere around was seen evidence of wealth—magnificent horses, handsome carriages, horses champing the bit in pure pride of blood, liveried servants, and all the other outward and visible signs of unstinted luxury. And all this, while millions were in a state bordering upon starvation; and all this within from half-an-hour to an hour's walk of abodes more filthy, more squalid, more wretched than could be found

in Little Ireland or the miserable courts in George's Road.
What could the inhabitants of these palaces know of their
neighbours? They lived in an atmosphere of their own.
They were in a Goshen, where the plagues of Egypt might
not come. Of the doings and the sufferings of some million and a half of their fellow-citizens they were as ignorant
as if separated by the wide Pacific. They did not even
hear of the sufferers, but occasionally as grumblers, discontented with the fate assigned them. *Brothers!* Could
the inhabitants of this great mansion, with all its well-
ordered and luxurious appointments, recognize a dirty,
potato-fed, half-naked, unshaved, and unwashed Spitalfield
weaver as his *brother?* Could he sympathize with such?
And were one of the palace-inhabiting, Goshen-sheltered
men to be asked what he had done for his brother in
Spitalfields, there would be the expression of astonishment
like that of Cain, that the welfare of that brother should
ever be considered a matter with which he had anything to
do. Not that there was utter heartlessness. But there was
complete separation of classes. A separation as complete as
if they dwelt not in the same world—as destructive of all
mutual sympathies—and thus the extremes of luxury and
wretchedness were next-door neighbours, who knew not
each other, and never interchanged a kind word. It was
in this territory of exclusiveness that the "representatives"
of the people, as they call themselves, resided. There
were the abodes of the possessors of the "hereditary
wisdom" that, with the title to which it is attached, is
the qualification for a seat in the legislature. Could it
be wondered at that legislation should be a class legislation when it proceeded from those who knew nothing beyond the little world in which they moved,—said nothing
—heard nothing,—not willing to see, or hear, or know
anything of suffering poverty? Substantial remedies for
deep-felt national evils were not to be expected from such
men. Were multitudes complaining for want of food?

"*Send them abroad to find it*," was the reply. Had farm-labourers insufficient wages? "*Let to them half an acre of land for fifty shillings that now yields us nothing!*" Were parents compelled by sheer want to send their children to the coal pit or the factory? "*Do not let them be received.*" Did poverty drive families into cellars? "*They shall not live there—they must find better dwellings.*" Did the man who could not purchase a donkey, yoke a dog to his hand cart? "*We cannot allow cruelty to dogs.*" Did children grow up ignorant of their social and religious duties? "*Teach them the Church Catechism.*" Had we crime, the usual concomitant of poverty? *Build new churches.* Sharman Crawford, Joseph Sturge, what chance had you to persuade such men of the reasonableness of having a vote in the choice of representatives? Richard Cobden, John Bright, what chance had *you* to persuade such men to allow the Padiham weaver to exchange his piece of calico for a bushel of good American wheat? The confident answer was: "*Let the oppressed many make the ruling few uneasy.*"

And the ruling few did begin to become uneasy at those magnificent weekly demonstrations of the League in Drury Lane Theatre. The *John Bull* called the landowners to the rescue; warned them of the consequences of permitting it thus to form a strong public opinion; and told them plainly that if they did not instantly counteract the mis-chievous doings of the free-traders, they would richly deserve the ruin that was sure to befal them.

The meeting on Wednesday, April 5th, was quite as numerous and enthusiastic as any which preceded it, and there was abundant evidence that were every theatre in London to be opened on the same evening, for expositions of the injustice of monopoly, every one of them would be filled. George Wilson discharged his duties, as chairman, with more than his usual ability. Hitherto he had been too careful and too fastidious in utterance. That night, seemingly more at ease with his great audience, he

delivered a really effective speech. Joseph Hume seemed
inspired with new hope and new energy by the sight
before him, and gave the promise of fresh life in the
redress of the wrong against which he had so long battled.
I had experienced some difficulty in obtaining his promise
to take part in the meeting. He had been almost hopeless of moving the indifference of the House of Commons,
and did not think that his aid would contribute much to
the furtherance of free trade. I reminded him of the good
already done by the publication of the evidence brought
before the Import Duties Committee, of which he had
been chairman, laid before him a small neatly bound
volume, and said, " The man who has been instrumental
in reducing that book from three shillings to one shilling,
ought not to despair of any thing ; I had it yesterday from
John Childs, as part of the results of the abolition of the
Scotch Bible monopoly.* He smiled, and promised me
that he would address the meeting ; and I rejoiced to see
the cordiality of his reception, and to mark the spirit with
which he spoke. Joseph Brotherton made a good speech,
which was well received. He wanted the vivacity which
tells on such assemblies ; but the plain common-sense
view of the question was taken, and his obvious earnestness made amends for any lack there might be of exciting
oratory. Mr. Milner Gibson was more effective than I had
ever heard him before ; he was earnest even to fervour,
and his speech, full of argument, well and very cleverly
put, elicited repeated bursts of cheers   John Bright, who
had just returned from a manly and closely-run contest
with a monopolist at Durham, was the last speaker ; and
his speech fully justified the approbation with which he
was received ; and he was repeatedly and enthusiastically
cheered during his stirring address.

While the more prominent members of the League were

* See Tax on Bibles at the end of this volume.

occupying the boards of Old Drury, Mr. Paulton and I thought we would try what sort of audience we could have at the Sadlers Wells Theatre, capable, from the great size of the stage, of holding some 2,400 persons. When we arrived there, the place was completely filled, and in the attendance was a great number of ladies. Mr. Lawrence Heyworth, of Liverpool, having been called to the chair, opened the business, and took a broad general view of the question, in its political, moral, and religious aspects. Mr. Paulton very effectively answered the fallacy that a low price of provisions was attended by low wages, and showed that land in Russia, Austria, and France, paid a much greater share of the general taxation. He was loudly cheered throughout his speech; and I found, when I began to speak, that he had prepared the audience to be very favourable to me; and I certainly never saw a more enthusiastic meeting. Mr. George Wilson, making way to the back of the stage about the middle of the proceedings, heard a tumult within, which led him to conclude that the chartists of Finsbury had overpowered us, and were triumphing in consequence, and he was greatly relieved when the scene was completely before him. From this meeting I could judge that the various assemblages in large rooms and halls throughout London, under the direction of the Metropolitan Association, had not been without their fruits.

The fifth weekly meeting was held in Drury Lane, April 12th, Mr. George Wilson in the chair. In the course of his address he said :—

" During the last week some little diversity has taken place in this agitation. We observe that the enemy have had their meetings. There has been a county meeting in Buckinghamshire. (Laughter.) It was called a county meeting, but certainly no member of the county was present on the occasion. The Duke of Buckingham—(hisses and laughter)—the farmers' friend—(renewed hisses)—declined to have anything to do with it, and the only distinguished orators were that most excellent, but certainly most misguided peer, the Earl Stanhope, who was the great knight, and Dr. Sleigh, our old acquaintance, who was his lordship's trusty squire on that occasion. That meeting being attended with such discouraging circumstances will not, I think, incline these gentlemen to have another. But on that same day the League had a meeting, not in Buckinghamshire, but in Somersetshire, at Taunton, and which meeting was addressed by Mr. Cobden, Mr. Bright, and Mr. Moore. The Shire Hall was thronged to suffocation. There were upwards of 800 farmers present, besides a large attendance of the townspeople, while nearly 1,000 persons were at the doors, unable to gain admission. The farmers, after the information which these gentlemen conveyed to them, passed a resolution condemnatory of the Corn Laws. (Loud cheering.) That is the second meeting which we have held within the last fortnight of this description. We shall hold a similar meeting in every county in the kingdom, on each succeeding Saturday, and Mr. Cobden has pledged himself to attend every one of those meetings (loud cheers); and this system of agitation will be pursued until the whole country has been visited. (Cheers.) We now begin to experience the effects of the distribution of the tracts among the farmers. We see the weakness of our opponents in those strongholds of the monopolists. We are determined to prosecute the war even in their own camp, and we will wring from out their own hands that political influence which they have so much abused in destroying the industry of the country. (Loud cheers.)

Dr. Bowring followed, and said that the fame of the League had gone out throughout the world; that China rejoiced in the expectation of more commercial intercourse with us; and that Egypt, the granary of the ancient world, was anxious to supply our starving multitudes out of its overflowing granaries. He contrasted the effects of free trade in Holland and Tuscany, with the effects of monopoly in Spain and the Roman States, and concluded by saying:—

"What is shown by such magnificent meetings as these? What, but that you understand the language which the prime minister of England has uttered; and that you will require that that language shall not be a mere idle theory, falling to the winds, to be inherited and applied by nobody, but that you have taken it up, that you understand Sir Robert Peel, and that you will keep him to his declaration (cheers); that the parliament of England, within the walls of the legislature, should not be less interested, less energetic, than the people without. (Cheers)

My friends, in that House of Commons it is said that our numbers are helplessly small; but there are there many who have done admirable service in the popular cause, and whose energies have never been wanting, and whose voices have never been stifled, and whose votes have never failed; and who always call out to you to march onward, and more onward, to the goal towards which our cause is impelling. (Cheers.) But, after all, we, my friends, are the few, and you are the many. (Loud cheers.) And it is for you to decide whether the interests of the many, and the voices of the many, and the will of the many are to predominate, or whether that house is to continue blind, and deaf, and careless, reckless of the misery that is everywhere around them (cheers); indifferent to all that you see, and all that others suffer. (Hear.) I, for one, have better, and higher, and more consoling hopes, for I believe that the firm will of England has but to declare itself, as it is now declaring itself, and nothing can or could resist that will. I am afraid that I have spoken to you at too great a length. (Cries of 'No, no.') Let me then just address to you one parting word :—

'How oft on this illustrious stage
The words of fire from Shakspere's page
Your passions rouse, your souls engage.
 Here truth shall make
A still more eloquent appeal
To all who think—to all who feel
The public woe, the public weal,
 Are now at stake.

'To us no mimic art belongs,
Not fictious scenes, nor fancy's songs;
We speak of real right and wrongs
 To thoughtful men:
For myriad sufferers here we plead,
For those who weep, for those who need;
Ours is a holy cause indeed:
 Uphold us then!

'To you we look; on you we call;
Say! will you burst the ignoble thrall?
Answer, ye men of England, all;
 Ay, answer now!
Pledged all; leagued all; the vow imprest
In every mind, in every breast.
Pledge! and Heaven's benison shall rest
 Upon the vow.

'The vow! that leagued in heart and hand,
One purpose ours, erect to stand,
Each bound to each, a plighted band,
 Whom nought shall sever,
Till the unfettered world shall see
Labour, and trade, and industry,
Free as the winds of heaven are free,
 Free, free, for ever.'

Mr. H. Elphinstone, the member for the borough of
Lewes, was the next speaker, and expressed his decided
conviction that the landlords were greatly injuring their
own interests by their support of monopoly. The Rev.
John Burnett, of Camberwell, followed, and claimed the
right of every dissenting minister, and every Christian, to
interfere in all and every thing that affected the welfare
and happiness of their fellow men; for they read in their
Bible, and they thought, as Christians, that all men are brothers; that God had made them all of one blood; that all
the races of men, and all inhabitants of all nations of the
earth, were to be practically held as brothers, whatever
might be their clime, their origin, or their colour; and that,
holding to that principle, they protested against the Corn
Law as flagrantly opposed to it. The meeting closed after
brief speeches by Mr. L. Heyworth and Mr. T. M. Gibson.

CHAPTER V.

THE AGRICULTURAL DISTRICTS.

Merchants and manufacturers were now universally convinced that they could have no sound and prosperous trade while they were limited in their returns by a selfish legislation, which excluded the articles that would otherwise find an extensive market in this country; working men also were now almost universally convinced that the corn and provision laws, which lessened the demand for their labour, and raised the price of their food, were unjust and iniquitous ; and their only difference with the League was as to the *means* by which the redress of their grievances was to be obtained. Seeing this—seeing that their labours had been so far successful—and seeing that the great "unsettlement" which the new Corn Law and the tariff had made, and the general belief that monopoly was tottering to its fall—they determined to carry the war into the enemy's stronghold, and to raise the demand for free trade from the tenant-farmers who had hitherto lent their aid to support landlord aggression. A double number of the *Norwich Mercury*, of Saturday, April 28, contained no fewer than twenty columns of a report of meetings held in the county town of Norfolk, at which Mr. Cobden, Colonel Thompson, and Mr. Moore completely and triumphantly demolished the landowners' fallacies, and convinced the farmers that what is called "protection" had been grievously injurious to their interests, and that nothing but free trade could prevent their ruin. The *Mercury* said :—"The thousands who were rivetted into silence, and reasoned into acquiescence, will go forth and attest these truths. It will henceforward be as impracticable and hopeless, as it has hitherto been ungenerous and unjust, to attempt to stigmatize the cause or abuse the men. So far as public opinion in Norfolk is concerned, the question is set at rest. The feeble opposition which can hereafter be offered will be confined to inconvertible prejudice or immoveable self-interest."

Mr. Cobden, Mr. Bright, and Mr. Moore, were in like manner successful at Taunton, where the Somersetshire farmers had congregated in great numbers. At first the deputation was received somewhat coldly, but conviction gradually stole upon the audience, and before the meeting terminated, the farmers testified their approbation of what fell from the real " farmers' friends " by enthusiastic cheering. Several of the landlord class, who, at the commencement of the proceedings, had formally claimed a right to reply, seeing all their arguments knocked upon the head, slunk away from the meeting, and there was not a single man, lay or clerical, bold enough to stand up amongst farmers, and contend that either they, or farm labourers, were benefited by the " protection " with which the legislature had favoured them.

A curious evidence of the state of opinion in that purely agricultural county, Suffolk, was afforded to myself on the following week. . In consequence of the death of Sir Broke Vere there was a vacancy in the representation of the county, and Lord Rendlesham, a tory, and Mr. Shafto Adair, a whig, were candidates. I was on a visit to my friend Childs, in Suffolk, and had been announced as intending to address the farmers attending the Ipswich market, and it happened that Mr. Adair had announced the same place and hour to address the electors. Of course the candidate had precedency. He was received without a single cheer; he spoke for an hour and three quarters without a cheer, and he retired without a cheer. He talked of broken pledges on the part of the tories on the Corn Law and New Poor Law, without a response; he abused the New Corn Law, without a response ; he praised the whig eight-shilling duty proposal, without a response ; he promised fixed and " *adequate* protection," without a response. All was silent as the grave. Never before was seen so dead an audience at any election. Never before was seen a meeting of electors without a single partizan to raise a shout. It was obvious that the farmers cared nothing about whig and tory, and that they expected nothing to relieve their distress from either faction. But the moment I began to speak from the other side of the Corn Hill, the whole audience instantly turned round, eager to hear what could be said in favour of *entirely free trade;* and their attention was soon rivetted, and continued to be so during the whole of my address, which was interrupted only by audible expressions of assent to my arguments, or loud laughter at the devices of the fixed-duty and sliding-scale men to prevent the farmers from seeing what was really the cause of their distress. The consequence of this state of opinion, this utter distrust of both whigs and tories, this conviction that landowners had legislated only for their own interests, made it obvious that a great many farmers, and a great many freeholders in the towns would hold aloof from the contest altogether.

Advantage was taken of the adjournment of parliament during the Easter holidays, a period at which the working men of Manchester usually take a few days' relaxation from their toil, to have a great tea party of that class, numbering between three and four thousand, at which an address was presented to Mr. Cobden, signed by 11,372 working men. He spoke with his usual ability, and was evidently moved by the striking testimony of esteem from so many of his fellow-countrymen ; and the intelligence of the audience was manifested by their evident appreciation of the arguments of Mr. Bright, still, rather unnecessarily, styled as "of Rochdale," Mr. Thomas Bazley, and Mr. Lawrence Heyworth.

There were two more great weekly meetings in Drury Lane in which the Rev. Thos. Spencer, Mr. Ewart, M.P., Mr. Bright, the Rev. Dr. Cox, Mr. Cobden, Mr. Latimore, a practical farmer of Hertfordshire, and Mr. Moore, took part. The use of the Theatre had then to be relinquished, for the Earl of Glengall, and the committee of shareholders, prohibited Mr. Macready from letting it for political purposes! Refused admittance into Exeter Hall, and driven out of Drury Lane Theatre, the League had to find other places of meeting, and were not long in finding them.

In the House of Commons, April 25th, Mr. Ricardo moved a resolution expressing the opinion that England ought not to postpone the remission of her import duties with a view to negociations for reciprocity. Sir Robert Peel, speaking in reply, and of pending commercial treaties, said:

"We have reserved many articles from immediate reduction, in the hope that ere long we may attain that which we consider just and beneficial to all; namely, increased facilities for our exports in return. At the same time, I am bound to say that it is for *our interest to buy cheap, whether other countries will buy cheap or no*. We have a right to exhaust all means to induce them to do justice; but if they persevere in refusing, *the penalty is on us, if we do not buy in the cheapest market*. I feel certain that the example of England, adopted at a time of commercial and financial difficulty—our determination to pursue our path in the right course—will operate on foreign nations; but if we find that our example is not followed, if we find that instead of reducing the duties on our manufactures they resort to the impolicy of increasing them; still *this ought not, in my opinion, to operate as a discouragement to us to act on those principles which we believe to be sound*—those principles which will not only be immediately profitable to us, but the example of which will ultimately ensure that general application of them, which will confer reciprocal benefit on ourselves and all those who are wise enough to follow it."

" It is for our interest to buy cheap, whether other countries will buy cheap or no," was a large admission for a minister who had been peddling to obtain that by treaties which could be had at once by common-sense legislation. Sir Robert said that if the Brazilians chose to pay an artificially high price for cotton and woollen cloths, that was no reason why we should pay a high price for sugar and coffee ; and yet he sent out Mr. Ellis to tell them that if they would abandon a part of their folly, we would abandon a part of ours ; that if they would cease punishing themselves, we would cease punishing ourselves. From the minister's admissions Mr. Ricardo had been endeavouring to draw out some practical result. He had been repeating Sir Robert Peel's declaration, that " *the penalty is on us if we do not buy in the cheapest market ;* " but the expediency minister clung to his old practice of opposition to his new theory, and found enow of supporters to negative Mr. Ricardo's motion by a majority of about two to one.

Lord Howick ably supported Mr. Ricardo's motion ; and as Lord J. Russell took the same side, it was concluded that the whigs were preparing to make some nearer approach to free-trade principles than, in their timid and vacillating policy, they had hitherto made. Mr. Cobden, who spoke after Sir Robert Peel, disposed of the whole question in a few pithy sentences :—" Let us settle our own duties and our own commercial policy for ourselves ; and leave other countries to do the same. The moment they went to Brazil, and asked that government to reduce their duties, they placed themselves at the mercy of every country on the earth. It would be in vain to agitate for a remission of duties at home, if the executive government were to be allowed to go all over the world, creating obstacles, in order to make use of those obstacles, as an argument

against removing the impediments to increased trade, which
existed at home.   Another commercial treaty had been
projected with Portugal. He did not lay this to the account of the present government, because it had been
begun by the late ; but it had been followed up by the
right honourable baronet opposite. He did not wish to
say anything offensive of another country, but Portugal
was the poorest and most beggarly country in Europe.
Where was the sense of thinking that a treaty with that
nation could resuscitate the commerce of a country like
England, or of talking about encouraging British trade by
reducing the duty on port wine ? *The country did not want
a reduction of those duties on luxuries.* He spoke as a free
trader, having a pretty large connexion with commercial
reformers, and he said that they had not clamoured for a
reduction of the duties on *luxuries*, but for a reduction of
the duties on *corn, sugar,* and *coffee;* and those duties the
reduction of which would not impair the revenue, but
supply, according to the testimony of individuals connected with the Board of Trade, £3,000,000 or £4,000,000
of extra revenue, and at the same time create all the trade
that was wanted."

On the 9th of May, Mr. Villiers brought on his motion :
" That this house resolve itself into a committee, for the
purpose of considering the duties affecting the importation of foreign corn, with a view to their immediate
abolition." The motion excited great interest, not on
account of what might be said in favour of repeal, but to
know how it could be opposed, as all argument seemed to
be on the other side   Mr. Villiers said that the Corn
Law had been tried, considered, and condemned, out of
doors, and it now only waited the final sentence of that
house, or to have cause shown why final sentence of condemnation should not be passed against it. He asserted
that crime, misery, and social demoralization, were its
result ; that no language was too strong in condemning

it; that, of the whole population, there were ten millions that did not consume wheaten bread, while six millions "rejoiced in potatoes;" that farmers had no benefit from the monopoly; and that so far from there being peculiar burthens upon land, there were some shameful exemptions in its favour. Mr. V. Stuart seconded the motion. And then Mr. Gladstone rose, as able as any man in the house to give an argument for the monopoly, if any was to be found. It is curious now to refer back to what was then said by such a man. The Corn Law, he said, was not to be repealed, because on former motions Mr. Villiers had only some 90 votes; further change would be a breach of faith on the part of the government and the house, and, after the act of the previous year, a proof of the grossest imbecility; that act ought to have a fair trial; prices were lower than they were in 1835; repeal would throw the agricultural labourers out of employment; it would introduce more corn, he admitted, but *if* it were paid for in bullion, it would very seriously injure the currency; and that the revenue of the country would suffer severely! Mr. Trelawney did not think the repeal of the Corn Law would be a panacea for all evils; but he believed its effect was to undermine the best interests of the country. Mr. Christopher opposed the motion, because duties had already been lowered. Mr. Roebuck said he agreed with neither side of the house; but he did good service to the cause of free trade by some good argument. As to the draining of bullion from the country, he reminded Mr. Gladstone that bullion itself could be paid for only by manufactures. The house then adjourned.

Mr. Miles resumed the debate on the following night. Forgetting the formal and often-repeated resolutions, disclaiming all protection to manufactures, made at the meetings of the League, he said he could give that body more credit for sincerity if it called not only for the repeal of the Corn Law, but of all import duties. Mr. G. Ward

ably exposed the inconsistency between the Mr. Gladstone
of free-trade opinions and the Mr. Gladstone of parliamentary evasions. Captain Maurice held that free-trade
would convulse the land to its farthest end. Sir C. Napier
said he would vote for the motion, if nobody moved for a
fixed duty, which he would prefer. Mr. B. Cochrane gave
the League credit for energy and boldness, but counselled
that they should be met boldly and energetically. Sir
George Strickland said that unless the house showed
some sympathy with the people it would forfeit their
affections. Mr. H. J. Bailey, described as of Inverness,
never afterwards heard of, did not believe that any
government would be ever induced to withhold protection
from agriculture. Mr. Gisborne, as a practical farmer
himself, denied that protection benefited agriculture.
Mr. Colquhoun, of course, opposed the motion. Lord
Howick would have preferred a small fixed duty, but
would vote for the motion. Mr. Blackstone made some
commentaries on the advantage of protection, which much
amused the house. Mr. Wallace counselled the free-
traders to accept of no compromise. Mr. A. Campbell
had no fears of free-trade, if brought about gradually.
And so the second night's debate terminated.

The debate was resumed on the third night by Mr. P.
Borthwick, who accused the League of practising delusion
on the people. Mr. Wrightson said the Corn Law was
the most anti-national that could have been devised by
man. Mr. Robert Palmer did not believe that the farmers
were beginning to be advocates of free-trade. Mr. Marsland said that the farmers had no confidence in the
ministry, and none in the stability of the present law.
Sir E. Knatchbull, one of the ministry, contended that the
existence of the League was unconstitutional; and that
certain burdens had been entailed on land, marriage
settlements for instance, which could not be liquidated if
the Corn Law were repealed! Lord John Russell said he

would be ready to support or originate any motion for the re consideration of the Corn Law, but could not vote for the present motion. Mr. Danby repeated the old assertion that free trade would throw land out of cultivation. And so the third night's debate terminated.

The fourth night's debate was opened by Mr. Joseph Brotherton, who, after some correction of misrepresentations of what he had said on former occasions as to the effect of a fixed duty, went into the general question. He respected the rights of property, but some consideration was due to the rights of industry; the commercial community contributed more than one-half of the Income Tax and other taxes; and the prosperity of the community was to be mainly measured by the degree of comfort in which the middle and labouring classes could indulge. Mr. Hampden said that free-trade without reciprocity would be at once a solecism and a delusion; and no greater error in legislation could be committed, than to regulate the affairs of a highly artificial state of society, by an unbending adherence to abstract principles. Mr. James was opposed to the Corn Law, but was not prepared to support its total and immediate repeal, being disposed rather to advocate a moderate fixed duty. He should, therefore, abstain altogether from voting on the motion. Captain Thomas Gladstone admitted that the Corn Law raised the price of food, but he denied that it was the cause of those fluctuations which were attributed to it. There were peculiar burdens on the landed interest, under which they could not stand a free competition in corn; and on this, and other grounds, he opposed the motion. Mr. Aldam did not undervalue treaties of commerce; but foreign nations, as in the case of France and Portugal, were jealous of us, and fearful that we wished to cheat them. But if we opened our ports, and let them enjoy the advantages of our trade, we should speedily cure them of their reluctance to reciprocate. Mr. Benet said that the first effect of the repeal of the Corn Law would be to hand over the estates of the landowners to their monied creditors, the holders of ancient mortgages! Mr. Hume said we had been enabled to maintain our extravagance so long as we possessed a monopoly in the market of the world for the sale of our manufactures. But we could not retain it any longer; and we must prepare to return to a natural state, by reducing our prices to a level with those of other countries. This we could only attain by free-trade in everything, only raising what was requisite for the revenue. Protection to any one class whatever was robbery; and every man who upheld monopoly was a patron of robbery. Sir John Tyrrell said that the reduction of protection which had taken place, by the recent measures of the government, instead of benefiting the revenue, as the advocates of total repeal contended would be the result of their favourite policy, had rather injured it. Mr. Henry Berkeley supported the motion. Sir Walter James, considering himself in the same boat with the landowners, thought, nevertheless, that the time was now come when all the middle and upper classes must take a step in advance to save the labouring class. Lord Worsley said that the agricultural interest had made large sacrifices to place the present government in office, and they were entitled to a specific declaration, whether or not, after the brief trial of one year, they were dissatisfied with the Corn Law.

Hitherto the debate had produced nothing new in defence of the Corn Law. There was the old often-refuted argument, and the old often-contradicted assertion. The old dog had not even a new doublet. Would Peel make anything better of the defence? If not better, would he introduce any novelty into the threadbare discussion? Here is an abstract of his speech:—

"Sir Robert Peel said the progress of the debate had confirmed him in the impression he had formed at its commencement, that the subject was exhausted, and nothing new could be adduced. It was, therefore, his position alone which overcame his reluctance to address the house. The motion of Mr. Villiers was fairly stated and proposed; there was no subterfuge involved in it. But he thought that the principle must be applied generally and universally to every article on which a duty was levied. They could not stand on the single article of corn. By the adoption of the motion, they would sound the knell of protection, and they must immediately proceed to apply the principle to practice. This would at once upset the commercial arrangements of the last year. The whole of our colonial system must be swept away, without favour, and without consideration. Could any sane man commit himself to such a course, and trifle with the vast interests of our colonial empire, by the adoption of an abstract resolution? The supporters of the motion ought to act as if they were certain of being in a majority, for it would not be honest to vote for it in the hope of escaping from its consequences by the certainty of being in a minority. Even granting that our legislation was based on false principles, and ought to be altered, who would adopt the responsibility of its immediate repeal? Confining attention to the trade in corn, he agreed mainly in opinion with Lord John Russell as to the principles by which it should be governed, but he differed with him as to the mode of arriving at them. Mr. Gladstone had certainly used the word 'sinecure,' but an unworthy advantage had been taken of it; he was merely arguing that even in dealing with the most obnoxious of exclusive interests compensation was allowed, but he did not class the landlords as 'sinecurists.' The land did bear peculiar burdens, which justified protection; even the malt tax was of the nature of a peculiar incumbrance on the agricultural interest; and though it might be said that it fell on the consumer, the manufacturer would at once feel the peculiar weight of a similar burden, if it were laid on him. A fixed duty on foreign corn, from which domestic corn was exempted, would be, in fact, protection under a mask; and its imposition would not satisfy or silence the anti-corn-law agitation. Why should domestic corn be exempted from such a tax? Did they not tax home-grown barley? The government, in proposing their commercial reforms of last year, had in view the general welfare of the community. He was satisfied with their operation, and he stood by the principles on which these changes had been framed; but in doing so, he had no concealed or lurking intention of repealing the Corn Law, and he did not contemplate any immediate alteration. Beyond this decided declaration of no present intention to alter the law, he would not go, for he would not commit himself to any commercial law, or make declarations for the sake of conciliating political support. He did not think that the Corn Law was a bad law; it remedied the defects of the preceding one. But he was taunted with having promised that the law would keep prices between 54s. and 58s., and because they were now lower, the farmers were called on to withdraw confidence from him. To disprove this, he read an extract from his speech of last year, which showed that he had expressly disclaimed the possibilty of guaranteeing by legislation a remunerating price for corn. It was not the law which had caused the fall of prices—that he attributed to the depression of trade and commerce, the prosperity of which would better secure prices than any Corn Law whatever. It was hardly fair to try the present law by the circumstances of last year, during which great speculations in corn had been undertaken, on the faith that the harvest would be a defective one, a belief which had been much encouraged by motions and speeches in the house. Lord Palmerston, in July last, had ventured to predict that if parliament did not meet in the ensuing November, the government would have to let out the bonded corn. Under such circumstances of encouragement to undue speculation, the law had not received a fair trial. And as to the objection that it operated unfavourably to the employment of British shipping, returns showed that it had a fair share and chance. The Canada Corn Bill was a part of the measures which had been planned last year; and though they were aware that the re-agitation of the question would be disagreeable, they had resolved to keep faith with the people of Canada. On the whole, he contended that they had been actuated by regard to the public interests in the proposition of their measures, and had thereby risked political friendship and support; and they were now acting in good faith, and were not seeking to provide for themselves a shelter from political storms."

It was twelve o'clock before Sir Robert concluded this speech. The scene that ensued is thus described in the papers of the time :—

"By this time the patience of the monopolists was completely exhausted, and although Mr. Cobden was expected to reply, it is not at all probable that he would have been listened to with even ordinary patience, notwithstanding the vehement protestations made to the contrary. Accordingly, Milner Gibson moved an adjournment of the debate, on the ground that members representing large manufacturing constituencies were not only anxious, but bound in duty to assign reasons for the vote they intended to give. This he considered no more than fair, considering the indulgence extended to the other side of the house; but however proper these remarks may appear to impartial observers, they proved the prelude to a measure of turmoil, noise, and confusion, such as has rarely, if ever, been witnessed in the House of Commons. In the *Sun* of Saturday we find the following sketch, penned, no doubt, by an eye-witness :—

'Those of our readers who may happen to have visited Exeter 'Change—now alas! numbered with the things that were!—cannot fail to remember the strange scenes of uproar that used to be presented in the menagerie, at feeding time. The wild beasts on both sides the exhibition-room were all in the fiercest state of excitement—yelling, braying, roaring, each vieing with the other in the manifestation of impatience and irritability. Just such a scene was presented last night in that political menagerie, for we can give it no better term, the House of Commons. On a motion being made by an honourable gentleman, an uproar took place such as has not been witnessed since the night of the memorable division on the Reform Bill. There was cock-crowing in its highest perfection, the bleat of the calf, the bray of the ass, the hiss of the goose, together with divers supplemental sounds, to which Mr. Cobden did no more than strict and impartial justice, when he described them as being 'the most extraordinary and inhuman noises' that he had ever heard. Mr. Plumptre proposed 'mutual concessions,' whereupon the clamour became more furious than ever; and Mr. Mackenzie, at an early hour in the morning, suddenly found himself, like a true Highlander, in the possession of the 'second sight,' and announced to the Speaker that he saw 'strangers in the house!'—a discovery which might have been made, had the vision been vouchsafed, at least four hours before! On the whole, the scene was one of the most absurd, uproarious, and degrading to the dignity of the house, that ever yet took place in parliament. Surely Sir Robert Peel must by this time be heartily ashamed of his monopolist supporters.'

"When the tempest was at its height, the leaders, Sir R. Peel and Lord J. Russell, left the house; and, thus freed from all restraint, the belligerents became fiercer than ever; the blood of both parties was fairly up; for nearly two hours, declamation roared while reason slept; and during the vociferous display, the voice of the Speaker was little more regarded than a whisper amidst a storm. The minority were aware that the remaining speeches, even if delivered, could not be reported, and for that and other reasons, were in their resolves so resolute, that although outvoted in sundry divisions, the question was just as often re-moved and seconded. At length Mr. Ross told Lord Dungannon, that if he were contented to sit till eight o'clock, himself, and such as acted with him, would willingly sit till nine; and it was at this stage that Sir Charles Napier slyly suggested that they should divide themselves into three watches, after the fashion of a ship's crew. This arrangement would afford ease to all excepting the Speaker, to whom he was sorry he could not afford the slightest relief. Worn out at length by the violence of their exertions, and despairing of victory, the majority yielded."

On Monday, May 16, the fifth night's debate was opened
by Mr W. O. Stanley, who supported Mr. Villiers' motion
in a short speech.   Dr. Bowring followed.   He said that
Sir Robert Peel must soon make his final choice whether
he would stand by the producers or the consumers ; he
could not long go on vibrating between the two interests.
He lamented the bad example England was setting to all
other nations by the maintenance of the Corn Laws.   He
had heard it urged that their maintenance was rendered
necessary by the weight of our public burdens, but he
could not understand how these were to be alleviated by
adding to them this other burden heavier than all.   Mr.
Ewart dilated upon the inadequacy of the ministerial measures of free trade, and the futility of hopes held out by
government that affairs would improve.   The people were
growing wise upon this subject, thanks to the League.
The country gentlemen, who used to be silent from contempt, were now silent from apprehension, as the inferior
creatures recognize in dumb amazement the approach of a
storm.   Mr. Childers, in advocating a free importation of
foreign corn, contended that such a measure would not
lower the price in England so much as was commonly
supposed, or as he himself desired.   Captain Layard said
that a total repeal of the Corn Laws would not be so injurious as the present state of uncertainty.   He himself was
friendly to a small fixed duty ; but, seeing no chance of
that, he would vote for this larger proposal.   Mr. E. Buller
could not go the length of a total abolition ; but he would
vote for the committee because he could not approve the
existing law.   The tax imposed, if imposed for revenue,
was too heavy.   The peculiar burdens on land were no
doubt a reason for protection ; but then we ought to have
been told what those burdens were ; we ought to have had
that committee upon them which the house had refused.
It was not true that tithes were a burden on the land, except when paid in kind ; neither was the land-tax, which

he affirmed to be merely a quit-rent substituted for the ancient feudal services. Sir C. Burrell opposed the motion. He insisted on the vast numerical superiority of the agricultural labourers, and the large proportion of poor-rate borne by the land, as reasons for continuing protection to agriculture; and he enumerated a list of manufactures which also enjoyed protections of their own. Mr. Poulett Scrope explained his views upon the general principles of taxation. If a man laid out £100 in producing a quantity of corn, half of which he sent abroad, taking foreign goods in exchange; and laid out another £100 in manufacturing a quantity of goods, half of which he sent abroad, taking foreign corn in exchange: the foreign corn so taken by him was just as much the produce of English industry as the corn which he had grown at home, and why should one be more protected than the other? Colonel Wood (Brecon) observed that if free trade was to be the order of the day, we ought also to have free cultivation; and would you allow the English farmer to grow his own tobacco, and make his own sugar from his own beet-root, and his own malt from his own barley? The agriculturists did not desire to buy at the cheapest rate; for that was to give low wages to the agricultural labourer. Nor did they desire to sell at the dearest rate. The farmers sought to live and let live, and the landlords felt the truth of the proposition, that property has its duties as well as its rights. Mr. Thornley said he had visited America last autumn, and had found the Americans with whom he had conversed, merchants, statesmen, and the President himself, all answering, when he urged the relaxations of last year's tariff, that these availed nothing while the duty was maintained against American corn. He did not believe that any quantity of American corn considerable enough to be worth mentioning, would be let in by the proposed regulations respecting Canada. Mr. Strutt said that tithes were not amongst land burdens; for if, upon the question of church rate, the dissenter was justly told that the amount of the rate formed no deduction from his property, the same argument must apply to the landlord and the tithe. He was convinced that the present Corn Law could not long be maintained. Sir H. Douglas expressed, as the representative of Liverpool, his apprehension that the doctrine of free trade, pushed to its extreme, would work anything but welfare to the great interests of the country. He valued all the three great interests, trade, manufactures, and agriculture,; but agriculture was the root of all. He believed that England was England's best customer; and that the distress now prevalent was attributable to our having already opened the sluices of free trade too wide. Mr. Muntz meant to vote with Mr. Villiers, not because he thought the protection to agriculture too large, but because he thought it too exclusively confined to land. It ought to have extended to labour also; whereas the labour of the cotton-spinners was now reduced by four-fifths of its value. He was grieved to say that the distress in Birmingham was undiminished, and that there appeared not even a prospect of its diminution. There was some little improvement in the trade of some other towns, but it was only speculative, having reference to India and China, where no permanent demand could be expected.

Mr. Cobden's speech was what might have been expected from a man of intellect and humanity; the one insulted by stale fallacies, the other outraged by the total want of sympathy with the people,—and all this endured for five weary nights. It is not astonishing that some acerbity was exhibited, and that the tone was that of one who felt little respect for the house which he addressed. He tore to very shreds the fallacies and pretences of the monopolists, and showed that their legislation was purely selfish, and as injurious to their own tenants and their labourers as to the interests of trade. This he did in a bold, manly, and honest manner, that carried the war right into the enemy's camp, and struck terror into them even behind their entrenchments. He said that—

"Throughout five nights of debate, hardly anybody had touched upon the main question, which was, whether you had a right to keep up a law, having for its object to inflict scarcity on the people. For whose interest? Not that of the farmer—not that of the agricultural labourer —but that of the landlord. When prices were at the highest, the condition of the farm labourer was at the worst. If such a law was ever to benefit the farm labourer, it should have benefited him in 1840, when there had been three successive years of high prices. Since 1840, the matter was still worse, and the increase of petty crime so great, that it was found necessary to wink at it instead of punishing it. Then as to the farmer, what benefit had he ever derived from the Corn Laws? From 1815 to 1841 there had been a series of these laws, but they had not shut out repeated seasons of agricultural distress. You might send a copy of such laws to another planet, if you could find a conveyance; and the inhabitants of that planet would at once remark, ' These enactments must have been made by landowners.' He would not say that the landlords were not perfectly entitled to get the best rents they could; but he would say they were not entitled to come to parliament for the purpose of artificially raising those rents. The rents of England had at least doubled in the last fifty years. Into that increase it was now the business of the legislature to enquire. A ' farmer's friend' cry had been raised to bring in the present ministers; there they were now, on the Treasury bench; they had obtained the power and patronage of the government, but what had the farmers got? It was his cue to show the farmers how they had been cajoled. They had been driven up to the poll by their landlords, and in many counties farming was kept at the worst, because landlords refused to grant leases, in order to retain their tenants under their political influence. This must not be treated as a farmer's question any longer, and the farmer knew it now. Sir Robert Peel had stated that the effect of this new Corn Law would be to lower prices; but nothing was said by the landlords about lowering the rents. The farmers were tired of their old friends; they had now shaken hands with the manufacturers; but in order that the farmers might understand the manufacturers to have no designs for themselves, he wished to explain that he sought to improve, not to impair, her Majesty's revenue; indeed the whole amount of the protecting duties to the manufactures was under two millions sterling. At present the public mind was arrayed solely against that key-stone in the arch of monopoly, the monopoly of agriculture; but it should not disperse until it had destroyed monopoly of every other kind. There were men in that house ever stirring in

matters of charity; would those charitable persons allow their names to
be seen in a division list against the good of the people ? If they should,
they would lose all their credit with the working classes, and consequently all their usefulness.   The people, as their numbers multiplied
without proportionate addition to the corn that should maintain them,
descended to live on potatoes; thus the price of their labour was
lowered, and the landlords, getting it so much cheaper, were interested
to keep up the law that excluded corn.

Colonel Sibthorp gave an exposition of the friendly
feeling that subsisted between him and his tenants, whose
forefathers had lived for successive generations on his
estate, and always without leases. He reprobated the
"folly and humbug" he had heard. Mr. Milner Gibson
warned Sir H. Douglas, whom he considered to have
made a most anti-commercial speech, that his constituency
at Liverpool were tending fast towards the opinions of
free trade. With respect to the analogy which had been
suggested between the sinecurist and the landowner, he
thought the landowner the more formidable incumbrance
of the two; for any member could ascertain the amount of
the sinecurist's pension; but no man could tell the amount
of the mischief produced by the legislation in favour of the
landowner. The manufacturers desired no monopoly;
when Mr. Huskisson proposed his great reductions of duty,
they supported his measure. The maintenance of the
church by the land was no argument for a Corn Law; if
the church were abolished, her interest in the land would
not devolve to the landlord. Mr. Villiers replied. He did
not regret the length of time which the discussion had
occupied. It would induce reflection, and must work for
good. Its protraction had been blamed as impeding
business; but he knew of no other business so important.
He defended himself for having brought forward this
monopoly, unconnected with others on which a repeal of
duty would be equally desirable. He had taken it singly,
because it had always been said by its advocates to depend
on considerations peculiar to itself. He then went into the

general question ; but this, after a long speech in opening,
and five nights of subsequent discussion, was too much
for the virtue of the house at between one and two in the
morning, and they expressed their dissatisfaction by frequent and loud interruptions.

At length they divided—

Against the motion	381
For it	125

Majority against the motion 256

This division marked some progress. An advance from
90 to 125 would have been little encouragement had it not
been for the acknowledgment of free-trade principles,
which promised their adoption in practice. The League
was not discouraged by the formidable majority arrayed in
favour of monopoly. Its hope was in the constituencies,
and to their further instruction it resolved to devote its
labours.

CHAPTER VI.

THE DIVISION ON MR. VILLIERS' MOTION.

Of the Lancashire and Cheshire members who voted in the minority on Mr. Villiers' motion, we find the names of

Bowring, Dr.	Hindley, Charles
Brotherton, Joseph	Jervis, J.
Cobden, Richard	Johnson General
Crawford, W. Sharman	Marsland, Henry
Fielden, J.	Philips, Mark
Fleetwood, Sir Hesketh	Standish, Charles
Gibson, Thomas Milner	Strickland, Sir George
Grosvenor, Lord R.	Walker, Robert

Of the Lancashire and Cheshire members who voted in the majority with the monopolists, were the names of

Blackburne, John Ireland	Greene, Thomas
Cardwell, Edward	Legh, G. C.
Douglas, Sir Howard	Patten, Wilson
Egerton, W. T.	Sandon, Lord
Egerton Sir P. G.	Tollemache, J.
Fielden, William	Wilbraham, Richard Bootle

A majority of the electors of Macclesfield had requested both their members to vote for Mr. Villiers' motion, but both were absent. A majority of the electors of Bolton asked Mr. Ainsworth to support the motion, but Lord Stanley, who had clapped him on the shoulder and called him "Peter," was more regarded than his constituents. All the Lancashire county members voted in the majority, except Lord Francis Egerton, who was not present, but who, if he had been present, would have voted with the monopolists. In the list of the majority were found the names of

Lord John Russell and Sir Robert Peel ;
Viscount Ebrington and Peter Borthwick ;
H. Labouchere and Lord Castlereagh ;
Lord Palmerston and Sir James Graham ;
Honourable G. Cavendish and Busfield Ferrand.

It is but justice, however, to the gentlemen connected with the late whig ministry to say that there were not many of their names to be found in such companionship, and that the following were in the honourable list of the minority :—

Buller, C.   Howick, Viscount
Dalmeny, Lord   Macaulay, T. B.
Ellice, Right Hon. E.   Maule, Honourable Fox
Grey, Sir George   Smith, Vernon

I subjoin some notices of the protracted debate :—
From the *Morning Post :*—

" Melancholy was the exhibition in the House of Commons on Monday. Mr. Cobden was the hero of the night. Towards the close of the debate, he rose in his place, and hurled at the heads of the parliamentary landowners of England, those calumnies and taunts which constitute the staple of his addresses to farmers. The taunts were not retorted. The calumnies were not repelled. No ; the parliamentary representatives of the industrial interests of the British empire quailed before the founder and leader of the Anti-Corn-Law League. They winced under his sarcasms. They listened in speechless terror to his denunciations. No man among them dared to grapple with the arch enemy of English industry. No man among them attempted to refute the miserable fallacies of which Mr. Cobden's speech was made up. * * * * * * Melancholy was it to witness, on Monday, the landowners of England, the representatives by blood of the Norman chivalry, the representatives, by election, of the industrial interests of the empire, shrinking under the blows aimed at them by a Manchester money-grubber; by a man, whose importance is derived from the action of a system, destructive in its nature of all the wholesome influences that connect together the various orders of society. Well; the cycle approaches its completion; the wheel has nearly effected its revolution;

and the foul and pestilential principles which, by their action, began, forty years ago, to consign to beggary hundreds of thousands of harmless and ingenious hand-loom weavers, seem destined, if not speedily resisted, to sweep away all the barriers that still remain to shelter productive industry from the encroachments of those classes of men, to whom the abasement of industry is the source of increased power and influence.''

From the *Times* :—

" Mr. Cobden's speech was clever and pointed. It was creditable to his talents, as evincing an aptitude of mind and an ability to adapt his style to the air of the place and the tastes of his audience; but we do not think it was equally creditable to his judgment. A stronger impression might have been made, had he abstained from personality and *persiflage*. Still, allowance must be made for a man who had to repeat a tale for the nine hundred and ninety-ninth time, and who, therefore, was compelled to adapt it to the palate of his hearers. * * * * * But the debate is over; the question is settled; for how long? How many even of the majority are satisfied with the working of the sliding scale? How many of the minority would be gratified by an utter and immediate abolition of ALL corn duties? These questions may perhaps be answered before June, A.D. 1844. Meantime, the legislature reposes from much operose and futile talk; and time is given to Mr. Cobden to ingratiate himself with his new friends, the farmers; to Col. Sibthorp, to point new and delicate jests; to Mr. E. Buller, to cull new and *à propos* quotations.''

From the *Spectator* :—

" Mr. Blackstone and his class are in despair, and almort disposed to give up the struggle; other agriculturists, like Mr. Campbell, boldly embrace Peel free-trade, with the sound of which ministers continue to familiarise their followers, as if in preparation for future contingencies; Mr. Gladstone being the eloquent asserter of their principles, and the adroit special pleader for not applying them yet. Lord Howick is prepared to support total and immediate repeal, if he cannot establish a fixed duty of four or five shillings. Lord John Russell, less in advance, adheres to his fixed duty, with a manner that says he will be obstinate as long as he can. The doom of the Corn Laws is to be learned in these indications, from the mouths of agricultural members and of tenant farmers.''

From the *Morning Chronicle* :—

" The elevation of Mr. Gladstone to the head of the Board of Trade will be viewed by the country as a satisfactory proof of Sir Robert

Peel's tendencies on commercial questions. Of course the country gentlemen will dislike it on that very account. Mr. Gladstone's name is regarded by them as almost synonymous of free trade; and very unpalatable to them it consequently is. And the appointment, therefore, is the best possible evidence of the very little account which Sir Robert makes of his supporters, and of his determination to follow his own course, in spite of their discontent. He has marked his reliance on Mr. Gladstone at the risk of offending powerful and jealous competitors. For, in the ordinary course of official information, both Lord Granville Somerset and Lord Lowther may be regarded as having had prior claims to a seat in the Cabinet. The preference of Mr. Gladstone is, therefore, a mark not only of the superior estimation in which his abilities are held by the Prime Minister, but of the adoption of his commercial policy by the Cabinet."

The following are the names of members who voted in the minority—a list often looked at afterwards when candidates stood for election :—

Aglionby, H. A.	Currie, Raikes	Grosvenor, Lord R.
Aldham, W.	Dalmeny, Lord	Hall, Sir Benjamin
Bannerman, A.	Dashwood, G. H.	Hastie, A.
Barnard, E. G.	Dennistoun, J.	Hawes, Benjamin
Berkeley, Hon. C.	D'Eyncourt, Right	Hay, Sir A. L.
Berkeley, Hon. Captain	Hon. C. T.	Hayter, W. G.
Berkeley, Hon. F. H.	Duncan, Viscount	Heron, Sir R.
Blewitt, R. J.	Duncan, G.	Hindley, Charles
Bowring, Dr.	Duncombe, Thomas	Hollond, R.
Brotherton, Joseph	Dundas, Admiral	Horsman, E.
Browne, Hon. W.	Ellice, Right Hon. E.	Howick, Viscount
Buller, C.	Ellice, E.	Hume, Joseph
Buller, E.	Ellis, W.	Jervis, J.
Busfield, W.	Elphinstone, H.	Johnson, General
Byng, Right Hon. G. S.	Ewart, William	Johnston, A.
Chapman, B.	Fielden, J.	Langston, J. H.
Christie, W. D.	Ferguson, Colonel	Langton, W. G.
Clive, E. B.	Fitzroy, Lord C.	Layard, Captain
Cobden, Richard	Fleetwood, Sir P. H.	Leader, J. T.
Collett, J.	Forster, M.	Lord Mayor of London
Collins, W.	Fox, C. R.	Macaulay, Right Hon.
Corbally, M. E.	Gibson, Thos. Milner	T. B.
Craig, W. G.	Gisborne, T.	Marjoribanks, S.
Crawford, W. S.	Grey, Right Hon. Sir G.	Marshall, W.

Marsland, H.	Pulsford, R.	Tancred, H. W.
Martin, J.	Ramsbottom, J.	Thornley, T.
Maule, Right Hon. Fox	Ricardo, J. L.	Towneley, J.
Morison, General	Rice, E. R.	Trelawny, J. S.
Muntz, G. F.	Roche, Sir D.	Tufnell, H.
Napier, Sir Charles	Roebuck, J. A.	Turner, E.
O'Brien, J.	Ross, D. R.	Vivian, J. H.
O'Connell, M. J.	Russell, Lord E.	Wakley, Thomas
Ord, W.	Scholefield, J.	Walker, R.
Oswald, J.	Scott, R.	Ward, H. G.
Parker, J.	Scrope, G. P.	Wawn, J. T.
Pechell, Captain	Seale, Sir J. H.	Williams, W.
Philips, G. R.	Smith, B.	Wood, B.
Philips, Mark	Smith, Right Hon. R. Y.	Wood, G. W.
Phillpotts, J.	Standish, Charles	Yorke, H. R.
Plumridge, Captain	Stansfield, W. R. C.	TELLERS.
Ponsonby, Honourable C. F. A. C.	Stanton, W. H.	Villiers, Honourable C.
	Stuart, Lord J.	Stuart, W. V.
Ponsonby, Hon. J. G.	Strickland, Sir George	
Protheroe, E.	Strutt, E.	

Deputies from a great number of anti-corn-law associations throughout the kingdom had congregated in London, and during the debate on Mr. Villiers' motion had met daily at Herbert's Hotel, to watch the proceedings in the house over the way, and daily to demolish the fallacies and the falsehoods uttered there. Resolutions were passed not only against the Corn Law, but against every commercial monopoly, and recommendatory of a registration of members of the League, the adoption of weekly, monthly, and other periodical subscriptions, and urging a complete parliamentary registration of all free-traders in the boroughs and counties, in order to bring into united action the whole of the free-trade constituencies of the empire. Nor did the exclusion from Drury Lane prevent a continuation of the meetings which had been commenced. On the 13th of May one was held at the English Opera House, which was addressed by Mr. George Wilson, Mr. W. J. Fox, and Mr. Cobden. On the following week, the meeting was held in the Hall of Commerce, and was

addressed by Mr. Villiers, Mr. Ward, M.P., Mr. Bright, and
Mr. Moore. On Monday, May 29th, another meeting was
held in the Hall of Commerce, which was addressed by
Earl Ducie, Mr. Moore. and Mr. Cobden. It is not to be
supposed that those numerous meetings in the metropolis,
every one of them instructive, every one of them exciting
to determined action, could be seen with indifference by
Lord John Russell, one of the members for the city of
London, and without the conviction that at the next
election free trade would form the main question. On
the 12th of June, his lordship, who would not vote for Mr.
Villiers' motion for inquiry into the operation of the Corn
Law, with a view to its repeal, moved simply for an
inquiry. The debate was a languid one in a thin house.

On the division there were 145 for the motion, and 244
against it. Lord John had only twenty more supporters
than Mr. Villiers had, showing that the fixed-duty whigs
had complained very unreasonably of the 125 who had
refused to stop at the half-way house with so small a company. The *Globe* was very witty upon the tories for
standing on the shibboleth of two words, " sliding scale ; "
not seeing how it might be retorted that the whigs could
also be taunted with standing on two words, " fixed duty."

The numerous meetings held in London did not inter-
rupt the movement that had been going on in the provinces.
On Saturday, April 29th, Mr. Cobden, pursuant to public
announcement, appeared at Hertford to address the farmers. As the Shire Hall could not hold the number that
had congregated, the meeting was adjourned to Plough
Mead, where two thousand persons attended, including a
large number of horsemen, among whom were Baron
Dinsdale, the Hon. W. Cowper, Sir Minto Farquhar,
G. S. Bosanquet, Esq., W. Stratton, Esq., T. Booth, Esq.,
T. Mills, Esq., and several other influential gentlemen of
the county. Mr. Welford, of Northaw, being called to the
chair, Mr. Cobden addressed the meeting with great effect.

Mr. Bennett, a tenant farmer, of Luton, moved that the repeal of the Corn Law would spread inevitable ruin throughout the rural districts. The motion was seconded in a bitter speech by Mr. Maydwell. Mr. Lattimore, another tenant farmer, moved: "That it is the opinion of this meeting that the existing Corn Laws have proved highly injurious to the independence and welfare of the tenant farmer, and that they ought to be abolished." The amendment was put and carried triumphantly, only about ten hands being held up for the original motion. Another open-air meeting of farmers, held at Cambridge, on the same day, and addressed by Mr. Bright and Mr. Moore, had a similar result. On Saturday, May 6, Mr. Cobden and Mr. Moore attended a crowded meeting in the County Hall, Aylesbury, Lord Nugent in the chair. It had been announced that Dr. Sleigh, a pro-corn-law lecturer, would be there to oppose the free traders, but he did not make his appearance, and a vote of thanks to their visitors, and of approval of the principles advocated, was passed by the whole assembly except five persons—"amongst the faithless faithful only they,"—and this in the stronghold of the Duke of Buckingham. On the following week, Mr. Cobden and Mr. Moore addressed the farmers at Uxbridge, and Mr. Bright and Mr. Moore the same class in the county town of Dorsetshire, and at both places resolutions were passed condemnatory of the Corn Law.

On Friday, May 19th, a meeting was held in the Sheep Market, Lincoln, to hear an address from Mr. Cobden and Mr. Bright upon the Corn Laws. This meeting, like all the others in the agricultural districts, had been advertised and placarded for three weeks previously throughout the county, so that it might in the strictest sense of the word be called a county meeting. It was attended by many farmers and others from a distance of nearly thirty miles, and great interest was felt in the result, from the confident expectation entertained by the monopolist party, whatever might be the result in other places, Lincolnshire would be found true to the principle of protection. The result proved most disastrous to the bread taxers. At three o'clock, the appointed hour of meeting, upwards of three thousand persons assembled round the commodious hustings which had been constructed for the occasion, and which was crowded with the more influential persons of the city and neighbourhood. As Mr. Cobden had been detained in town by his parliamentary duties the evening previous, he arrived from Nottingham at half-past three only. Mr. Bright opened the proceedings with a long and able address, which was followed by Mr. Cobden, who went through the argument exclusively applicable to the agriculturists, and clearly proved that neither farmners nor farm labourers had the slightest interest in maintaining the Corn Laws. The audience, which was at first cautious and doubtful, gradually threw aside its reserve, and warmed into enthusiasm as the speakers unfolded their views of the question, and at the conclusion of their speeches it was quite evident which way the judgment of the auditory would go. A motion having been submitted by Mr. Norton in favour of the immediate abolition of the Corn Law, an amendment was proposed by Mr. Moore, of Redburn, a respectable farmer, in favour of protection, upon which a discussion took place, at the close of which the decision of the meeting was taken by a show of hands, when at least five to one declared in favour of free trade.

On Wednesday, June 1st, a great meeting of the Liverpool Anti-Monopoly Association and the friends of free trade was held in the Music Hall, which was addressed by Mr. Chas Holland, Mr. Lawrence Heyworth, Mr. Thomas Baines, Mr. Christopher Bentham, Mr. Richard Sheil, Mr, Leech, and by myself as a deputy from the League. I took the opportunity of expressing my conviction, afterwards proved to be well-founded, that South Lancashire might return two free-trade members.

On the following Saturday, Mr. Cobden and Mr. Moore
visited Bedford, pursuant to advertisement, for the purpose
of discussing the question of the Corn Laws with the'
farmers of Bedfordshire. Much excitement had prevailed
in the town for some days previous, and every possible
exertion had been made by the pro-corn-law party to defeat
the advocates of free-trade principles. The farmers for
miles round had been canvassed by influential agriculturists
and landholders, and entreated to attend for the purpose
of putting down the representatives of the Anti-Corn-Law
League at Bedford. Lord Charles Russell was appointed
chairman, by acclamation. Mr. Cobden then came forward, and was received with considerable applause. He
was followed by Mr. Pym, who, in a long speech, and
which, from the applause of his own party and the opposition of a large portion of the meeting, was rendered almost
inaudible, proposed: " That protection to native industry,
particularly to the agriculture of the country, is essential
to the well-being of the state, and any attempt, however
plausible, to abolish that protection, and further depreciate
the productions of our own soil, will only end in the spread
of inevitable ruin throughout the rural districts, and ultimately deprive the manufacturers of their best and surest
customers." Mr. Bennett, of Luton, seconded the resolution in a long harangue vituperative of the Anti-Corn-Law
League. Mr. Metcalfe, in a brief speech, moved the following amendment to the resolution proposed by Mr.
Pym: " That in the opinion of this meeting, the corn law and
every other law which protects one class at the expense of
other classes, must prove injurious to the national prosperity; and, therefore, all monopolies, whether passed
under the pretext of benefiting the agricultural, colonial,
or manufacturing interests, ought to be immediately abolished." Mr. Lattimore seconded the amendment. Mr.
Biggs next addressed the meeting against the amendment,
which was supported at great length by Mr. R. R. R. Moore.

The amendment in favour of free-trade principles having been put, the Chairman, amidst the greatest applause, declared it to be carried by a large majority. The defeated monopolists, however, not satisfied with the decision of an avowedly pro-corn-law chairman, persisted in retiring to one side of the field, thus giving a further demonstration of the numerical weakness of the monopolists; for on the division the numbers appeared to be at least two to one in favour of the total and immediate repeal of the Corn Laws. This discomfiture was obviously most unexpected, as throughout the whole proceedings the pro-corn-law party . seemed to calculate upon a sure and decisive victory.

On Saturday, June 10th, Mr. Cobden and Mr. Moore visited Rye, in the eastern division of Sussex. Placards had been issued entreating the farmers to be aware and not to be misled by Mr. Cobden who, though the son of a Sussex farmer, was a manufacturer and a member of the League. A great number of that class, however, attended, and there was the necessity to adjourn from the Town Hall to the Cattle Market. The *Brighton Herald*, giving an account of the meeting, said: "Though there was evidently a hostile feeling towards Mr. Cobden, because it was known that he was an advocate for the total repeal of the Corn Laws, yet his success was most complete, and before he had half finished his first address, we do not believe there was a man present who was not convinced in his own conscience that the views taken by Mr. Cobden were sound and correct, and that there really was no answer to him." Mr. Moore followed, and then Major Curteis said that he went two thirds of the way with those gentlemen, but he lived in a part of the country where they had not good land, and the tenant farmers were in as bad a state as the labourers were themselves ("Granted"), and if there was an immediate repeal of the Corn Laws, two out of three in his parish would be obliged to leave their farms; and he asked if two-thirds of the tenant

farmers were to give up their farms, how many of their
labourers would be thrown out of work? (A Voice: If
these tenant-farmers and labourers are in such a distressed
condition, does it not arise from the enormous rents they
pay?) Major Curteis replied that he believed some of them
paid no rent at all, because they could not. He disagreed
with Mr. Cobden that there were no exclusive burdens on
the land, for he believed there were. He would go for
repeal to-morrow, but when he knew that two-thirds of his
neighbours would be thrown into great distress, he could
not advocate an immediate repeal. Mr. H. B. Curteis,
M P., said he stood there boldly to contest the ground with
Mr. Cobden. The point was not whether there should be
a sliding-scale or a fixed duty, but whether or no there
should be any protection to the English farmer. Mr.
Cobden said, something like a challenge had been thrown
out by a gentleman to the right, regarding a motion to be
moved on this occasion. He was not generally anxious
about having a motion : he was content to state a few facts
and leave them. It did not become him to move a resolution; but he would claim his right, as a Sussex man, to
move for a total and immediate repeal of the Corn Laws.
He then went in detail through Major Curteis's exclusive
burdens. The tithes, he contended, belonged to the
church, not to the landlords; they could not be a burden:
other classes were subject to the poor and county rates;
and with regard to the land tax, the wisest course the
landowners could take was to say nothing about it. After
answering several questions from Major Curteis, he concluded by moving: "That in the opinion of this meeting
the Corn Law is injurious to the interest and independence
of the tenant farmer, and farm labourer, and that it ought
to be totally and immediately repealed." Major Curteis
moved an amendment, "That in order to prevent the de-
preciation of the property of the tenant farmer, which must
ensue from an immediate repeal of the Corn Laws, a fixed

duty is desirable for the present." Mr. Selmes seconded
it. On a division, the original motion, for a total and
immediate repeal, was carried almost unanimously.

On the following Saturday, Mr. Bright and Mr. Moore
visited Huntingdon, where great pains had been taken to
get up an opposition to their object. After Mr. Bright's
address, Mr. J. Rust, a banker of Huntingdon, moved:
" That while the present charges on land remain, the home
growers of corn cannot compete with the foreign grower
without a protecting duty." Mr. R. R. R. Moore followed
in a lengthened and eloquent address in favour of a total
and immediate repeal, amid much opposition from the
pro-corn-law party, and loud cheers from a portion of the
meeting. He concluded by moving the following amendment: " That in the opinion of this meeting, the Corn
Law and every other law which protects one class at the
expense of other classes, must prove injurious to the national prosperity, and, therefore, all monopolies, whether
passed with the object of benefiting the agricultural, colonial, or manufacturing interests, ought to be immediately
abolished." Captain Duberley, a landed proprietor in the
counties of Huntingdon and Cambridge, seconded the
amendment in a long speech. Mr. Day (a legal gentleman, highly respected by the Whig party at Huntingdon)
then rose and spoke at great length in favour of the
original resolution, and the influence of this gentleman
being thrown into the scale of the pro-corn-law party, was
supposed to have been the moving cause of their subsequent equivocal success. A division was taken at the
conclusion of this gentleman's speech upon Mr. Moore's
amendment, which the chairman declared was negatived
by the meeting. It is right to say, that this decision was
protested against by the anti-corn-law party, who strenu-
ously insisted that the victory was on their side.

This very equivocal victory was counterbalanced by unequivocal proof of division amongst the landowners in

another quarter. A large number of tenant farmers connected with the fertile Vale of Clwyd, wincing under the
pressure of a limited demand and low prices for their
produce, fixed a meeting to be held in the County Hall on
Wednesday, June 28th, to which they invited the county
landowners, in order to consider the existing state of
things, and also the means best adapted to procure "*protection.*" The greatest publicity was given to this meeting,
and every landowner and considerable tenant was warned
of it by circular. Several influential landowners and a
great number of the tenant-farmers did attend, and others
sent letters. Amongst the latter was Mr. Myddelton Bid-
dulph, the Lord Lieutenant, who went at some length into
the question of protection, showing how futile it had
hitherto been, and pointing out that the existing as well as
all past protection had only produced uncertainty, and not
prosperity; and that what the agricultural interest was
now mainly suffering from was, "decreased consumption."
After some four or five hours' debate, a thorough free-trade
resolution, advocating the removal of *all* restrictions on industry as the remedy for the existing distress, was adopted
by a large majority. An objection was taken, that that majority was not composed of owners and occupiers of land,
which was the fact; and the mover withdrew it, in order
that the owners and occupiers present might go to a division on the moderate revenue-producing duty principles
propounded by the Lord Lieutenant, and the ultra pro-
corn-law resolutions of Mr. Griffith. The result was, that
just three persons, including Mr. Griffith and his seconder,
voted for the latter; and the meeting then adopted petitions to parliament, founded upon the Lord Lieutenant's
letter.

A more decided victory was obtained over the ultra
protectionists at Aylesbury. Dr. Sleigh, supposed to be
employed by the Duke of Buckingham, had announced
that a meeting would be held in the County Hall. The

advertisement included "the inhabitants and electors of Aylesbury," but stated that Dr. Sleigh would not submit that any resolution should be put to the meeting. A counter advertisement had been issued by Mr. Jno. Gibbs, in which that gentleman contended for his right to express his opinion, and to propose any declaratory resolution he might think proper. Dr. Sleigh asserted that the insatiable thirst for wealth was the cause of the reduction of wages, and that those persons who had been reducing wages were the very persons who were now raising the cry for cheap bread. Mr. Jno. Gibbs exposed all the fallacies of the lecturer, and moved a resolution in favour of the entire freedom of trade. The resolution was put by the chairman, after a protest against such a proceeding had been read by Dr. Sleigh. It was carried almost unanimously a thousand hands being held up for it. A vote of thanks to the chairman was then carried by acclamation; three loud and lusty cheers were given for free trade, and Dr. Sleigh retired from the hall discomfited.

On the 29th June, the market day at Maidstone, a meeting was held on Penenden Heath, attended by about three thousand persons, including many farmers, to hear an address from Mr. Cobden. He was received with loud cheers, and successfully attacked the fallacies of the landowners with regard to the operation of the Corn Law upon the interests of agriculture. At the conclusion of his speech, Captain Atcherley spoke for some time, very little to the purpose, and then Mr. J. Osborn, jun., of Marden, an influential landowner, who said that free trade would admit a deluge of corn, and reduce wheat from 60s. to 40s., which his audience said would be a good thing. The tenant farmers, he asserted, would lose a third of their capital, and the farm labourers a third of their wages. The Hon. C. P. Villiers took a manly part in the out-of-door day's work, and was as effective there as in the House of Commons, and sarcastically and effectively demolised Mr.

Osborn's statements and arguments. Colonel Thompson
followed, and his racy remarks excited much applause.
Mr. Beacon proposed petitions to both houses of parliament for the repeal of the Corn Laws, which were carried
with only two dissentients.

On the following Saturday, Mr. Cobden and Mr. Moore
met the farmers on the Barrack Field, Guildford, Mr. R.
D. Mangles, M.P., occupying the chair. Mr. Cobden addressed the meeting for two hours, after which Mr. Maydwell attempted to reply to him, but not at all to the
satisfaction of the farmers. A number of questions were
put to the two free traders, and then a resolution in favour
of the repeal of the Corn Law was put and carried almost
unanimously.

These victories, in county towns, on market days when
crowds of agriculturists could attend, were alarming to the
landowners, and every effort was made to make a successful stand against the triumphant free traders. It had been
known that Mr. Cobden and his fellow-labourers were
about to visit Essex. Their exploit was said to savour
rather of courage than discretion, and many a prophecy
was hazarded as to the amount of the majority by which
the free traders were to be defeated. Wherever else Mr.
Cobden might have triumphed, in Colchester, at least, the
protectionists were secure. In other places the champions
of free trade might have succeeded; here they would in all
probability shrink from the contest, or if they appeared, it
would only be to retire discomfited from an honest agricultural population. Advertisements were inserted in all
the county papers calling upon the farmers to attend.
The local agricultural associations marshalled all their
forces. The clergy of the county canvassed eagerly on
behalf of those Corn Laws by which their income was measured. Sir John Tyrrell himself, at a dinner given at
Maldon but three days previously, declared that "it was a
great question on which they were to go to the meeting at

Colchester, and that from what he had seen in the united press of the county and in all parts, the agricultural body would feel it their duty to attend." *Six thousand* people assembled, with but very few mechanics among them. A chairman was appointed, who confessed that he entertained very strong feelings in favour of protection. Mr. Cobden, after an address more than usually effective, deviated, at the request of his adversaries, from his usual custom, and proposed a resolution attacking in direct terms the Corn Laws and all class legislation. Sir John Tyrrell, the friend of the agricultural labourers, did not wish somehow to wait for the hour at which those labourers could attend, but took a division, without the help of the chairman, upon an amendment of his own, which was not fortunate enough to be seconded, and was beaten by such a majority that he thought it prudent to withdraw his proposition upon the ground of its admitted irregularity. The meeting proceeded. Sir John Tyrrell harangued, and the notorious Mr. Ferrand howled, but an overwhelming majority—there being but twenty-seven dissentients—scouted protection ; and, smarting under the most signal defeat which they had yet sustained, the monopolists went discomfited from their chosen field. The Hon. C. P. Villiers accompanied Mr. Cobden, and made an admirable speech, his sarcasm telling most effectually on Sir John Tyrrell.

Mr. Bright was also in the field, carrying into the north the principles which had been so successfully urged in the south. The following is a brief account of a meeting at Kelso, surrounded by the finest agricultural district in the whole island :—

"On Friday evening last a very large and influential meeting was held in the Secession Church, Kelso, to receive a deputation from the League. Messrs. Bright and Prentice attended, and were most cordially received. It was intended to have held two meetings in Kelso, one in the middle of the day for the farmers, attending the market, and one in the evening for the town's-people. The bailie, or magistrate, an officer appointed by the Duke of Roxburgh, refused the use of the Town Hall, and no other suitable building being to be had, the evening meeting only was held, and to this the farmers were invited, and many most respectable and influential farmers attended. A letter was read from Sir Thomas M. Brisbane, expressing his hearty concurrence in the objects of the meeting and his regret that he could not attend, his delicate health alone keeping him away. The Earl of Buchan had agreed to take the chair, but being called off suddenly to Edinburgh on business which admitted of no postponement, he was compelled to be absent, and a note from his lordship was read stating his full agreement with the object of the meeting. Mr. George Thomson was called to the chair. This gentleman is a large farmer, and the condition of his farm proves that he has not relied upon an act of parliament for his success as an agriculturist. Mr. Prentice first addressed the meeting, and speaking as the son of a Scotch farmer, his speech evidently produced a good impression. Mr. Bright followed in a long speech, in which the deadening effects of 'protection' on the prosperity of agriculture were forcibly exposed. The chairman asked if any person had any questions to put to the deputation, when Dickinson, a Chartist from Manchester, mounted a form and proceeded to speak in the usual strain of the men who have been hired to support the monopolists under the garb of friends of the working classes. The chairman requested Dickinson to keep to the subject, and to confine himself to questions. He then asked Mr. Bright if he did not think that machinery was the cause of the distress of the country? Mr. Bright then entered on the machinery topic, and demonstrated the fallacy of the miserable pretences on which the dislike to machinery was founded. He showed, by reference to the condition of Ireland and the agricultural counties of England, how foolish it is to suppose that the comforts of the people are greatest where no machinery exists. He enforced his arguments by a reference to the cotton trade, showing how the numbers employed in it have increased thirty fold since the discoveries of Watt and Arkwright, whilst the wages of those employed have been also greatly increased during that period. He alluded to the fact that the democratic countries of Switzerland and America encourage machinery as much as possible, and finally, he asked Dickinson if he had not attempted to introduce his anti-machinery claptraps at a meeting held in the theatre, Rochdale, last November, at the close of Mr. Buckingham's lecture, when the working men then assembled refused to hear him, and he was turned out of the meeting. To this Dickinson had nothing to reply. Mr. Prentice then asked him if the Corn Law was a just law? After a pause, Dickinson replied, ' No ! ' At this the meeting laughed and cheered, and the degraded tool of the bread taxers, the pretended working man *who will not work,* but prefers to sell the dearest rights of working men, was forced into silence. A resolution condemning all protection was passed, with only five dissentients, also a vote of thanks to the deputation, and the meeting separated with repeated cheers for the League."

The next movement was upon Alnwick, where the land owners had been using strenuous endeavours to defeat the free traders :—

"Mr. John Bright and Mr. Archibald Prentice, two talented deputies from the National Anti-Corn-Law League, will address the farmers of Northumberland, on Saturday next, at Alnwick. Their auditory, we are quite sure, will be both numerous and attentive ; and we are just as sure that the 'seeds' which will be that day 'scattered' will bring forth goodly fruit in abundance in due season. We shall give as much as possible of the proceedings in a third edition. In the mean time, however, and without entering upon the general question, we wish to call the attention of the public to the following atrocious paragraph, which appeared in the *Newcastle Journal* on Saturday last: 'It is stated that Bright, the anti-corn-law agitator, is expected to visit the wool fair which will be held at Alnwick shortly, in order to scatter the seeds of disaffection in that quarter. Should he make his appearance, which is not improbable, (for the person has impudence for anything of this sort,) *it is to be hoped there may be found* SOME STALWART YEOMAN *ready to treat the disaffected vagabond as he deserves.*' This abominable invitation to violence, this finger-post to assassination, is published, be it remembered, in a newspaper which was established at Newcastle, a few years ago, under the immediate auspices of the Duke of Northumberland and of Mr. Matthew Bell, the present tory member for South Northumberland. It is well that the public should be acquainted, not only with the paragraph, but with the godfathers of the 'physical force' publication in which it appeared."—*Gateshead Observer.*

On Saturday, Mr. Bright and I proceeded across the border country from Kelso to Alnwick, where we found a great audience, consisting principally of agriculturists, many of them landowners and extensive farmers. Notwithstanding the appeal to the physical force of the "stalwart yeoman," we had an enthusiastic reception, and a most satisfactory meeting, Mr. Bright's speech being exceedingly effective. He and I then took different routes :

"LANARK, 12th July.—On Mr. Prentice's arrival here yesterday by the Edinburgh coach, he was surrounded by a number of the inhabitants of Covington, his native parish, who had come seven miles cordially to welcome him, and to hear an address from a son of the much-respected 'Gudeman of the Mains.' He was accompanied to the Town Hall by the provost, the Revs. Messrs. Borland and Johnstone, some of the bailies, and other gentlemen. The hall was so crowded as to be inconveniently hot, but the audience, of whom two-thirds were respectable farmers, were so far interested, that all remained throughout the proceeedings. The novelty of a farmer's son undertaking to prove that the Corn Law, instead of being beneficial, had been extremely injurious to practical agriculturists, and the well-known character of the speaker's father and relatives, had secured a good attendance and most respectful attention. The conversation, when the farmers had spread over the town after the lecture, was invariably upon the subjects treated of. What one man said may represent the state of opinion amongst them : ' He made everything very plain, and said naething but what was perfectly true, and proved that the Corn Law did us nae guid, and that its repeal would do us nae ill; but its of nae use to convince us unless he convinces our landlords too, for we maun just do as they bid us.' A considerable sensation, however, was excited, and the subject will be earnestly discussed in all the country round this, many active-minded men having come ten or a dozen miles to hear Mr. Prentice's address, and some having gone home convinced, who came determined not to be convinced."

"GLASGOW.—According to announcement, Mr. Prentice, editor of the *Manchester Times*, and one of the members of the National Anti-Corn Law League, lectured on Thursday evening in the Trades' Hall, on the question of the Corn Law, and its bearing on the agricultural interests of the country. There was a pretty good attendance, but owing to the holding of the fair, and the season of the year, the turn-out was not so numerous as might have been anticipated. Alex. Couper, Esq., occupied the chair, and was supported by Mr. Alex. Graham, Councillors Hamilton and Turner, Mr. Ure of Croy, Rev. Mr. M'Tear, Bailie Hastie, Mr. J. P. Reid, and a few others of the members of the Glasgow Anti-Corn-Law Association. Mr. Prentice, on coming forward, was loudly applauded. He commenced his address by referring to the progress which the repeal cause had made amongst the mercantile, compared to the agricultural classes, and after an able address, resumed his seat amid loud and continued applause. On the motion of Mr. Alex. Graham, seconded by Mr. Turner, of Thrushgrove, a hearty vote of thanks was awarded to him for his very able and instructive address, and the meeting broke up shortly after ten o'clock."

Mr. Bright proceeded to Newcastle, where a great meeting was held in the Nelson Street Lecture Room, Mr. T. M. Greenbow in the chair. There was no attempt to controvert his arguments, no "stalwart yeoman" to meet him with the reasoning of an ash-stick, and thanks were passed to him enthusiastically. His next visit was to Sunderland, where he met a large audience, the mayor in the chair, and where his address produced a great sensation. We next hear of him at Winchester, in company with Mr. Cobden and Mr. Moore, instructing the farmers of Hampshire, the meeting passing resolutions against protection as unsound and injurious. Similar success attended Mr. Cobden amongst the farmers at a large meeting held at Lewes in Sussex.

CHAPTER VII.

MR. BRIGHT'S RETURN TO PARLIAMENT.

During these movements on the agricultural districts, an election committee had unseated Lord Dungannon, one of the members for Durham, for bribery. Mr. Bright was invited to offer himself as a candidate, and accepted the invitation. His opponent was Mr. Purvis, a conservative who had much influence in the city and its neighbourhood, but at the close of the poll (July 25th), the free trader had a majority of seventy-eight. "*The Quaker Bright has many friends in Durham,*" said the *Morning Herald*, preparing the monopolists for a defeat in that Cathedral City. So it proved; but of the friends who carried his election triumphantly, there was not one who knew him personally before the previous April. At that time he went into the city a perfect stranger, and, without preparation, almost without a canvas; his honest, straightforward advocacy of free-trade principles—"the principles of common-sense," as one said who admitted a truth but dared not act upon it—balanced the strong aristocratic influence that previously had been all-powerful, and would have secured his return but for the wholesale bribery that was resorted to. Before three short months had elapsed the aristocratic member who represented bought votes was unseated; and, in spite of every attempt to intimidate, it having become dangerous to bribe the electors, the free-trade candidate, without any other influence in the city than the influence of principle

upon the minds of the constituency, headed the poll from
the first, continued to head it to the last, and was returned
by a majority of *seventy-eight*, having recorded 488 votes,
whilst the Peel candidate, with all his weight of local influence, could command no more than 410. The enemies
of free trade and reform endeavoured to lessen the value of
the victory by saying that had the Marquis of Londonderry
exerted his power the result would have been different ;
that is, if a peer had *illegally* interfered in the election, the
monopolist candidate might have been elected. With
equal propriety they might have attributed the defeat to
the fear of using their usual auxiliary, the corruption of the
voters. The talk was that of the wrestler, who would say :
" You could not have thrown me if I had chosen to stab
you with my knife." My comment on this victory at the
time was : " Greater than the accession to the House of
Commons of an additional advocate of freedom of trade,
freedom of conscience, freedom of representation, and universal peace, able, vigorous, and eloquent though he be,
must be the results of John Bright's election. It has
proved that a *principle* is much more influential than a *name*.
He has achieved a victory which could not have been attained by any one even of the very *élite* of the whig aristocracy. Lord John Russell, Lord Morpeth, Lord Howick,
would have failed where the Rochdale cotton-spinner has
been successful. They would have found that the party-
name was no longer one to conjure with. The electors
who rallied round Mr. Bright, listening with breathless
attention to his exposition of the real causes of national
distress, despising every allurement and every threat, and
struggling for his success as if their very existence were
involved in the contest, would have remained unmoved as
the stones in the market-place to speeches upon the comparative merits of whig and tory administrations. The
lesson will not be thrown away. The Walsall election, by
showing how powerless were the aristocratic influences of

the neighbourhood, drove the whigs in office to their retiring declaration in favour of partially free trade; the Durham election will show them that they must go much further if they would acquire the confidence of the country; it will show them the value of Lord Sydenham's advice, to offer the people *something worth struggling for*, if they would have their aid; and, much more than the benefit of any whig conversion, it will show honest men, really desirous to benefit their distressed country, that a bold reliance on a principle, regardless of party names, and of local influences whose sole strength is in the belief of their strength, is, even with seemingly indifferent, or suspectedly corrupt constituencies, the best recommendation of a candidate."

The new member took his seat in the Commons in time to make his first speech there before honourable members abandoned legislation for grouse shooting and leaving to have "a trial" Peel's corn bill, which imposed a duty of twenty shillings a quarter on wheat then at forty-five shillings. On the 7th August, on the motion for going into a committee of supply, Mr. Ewart submitted the following amendment: "That it is expedient that the principles and suggestions contained in the evidence taken before the Import Duties Committee of session 1840, be carried into general effect; and that the trade and industry of the country require further and more effectual relief by the removal or reduction of duties which press upon the raw material of manufacture, and on articles of interchange with foreign nations, as well as on the means of subsistence of the people." The discussion was a short one, and in a thin house, most of the members being away to prepare for the moors. Mr. Bright rose before probably the smallest audience he had addressed for years, and seemed a little nervous at first, but gained confidence as he went on, and convinced many of his hearers of his manly nature, and that he would not be deterred by the conventionalities of the place from giving honest and forcible

utterance to his opinions.   In a house of 77 members 25
voted with Mr. Ewart

On the 24th of August, parliament was prorogued.
Ministers were obviously waiting the chapter of accidents.
There *might* be a good harvest—that is, such a harvest as
would neither make prices so low as to add to the discontent of the agriculturists, nor so high as to add to the discontent of the industrial classes ; there *might* be such a
division in Ireland of federalists and repealers as to lessen
the fears of a general revolutionary movement; there *might*
be such divisions in the Free Church of Scotland as to
restore the tory administration to its lost place in that part
of the kingdom ; there *might* be some such revival of trade
as to make the operations of the League less effective ;
there *might* arise some such unforeseen demand for iron
as would give employment to the almost despairing people
of Bilston and Dudley, Gartsherrie and Dundyvan ; the
Welsh farmers *might* tire of knocking down toll gates ;
there MIGHT, *should all those things happen*, be such a consumption of spirits, wines, malt, sugar, coffee, and tea, as
to supply the deficiencies of the exchequer ;—in short, the
fire *might* go out of itself without the use of Sir Abel Handy
Peel's patent engine—the patient might recover without
the use of his patent pill.   In such hope, the "strong
government" prorogued parliament, utterly regardless of
the distressed condition of the country—prepared, however, as the Duke of Wellington said, to meet energetically
any movement that might arise out of the universal discontent,—to meet with steel the demand for bread !   The
members of the late whig administration had also *their*
reliance on the chapter of accidents.   If the fire did not
go out of itself they might be called in to put it out.   If
Sir Robert's pill was found useless, Lord John's might
effect a cure.   If the machinery of government stood still
the whigs might be called in to put it in motion again.
They were waiting the favourable occasion for making their

bid. They expected that the people would come to *them*, quite unconscious that the reply was: "You must come to *us*." Although they abandoned their public duties the moment they were deprived of office, they expected that the public would back them when there was a chance of their return to office. Although they did nothing when they had the power, they expected to be carried into power again—again to do nothing.

Ministers, previous to the prorogation of parliament, asked for and obtained the power of calling out, arming, and training TEN THOUSAND MEN, to be picked from the whole of the Chelsea Pensioners. They justified this extraordinary increase to the effective force of the standing army, on the ground that it was well to be prepared for any emergency; and Sir Robert Peel refused to allow the limitation of this new power to five years, because *any* limitation would be an acknowledgment that it was an unconstitutional one! He was about, as he was two years before, to retire to Drayton Manor for five months, there to consider what further prescription would be necessary for the suffering patient whom, meanwhile, he left under the Castlereagh regimen. This extraordinary measure for supplying the means of coercion, had the additional discredit of being introduced at the very close of the session, when few members remained in town except the officials, whose votes were at the service of Ministers. Some twenty members, and amongst them Mr. Cobden and Mr. Bright, had manfully resisted this extra-arming act, to put down any expression of that universal dissatisfaction which was the result of misgovernment; but where were all the rest of the so-called *liberals*, that they did not return to their places in opposition? There was one comfort in all this indifference on one side and of encroachment on the other, that things were rapidly drifting on to that state of public opinion which made the first great inroad upon the rotten borough system. The refusal of *corn* had wonderfully increased the demand for *votes*.

Immediately preceding the prorogation of parliament, Mr. Cobden and Mr. Bright visited the cathedral city of Canterbury, where great preparations had been made to defeat the free traders ; but when they arrived the courage of the monopolists oozed out at their fingers' ends. They had met at the Corn Exchange, Sir Brooke Brydges in the chair, to consider whether they should or should not offer any opposition. A resolution was passed, "That the farmers of East Kent do not consider it expedient to enter upon a discussion of the Corn Laws at a meeting called by or at the request of any person unconnected with the county." No, it was not *expedient*, it was not *prudent*. The motion was seconded by Mr. James, the novelist, although he declared he could see through some of Mr. Cobden's fallacies and answer them ! In spite of the remonstrances of several persons present, who first desired that Messrs. Cobden and Bright should be invited to discuss the question in the Corn Exchange before the then assembly, and afterwards that they should be met upon their own ground in the Cattle Market, no terms could be arranged, and it was ultimately determined *not to meet* Messrs. Cobden and Bright, the above resolution being carried with only a few dissentients. Notwithstanding this avowed determination, it was observed that nearly the whole of the assemblage instinctively moved off in the direction of the Cattle Market, where the meeting was then about to commence. The free-trade resolution was carried, with only one or two dissentients, amid loud applause.

Where were the *farm labourers* all this while ? If each farmer at this Canterbury meeting had been attended by four or five labourers, there would have been a majority of countrymen, and the country interest would have been victorious. Time was when the labourers were sent to meet the arguments of the early lecturers of the League with blows ; time was when they were employed to ring bells, fire guns, play the fire engines, throw eggs, and

stones, and mud, and exercise their lungs with groans and
hootings.   But they were not now to be enlisted in such a
warfare.   They did not find that they were the happy
Arcadians the landowners would have them supposed to
be.   They had indeed, "the clear sky above them and the
green fields before them ; " but they had poverty and
wretchedness in their hovels.   They now saw plainly
enough that corn-law legislation had done nothing to improve their unhappy condition.   They would not now
listen to descriptions of the dirty avocations pursued in
smoky and unhealthy towns.   They would rather have had
such employment than starve, or be transported to the
colonies, or imprisoned in the Union Workhouses.   "What
is the reason " asked Mr. Cobden, " that agricultural labourers troop into the manufacturing districts ?   Simply
because the wages in those districts are better, and the
employment more continuous, than in the agricultural
districts.   When the landowners denounce the manufacturing system, let them bear in mind that *there must be
something worse behind* to induce the agriculturists to come
in crowds to seek work in the manufacturing districts."
The labourers knew all this, and therefore they were no
longer to be compelled to oppose, with offensive missiles,
or strong lungs, men whom they now believed to be more
really their friends than those who professed to be legis-
lating for their especial benefit.

The defeats in towns surrounded by a purely agricultural
population were not to be attributed merely to the greater
ease with which a town's population was mustered.   No
coercion could bring the labourers, or if it could, it would
not then be resorted to, for it was known that they would
only add to the number who voted for "the principles of
common sense."   And when the farmers were brought
together the result was only that they were converted.   At
Canterbury they met and peaceably joined in a vote, that
it was *inexpedient* to have any discussion with Messrs.

Cobden and Bright; and then they, one and all, and at once,
proceeded to hear those gentlemen's speeches, and voted
in favour of the free-trade resolution.

And, for a moment, supposing that those defeats arose
from no other cause than the facility of mustering a town's
population, what would that fact have declared? Why,
that, contrary to the reiterated claim of the landowners, to
have the inhabitants of towns so situated included as a
part of the agricultural population, being solely employed
in supplying the wants of the agriculturists, they had re-
nounced the allegiance and denied the alliance. When
the object was to represent the great importance of the
agricultural interest, every tradesman not absolutely a
manufacturer of iron, or wool, or cotton, or silk, was
claimed as a part of that interest. Towns where those
anti-corn-law meetings had been held—Norwich, Colchester, Chelmsford, Taunton, Aylesford, Hertford,. Huntingdon, Alnwick, Kelso, Salisbury, Canterbury, Knutsford—
were always claimed by the landowners as a part and
parcel of their own interest. The mantle of "protection"
was claimed for them as being indissolubly connected with
the owners and cultivators of the soil, their neighbours
and their sole employers. But when a meeting was held,
and when those tradesmen voted according to their conscience,—when, seeing that *they* derived no benefit from
landlord legislation, they voted for free trade—they were
spoken of as a factious "town-population," more easily
gathered together and more easily led to mischief than
their agricultural friends and customers. "*They are all
ours,*" said the landlords, when they wished to swell out the
numbers of the agricultural population. "*They are none of
ours,*" was the cry when they voted against landlord legislation.

But where were the members of the high aristocracy of
the counties in which those contests so singularly inglo-
rious to the monopolists had taken place. Where were

the men whose rank, wealth, and personal virtues gave them an influence irresistible when exerted in a good cause, and too often resistless in a bad one? Surely *they* might have turned the tide of action if not of opinion. Surely *they* might have arrested in some degree, the progress of dangerous principles in their various localities. Why did not *they* appear? The truth seems to be that they were ASHAMED to appear in the companionship of men who admitted that the Corn Laws were passed to *raise rents*, and retained to *pay off mortgages*, to fulfil *marriage settlements*, and to keep honourable baronets in their *proper station in society*. They had their title-deeds in their own family chests, and would not appear in company with men mortgaged to the lips by extravagant, perhaps profligate expenditure; they could fulfil their marriage settlements without robbing the community; and they could sustain their station in society without putting their hands into other men's pockets; they would not make common cause with the desperate of fortune, who urged their private engagements as an excuse for public robbery. Besides, there was, at the bottom, a growing conviction that the Corn Laws were doomed to destruction; and men of wealth, rank, and a character for justice and humanity, would not hazard the diminution of their legitimate influence by exerting it in so doubtful a cause.

Seeing then that farmers and farm labourers were beginning to discover that "protection" had been of no benefit to them; that tradesmen in what are called agricultural towns did not identify their interest with that of the landowners; and that the really respectable members of the aristocracy would take no active part in a cause of doubtful justice; it was not surprising that the course of the able, eloquent, and indomitable leaguers, should be a course of triumph from the first small meeting with the farmers at Over in Cheshire, to the last great meeting at Canterbury in Kent. And yet the strength of the free traders in the House of Commons was only 125 out of 658 members. Further means were needed to bring that body into accordance with public opinion.

Five years had elapsed from the time at which the Manchester Anti-Corn-Law Association had been established. Three years had elapsed from the time at which the League, representing hundreds of local associations, had begun to exercise some influence upon elections. During that time thirty-five members had been added to the free-trade party in parliament. That fact marked progress ; very slow progress indeed ; but there was reason to believe that the increase of strength there would go on in an accelerating ratio. Fifty thousand pounds had been readily given to carry on the operations of the League for one year, and the council had faith that the public would accede to the claim of means to carry on, at the same rate, the wholesome agitation for two years more. It was resolved to raise a fund of one hundred thousand pounds, to engage Covent Garden for fifty nights, although it was known that the rent would be three thousand pounds ; to expend ten thousand pounds a year in distributing amongst ten thousand subscribers, of one pound and upwards to the fund, a full sized-weekly newspaper, to be called *The League*, instead of the small fortnightly publication called the *Anti-Bread-Tax Circular;* and that in addition to the constant labours of some twelve or fourteen lecturers, and the incessant and liberal distribution of tracts to electors in counties and boroughs, members of the League should be invited to become deputies, whensoever any locality invited aid in the work of public instruction ; for now requisitions for the services of Cobden and Bright had become so numerous, that, ubiquitous as those gentlemen seemed to be, it was impossible that they could comply with one tenth of the demands made upon them.

The first number of *The League*, published in London, under the able editorship of Mr. Paulton, appeared on

Saturday, September 30th; thenceforward to be a faithful recorder of every movement of the body down to its smallest ramification, and remorsely to demolish every sophistry, every fallacy, every misrepresentation, and every falsehood uttered in defence of monopoly ; and there, now, in its three thick volumes, which ought to be found in every public library in the kingdom, is the whole History of the League, during its three further years of struggle, with every argument for and against the principles of free trade. From the commencement of that publication, easily accessible to the future historian, my notices of the movement need to be no more than of such of its phases as marked the onward progress to ultimate triumph.

Previous to the commencement of the great meetings in Covent Garden, the Council of the League prepared an address to the people of the united kingdom, giving an account of what had been done during the year ; and the following were the means which were contemplated for forwarding the cause :—

" 1. Copies will be obtained of the registration lists of all boroughs and counties throughout the kingdom, and the collection lodged at the Metropolitan Office of the League, as a central place of deposit, to be consulted as occasion may require.

2. An extensive correspondence, by means of the post, and of stamped publications, will be kept up with electors, in all districts, upon matters connected with the progress and success of our cause.

3. It is intended that every borough in the kingdom shall be visited by deputations of the League, and meetings held, which the electors will be specially invited to attend.

4. Prompt measures will be taken to ascertain the opinions of each elector in every borough, with the view of obtaining an obvious and decided majority in favour of the total and immediate repeal of the Corn Laws.

5. Every constituency, whose representatives have not hitherto supported Mr. Villiers's motion for the repeal of the Corn Laws, will be invited to memorialise its members to vote for such motion when next brought forward.

6. Whenever a vacancy occurs in the representation of any borough, the electors will be recommended to put a free-trade candidate in

nomination; and the League pledges itself to give such candidate every possible support, by deputations, lectures, and the distribution of publications.

7. In the event of any borough being unable to procure a suitable candidate, the League pledges itself to bring forward candidates, so as to afford every elector an opportunity of recording his vote in favour of free trade, until the question be decided."

In the report prepared it was stated, that during a very considerable portion of the year there were employed in the printing and making up of the Electoral Packets of Tracts, upwards of 300 persons, while more than 500 other persons were employed in distributing them from house to house, among the constituencies. To the parliamentary electors alone of England and Scotland there had been distributed, in this manner, of tracts and stamped publications, 5,000,000. That, besides these, there had been a large general distribution among the working classes and others, who are not electors, to the number of 3,600,000. In addition, 426,000 tracts had been stitched up with the monthly magazines and other periodicals, thus making altogether, the whole number of tracts and stamped publications, issued by the Council during the year, to amount to 9,026,000, or in weight upwards of one hundred tons. That the distribution had been made in twenty-four counties, containing about 237,000 electors, and in 187 boroughs, containing 259,226 electors, making in boroughs and counties together, the whole number of electors supplied, 496,226. That the number of lecturers employed during the year had been 14, and that their labours had been spread over fifty-nine counties in England, Wales, and Scotland, and they had delivered about 650 lectures during the year. That a large number of meetings had been held during the year in the cities and boroughs, which had been attended by deputations of members of the Council. Exclusive of the metropolis, 140 towns had been thus visited, many of them twice and three times; and that such had been the feeling existing in all parts of the kingdom, that there was scarcely a town which had not urged its claim to be visited by a deputation from the Council of the League.

The heads of expenditure were stated as follow :— Printing 9,026,000 tracts, and stamped publications, and distributing the same.—Lecturers' salaries, and expenses of hiring rooms, printing, &c., for 650 lectures.—Expenses of deputations to 156 meetings in counties and boroughs. —Expenses of agricultural meetings, including printing, placarding, and distributing reports, &c.—Expenses of deputations to boroughs on parliamentary registration.— Expenses of weekly meetings of the League, and Metropolitan meetings.—Rent, taxes, gas, and office expenses, in London and Manchester.—Advertising, including 426,000 tracts in magazines.—Wages, stamps, postages, and incidental expenses.—Local expenses in collecting the League Fund.—Total expenditure, £47,814 3s. 9d.—Balance of cash in hand, September 9th, 1843, £2,476 10s. 3d.

A stronger proof could not have been given of the confidence of the Council that they would receive public support than that, with so small a sum " in hand," they should have commenced preparations involving so great an expenditure.   The following description of the Covent Garden meeting is from the *Morning Advertiser* :—

" The recommencement of the Anti-Corn-Law agitation in the metropolis, was made last night, September 28th, in Covent Garden Theatre. And nothing could exceed the enthusiasm with which that recommencement was hailed by the largest and most brilliant metropolitan meeting which has yet taken place on the subject. Mr. Wilson, the chairman, briefly opened the proceedings of the evening—glancing at the past operations of the League, and referring to their future prospects. He hurled defiance at the opposition of the oligarchy, and proclaimed amidst deafening plaudits, that the doom of the bread monopoly might now be fairly considered to be sealed, and that a very short period would suffice to see the Corn Laws erased from the statute-book of England. Mr. Paulton, the secretary, read the report. It details the past proceedings of the League, and adverts to the plan of their future operations. No one can attentively read this document without being struck with the

surpassing skill and untiring energy with which the League have prosecuted their labours. Neither can any man doubt the issue of the great
struggle, when he considers the points in dispute, the condition of the
country, the state of public feeling, and the means at the disposal of the
League for prosecuting the war in which they have embarked. Mr.
Cobden, who was received with, if possible, greater applause, than ever,
plunged at once into the marrow of the question. He commenced by
grappling with the argument against the abolition of the Corn Laws
which has been so often, of late, urged by the monopolists—namely,
that, notwithstanding the existence of these laws, trade is confessedly
reviving. He first demonstrated that the revival of trade is only partial,
and then that even this partial resuscitation is solely the result of a
reduction of prices, consequent on two favourable harvests. The hon.
gentleman entered into various statistical details in proof of his position,
which he established with the conclusiveness of mathematical demonstration, and amidst the loudest plaudits that ever greeted the eloquence
of a public speaker. Mr. Cobden adverted at considerable length to the
League's plan of operations for the future. Anything better adapted
to accomplish its purpose was never devised by human ingenuity. The
announcement of Mr. Cobden, that it is not the intention of the League
to recommend any further petitioning to parliament, produced a sensation exceeding anything we ever before witnessed. The immense
assemblage—there must have been fully 5,000 present—simultaneously
rose to their feet, and gave expression to their joy in thunders of applause.
We wish that all the members of the corrupt Commons had been present
to witness this expression of the estimation in which they are held by
the country. Mr. Bright, in a speech displaying more than his wonted
eloquence and power, proceeded throughout on the assumption that the
corn monopoly is tottering to its fall. Even already, as he justly remarked,
there are thousands of families in England who are deriving actual
happiness from the labours of the League, merely from the confident
expectation that the entire extinction of the monopoly is at hand. Mr.
Fox followed Mr. Bright. His speech was one of the best he ever
delivered, and was received with continued bursts of applause. The
speaking was equal, on the whole, to anything we have heard since the
commencement of the Anti-Corn-Law agitation. But what is of more
importance, the arguments were conclusive in themselves, and were
brought forward with irresistible effect. No monopolist sophistry was
left unexposed—no point was omitted which could place in a strong and
striking light the terrible effects which have been produced by the
operation of the Corn Laws. If, indeed, the decision of the points at
issue depended on the awards of justice, reason, and utility, the question
might have been fairly considered to have been last night settled."

A vacancy in the representation of London had been occasioned by the death of Sir Matthew Wood. The conservatives and the monopolists had invited Mr. T. Baring, and the reformers and free traders Mr. Pattison, to become candidates. Mr. Bright alluded to this opportunity given to the citizens of London :—

" Landlords ! They built not this magnificent metropolis—they covered not these forty square miles with the great mass of human dwellings that spread over them—they crowd not our port with shipping —they filled not your city with its monuments of science and of art, with its institutions of literature and its temples of religion—they poured not that stream of commercial prosperity into the country, which during the last century has made the grandeur of London, quadrupling its population, and showing that it has one heart with the entire community. They ! Why, if they were to spend—if you could impose on them the laws which they would impose upon you, and they were bound to spend in this metropolis all they received in their rents; if there were no toleration for French wines or foreign luxuries; if they were prohibited from storing and locking up in their remote galleries works of art, real or pretended, which they prize as property; if here, amongst the shopkeepers of London they were bound to spend that which they had obtained by their rents : it would be wretched repayment to you for what you have forfeited by the absence of free trade. (Loud cheers.) It is as it were to make war upon towns and cities, to cut off their supplies of food, to limit their resources, to levy upon them other taxation : for in the vast spread of this metropolis, where there are nearly two millions of inhabitants probably, not less than six or eight millions sterling is wrung from your resources in different ways, not going into the pockets of the landlords, but being lost by the way, a great portion of it, in order that their extortion may keep up a veil on its horrid countenance, and have something the show of legitimate taxation, instead of being apparent and downright plunder. (Loud cheers.) The time is opportune for the appeal which has been made to the inhabitants of this metropolis, and for the appeal to those among you who enjoy the franchise of the city of London. (Cheers.) There will, in a very short period, be an opportunity for you to show decidedly that the principle of free trade is consecrated in your hearts, and guides your votes. (Loud cheers.) I trust the contest will be by no means a personal one, but one wholly of principle, and that no ambiguous pretensions, no praise of free trade, with certain qualifications and accommodations necessary to the hustings, will be tolerated for an instant; but that the plain and simple test will be—the complete, total, and immediate abolition of the monopoly of food. (Cheers.) I know not why one should hesitate to say, upon such an occasion as this, that the placards which I see round about this theatre express the feeling and preference that I think may be honestly entertained for Mr. Pattison as the representative of that great city. (Tremendous cheering.)

Liverpool, in its great and growing commerce rivalling London, was doing what it could to counterbalance its want of representation, or rather its misrepresentation in the House of Commons. The monthly meeting of the Anti-Monopoly Association was held, October 4th, at the Amphitheatre; and the enthusiasm manifested by a crowded audience of between 5,000 and 6,000 persons equalled, if indeed it did not surpass, anything ever before witnessed in Liverpool. The house was splendidly decorated for the occasion; gorgeous banners and free-trade devices ornamented the stage, while the boxes were surrounded by pithy mottoes. Mr. Charles Holland was called to the chair, and the meeting was addressed by Mr. Thomas Blackburn, during whose lucid and argumentative speech the most perfect silence reigned throughout the house; and the clear apprehension and ready assent given to each successive point in his most logical train of reasoning, evinced that the audience fully understood the functions, and took upon themselves the responsibilities, of a deliberative assembly; and their vote, unanimously given, that whatever the course other nations might pursue, it was our duty at once and for ever to abolish all restrictions on our commerce, set at once a noble example to the country at large, and read a valuable lesson to its rulers. This motion was followed by a well-timed resolution, calling upon the electors of London to do their duty, and discharge worthily the heavy responsibility devolved upon them, by sending to parliament as their representative a thorough uncompromising corn-law repealer. The speech of Mr. W. J. Fox, which followed, was brilliant in the extreme, and during its delivery that accomplished orator was frequently interrupted by the most enthusiastic cheers from all parts of the house ; the whole assembly repeatedly rose in a body, and at its close several distinct rounds of applause testified the delight with which his address was received.

On Saturday, October 7th, Mr. Cobden and Mr. Bright met the agriculturists of Worcestershire, in the Guildhall, Worcester. The meeting was convened by public placards posted throughout the county, inviting the farmers, land-owners, and freeholders, to hear the general question of free trade and the influence of the Corn Laws on the interests of farmers and farm-labourers fully discussed. The meeting was a highly respectable one, attended by large numbers of the tenantry of the county, and was quite equal in importance and interest to any of the agricultural county meetings convened by the League. The chair was taken at half-past twelve, by E. Holland, Esq., a large landed proprietor, and late high sheriff for the county. The Guildhall was crowded in every part with from two to three thousand persons, and though a very great proportion was composed of farmers and landowners, the speakers were listened to throughout with the most intense interest, and frequently interrupted with the reiterated cheers of the auditory ; and the resolution in favour of free trade, moved by Mr. C. E. Hanford and seconded by Mr. W. B. Collis, was carried by an overwhelming majority.

CHAPTER VIII.

MR. PATTISON'S ELECTION FOR LONDON.

The meeting in Covent Garden Theatre, October 12th, was an extraordinary one, for there was the excitement occasioned by the preparation for the city election, and the promise of addresses from Mr. Villiers, Mr. Cobden, Mr. J. Bright, and Mr. W. J. Fox. Crowded is a weak word to express the condition of the house. Stage, pit, boxes, and galleries were crammed, and every entrance, public and private, was besieged by crowds of eager applicants for admission, but for whom no room could possibly be found; although an additional gallery had been re-opened for the occasion, capable of seating from five to six hundred persons. As had been previously announced, the Hon. C. P. Villiers, M.P., presided, who, with Mr. Cobden and Mr. Bright, in the course of eloquent and argumentative speeches, strongly recommended active exertions on the part of every free trader to secure the election of Mr. Pattison. Mr. Fox, in reply to the vituperation against the League for its "interference" in a London election, said:

" I had imagined that if there were men who could point the path of improvement, which could lay their hand on a law and say this is bad, wrong in principle, and injurious in operation, and ought to be repealed —that when they could say that such is the course by which commerce may be extended, labour more amply rewarded, and industry more sufficiently encouraged, I should have supposed that the home of such men, their natural abode, should have been in London. I had supposed that when there was an appeal to be made against the infliction of wrong—

that when the cry of justice was to be raised—that when the favouring spirit of public opinion, manifested by the daily organs of the press, or by the voices of assembled multitudes—was it not to be looked for that those who sought such things, and entertained such objects should be sure of finding their homes in London? (Cheers.) Such, I trust, will London be, and not a cistern for the foul toads of monopoly to knot and gender in. (Loud cheers.) The feeling of the people with these men of Lancashire has crowned their heretofore honourable labours; and it now will, I trust, add a more brilliant victory than any which they have yet achieved as preparatory to the great final triumph. In our response to the appeal of these people I feel that their home is wherever the principles of truth and justice can prevail. (Cheers.) They are not for abstract justice merely—the meaning of which I take to be simply an abstraction of justice from the people: and wherever knowledge penetrates; wherever the multitudinous tracts which they put forth find their way to men's intellects and hearts; wherever, by the growth of information, sound principles are generated, and the progress of social improvement is advanced—there the League has its home. Wherever there is hard endurance of imperfectly remunerated toil; wherever the artisan in the populous city has to grieve over the pittance which is all that he has to bestow on his family; or, in remoter districts, wherever the agricultural labourer looks around on the tattered vestments of his wife and children, and feels that they cannot even appear decently at church to receive the ordinances of their religion—there is the home of the League, to inspire despondency itself with hope, and to give the prospect of relief. Wherever in distant regions nature's fertility runs to waste—where, for want of a demand for the power of human labour, ingenuity is not put forth, but the soil is doomed to artificial barrenness through the power of monopoly in this country, preventing the interchange for that which the cultivator would gladly make—there, too, is the home of the League, bringing the promise of richer harvests; there to clothe the distant cultivator, and to feed the artisan. (Cheers.) And wherever, on all future occasions, the battle of principles is to be fought in the electoral contests; wherever monopoly may raise its head and make its last expiring efforts against free trade—there will be the home of the League, to see fair play, to encourage the timid, and to cheer on the candidate who shall honestly advocate those measures which shall ensure food to the hungry, clothing to the naked, and give life, spirit and power to all classes of society, and thereby showing that this country, has yet to run its career of prosperity and glory. (Loud cheers.) And I trust that the result of this election will be to show that where there is a legislature having in its hands the destinies of a great empire, there likewise will be the home of the League, proving that justice—no longer an abstraction—justice to all classes, from the highest to the lowest, is the surest guidance of legislative enactments, as it is the amplest resource of national prosperity."

The London election occupied the attention of Manchester also, and at a great meeting held in the Free Trade Hall—every meeting there was a great meeting—and, after a report of progress by Mr. Wilson, the chairman, and a good speech by Mr. Benjamin Pearson, Mr. Cobden adverted to the necessity of securing free-trade representatives for all the great towns by attention to the registration, and especially for London. He referred to a recent adhesion to the cause of free trade : " I hope that such a manly example as has been set by Mr. Samuel Jones Loyd, in London—for most manly it was in a gentleman of his reputation, and of his notorious wealth, to join the League at the very moment that it was suffering under the opprobrium attempted to be fastened upon it by a millionaire of the city—a most manly act it was of Mr. Samuel Jones Loyd at that time to throw himself into the ranks of the leaguers ; and, I say, I hope the example of such men as my Lord Fitzwilliam and Mr. S. J. Loyd will be followed by others nearer home, in Manchester. I can make allowance for, and can duly appreciate the causes which may deter gentlemen of influence, gentlemen to whom parties look up, whom a wide circle respect and follow in every movement ; I can make allowance for the caution with which they may hesitate to join such a body as the Anti Corn-Law League ; but I put it to them, whatever their political opinions may be, whether the time is not now come that they can with safety and propriety join us as a body, and whether we have not given them guarantee sufficient by the prudence and the caution, and, I will say, the self-denial with which we have carried on our proceedings ; that they will run no risk, whatever opinions they may have on other subjects than that of free trade, o having those opinions in the slightest degree offended, or prejudiced in any way by joining us forthwith in this agitation."

The adhesion of Mr. Loyd was really important at the time. The monied class of London had been tardy in its movements. It needed an example. A subscription of £50 from one of Mr. Loyd's enormous wealth was nothing; but it was a great thing that a man of such cold caution and of so instinctive prudence should have given name and money to promote the object of the League, abused as it was for going too far and too fast. Natures the driest, hardest, and most calculating, might follow when Mr. Jones Loyd led the way, without the fear of being called impulsive and rash.

Earl Fitzwilliam's adhesion had an influence on another class of persons—those who desired that justice should be done, even if the doing were to be injurious to their own interests. His lordship took the field along with Cobden and Bright. The open-air arena was on the Vicarage Croft, Doncaster. By invitation from Earl Fitzwilliam, Mr. Cobden slept on Friday night at Wentworth House (Mr. Bright, having been detained in London, was obliged to travel all night to the place of meeting); and on Saturday forenoon, accompanied by his noble host, they passed through Doncaster to the seat of J. W. Childers, Esq., M.P., of Cantley, where they lunched. A little before two o'clock, Earl Fitzwilliam, with the deputation, and John Parker, Esq., M.P.; W. B. Wrightson, Esq., M.P.; and J. W. Childers, Esq., M.P., arrived in Doncaster. The meeting was formally constituted in the Town Hall, where Thomas Johnson, Esq., the late mayor (in consequence of the illness of the then mayor), was called to the chair. Mr. Milner then moved the adjournment of the meeting to the Vicarage Croft, which was seconded by Mr. Childers, and carried. After able speeches had been delivered by Mr. Bright and Mr. Cobden—the former expounding the principles of free trade generally, and the latter applying them more directly to the cases of the farmers and farm labourers—who were listened to with an attention only interrupted by repeated cheering, a resolution was moved by Mr. W. B. Wrightson, M.P., in a speech of remarkable clearness and ability. Earl Fitzwilliam then addressed the meeting with great ability and vigour. In proving how deeply agriculture was affected by trade, he said :—

" I think it very probable many of the farmers present will be surprised when I tell them that there pass up the Don from Doncaster every year no less than 100,000 quarters of wheat. These 100,000 quarters pass through Doncaster, and are the produce of the fertile soil on the borders of Yorkshire and Lancashire. Why are these 100,000 quarters wanted? Why is it that what is represented on the old maps as Hatfield chase and Thorne waste, has been cultivated? and why does that corn traverse the Don? Is it not for the support of the 120,000 people who throng the streets of Sheffield? Now, gentlemen, what do you think is the state of Sheffield now? Do you think it as good a market as when it had a prosperous trade? Do you know how many houses there are in Sheffield? I will tell you. There are 20,000 houses in Sheffield; and how many of these are unoccupied? Two thousand of them. That is, one-tenth of the houses in Sheffield were unoccupied the last time I inquired. There were 2,000 houses unoccupied, and I am informed the number is now 2,800; and do you think that the state of things in Sheffield can cause as active a demand for food in the Doncaster market as when there is an active trade; do you believe that? (No, no.) Do you think that when the men who lived in the front houses have been driven into smaller, and the men who lived in smaller into cottages, and those who lived in cottages into lodgings—do you think that, under these circumstances, there can be the same demand for agricultural produce as when the trade is prosperous? Now, gentlemen, I will go a step further, and endeavour to lead you to a consideration of the reasons why the town of Sheffield is not prosperous. Somewhere about the year 1820, a little before or a little after, I forget which, the United States were framing a new tariff. You know what tariff means? (Laughter.) That tariff was hostile to English manufactures. Now, why was it hostile? I suppose you will believe our ambassador, and these are the words on that subject of Mr. Addington, our minister at Washington, while that tariff was under consideration. Writing to the ministry in England, he said : ' The hostile character of the tariff now being enacted arises entirely from your Corn Laws.' Why then, I say, what has the hostile tariff of America effected? It has robbed Sheffield of its trade. What is the article most wanted in America? The tool necessary to destroy the forests, and to turn them into cultivated plains. That tool is the axe, and the axe trade of Sheffield has been lost. The axes which are now wielded in the destruction of the forests in the back settlements are not now manufactured in Sheffield, but in Pennsylvania. It is thus that to the Corn Laws Sheffield owes the loss of one of its trades. This it is that has caused 2,000 of the houses of Sheffield to be uninhabited; and the loss of the prosperity of that population injures—I will not exaggerate —injures—I will not say destroys—the market of the farmers, and reduces their prices. I think I have proved to you that this restrictive Corn Law, pretending, as was truly said by Mr. Bright, to be enacted for the benefit of the farmer, but in the belief of those who enacted it, though not in my belief, for the benefit of the landowner; I say not in my belief, for I do not believe that, although it may temporarily produce a somewhat higher rent to the landlord, but I do not believe that in the long-run even the landowner is benefited by this law. (Loud cheers.) Therefore, I say this law, that has been enacted on pretence of benefiting the landlord, does not benefit the landowner or the farmer, and is unjust to the manufacturer, and therefore to all the best interests of the country."

On these grounds his lordship moved a resolution that all protective duties should be promptly abolished, which was carried by an immense majority.

The nomination for London took place on the 26th of October, and the election the following day. At ten o'clock Mr. Pattison's majority was 345; by desperate efforts on the part of the monopolists, aided by active canvassing on the part of government officials, the majority was reduced at twelve o'clock to 43; but the tide began to turn, and at the close of the poll the numbers stood :—

Pattison 6,535
Baring 6,334

Within twenty-four hours of the result becoming known in Manchester, an announcement appeared on the walls that there would be a meeting in the Free Trade Hall to congratulate the electors of London on their triumph. Notwithstanding the shortness of the notice, the wetness of the evening, and the certainty that neither Mr. Cobden nor Mr. Bright could be present, those gentlemen having gone, accompanied by Mr. Henry Ashworth, of Bolton, to attend at meetings in Durham, Cockermouth, Alnwick, Haddington, Berwick-upon-Tweed, and Kendal, there was a gathering of 5,000 persons, which would be considered a very large assemblage anywhere but in Manchester. The speakers were Mr. Alderman Callender, Mr. Alderman Brooks, Mr. Thomas Bazley, Mr. Brotherton, M.P., and myself, and the congratulatory resolution was passed with great enthusiasm. On the following Friday there was a most crowded and enthusiastic meeting in Covent Garden Theatre, addressed by Mr. Wilson, Mr. Villiers, Mr. Milner Gibson, Mr. Heppell, one of Mr. Pattison's committee, and Mr. Moore, and a congratulatory address to the citizens of London was passed unanimously.

The mode adopted to raise the £100,000 fund was, in each place, to originate the subscription at a public meeting. Each meeting was in itself a formidable agitation, for the best inducement to give was an exposition of the wretchedness occasioned by the monopoly. The Manchester meeting, held in the Town Hall, November 14th, was addressed by Mr. Robert Hyde Greg, Mr. Henry Ashworth, Alderman Callender, Alderman Kershaw, Mr. James Chadwick, Alderman Brooks, Mr. Robert Gardner (father of the now member for Leicester), Mr. Bright, and Mr. Brotherton. The amount subscribed in an hour and-a-half was Twelve Thousand Pounds. Amongst the subscribers were, for £500 each, Messrs. James Chadwick, Jacob Bright & Sons, John Brooks, Robert Munn, Samuel Greg & Co., and Robert Ashton. For £400 each, Messrs. Thomas Ashton, and Robert Lees & Sons. For £300 each, Messrs. Wm. Bayley & Bros , John Lord, J. B. Reyner & Bros., John Whittaker & Sons, Samuel Ashton, and Geo. Cheetham & Sons. For £250, Messrs. Thomson, Bros., & Sons. For £200 each, Messrs. Henry & Edmund Ashworth, Richard Cobden & Co., Richard Ashton, Booth

& Hoyle, J. Hoyle & Son, Callender Bickham & Cross, Eccles Shorrocks & Co., Sir Thomas Potter, Jas. Wrigley, A. & J. S. Buckley, Jas. Kershaw, Alex. & Saml. Henry, and Oxford Road Twist Company. There were thirty-one subscribers of £100 each.

Mr. James Chadwick, of Eccles, had told me before the meeting that he would give £1,000. I begged that he would not, because we wanted twenty subscribers of £500 each, and could not expect to have so many if he began with so large a sum. "Well, well," he said, "mind if another fund is required, I shall have another five hundred ready." A correspondent of *The League* says: "Mr. Chadwick's speech was a fair representation of the spirit that animated the meeting. He is a homely, business-like, prudent man in appearance, and I was very much struck with his style of dealing with the Corn Law. 'I have no idea of paying other people's marriage settlements,' said he, and then, as if checking himself in the outset of a speech with the mental remark of 'pooh! pooh! what's the use of speechifying?' he threw to the chairman a bundle of bank notes, with the words 'There's my £500 for the League!' and sat down. I have heard Brougham, Canning, and all our best orators, but never heard a speech that produced the effect of Mr. Chadwick's. It would be impossible to describe the excitement that followed as successive contributions were handed in, varying in amount from £500 downwards. One subscription, from Mr. Robt. Ashton, elicited a burst of applause. I have heard of an interesting description of the scene when that munificent gift was promised to the League. Mr. Brooks called upon Mr. Robert Ashton a few days ago to ask him to attend the meeting. He found him sitting with his lady, and solicited his subscription to the fund. 'I gave you £100 last year, and shall give you £200 now,' was the answer. 'Give him £500, Robert,' was the quiet suggestion of the lady; and Mr. Ashton, who is worthy of such a wife, at once assented.

This was too much for the warm-hearted, susceptible Mr. Brooks, whose irrepressible emotions found vent in a burst of tears."

The Rochdale meeting, held November 28th, was addressed by Mr. Cobden, Mr. W. J. Fox, and Mr. Bright. Amongst the subscribers were Messrs. Jas. King & Sons, £200; Mr. John Fenton, £100; Messrs. James Tweedale, Robert Schofield, James Midgely, Robert Kelsall, George Ashworth, and Chas. Haigh, £50 each. Before the meeting terminated, the sum subscribed amounted to £1,574, making with the £1,150 subscribed at Manchester by Rochdale gentlemen, the sum of £2,724 from that spirited town.

The meeting of the Liverpool Anti-Monopoly Association, held in the Amphitheatre, December 6th, was addressed by Mr. Thornley, M.P., Mr. Cobden, M.P., Mr. Lawrence Heyworth, Mr. William Rathbone, Mr. C. E. Rawlins jun., and Mr. Bright, M.P. Amongst the subscribers were Mr. Lawrence Heyworth, £300; Messrs. H. & H. Darby, £200; Messrs. Christopher Rawdon, Jas. Harvey, James Mulleneux, James Muspratt, J. R. & D. Mather, Wm. Fawcett, G. Crosfield & Co., Wm. Rathbone, Watson Brothers, Thomas Thornely, Geo. Armstrong, J. D. Wood, Victor Poutz, James Mellor, Edward Wilson, G. Holt & Co., and William Brown, £100 each. There were nineteen subscribers of £50, and the amount raised before the meeting separated was £4,600.

The meeting at Huddersfield, held December 7th, was addressed by Mr. F. Schwann, Mr. W. Willans, Mr. J. T. Clay, Mr. Cobden, M.P., and Mr. R. R. Moore. Amongst the subscribers were Mr. F. Schwann, £200; Messrs. Mallinson & Sons, George Crossland & Sons, and Mr Joseph Kaye, £100 each; and Mr. J. T. Clay, £50. The amount subscribed before the meeting separated was £1,322. On the following evening Mr. Bright and Col. Thompson attended at Holmfirth where the amount subscribed was £105.

The meeting at Glasgow, held December 9th, the Lord
Provost in the chair, was addressed by Mr. Alex. Graham,
Mr. John Tennant, Mr. Walter Buchanan, and Mr. Hig-
ginbotham. Amongst the subscribers were Messrs. A. & J.
Dennistoun, Charles Tennant & Co., William Dixon, Saml.
Higginbotham, and Dunlop, Wilson, & Co., £200 each ;
the Lord Provost, and Buchannan, Hamilton, & Co., £100
each ; a friend, £60 ; Neale Thomson, James Scott, Alex.
Graham, D. Mc.Phail & Co., Wm. Stirling & Sons, and
S. R. & T. Brown, £50 each.   The amount subscribed
before the meeting broke up was £2,531.

The meeting at Halifax, held 11th December, was ad-
dressed by Mr. Jonathan Akroyd, Mr. C. Wood, M.P.,
Mr. E. Ackroyd, Mr. Cobden, Mr. J. T. Clay, Mr. Bright,
Col. Thompson, and Mr. R. R. Moore.   Amongst the sub-
scribers were Messrs. James Ackroyd & Sons, £300 ; Josh.
Stocks & Co., John Crossley & Sons, and John Hadwin &
Sons, £100 each ; Henry Ambler, Thomas Taylor & Sons,
and J. T. Clay, £50 each.   The total amount was £1,430.

The meeting at Leeds, December 12th, was addressed
by Mr. Hamer Stansfeld, Mr. James Garth Marshall, Mr.
Henry Ashworth, Mr. Carbutt, Mr. Cobden, Mr. Frederic
Baines, Mr. Bright, Col. Thompson, and others.   Amongst
the subscribers were Messrs. Marshall, £500 ; John Marshall, £300 ; Stansfeld, Brown, & Co., £150 ; Peter Fair-
bairn, J. Wilkinson & Co., and W. Lupton & Co., £100
each ; and Beverley & Simpson, E. Baines & Sons, John
Waddingham, and Benjamin Walker, £50 each.   Before
the meeting separated the amount subscribed was £2,110.

These, be it recollected, were only beginnings.   The
success furnished subject for reasonable congratulation at
a second meeting in Manchester, at which it was reported
that the subscription there had reached £20,280.   Amongst
the subscribers since the previous meeting were, Messrs.
J. & N. P. Philips & Co., £500 ; Alfred Orrell, William
Walker, and Geo. Foster, £200 each ; John Kenworthy &

Co., Wm. Ross, Thomas & Robert Barnes, Jas. Heywood (afterwards M.P. for North Lancashire), and Alfred Binyon, £100 each; and Mr. Alex. Kay, the mayor, £50.

A meeting was held at Wigan, December 14th. The speakers were Mr. R. Thicknesse, Mr. H. Ashworth, Mr. Cobden, and Mr. Moore; and the subscriptions, including £100 from W. Thicknesse, and £50 each from Messrs. Joseph Acton, and T. Taylor and Brother, amounted to £434.

A meeting was held at Bradford, Yorkshire, December 19th, Mr. W. Rand, a gentleman of conservative politics, in the chair, who addressed the large audience very effectively. He was followed by Mr. Cobden, Mr. Moore, and Mr. H. Ashworth. Amongst the subscribers were C. H. Dawson, and Milligan Forbes & Co., £200 each; H. Leah, £100, John Russell, £50, Titus Salt, £100, R. J. Garrett, £100, E. Ripley and Son, £100, S. Smith and Brother, £100, D. Bateman and Sons, £50, W. Rand, £50, and Saml. Field, of Pudsey, £50. The amount subscribed was £1,709, which in a few days was increased to £2,002.

Other meetings closely followed, where the sums subscribed were, at Barnsley, £183; at Warrington, £340; at Todmorden, £563; at Macclesfield, £131; Nottingham, £580; Leicester, where £500 was subscribed by the Messrs. Strutt, £965; Accrington, £200; Dewsbury, £200; Oldham, £860; Bolton, £1,205; Pudsey, £112; and Coalbrookdale, £350.

The first meeting at Manchester to originate the £100,000 fund went far to convince the metropolitan press that the agitation would last while any Corn Law lasted. The *Times* acknowledged that the League was a " great fact." The seeming accession of that " leading" journal was looked upon by many as an opportune event; not that parties were so nearly balanced as that such a *pronunciamento* should give victory to one side or the other, but that it was regarded as an indication of public opinion, which the *Times*

was supposed to be more inclined to follow than to lead.
In that point of view, however, it could only be looked upon
as the result of a shrewd guess as to the party which should
be ultimately victorious. The *Times*, however, had an influence beyond what could be exercised by a journal
notoriously *following* public opinion and changing as that
did. It was representative of the feeling of the English
people rather than of their opinion. It represented their
benevolence, veneration, and combativeness, and it was
powerful because it appealed to those feelings. In this
respect it was not unlike Cobbet, who, whatever might be
his errors, was always English. Nor did the *Times* slavishly
follow public opinion. Without waiting for such expression, it denounced, in unmitigated terms of indignation
and horror, the actors in that Manchester tragedy of 16th
August, 1816 ; it supported the cause of Queen Caroline
when the influential in society were against her ; it threw
its powers heartily into the contest for the Reform Bill,
and did not abandon the whigs till they had abandoned a
great part of their professed principles ; it had, in opposition to the opinions of the great and small aristocracy,
boldly supported the right of the poor to assistance without
the rigid tests prescribed under the New Poor-Law Act ;
even upon the Corn Law question it had done more than
many of the recent converts of the press, by continuing,
for a quarter of a century, almost uninterruptedly, to pub-
lish the comparative prices of corn in the home and foreign
market, and thus to supply a constant argument against
the monopoly ; and it was confessedly, *unpurchaseable.*
With this character it had an influence, for good, beyond
that of any other journal ; and its onward movement in
the right direction was hailed, as likely, although it did
not give in its adhesion to the grand single principle of
the League, to give a fresh impulse to the agitation against
the then existing Corn Law. The following is from the
leading article of November 18th, which much excited the
fears of the monopolists :—

"THE LEAGUE IS A GREAT FACT. It would be foolish—nay, rash to deny its importance. It is a great fact that there should have been created in the homesteads of our manufactures a confederacy devoted to the agitation of one political question, persevering at it year after year, shrinking from no trouble, dismayed by no danger, making light of every obstacle. It demonstrates the hardy strength of purpose—the indomitable will—by which Englishmen, working together for a great object, are armed and animated. It is a great fact that at one meeting at Manchester, more than forty manufacturers should subscribe on the spot each *at least* £100, some £300, some £400, some £500, for the advancement of a measure which, right or wrong, just or unjust, expedient or injurious, they at least believe it to be their duty or their interest, or both, to advance in every possible way.

"These are facts important and worthy of consideration. *No moralist can disregard them; no politician can sneer at them; no statesman can undervalue them. He who collects opinions must chronicle them. He who frames laws must to some extent consult them.*

"These things are so. It matters not that you tell us, as you may tell us with truth, that the League has another character, and other objects, than those which it now professes. The League may be a hypocrite, a great deceiver, a huge Trojan horse of sedition. Be it so. But we answer—THE LEAGUE EXISTS. You may tell us, and with truth, that there are men in the League sworn foes to church and crown—to peers and dignities—to bishops and judges: that, now speaking and declaiming, and begging, and taxing, and, an' you like, plundering men to resist the Corn Laws, this monster-being will next raise its head and subdue all laws beneath it. You may tell us, that its object is not to open the ports, to facitate commerce, to enrich England, but to ruin our aristocracy, whom Leaguers envy and detest. You may tell us that no men of honesty or intelligence could, consistently with their honour and their knowledge, seek to rifle an embarrassed State of that just subsidy which all States impose upon articles of the most necessary consumption. You may tell us, that, whatever be the specious pretext which they hold out, or the disguise under which they work, they can really only look forward to that disastrous crisis in the annals of a kingdom when indiscriminate plunder consummates the work of hopeless and inextricable confusion. You may tell us, that the League has whined and canted about the sufferings of the poor; that its orators wink with malicious cunning at the 'point' they make about the miserable victims of landlord legislation. In all this there is, doubtless, much truth.

"But, we ask, tell us this :—Who created the League? Who found the ribs and planks of this *'infandum monstrum?'* Who filled it with armed men, and introduced its perilous presence within the walls of the constitution? We answer—*experience set at nought—advice derided—warnings neglected*—these brought the League into existence—these gave it power and motion, and vital energy—these gave it an easy and unresisted ingress into the very sanctuaries of our domestic life—

> ' Scandit fatalis machina muros
> Fœta armis : *pueri circum innuptæque puellæ*
> *Sacra cánunt,* funemque manu contingere gaudent.
> Illa subit, mediæque minans illabitur urbi.'

A NEW POWER HAS ARISEN IN THE STATE ; and maids and matrons flock to theatres, as though it were but a new 'translation from the French.'

" Let no man say that we are blind to the possible mischiefs of such a state of things. We acknowledge that we dislike gregarious collections of cant and cotton men. We cannot but know that, whatever be the end of this agitation, it will expire only to bequeath its violence and its turbulence to some successor."

The League could forgive the allusion to "gregarious collections of cant and cotton men." It could forgive being called deceiver, hypocrite, huge Trojan horse of sedition. IT WAS A GREAT FACT, and it would remain a great fact in spite of railing. It had produced facts, too, important and worthy of consideration. The *Times* had recorded that " no moralist could disregard them ; no politician could sneer at them ; no statesman could undervalue them ; he who collected opinion *must* chronicle them ; he who framed laws *must*, to some extent, consult them." The *Times* had acknowledged this ; it had declared that " A NEW POWER HAD ARISEN IN THE STATE," and the League could forgive its habit of calling names. The *Morning Post* also admitted that the League had become "a great fact," but attributed its power to the inertness of the landed interest :—

" The Anti-Corn-Law League is described by the *Times* as 'a great fact,' which owes its existence to the eventual combination of moderate men to effect, by an organization of numbers, that which their isolated efforts had failed to compass. We cannot agree to this theory of the League. We admit that it has become ' a great fact,' but from the beginning it was the work of violent and selfish men. They have the merit of great activity and great perseverance. We deny them any other merit. The *Times* thinks the progress of the League is owing to the real soundness and reasonableness of the purpose in which it had its origin. To this we cannot agree. We think it owes its progress to the discovery of the active, selfish, ambitious men at its head, and the antagonist influence which they had to overthrow was little better than a *vis inertiæ*, which probably might be overcome by great activity and great effrontery. They discovered that the landed interest was not likely to be defended by the owners of land with such weapons as in these days prevail, and that they had placed their championship in the hands of political leaders, who were more likely to give up the battle upon a fair excuse, than to fight it out from a sense of duty. The League managers saw there was a chance to win, and, inspired by *that*, they have persevered, and the League has become 'an important fact.'"

" More likely to give up the battle on a fair excuse than to fight it out from a sense of duty !" This was a flattering character of the premier! The *Morning Herald* called the landowners and the conservatives to the rescue of Sir Robert Peel's cabinet:—

" If the rise and advance of the present power of the Anti-Corn-Law League were so easily augured years ago, why was Sir Oracle then dumb—why was the prophet after the event silent before its occurrence —why, if the refusal of a fixed duty was foreseen to lead to the present condition of things, did the *Times* join in placing in power a cabinet bound in honour and honesty to refuse it?—why did it formerly speak as the organ of a party nearly unanimous in opinion against such a corn-law scheme?—why has it continued down to the present time to support, more or less, an administration still pledged to resist a fixed duty ?

" But the manifest and dishonest inconsistency of that journal is unimportant in comparison with the present strength and future prospects of the League. That confederacy *is* powerful; its inherent power is increased by the supineness of those whose great interests it assaults; and its ultimate success is certain, unless vigour and unanimity be re-infused into the conservative party. The sincerity of its leading men is testified by their subscriptions; and the determination of its moving men is certified by their indomitable perseverance, their incessant activity, and their remorseless unscrupulousness. Flushed with triumphs at London and Kendal, the League now assails Salisbury, threatens to invade every vacated borough, and has an organised correspondence in every town and village. It has its corps of reporters who note down every syllable that falls from the lips of its spouters; it furnishes gratuitously elaborate reports to the whig and radical papers of the metropolis and the provinces; and it gains their editorial assistance by the community of its opposition to government, and still more by the lavish purchase of the papers containing the reports of its proceedings. Two or three years ago, Acland and Smith were its itinerant orators; this year Cobden and Bright are its travelling agents. Then the former were kicked out of agricultural towns, now the latter address large audiences therein without interruption, and, we fear, with applause; then the farmers were indignant, now they are listening; then the landlords were, comparatively speaking, active, now they are quite supine; then there were few men of wealth or respectability, without the circle of Manchester and its satellite towns, subscribers to its funds, now our Jones Loyds, and Raikes Curries, contribute to its rent; then it raised £50,000, now it is demanding £100,000; and those who were then ashamed are now proud of their membership. * * * County meetings or agricultural petitions against the present law must strengthen the League; we last year warned the farmers that by their adoption of Earl Stanhope's excitement against the sliding scale of 1842, they were playing into Mr. Cobden's hands; and we now repeat the advice we then gave them; that in union to support the present Corn Law and the present ministry alone is their safety. If the present law cannot be maintained, substantially all protection is abandoned; if the present cabinet cannot be sustained in power, that law cannot be maintained. In expressing dissatisfaction with ministers, farmers are lessening the power of their only friends; in assisting to overturn the present cabinet they are striking away the plank beneath their own feet. In Mr. Cobden's triumph there is ruin to the conservative party. Will not, then, the rapid progress he has lately made recompose its differences and reunite its ranks in earnest and cordial support of government? The League triumphant, ' other alterations,' said Friend Bright lately, ' will quickly follow!' Who doubts it? The aristocracy? The fundholder? The Church ?"

Here were admissions from the paper whose pride it had been to enjoy the confidence of the agricultural classes! The *Herald* was about as ready as the *Times* to acknowledge the existence of the GREAT FACT. The confederacy *was* powerful; it *had* inherent power; its ultimate success *was* certain, unless some impossible event occurred; its leading men *were* sincere, determined, of indomitable perseverance, and of incessant activity. Nothing then could obstruct the course of such men but to rally round Sir Robert Peel and his cabinet. Alas, for the *Morning Herald's* forlorn hope—the agriculturists had little faith in that quarter. They wanted a better leader. Here is what the *Bucks Herald* said, no doubt in reference to the "no-surrender" Earl Stanhope :—

"AGRICULTURAL APATHY.—We do not fear so much from the activity of the League, although it is too formidable to be despised, as from the torpor of the agricultural body. They seem to have relapsed into a state of somnolence, from which there is no waking. When *the time was*, and they had a leader ready, able, and willing to head them, they were shy, frightened, and backward; and now they will find their error when it is too late to retrace their steps, and discover in the progress and results of free trade that ruin which they were forwarned of, but which they either did not believe, or, believing, were too much scared to attempt to repulse."

The *Manchester Courier*, the most reckless of its tribe, had the hardihood to assert that public feeling in that town was fast cooling towards the League! It said :—

"Now, considering the amount of money promised—upwards of £11,000 we are told—the meeting was an exceedingly small and unimportant one, occupying only the small space of the Cross-street end of the Town Hall. The requisition contained only seventy names and firms, collected in the town and neighbourhood; but then the meeting was fixed for *the* market day, when the manufacturers from the surrounding country flock into the town. This alone ought to have ensured a large meeting, and doubtless it was designed to do so. Nothing, however can be more palpable than that public feeling in this town, and more particularly in this season of revived commercial activity—*the fruits of Sir Robert Peel's sound and comprehensive policy*—is fast cooling towards the League. True, the remark will not apply to the prime movers, whose activity and zeal seem rather to have increased; but this may arise, and probably does arise, out of a pressing consciousness on their parts that it behoves them to make up by their own personal exertions for the ground which they are undoubtedly losing with the public."

The *Courier* was eagerly quoted by the *Morning Herald*, but the statements, so much at variance with the admissions of the *Herald*, were laughed at where the paper was known, and well answered by the fact that the £11,000 subscription had in a few days swelled to £20,000. I subjoin a few of the bellowings and bleatings of two more of the newspapers in the interest of the monopolists. The straw had begun to rustle.

From the *Yorkshire Gazette :—*

" We are not disposed to overlook the danger in which the landed interest of this country is placed by this fearful confederacy; and we would hint, that unless there is more zeal and more energy displayed by those who are more immediately interested in British agriculture, the time may come when resistance will be in vain, and we shall see British industry laid prostrate by the machinations of selfish and avaricious manufacturers."

From the *Gloucestershire Chronicle :—*

" What are the conservatives doing? NOTHING. The contrast between the two parties is most striking. The conservatives seem steeped in criminal apathy. In vain do we and our fellow labourers of the conservative press sound the alarm; in vain do we point to the actions, the objects of the League. There is no evidence of any response. It is not that men are insensible to the existence of danger, although they greatly underrate the greatness of the ultimate danger. It is that men are indolent—satisfied with Sir Robert Peel's present large majority—listless as the satiated Indian over his hardly-gained spoils of the chase. That the operations of the League are magnified on paper, to serve an obvious end, is likely enough; but there is no longer room for doubt that they are a most formidable and mischievous body."

I conclude the notice of movement during the year 1843, by quoting the following from *The League,* of Dec. 30th :—

" Last year the men of mark for ample wealth or high rank, who associated themselves with the League, or who became publicly pledged to its principle, were very few indeed. The scruples which kept them aloof have been removed. The example of Mr. Jones Loyd has had its effect on the capitalists. Earl Fitzwilliam has strengthened the impression previously made by Lord Radnor. And the late avowal of Earl Spencer shows that even the notion of an Anti-Corn-Law Cabinet is not so utterly preposterous and chimerical as some had represented.

" And if, last year, the distinguished few were yet holding back, neither had the numerous classes given more than a fraction of that general and hearty co - operation which they have since afforded. Chartist traitors were still enabled to earn the wages of corruption by the disturbance of public meetings. Now, their occupation's gone; or, at any rate, their employers must be easily satisfied if they think they get money's worth out of such agencies. The working people are instructed. They have risen into a perception of their real interests. The fallacy of dear, bread and high wages is exploded. Anti-corn-law meetings, in populous places, are not merely secure from interruption, they are sure of enthusiasm. In the metropolis the League, as a distinct and organised body, scarcely showed its face till the present year. It chiefly appeared as merged in the annual Anti-Corn-Law Conference. The series of meetings at the great theatres is wholly unprecedented. They are an event in the record or demonstrations of public opinion.

"Agricultural meetings have taken a new character. Landlords suggest improvements, and tenants hint at rents. Protection is no longer the infallible panacea, and duties are coming down to a discount. The note of warning and preparation is everywhere sounded. Farmers more than half suspect that they have been taken in, and begin to run restive. A noble chairman is occasionally pelted with awkward questions from remote corners of the room. Successful candidates at cattle shows turn bitter on Sir Robert Peel, and grow ironical on ' the best bull in Birmingham market.' They reckon it no better than an Irish bull. ' Adjustment of rents' is gaining currency as a phrase, and coupled with the repeal of the Corn Laws.

" Amongst the most marked features of the change which has taken place, is the complete subsidence of discussion about the merits of the sliding scale. Nobody talks of it; nobody seems to think of it. The time for praising it has entirely gone by. It is *hors de combát.* Controversy has shifted its ground. Even Mr. Baring, when standing for the city as a Peelite, and supported by all the influence of the government, hinted his preference of a fixed duty. And thus it is that the battle of argument now rages, so far as there is any such battle, between a fixed duty and total abolition. The present system is contemptuously passed over with tacit condemnation. Approaching change is taken for granted. But we cannot believe that the imposition of a fixed duty is at all the nearer on that account. What farmer will have faith in it? Who will speculate on its permanence? Where are the converts to it? Converts *from* it are all of which we have any intelligence. It would satisfy no party. In the last session of Parliament, Lord John Russell's motion for considering the Corn Laws, with the view of substituting a fixed duty, was supported by just twenty members more than voted for Mr. C. Villiers' motion for such consideration with a view to total repeal. And it was so framed as to allow the total repealers to vote for it.

The parliamentary strength of a fixed-duty party (regarded exclusively) we take to be little more than this increment of twenty. Out of the house, the proportion is much smaller. We scarcely know where to find it at all. Total repeal is the principle of the agitation; and the present argument of its advocates is mainly against a fixed duty as the only other alternative to the present system.

" Hopefully, then, shall we enter on the new year. Hopefully; and yet with saddened feelings that justice, however certain in the end, is still delayed. For, as the old proverb has it, ' while the grass is growing, the steed starves.' Every month of delay is the prolongation of indescribable wretchedness. We begin another year of multiplying bankruptcies and blighted hopes; of terrible sufferings and terrible crimes; of overflowing workhouses and blazing barns. Rest the responsibility where it may, it is an awful one. The greater be our exertions. Lancashire and Yorkshire have evinced their zeal nobly. We shall soon have to record the emulation which they excite. The last forlorn hope of monopoly has failed, in the failure of the partial revival of trade, through the comparative cheapness of food, to distract the attention, mistify the minds, or abate the earnestness of corn-law repealers. The League has wintered and summered it, ever making progress. And now for one great effort more, to vindicate the rights of industry, lessen the burdens of poverty, and secure the just recompense of honest labour. Heaven crown it with success ! "

CHAPTER IX.

THE CAMPAIGN OF 1844.

The year Eighteen Hundred and Forty-Four opened hopefully so far as regarded the means of agitation for free trade. The League was certain of its £100,000 fund. Amongst its supporters it had, in Mr. Samuel Jones Loyd, the wealthiest individual of the monied interest; in Mr. Marshall, of Leeds, the wealthiest of the manufacturers; and the first day of the new year gave it the wealthiest of the nobility. On that day the following letter was received:

"Eaton Hall, Jan. 1, 1844.

"Sir,—Having, on a former occasion expressed to you my anxious wishes for your success in the arduous contest with monopoly in which you are engaged, I cannot refuse myself the pleasure of congratulating you upon the rapid progress you have since made in the struggle with that formidable adversary.

"As you have found your foe to be daring and resolute, so have your energies increased in a wonderful manner; and, in spite of opposition, you have carried the war most effectually into the enemy's strongholds. With such vigorous and sustained efforts the victory must be yours; and my hopes of ultimate triumph, and that at no very distant date, therefore, much exceed my fears of failure.

"As to the duty—that it is said, would be lost to the country, if not insisted on, I am satisfied that such would be the prosperity of all classes from the abolition of this impost, such the advantage that would accrue to all the monied concerns of the community, that, in a very short time, the general wealth would be so far augmented that the national revenue would outrun the amount of any duty that has been proposed, whether 3s., 5s., or 8s.

" It may be all very well, at agricultural meetings, to talk of the advantages of long leases, of tile-draining, &c., and to drink the health of the labourers; but to what good effect? Long leases are, in certain districts, and under certain well-known circumstances, desirable enough; good draining has long been understood and practised, where there have been sufficient means, sufficient enterprise, and a soil requiring it; praise has no doubt been deservedly lavished upon the farm labourers; but there is something still to be done much more important to them, which is, to give them the means of obtaining an honest and independent livelihood—solid pudding being preferable to empty praise—and this cannot be effected without the abrogation of these mischievous enactments.

" I have much pleasure in sending a contribution of £500 to your fund; and I venture to express a hope that you will not relax your endeavours until you have obtained from government, in whatever hands it may happen to be, the fullest measure of free trade compatible with what is due to the maintenance of public credit.

" I remain, sir, your most obedient servant,

" WESTMINSTER.

" George Wilson, Esq.,
Chairman of the Council of the National
Anti-Corn-Law League."

The League was as strong in the high character, the ability, the perseverance, and the energy of its leading members, as it was in its money resources. The Shibboleth of the "sliding scale" was undefended, and the demand of those who had used it was mitigated into a prayer that Peel's bill, substituting a 20s. for a 38s. 8d. duty, both equally exclusive of imports, should have a fair trial; and the other Shibboleth of a "moderate fixed duty" was used only to effect that sort of half-way-house compromise, through which a party *out* might become a party *in*. Why did not government yield under these circumstances? Simply because it had an unreasoning majority in both houses of parliament. The members of the Commons had been elected in 1841, while the landowners and the farmers were alarmed by the progress of the League, but before the League had made its power felt on the hustings. They were elected for seven years; and for the remainder of that term the ministry which they were sent to support felt itself safe, whatever might be the state of public opinion. Under triennial parliaments there might have been expected, in this eighteen forty-four, not a majority of free traders, but such a minority as, promising soon to become a majority, would have given it almost the power of a majority; but Peel's parliament might exist for four years more, and therefore Peel's ministry might "wait on Providence," and calmly look on the storm without: and the more calmly, perhaps, from the belief that a considerable portion of the free traders, with a four years' inert resistance before them, might compromise with the whigs for an eight or ten shillings fixed duty, and thus load themselves with an odium that would render them powerless.

With that resistance, provided by "matchless constitution," irremovable for four long years, the members of the League abated not a jot of faith or hope, energy or determination They felt that they had justice on their side. They saw that the instruction of the people had already done something, and they believed that it would do more; and they felt that even if the struggle should last for four years more, in addition to the five during which, with less hope of success, it had already existed, the benefit to the people would be worth all the labour expended.

The realization of the £100,000 fund went on most promisingly. On the 4th January a meeting was held at Oldham, attended by Mr Cobden, Col. Thompson, and Mr. Moore, at which the sum of £860 was subscribed. On the following evening one took place at Bolton, attended by Mr. Cobden, Col. Thompson, Mr. Moore, and Mr. W. Evans, at which the sum of £1,205 was subscribed, of which £200 was from Messrs. Callender, Bickham, & Cross; £200 from H. & E. Ashworth; £100 each from J. R. Barnes & Son, and Mr. Thomas Thomasson; and £50 each from R. & J. Lord, and Arrowsmith & Sons. On the 4th January, Mr. Bright and Col. Thompson attended a meeting at Bury, where the subscriptions amounted to £1,120. On the 8th, at a great tea-party at Ashton, addressed by Mr. C. Hindley, M.P., Col. Thompson, and the Hon. C. P. Villiers, the subscription, including several sums put down at Manchester by Ashton gentlemen, amounted to £4,338. At a meeting at Bacup, held on the the same evening, addressed by Mr. H. Ashworth, Mr. Cobden, and Mr. Moore, the amount subscribed was £245, in addition to £1,100 given at Manchester by Bacup gentlemen. On the evening of next day a meeting was held at Burnley, addressed by Mr. Cobden and Col. Thompson, at which the sum of £914 was subscribed. On the same evening a meeting was held at Ossett, Mr. Plint appearing as a deputy from Leeds, and the subscription amounted to £95. On the following evening one was held at Hebden Bridge, which was addressed by Col. Thompson and Mr. Moore, and the amount subscribed was £382.

The movement was now directed on Scotland. A great banquet was held in the City Hall, Glasgow, January 10th. The Lord Provost presided, and the Rev. Dr. Wardlaw invoked the divine blessing on the assembly. Mr. Fox Maule, M.P., Mr. Cobden, Mr. Alex. Graham, the Rev. Dr. Heugh, Mr. Bright, Mr. Oswald, M.P., the Rev. D. Willis, and Col. Thompson, addressed the company. The interesting proceedings lasted till a late hour, and no subscription was entered into, but in a few days it was announced that £3,000 had been raised.

On his way to Glasgow, Mr. Bright had stopped in Carlisle, where a spirited meeting was held, at which the subscription amounted to £403, of which £100 was from Mr. John Dixon, and £100 from Mr. Peter Dixon.

On Thursday, 11th January, the New Music Hall, the largest room in Edinburgh, was completely filled. Amongst the audience were thirty-four ministers of religion, and deputations from Leith, Dalkeith, and Musselburgh, and a good many tenants of large farms in East Lothian. The

Lord Provost was in the chair, and addressed the meeting at some length, after which he read the following notes which had passed between Mr. Duncan Maclaren and Mr. Macaulay, one of the members for the city :—

" Edinburgh, Dec. 21, 1843.

" Dear Sir,

" At a meeting of the committee, I was desired to send you the enclosed *soirée* ticket, and to invite you to be present at the meeting, without reference to the opinions you may hold on the question.

" I was likewise desired to request you to take part in the proceedings, on the condition that your opinions are such as to allow you to speak in support of the object of the meeting—the immediate abolition of all the duties on the importation of corn, and the propriety of raising a fund to aid the League in promoting this object.

I am, &c.,
D. M'LAREN,
Convener of Committee.

" The Right Hon. T. B. Macaulay, M.P., &c., &c."

"Albany, London, Dec. 23, 1843.

" Dear Sir,

" I have often expressed my opinion on the subject of the Corn Laws, and am not aware that I have anything to add, to retract, or to explain. You will not, therefore, be surprised at my saying that I do not think it right to attend the meeting of the 11th of January.

I have the honour to be, &c.
T. B. MACAULAY."

This curt letter from the representative of the Edinburgh lawyers excited much disapprobation. Mr. W. Gibson Craig, the other member, was more circumlocutory but not more satisfactory, for he held to the whig shibboleth of " a low fixed duty." The speakers were Mr. Cobden, Mr. Hunter (advocate), Mr. Bright, Mr. B. W. Jameson, W.S., Col. Thompson, and Mr. Moore, and the subscriptions amounted to £1,142.

The members of the deputation did not, as the Scotch phrase goes, let the grass grow at their heels. Next day they were at Perth, where in the North United Secession Church an audience of two thousand, including many agriculturists from the fertile districts in the neighbourhood, was waiting to give them a welcome. Mr. Fox Maule, afterwards Lord Panmure, being called to the chair, expressed his conviction that agriculture suffered by the corn monopoly. He was followed by Mr. Cobden, who took the same ground at greater length, and exposed the absurdity which would be apparent if manufacturers attempted to fix their price by act of parliament. He added :—"You need entertain no alarm, that if the Corn Law is abolished the landowners will permit any other monopoly to exist. Not long ago, I was in Macclesfield, a seat of the silk trade, which I found to be in a very depressed condition, although it enjoys a high 'protection;' and I will tell you an anecdote which will serve to show what will be the fate of all other protections when the most injurious of them all shall have been got rid of. I recently had a conversation with a conservative nobleman, who is a practical agriculturist, and knows how to buy and sell cattle in the market. This nobleman confessed to me, that, but for his party, he would be for the repeal of the Corn Law. I know, he said, protection to be all a humbug; I am satisfied that the Corn Law must be abolished, and when that event takes place, 'won't I have a go at those silk beggars!' (Cheers and laughter.) Then there are the sugar, coffee, and other monopolies, which could not exist a day but for the existence of the Corn Law. The Corn Law is the keystone of all the monopolies that afflict this country, and when once it shall have been knocked down, it will need no help from you, or from us, to bring down the whole structure." Lord Kinnaird, in the course of an able speech, said, " When following the remains of that distinguished nobleman (the gallant Lord Lynedoch) to his narrow house in the village of Methven, I was in conversation with a neighbouring proprietor, Mr. Smythe, who informed me that the population of the place had decreased by 300. On inquiring as to the cause of this diminution of the population,

I was informed that it had been produced by the decline in the Glasgow weaving trade, so that this lessening of manufacturing employment in the village of Methven gives 300 fewer customers to the farmers in the district than they formerly possessed, while those that remain are also less able to buy. (Hear, hear.) This is an isolated, but satisfactory, illustration of the injury that results to agriculture from an unprosperous condition of manufactures. I am a landlord myself, and if the Corn Law could be beneficial to any one, it would be so to me, inasmuch as the protection which it gives is principally a protection to wheat, and as my land is almost entirely what is called wheat land, or land upon which wheat is grown. Now, I find the Corn Law to be positively hurtful to me, instead of an advantage ; for it impoverishes my customers, and, consequently, has an injurious effect upon my profits." Mr. Kinloch, of Kinloch, at the opening of his speech, made interesting allusion to his patriotic father :—" It is about ten years since, at a meeting of the inhabitants of Dundee, I advocated a total repeal of every tax affecting the food of man. Upon the 14th of May, 1834, a meeting was held in the Magdalen Yard, and resolutions unanimously agreed to condemnatory of the Corn Laws—upon the same spot where, in 1819, my father presided at a meeting of the radical reformers of Forfarshire ; and for having done so, and there expressed his detestation of the instigators of the Manchester massacre, and his belief ' that as long as the House of Commons remained as then constituted, no effectual remedy to the distress of the people would either be proposed or applied by them,' he was forced to flee his country, and live for years in exile." Mr. Moore and Colonel Thompson followed " Kinloch of Kinloch," and then the meeting separated ; many of those who attended the meeting again assembling at a *soirée* given to the deputation, and which was also numerously attended.

The invitations from Scotland became so numerous that it was necessary to divide the deputation, Mr. Cobden and Mr. Moore keeping "east," and Mr. Bright and Col. Thompson going, in the phrase of the country, "away west." Afterwards, when a deputation was invited, two persons were sent, and sometimes only one when two could not be had. Mr. Brotherton, M.P., Col. Thompson, the Rev. J. W. Massie, Mr. C. E. Rawlins, jun. (of Liverpool), and Mr. T. Plint (of Leeds), were always ready when their other avocations would permit, and with one or other of them, and sometimes alone, I attended many meetings. The benefit of this subdivision of labour was not only the covering of a greater surface of ground, but the bringing out of a greater amount of local ability and action, all needful in the still to be protracted struggle.

Mr. Bright and Col. Thompson proceeded to a meeting at Greenock, where the provost presided, Mr. P. M. Stewart, M.P., and Mr. Wallace, M.P., taking a part in the proceedings; to Paisley, where the provost presided, Mr. Hastie, M.P., and Mr. P. M. Stewart, M.P., taking a part; to Ayr, where the provost presided; to Kilmarnock, where Sir J. Cunningham Fairlie presided; and to Dumfries, where Mr. David Armstrong presided. Mr. Cobden and Mr. Moore proceeded to Aberdeen, where a forenoon meeting was held in the Theatre, and one in the evening in the Temperance Hall; to Dundee, where Mr. Edward Baxter presided, and Mr. Duncan, M.P., took a part; to Montrose, where the provost presided; to Forfar, where a crowd assembled, and an extempore meeting was held; and to Cupar, where the provost presided, and where the deputation met deputations from Kirkaldy, Kettle, Leslie, Markinch, Pittenweem, and Auchtermuchty, and where the freedom of the borough was conferred on the two English visitors. At Leith, on their way "south," they were joined by Col. Thompson at an enthusiastic meeting. Mr. Cobden and Mr. Moore then proceeded to Hawick, where the

Earl of Buchan presided; and to Jedburgh, where his lordship, a thorough free trader, also presided.

Invitations had come from many places in Scotland which the deputation had not time to visit. In the course of the summer I went to meetings at Haddington, where the provost presided, supported by the greater part of the town council; at Linlithgow, where provost Dawson presided, similarly supported; at Lanark, where Dr. Shirley presided; and at Galashiels, where the Earl of Buchan (son of the celebrated Henry Erskine), who had been chairman at meetings in Kelso, Hawick, and Jedburgh, presided. His lordship had great merit in this zeal, for his income was slender in comparison with his high rank in the Scottish peerage, and was derived almost solely from "corn rents," and consequently would be diminished in proportion to any fall that might take place in the price of grain by the repeal of the Corn Law. At his very beautiful residence at Dryburgh Abbey, I had the opportunity of renewing a sort of old feudal connection with the Erskine family. My great grandfather was a tenant of his lordship's great grandfather. Both were driven into exile in the hot persecution which followed the battle of Bothwel Brig, in 1679. At the Revolution of 1688, Lord Cardross returned from Holland with the Prince of Orange, and resumed the possession of his estate in Linlithgowshire, and Alexander Reid returned from England, where he had sought refuge, to the occupation of his farm. I told the meeting that I was glad to stand on the platform with one whose ancestor had, with mine, contended for the religious liberty of his country, and who now, with me, was contending for its commercial liberty, as his father had, with mine, contended together, at the commencement of the French war, for its political liberty.

On the 23rd, an exceedingly crowded meeting was held at Sunderland, the mayor in the chair, to receive Mr. Cobden and Mr. Moore; on the following day Col. Thompson and Mr. Moore attended one in Tynemouth; on the same day Mr. Cobden and Mr. Bright attended one at Sheffield; Mr. Edwd. Smith was chairman, and opened the subscription by putting down his own name for £200; on the 25th, Mr. Cobden, Mr. Bright, Col. Thompson, and Mr. Edwd. Smith (of Sheffield), attended a great demonstration at York; on the 26th, Mr. Cobden, Col. Thompson, and Mr. Bright, were at another at Hull, Sir W. Lowthorp in the chair; on the 29th, the same gentlemen were at Blackburn, where Messrs. Eccles, Shorrocks, & Co., contributed £200 towards a subscription which reached £713 before the meeting closed; and on the 30th, Mr. Cobden and Mr. Moore attended one at Stockport, where the sum of £984 was subscribed, in addition to £320 given at Manchester by Stockport gentlemen.

On the 31st, a West Riding social demonstration took place at Wakefield, the noble hall of the Corn Exchange being tastefully decorated for the occasion. The following localities were represented by their deputies:—Ossett, Halifax, Farsley, Gomersall, Cleckheaton, Heckmondwyke, Doncaster, Dewsbury, Yeadon, Horsforth, Guisely, Rawdon, Pudsey, Batley, Barnsley, Wakefield, Huddersfield, Lindley, Lockwood, South Crosland, Hanley, Kirkburton, Golcar, Dalton, Kirkheaton, Mirfield, Skelmanthorpe, Clayton West, Holmfirth, Molegreen, Kirkby, Bradford, Ottley, Morton, Clayton, and Leeds. Mr. James Garth Marshall, of Leeds, presided, and Messrs. H. H. Stansfield, George Craven, F. Schwann, and F. Carbutt, acted as vice-presidents. After the chairman had expressed his regret that Mr. Villiers, one of the greatest champions of their cause, had been unable to be present, Mr. Plint read letters of excuse from the Earl Fitzwilliam, the Earl of Radnor, Lord Kinnaird, Earl Dacre, Sir George Strickland; Edward Vavasour, Esq.; F. H. Fox, Esq., of Farnham; Sir Charles Tempest; Geo. Jno. Farquharson, Esq.; Redhead Yorke, Esq., M.P.; W. B. Wrightson, Esq., M.P.; Edwd. Baines,

Esq.; — Wrightson, jun., Esq.; Mark Philips, Esq., M.P.;
Thomas Birkbeck, Esq., of Settle; and Thomas Thornley,
Esq., M.P.; all of whom signified their approbation of the
objects of the meeting, and regretted their inability to
attend it. He then read a report, which embodied a statement of the amounts collected in the different districts of
the county in the present and the preceding year. The
totals of each district were as follow :—

Districts.	1843.	1844.
Leeds	£1743	£3876
Barnsley	100	255
Sheffield	——	1000
Doncaster	75	100
Bradford	1000	2768
Huddersfield	1805	2150
Halifax	1030	1835
Hebden Bridge	250	500
Brighouse	64	90
Wakefield	129	357
Holmfirth	——	212
Total	£6,196	£13,143

The chairman, after some introductory remarks, said
that the League had not gained the position it held by
any unworthy compromises, and he added :—

" It cannot, however, be other than a great encouragement to us to
find that men who are now our firmest supporters come from the ranks
of the noblest and wealthiest of the landed proprietors—(cheers)—from
the largest and most skilful agriculturists; as well as from the toiling
millions, both in town and country. (Cheers.) But whilst we are wel-
coming new converts, there is another welcome to be spoken of to-day.
Lord Morpeth—[Here the whole assemblage rose as one man, and
commenced cheering, characterised by the most intense enthusiasm,
which did not subside for several minutes. At times it appeared to die
away, and silence to be about to be restored, but again and again it was
renewed with redoubled energy.] Lord Morpeth is no new convert to
the principles of free trade. He is no new visitor of these large meetings of the West Riding. It is because we know him so well—because
we know him as a statesman and a man—because we know the qualities

equally of his understanding and his heart—(cheers)—it is for these reasons that the return of Lord Morpeth amongst us is welcomed with a degree of respect and of joyful cordiality that could not but have attended the fullest acquisition of the support of his distinguished name. I now, gentlemen, propose to you the health of the Right Honourable Lord Viscount Morpeth."

The toast having been drunk with the most unbounded enthusiasm, Lord Morpeth rose, and was received with a repetition of the cheering with which the mention of his name had been at first greeted. His lordship having acknowledged the kindness with which he had been received, and observed that he was bound to look to himself, that his coming amongst them should not appear to rest upon false pretences, said :—

"The chief object of this gathering, as I understand and interpret, is, upon the part of the West Riding of Yorkshire, to do honour and to give encouragement to the Anti-Corn-Law League, and to its deputation now present, and to promote, as far as in them lies, the abolition, the total and immediate abolition of the Corn Laws. (Immense cheering.) That you inform me is the object and meaning of your present gathering. ('Yes, certainly.') Well, then, I know it will be inquired both by friend and by foe—(hear)—'am I prepared to go so far?' (Hear, hear.) My last dealing, as you may probably remember, with the subject of the Corn Laws, was in the year 1841, as a member of the then existing government, and as being a party to the proposition for an 8s. duty. (Hear, hear.) In that proposition we failed, and we fell—(laughter and cheers)—because the upholders of the present Corn Laws, our opponents then, as they are your opponents now, thought that we proposed to concede too much, and that our proffer was over liberal to the consumers. Now, so far from being admonished by failure, so far from being covered by defeat, I think the day for the same terms is gone by —(here the meeting rose *en masse* and cheered vociferously)—and that what was considered by the constituents of the empire to be too much then, would be too little now. Moreover, the very fact of my coming here under the bond of no coercion, having remained aloof from public life for the last two years, without concert or consultation with any one, speaking entirely and exclusively for myself—all this, gentlemen, is a proof that I do not wish to withhold my acknowledgments for the zeal and energy which have been displayed by the Anti-Corn-Law League ; not, of course, pretending to indorse everything they may have said or may have done, or to withhold my sympathy for the struggle which you, my late constituents of the West Riding, are so gallantly, and, as we have just had a proof, so munificently carrying on, to promote the cause in which you conceive—and justly conceive—(immense applause)—your vital interests are deeply involved. But, gentlemen, though I feel that I might safely wrap myself up in vague generalities, and steer clear of using any expression which should run counter to the feelings even of him who feels the strongest and goes the farthest among you ; yet in your own presence, gentlemen, and in the presence of your distinguished guests—although I am aware that I may be somewhat checking those plaudits which have even now rung around me, and may be damping the warmth which seems to glow in your welcome of me—I do not scruple to avow that, as now advised, I am not prepared to debar myself, at any time hereafter—either if I should think that the necessary or best understood interests of the public revenue absolutely required it, or if I should see no other way of effecting a better settlement of the whole question than that which now prevails, or if I thought I was making a great advance in a right direction—in these or in such like cases, I do not debar myself from the power of acquiescing in a fixed duty of low amount. (Loud cries of ' No, no, that won't do,' and expressions of dissent.) I was prepared for the expression of some dissent to the liberty which I nevertheless must reserve to myself. I knew that in so doing I should not, as Mr. Bright thought of the West Riding formerly, come quite up to the mark, or as my friends the Americans say, with more expressiveness than refinement, I should not quite "toe the mark." But when I have said this, which I have thought it right as an honest man to do (cheers), not foreseeing what combination of circumstances might arise, I at once frankly add, that I am by no means bigoted to this measure of a fixed duty. (Cheers.) Indeed, when it is thus limited to a small amount, I am not inclined to attach to it the same importance, on one side or the other, which is sometimes done upon both. At all events, I demur to any intolerance with respect to this proposition, and sure I am, at least of this, that I would infinitely prefer a repeal, a total and immediate repeal, to a year's continuance of the law as it now subsists. (Immense applause.) And even if in the present year, a total and immediate repeal could be carried—as I suspect it would be, gentlemen, if the ultimate decision rested with you (cheers)—I should not be inconsolable, or long in making up my mind to the result. (Cheers.) His lordship then proceeded to remark, that he had shared in the satisfaction of the audience in the accounts of the progressive advances of free trade and free industry : and, having dwelt upon some general topics, trusted he would be excused for adding more in the way of preface to the toast—

' Prosperity to the West Riding, and may its agricultural, manufacturing, and commercial classes become convinced that their true and permanent interests are indissolubly united, and have their surest basis in freedom of trade and industry.' (Cheers.) His lordship having briefly painted, in glowing terms, the happy results of unfettered commerce, said:—I do not wish, gentlemen, upon such an occasion, to employ any serious or solemn terms, when at least our meeting, in its aspect, is entirely festive, though none can doubt the sober seriousness of your determination. ('Yes, yes, we are determined.') But what I want our opponents—the opponents of free industry—to lay to heart is, whether, in the course they are pursuing, they are not fighting against nature itself, and against the laws which guide and bind the universe? (Cheers.) For what, gentlemen—what is the obvious meaning, what is the inevitable inference of those arrangements which mingle on the surface of our globe—so much of want here, and so much of abundance there—here such utter destitution, there such prodigal profusion? Writers of fiction and fancy have been pleased, sometimes, to attribute voices to the winds, and to people with sounds the echoes of the hills; but the real words which Nature sends forth through all her wide departments are ' work' and ' exchange.' (Great cheering.) His lordship then illustrated this position by a reference to America, whose inexhaustible granaries could stay the advances of our own pauperism, and supply the hungry of England with bread. The English traveller in foreign climes found many grounds for exulting in the superior advantages of his own country; but his exultation was checked when he contrasted the fearful pressure, the destitution, and sometimes famine, which visited so many homes and families. He then expressed his warm sympathy with the League, and counselled them not to undervalue their opponents. He concluded as follows:—Yes, gentlemen, I know not what new forms of tactics the enemy may assume. Farmers may secede from useful agricultural societies. (Hear, hear.) The Anti-League may be rallying up to scatter the light chaff of your arguments with the heavy flail of their logic. (Loud laughter.) You may be accused of setting fire to ricks, or, resorting to another element, they may threaten you with submersion in rivers (laughter); but you will look upon all these ebullitions of hostility as evidences and omens that you are gaining ground, that you are making way, that you are making yourselves felt. And it is that I may be sure of indicating the principle which I believe embraces all our efforts, and of rivetting our allegiance to the cause which I believe the exigencies of our country, and the circumstances of the world make emphatically the cause of the day, that I propose to you to drink—" Prosperity to the West Riding, and may its agricultural, manufacturing, and commercial classes become convinced

that their true and permanent interests are indissolubly united, and their
surest basis in freedom of trade and industry."

Mr. Hamer Stansfield, mayor of Leeds, then proposed
"The healths of Richard Cobden, Esq., and John Bright,
Esq., the undaunted and untiring champions of free trade,
with the warmest thanks for their invaluable exertions."

Mr. Cobden, after speaking on the general question, said:

"We are not politicians or statesmen, and have never aimed at being
such. We were driven from our business quite unexpectedly to ourselves; for I declare solemnly, if I had thought five years ago that I
should have been gradually and imperceptibly brought to the station I
now occupy, and from which I see no way honourably to return (loud
cheers)—I say, if I had foreseen, five years ago, that the struggle in
this cause would have involved sacrifices of health, of time, of domestic
comfort—ay, and other sacrifices, too, which men of business can comprehend—I believe, much as I felt upon the question, I should not have
dared, in justice to myself, or to others to whom nature has given a
claim upon me, to have taken a part. (Loud cheers.) But our question
has been advancing until it has become a great national and a great
political question; and now, when we find our cause lifted to the first
rank in the senate, we want men there—men having established character as statesmen—men to whom privileges appertain, and to whom
the people are inclined to look as leaders, statesmen, and politicians.
We want these men in the House now, to take charge of this great
cause. (Cheers.) And if there was one sentiment that more pervaded
my mind than another, as I came to this place, it was the strong hope
which I entertained, knowing that I was coming here to meet the distinguished statesman to whom his countrymen are inclined to look as
much as—I had almost said more—than any other living statesman
(cheers) for the future conduct of the nation's interest in the House of
Commons;—I say, the sentiment which pervaded my mind most
strongly was, that coming to the West Riding of Yorkshire, I should
find the man who would be the Moses to conduct us through the desert
to the land of promise. (Loud and long-continued cheering.) I say it
most emphatically, in the name of my colleagues and myself, that most
happily should we surrender our cause into the keeping of such a man,
if he advocated our principles in the House of Commons. Most gladly
would we have toiled in the ranks out of doors, where we can be of
efficient service, and where we would have cheerfully aided such a statesman in identifying his name with the greatest commercial reform—nay,
the mightiest revolution that this world ever witnessed. (Cheers.)

Gentlemen, I do not despair. (Loud cheering for several minutes.) We will work on another year. (Cheers.) I think the noble lord said a year, a little year. We will work on gladly for him for another year (cheers); and then, when he has reflected on our principles—when he has considered the justice of our case—when he has brought his mind, by the unaided course of his own calm reflections and his high moral guidance, to believe that we are right and just in our object—when he shall have done this, I live in hopes that he, at the end of a little year, will yet come forward and and achieve the triumph of this great question in the House of Commons. (Cheers.) But, whilst we express that hope again, I must remind you that we are here as anti-corn-law leaguers. We are here pledged to our principles, and I must tell you in the West Riding, that it lies with you now to show to the people of England that we are honest in the avowal of our principles. You may be called upon to make sacrifices, greater sacrifices, of personal feeling, rightly directed and well merited—greater personal attachment than any constituency of this country ever was called upon to make. I neither hold out bribes nor threats to the noble lord. I know he is competent, by his own unaided intellect and right-minded integrity of character, to decide for himself. But we stand pledged not to whigs nor to tories, but to the whole people of this country that we are not politicians. (Cheers.) Mr. Cobden having mentioned the names of various eminent individuals holding conservative opinions who were with the League, said:—In conclusion, I say to the noble lord one word more. The noble lord has said to us 'God speed you; you are in the right path, and I hope that you will go forward under your advancing banner.' I say to him, he is in the right path, and God speed him whilst he makes progress in it."

Mr. Bright, on rising, was greeted with the same earnestness and warmth of feeling which had marked the reception of his distinguished colleague. The committee of management had requested him, said he, to propose to the meeting this sentiment—"The Abolition of the Sugar and all other Monopolies," and although it was not his custom to propose what were commonly called toasts, he had very great pleasure in proposing this sentiment, and was glad of being permitted to offer some observations upon it. The hon. gentleman then proceeded to discuss several bearings of the free-trade question; and commented at some length on the various meetings of the agricultural "protection" societies. Having next referred to his recent successful tour in Scotland, the honourable member said :—

"I have listened to the speech delivered by your late representative with feelings of mingled pain and pleasure : with feelings of pleasure at many beautiful sentiments, which were expressed and clothed in as beautiful language ; but with pain, that hitherto he has not seen it right to take up to the full extent the principle which we ourselves are now advocating; but I cannot conceal from myself, that from his speech there is in his mind so small a remnant of love of what is old in this matter, that it seems most extraordinary if it should remain there long at all. (Hear, hear.) I listened to his description of some portion of his journey on the American continent; to the glowing language in which he spoke of those vast prairies, which seemed as if some countless ages since the vast ocean had flowed over them, and that by some omnipotent fiat it had been at once suspended and changed into the solid earth ; and I heard his description of those large rivers which rise no one knows how, or knows really where they are in future centuries to lead as highways from the ocean to the people who inhabit their banks. I was pleased to hear all this, and when he spoke of the surplus produce of those vast countries, and of the want there is in this country, I confess that I did feel disappointed (loud cheers) that any bar should be proposed or permitted to be put, which should in any degree narrow the market and the circle out of which we might obtain a supply for the hungry people of this country. A small fixed duty might not be insurmountable by the corn growers of the nearest country ; but to America, distant only three thousand miles, and to those vast prairies distant five thousand miles, a fixed duty of very small amount would operate generally as an insurmountable barrier to a constant trade in corn between this country and that. I will not enter more into this part of the question. The League has put its hand to the plough, and it will not turn back. (Loud cheers.) The honourable gentleman concluded by proposing 'The total and immediate abolition of the sugar and all other monopolies.' "

Mr. Rand, of Bradford, proposed " The health of Geo. Wilson, Esq., the chairman of the Anti-Corn-Law League," and said :—

"As a Conservative, it was a source of satisfaction to his mind, that, at a period when strong political feelings were dividing the country into contending parties, some common ground could be discovered on which they could lay aside their party politics, and unite in the prosecution of one great question—a question so great, indeed, that it might well call upon them not to lay aside those politics merely for a season, but almost, if not altogether, to forget their existence. With respect to the charge brought against the League, that their object in endeavouring to procure cheap corn was to bring down wages, it was one which had often been refuted, and which he himself most distinctly denied. The firm to which he belonged employed 1,500 persons, and he could affirm that, generally speaking, their wages had been the highest when corn had been at the cheapest, and they had been the lowest when there had been a scarcity. (Cheers.) Much of the influence of every movement depended upon the character of those who took a leading part in it, and especially of those who presided over it. He had not the pleasure of knowing personally Mr. Wilson, the chairman of the League, but he had marked that gentleman's public course, and had read his addresses, and it was his firm impression that much of the progress of the League itself was to be attributed to the care, judgment, persevering energy, and unimpeachable character of Mr. Wilson, its chairman. (Great cheering.) He had, therefore, very great pleasure in moving the toast, ' George Wilson, Esq., and may the labours of the Anti Corn-Law League be speedily crowned with success.' (Cheers.) The toast was drunk with several rounds of applause."

In the absence of Mr. Wilson, whose duties at the council of the League, in London, prevented his attendance, Mr. H. Ashworth acknowledged the toast. Mr. Bazley proposed the health of the chairman of the meeting, which was drunk with great applause. The chairman returned thanks. The health of Col. Thompson was then proposed by Mr. Schwann. Col. Thompson acknowledged the compliment in one of his happiest modes, and concluded by proposing the health of Mr. Plint, who returned thanks. The meeting was protracted considerably beyond twelve o'clock, and the greater part of the company remained to the latest moment, special trains having been retained at the several railway stations, to convey parties to their respective homes.

The high character of Lord Morpeth gave a promise that his qualified adoption of the League's great principle would soon become unqualified. All who knew him knew that when he wished it " God speed " he would feel it to be his duty to help it onward to the best of his power. It was believed that no whig administration was likely to be formed—or if formed, not likely to continue in office—without his occupying a seat in the cabinet; and hopes were formed that some of his former colleagues would follow his example, if not from motives like his, of justice and humanity, from the conviction that without the assistance of the free-trade or people's party they would gain nothing, and that with it, they would at once gain office and popularity. But they continued aloof, abiding pertinaciously to their "fixed duty" Shibboleth; standing doggedly at their half-way house; believing that the *juste milieu* was equi-distant from obstruction and progression, toryism and radicalism. It was perhaps well that they thus stood. Had they at that time achieved such popularity as to carry them into office, they might have recoiled from the noise themselves had made, and, according to former custom, sought compromise. It was well, perhaps, that they should cling a little longer to their Shibboleth until its utter worthlessness should be demonstrated, until they saw that the old party cries were regarded but as chaff. That year of eighteen hundred and forty-four was still to be one of constant, unremitting toil on the part of the free traders ; not cheered by the hope of success then, but sustained by the conviction that their cause was a just one and that in the end it would prevail—prevail, very probably, by 1848 at the latest, when popular influence would operate strongly on the body of electors. The duty of the League was to go on instructing the people, and especially the constituencies which had any remnant of elective freedom. It had now the support of the best part of the press both in London and in the provinces. Every speech was reported, and millions of readers looked to the speeches at anti-corn-law meetings with more eagerness than they did to the proceedings in parliament. It was resolved that the meetings in Covent Garden Theatre should be weekly. There could be but two or three debates upon the great question in the course of the session, but in the same time it might be discussed thirty times before an audience ten times more numerous.

Parliament met on the 1st of February. The queen had been directed to say in her speech :—" I congratulate you on the improved condition of several important branches of the trade and manufactures of the country. I trust that the increased demand for labour has relieved in a corresponding degree many classes of my faithful subjects from sufferings and privations which, at former periods, I have had occasion to deplore." The course of the administration could easily be prognosticated from this. Trade was to be represented as thriving and the revenue as improving, and the inference was to be that there was no occasion for any change. Accordingly Lord Clive, who moved the address, and Mr. Cardwell, who seconded it, sung a song of triumph on the improved and improving condition of the country. The latter talked fluently about revival of the cotton manufacture, the improvement of the linen trade, the increase in the deposit banks, the decrease in the poor-rates, and the good prospects of the iron trade. Lord John Russell attributed such improvement as had taken place to the reduction in the price of bread :

" I have made some inquiries with respect to the effects produced in poor families by the reduction of the price of bread this year, and I have been told that in some families it has occasioned a saving of a shilling every week in the consumption of the family; and if we multiply the numbers of families that must be in this condition, it will show an amount of some eight or ten millions saved, in the article of food ; and can there be a ground for doubting that the application of the money thus saved to the acquisition of other objects, which are the obvious produce of the bounty of Providence, goes far to account for the improvement that has taken place." (Cheers.)

But Lord John Russell still contended for his fixed duty, as a revenue duty, and laid himself open to a rebuke from Sir Robert Peel :—

" If the noble lord intend it for revenue merely—if he think there is no claim on the part of the agricultural interest to protection in any shape whatever, then I retain my opinion that the noble lord will find it extremely difficult to resist the argument, that if this duty be laid on foreign corn for the purpose of revenue only, and not for protection, why not apply it to corn of domestic produce? (Loud cries of 'Hear, hear,' in which several of the free-trade members joined.) When the noble lord is defending his fixed duty on wheat, as a fixed duty imposed, not for protection, but for revenue, he will have the case of barley and of malt quoted against him (hear, hear); and would be told that with respect to other descriptions of corn, such as barley, we do raise a large revenue from our domestic produce, and that if you think it right to have a duty on wheat, not for protection, but for revenue, why not lay a tax on wheat ground at the mill, and not confine yourselves to taxes on the imports? (Loud cries of 'Hear, hear.') Why not pursue, with respect to wheat, the course you have taken with respect to barley, and subject both foreign and home produce to equal duties—provided you are sincere in enforcing your duty, not on account of protection, but really for revenue?"

Sir Robert went on to dispel the fears lurking in the "agricultural mind." After intimating that, should the agriculturists ever arrive at preference of a fixed duty over a sliding scale, it would devolve on Lord John Russell rather than on himself, he said :—" The experience we have had of the present law has not shaken my preference for a graduated duty; and although I consider it inconsistent with my duty, to make engagements for adherence to existing laws, under all circumstances, in order to conciliate support, I can say, that the government have never contemplated, and *do not contemplate any alteration in the existing law.*" With Sir Robert the contest was to be between entirely free trade in corn, and the existing law, which imposed a duty of 20s. a quarter on the importation of wheat, the price of which was then 50s. 9d. Lord Howick, with this distinction of contending parties, said he knew which side to take :—

" The controversy had been kept up so long that he almost doubted whether, even without that very significant speech which had fallen from the right honourable baronet that night, the time for a compromise had not passed, and that now every one must take his part in this question either on the one side or the other. If the right honourable gentleman, and those who thought with him, were of opinion that it was wise to lay this stress on all the objections to a fixed duty, it would be idle, and worse than idle, to make such a proposition. Then the question resolved itself into this—were they to have the existing Corn Law, or was the importation of Corn to be free? (Cheers.) That was the point to which the right honourable gentleman wished to bring the matter, and that was the question he wished to bring to issue. He (Lord Howick) adhered to the opinion from which he had never swerved, and which he had maintained at all times and at all places—in that House and on the hustings of a purely agricultural county; and when this question was brought to issue, his choice would be without hesitation, or one moment's delay, in favour of the free importation of corn."

Mr. Villiers with great force pointed out the degrading position of Sir Robert Peel in relation to the monopolists in the house and out of it. He said:—

" Whatever might be the consequences to the people, there had gone forth a decree from the landed interest that if there was the slightest change in the system, the least alteration, or if the protection was to be in any way diminished, the ministers would not be allowed to retain their places. (Loud cheers.) It might be said that this had been the practical working of the constitution, and such intimations might have been privately given to the minister, but he had never before known anything so indecent or haughty, and so dictatorial, as he had recently heard uttered at public meetings (ministerial cheers, and counter cheers from the opposition),—that a minister should be openly threatened with expulsion if he did not do what was most injurious to the community at large, unless he maintained such a system as would put most rent into the pockets of the great dictators themselves. (Loud cheers.) Noble dukes gave the sign, and the squireens followed. (Cheers.) There was not a term of abuse which was not lavished on the right honourable baronet. He (Mr. Villiers) had no objection to the right honourable gentleman. If any one were to administer such a system, no one could doubt either his competency or his capacity; his only regret was that *the right honourable baronet had not,* if he might use the term, *the spirit to turn round upon these people and show them their utter helplessness without him, their utter inability to admininister without him the government upon their own system.* (Cheers.) Now, with all their rank and property and pride, they would fall were it not for the person who had talents and experience and capacity. (Loud cheers.) If the right honourable gentleman had the courage to adopt the system which he himself believed to be sound, he would rally the people to his support, he would take that higher station which he represented as alone making office valuable to him. ' Cheers.) Those who had the power to declare his not doing this, had not the capacity to form a government. (Cheers.) Who were the victims of all this pride on the one side, and of avarice on the other; of this trial to maintain a consistency for a month or a year on the one side, and of a struggle to retain that to which they had no right, on the other? It was the people. (Cheers.) Could they wonder, then, that the honourable member for Rochdale should seek to stop the supplies when those crying grievances existed, without a hope of redress? Was his honourable friend, the member for Stockport, to be blamed when, with this before him, he was labouring from morning to night, not going to the extreme means of the honourable member for Rochdale, but trying to influence the constitution of the House of Commons, so as to make them do justice to the people? (Cheers.) Had they any right to blame him, or could they wonder at the organization of which he was the head? They knew that evils existed, for which it was now hopeless to expect redress; these were the justifications for his exertions, and if it were tried, with those evils existing, to prevent the expression of complaints, in his opinion a greater error could not be committed. (Loud cheers.)

How often was repeated now the remark of Poulett Thomson, in 1839—" Peel could do it, if he had the courage." But he had it not. He submitted to the indecent, haughty, and dictatorial declarations of the monopolists that he was nothing without them ; wincing, perhaps, under their insolence, but without the boldness to set them at defiance ; resolved, perhaps, at some favourable opportunity, to assert his independence, but not daring to *make* the opportunity. And all the while Lord J. Russell standing by and uttering his little Shibboleth !

CHAPTER X.

THE QUESTION BEFORE PARLIAMENT.

Previous to the next movement in parliament the following meetings were held in Covent Garden Theatre :—

February 1st.—Chairman, Mr. Wilson; speakers, Dr. Bowring, Colonel Thompson, and Mr. Bright.

February 8th.—Chairman, Mr. Wilson; speakers, Mr. Villiers, Mr. Cobden, and General Sir De Lacy Evans.

February 15th.—Chairman, Mr. Villiers; speakers, Mr. Hume, Mr. Christie (M.P. for Weymouth), and Mr. W. J. Fox.

February 22nd.—Chairman, Mr. Wilson; speakers, Mr. James Wilson, Mr. Daniel O'Connell, (whose speech excited great enthusiasm) Mr. Geo. Thompson (who had recently returned from India), and Mr. Moore.

February 28th.—Chairman, Mr. Wilson; speakers, Mr. Henry Ashworth (of Bolton), Mr. Milner Gibson, and Mr. Bright.

March 6th.—Chairman, Mr. Villiers; speakers, Dr. Bowring, Mr. J. T. Leader, M.P., and Mr. W. J. Fox.

In the House of Lords, on Monday, March 11th, the Earl of Radnor presented the county of Somerset free-trade petition, which raised considerable discussion. As it was impossible to deny that a free-trade petition had been adopted at a great county meeting, all efforts were directed to show that the majority at the meeting had been improperly constituted, and did not fairly represent the feelings of the county. The Duke of Wellington said that it would be an impolitic thing to disturb the Corn Law, because it had not yet had a fair trial, and the Duke of Richmond was of opinion that the Corn Law wanted no more discussion!

In the House of Commons on the following evening Mr. Cobden brought forward a motion, of which he had given notice, to inquire into the effects of protective duties on the interests of the tenant-farmers and labourers of this country. The *League* says :—" There was a dinner to be given to Mr. O'Connell on the same evening ; and the name of Mr. Cobden appeared amongst the list of stewards. It is impossible to describe the feeling of satisfaction which this little fact diffused amongst the monopolists in London. In Pall Mall and Piccadilly—in the Carlton, ay, and even in the Reform Club, for there are some monopolists there—the topic of discussion was whether or not Mr. Cobden would bring on his motion. ' Oh, is Cobden to bring on his motion to night ?' ' Don't know, but I should say he will not. He is advertised as one of the stewards to this O'Connell dinner.' ' Indeed ! I am right glad to hear of it. Of course there will be no House.' ' Well, but suppose we go down to see. These fellows have an ugly way of sticking to business, and I should not wonder if Peel and Gladstone were in the way, ready to make some of their confounded damaging admissions !' Down they come ; and are rather nettled, if not amazed, to find, not only a House, but a crowded one. The benches on both sides are full ; all the ministers are in attendance ; and, though a hum of conversation fills the atmosphere, there is evidently the expectation of a something. The speaker calls on Mr. Cobden ; instantly there is a profound silence ; and the Strangers' Gallery, which is crowded to suffocation, looks the very picture of excited satisfaction."

Mr. Cobden commenced his speech by saying that the motion might more properly have been brought forward by some county member, but he did not feel that he was precluded from taking a prominent part in a question affecting the interests of farmers and farm labourers, for whom he felt a strong sympathy.   He went on to state what he would prove before the committee :—

"I will not bring forward a single witness before that committee who shall not be a tenant farmer, or a landed proprietor, and they shall be persons eminent for their reputation as practical agriculturists.   The opinion which I shall hold on entering the committee is, that, 'protection,' as it is called, instead of being beneficial, is delusive and injurious to the tenant farmers; and that opinion I shall be prepared to sustain by the evidence of tenant farmers themselves.   I wish it to be understood I do not admit that what is called protection to agriculturists has ever been any protection at all to them; on the contrary, I hold that its only effect has been to mislead them.   This has been denied both in this House and out of doors.   I have recently read over again the evidence taken before the committees which sat previous to the passing of the Corn Law of 1815, and I leave it to any man to say whether it was not contended at that time that sufficient protection could not be given to the agriculturists, unless they got 80s. a quarter for wheat.   I wish to remind the hon. member for Wiltshire (Mr. Bennett) that he gave it as his opinion, before the committee of 1814, that wheat could not be grown in this country unless the farmers got 96s. a quarter, or 12s. a bushel for it, while now he is supporting a minister who only proposes to give the farmers 56s. a quarter, and confesses he cannot guarantee even that.   It has been denied that this house has ever promised to guarantee prices for their produce to the farmers.   Now, what was the custom of the country from the passing of the Corn Law in 1815 ?   Why, I will bring old men before the committee who will state that farmers valued their farms from that time by a computation of wheat being at 80s. a quarter.   I can also prove that agricultural societies which met in 1821 passed resolutions declaring that they were deceived by the act of 1815, that they had taken farms calculating upon selling wheat at 80s., while, in fact, it had fallen to little more than 50s.   In the committee which sat in 1836 witnesses stated that they had been deceived in the price of their corn; and I ask whether, at the present moment, rents are not fixed rather with reference to certain acts that were passed than the intrinsic worth of the farms?   In consequence of the alteration that was made in the Corn Law in 1842, the rent of farms has been assessed on the ground of corn being 56s. a quarter. I know an instance where a party occupying his own land was rated at a certain amount, viz., at the valuation of corn being 56s. a quarter, while, in fact, it was selling at 47s.; and, upon his asking why he had been so rated, he was told that the assessors had taken that mode of valuation in consequence of what the Prime Minister had stated was to be the price of corn. ('Hear, hear,' and 'Oh, oh.') Hon. gentlemen may cry 'Oh, oh,' but I will bring forward that very case, and prove what I have stated concerning it. What I wish in going into committee is, to convince the farmers of Great Britain that this house has not the power to regulate or sustain the price of their commodities. The right hon. baronet opposite (Sir R. Peel) has confessed that he cannot regulate the wages of labour or the profits of trade. Now, the farmers are dependent for their prices upon the wages of the labourer, and the profits of the trader and manufacturer; and if the government cannot regulate these—if it cannot guarantee a certain amount of wages to the one, or a fixed profit to the other—how can it regulate the price of agricultural produce? The first point to which I should wish to make this committee instrumental is, to fix in the minds of the farmers the fact that this house exaggerates its power to sustain or enhance prices by direct acts of legislation. (Hear.) The farmer's interest is that of the whole community, and is not a partial interest (loud cheers), and you cannot touch him more sensitively than when you injure the manufacturers, his customers. (Cheers.) I do not deny that you may regulate prices for a while—for a while you have regulated them by forcing an artificial scarcity; but this is a principle which carries with it the seeds of self-destruction, for you are thereby undermining the prosperity of those consumers upon whom permanent welfare depends. A war against nature must always end in the discomfiture of those who wage it. (Hear, hear.) You may by your restrictive enactments increase pauperism, and destroy trade; you may banish capital, and check or expatriate your population; but is this, I will ask, a policy which can possibly work consistently with the interests of the farmers? (Hear, hear.) These are the fundamental principles which I wish to bring out, and with this primary view it is that I ask for a committee at your hands."

He went on to show the absurdity of the assertion that wheat could be imported at 25s. or 30s., and instanced Jersey, where unrestricted importation was permitted, the average price for ten years had been 48s. 3d. ; and then went on to show that it was the speculator, and not the farmer, that received the highest prices :—

"A short time ago I met a miller from near Winchester, who told me the prices which he paid every year for the corn which he purchased before the harvest, and after the harvest, during five years. That statement I beg to read to the house :—

1839	August	Wheat..£19	10	Load of 5 qrs.
	November	Ditto.. 16	0	ditto
1840	August	Ditto.. 18	0	ditto
	October	Ditto.. 14	5	ditto
1841	August	Ditto.. 19	0	ditto
	October	Ditto.. 15	0	ditto
1842	August	Ditto.. 17	0	ditto
	September	Ditto.. 12	0	ditto
1843	July	Ditto.. 15	15	ditto
	September	Ditto.. 12	10	ditto

Thus in these five years there had been a difference of £3 18s. a load, or 15s. a quarter, between the prices of wheat in July and August, and in October and November in each year, showing, beyond dispute, that the farmer did not sell his corn at the highest, but at the lowest of the markets."

He reminded the agriculturists that every prediction then uttered with regard to corn had been uttered with regard to wool, all of which had been falsified. Similar predictions had been made with regard to the late tariff :

"It is said that the tariff has caused distress among the farmers. Why, I don't believe here has been as much increase in the imports of cattle as would make one good breakfast for all the people. (Laughter.) Did it never enter the minds of hon. gentlemen who are interested in the sale of cattle, that their customers in large towns cannot be sinking into abject poverty and distress without the evil ultimately reaching themselves, in the price of their produce ? I had occasion a little time ago to look at the falling off in the consumption of cattle in the town of Stockport. I calculated the falling off in Stockport alone for three or four years, at more than all the increase in the importation of foreign cattle. It appears, therefore, that the distress of that town alone has done as much to reduce prices as all the importation under the tariff. It has been estimated that in Manchester forty per cent. less of cattle was consumed in 1842 than in 1835; and it has also been estimated that the cotton trade was paying £7,000,000 less in wages per annum in 1842 than in 1836. How could you then expect the same consumption ? (Hear.) If you would but look to your own interests as keenly and as wisely as manufacturers look to theirs, you would never fall into the error of supposing that you can ruin your customers, and yet, at the same time, prosper in your pursuits. (Cheers.) I remember hearing Lord Kinnaird, whose property is near Dundee, state that, in 1835 and 1836, the dealers from that town used to come and bespeak his cattle three-months in advance; but in 1842, when the linen trade shared the prostration of all the manufactures, he had to engage steam boats three months in advance to bring his cattle to the London market. Hon. members who live in Sussex and the southern counties, and who are in the habit of sneering at Manchester, should recollect that they are as much dependent upon the prosperity of Lancashire as those who live in their immediate neighbourhood. (Hear, hear.) If graziers, on looking at the *Price Current*, find they can get a better price for their cattle in London than in Manchester and Stockport, will they not send their cattle up to London, to compete with the southern graziers?"

He then adverted to the subject of rent as a large item in the outlay of the tenant, regretting that there were no tenant farmers in the House, men of good practical knowledge, to set them right on that highly important part of the question :—

" The landowners, I mean the political landowners—those who dress their labourers and their cattle in blue ribbons, and who treat this question entirely as a political one—they go to the tenant farmers, and they tell them that it would be quite impossible for them to compete with foreigners, for, if they had their land rent-free, they could not sell their produce at the same price as they did. To bear out their statement they give a calculation of the cost per acre of growing wheat, which they put down at £6. Now, the fallacy of that has been explained to me by an agriculturist in the Midland Counties, whom I should exceedingly like to see giving his evidence before the committee for which I am moving. He writes me in a letter which I have received to-day, ' You will be met by an assertion that no alteration in rent can make up the difference to the tenant and labourer of diminished prices. They will quote the expenses on a single crop of wheat, and say how small a proportion the rent bears to the whole expense, but that is not the fair way of putting it. Wheat is the farmer's remunerating crop, but he cannot grow wheat more than one year in three. The expense, then, of the management of the whole farm should be compared with the rent, to estimate what portion of the price of corn is received by the landlord. I have, for this purpose, analysed the expenses of a farm of 400 acres—230 arable, 170 pasture.

'The expenses are :—

			£
Parish and county rates	..	.. ..	90
Interest of capital	..	.. .. ..	150
Labour	..	.. .. ..	380
Tradesmen's bills	..	.. .. ..	80
Manure and Lime	..	.. .. ..	70
Wear of horses	..	.. .. ..	20
			790
Rent	..	.. .. ..	800
			£1,590.'

So that, on this farm, which is very fairly cultivated, the rent is £800, the other expenses £790. (Cries of 'Oh, oh,' from the ministerial side.) Now, if it requires 55s. per quarter in an average year to enable the tenant to pay the rent, and make £150 profit, it is obvious that without any rent he would be able to pay his labourers and tradesmen as well, with a price of 30s., supposing other produce to be reduced in the same proportion. But I do not anticipate that wheat will be reduced below 45s., even by free trade, and meat, butter, cheese, will certainly not fall in the same proportion."

Nine years after this prediction wheat exceeded 45s., and the price of meat, butter, and cheese was higher than in 1844. Mr. Cobden went on to say :—

"It must not be imputed to me that I entertain the opinion that free trade in corn would deprive the landowners of the whole of their rents. I have never said so—I have never even said that land would not have been as valuable as it is now if no Corn Law had ever existed. But this I do mean to say, that if the landowners prefer to draw their rents from the distresses of the country, caused by their restrictive laws to create high prices through scarcity of food, instead of deriving an honourable income of probably as great, or even greater amount, through the growing prosperity of the people under a free trade, then they have no right, in the face of such facts as I have stated, to attempt to cajole the farmer into the belief that rent forms an insignificant item in the cost of his wheat, or to frighten him into the notion that he could not compete with foreigners if he had his land rent-free."

An honourable income, as great as it had been under restriction, was had from land after the repeal of the Corn Law. Mr. Cobden proceeded to state the condition of agricultural labourers under "protection:"

" Before I allude to the condition of the agricultural labourers, I wish to state that, whatever may have been the animus which influenced others in investigating the condition of the manufacturing districts, I am actuated by no invidious feeling whatever towards the agriculturists, for, bear in mind, that my conduct has been throughout marked by consistency towards both. (Hear.) Had I ever concealed the wretched state of the manufacturing operatives, or shrunk from the exposure of their sufferings, my motives might have been open to suspicion in now bringing before your notice the still more depressed condition of the agricultural poor. (Hear.) I was one of that numerous deputation from the north which, in the spring of 1839, knocked in vain at the door of this House for an inquiry at your bar into the state of the manufacturing population. (Hear, hear, hear.) I was one of the deputies who intruded ourselves (sometimes five hundred strong) into the presence of successive Prime Ministers until our importunities became the subject of remark and complaint in this House. (Hear.) From that time to this we have continued without intermission to make public in every possible way the distress to which the manufacturers were exposed. We did more. We prescribed a remedy for that distress. (Hear, hear.) And I do not hesitate to express my solemn belief that the reason why, in the disturbances which took place, there was no damage done to property in the manufacturing districts was, that the people knew and felt that an inquiry was taking place, by active and competent men, into the cause of their distresses, and from which they hoped some efficient remedy would result; and I would impress upon honourable members opposite as the result of my conviction, that if the labouring poor in in their districts take a course as diabolical as it is insane—a course which I am sorry to see they have taken in many agricultural localities —of burning property to make known their sufferings; if I might make to those honourable gentlemen a suggestion, it would be this—that if they had come forward to the House and the country as we, the manufacturers, have done, and made known the sufferings of the labouring population, and prescribed any remedy whatever—if that population had heard a voice promulgating their distresses, and making known their sufferings—if they had seen the sympathies of the country appealed to, I believe it would have had such a humanising and consoling effect upon the minds of the poor and misguided people, that in the blindness of despair they would never have destroyed that property which it was their interest to protect. (Hear, hear, hear.)"

He proceeded to state from the report of Mr. Austin, one of the assistant poor-law commissioners, the condition of agricultural labourers in Somersetshire, Devonshire,

Wiltshire, and Dorsetshire. The vicar of Colne was unable
to make out how they contrived to live on their wages ;
Mr. Bowman, a farmer in the Colne union, said that a
man, his wife, and four or five children, had to be supported on his wages of eight or nine shilllings a week ;
Mr. Hunt, a farmer in Gloucestershire, said it would not
be safe to feed the inmates of workhouses on so low a
dietary as the labourers had ; Mr. Austin measured a room
near Blandford, in which eleven persons slept, which was
only ten feet square, the roof being in the thatch and in
the middle only seven feet high ; Mr. Phelps, an agent of
the Marquis of Blandford, found twenty-nine persons
living under one roof; the Hon. and Rev. S. G. Osborne
saw, in a room thirteen feet square, three beds, one occupied by the mother, dying of consumption, one by a young
man of eighteen and a girl of twelve, and the third by a
young couple whom he had married two days before ; and
the same gentleman said that in Tarrant Hinton, a father,
mother, married daughter and her husband, an infant, a
blind boy of sixteen, and two girls occupied one bed room,
and that next door there were a father and six children
occupying one room. After enumerating other instances
both in England and Scotland of the miserable destitution
in the families of agricultural labourers, he urged upon the
House the humanity and the justice of an inquiry into the
truth of these allegations, and said :—

"You do not want acts of Parliament to protect the farmer—you
want improvements, outlays, bargains, leases, fresh terms. (Cheers.)
A farmer before my committee will tell you that you may employ more
labourers by breaking up land which has lain for hundreds of years in
grass, or rather in moss, to please some eccentric landowner, who prefers
a piece of green turf to seeing the plough turning up its furrows. This
coxcombry of some landlords would disappear before the good sense of
the Earl of Ducie. (Cheers, and cries of 'Oh, oh,' from the Ministerial
benches.) You may derive advantage from examining men who look
upon land as we manufacturers do upon the raw material of the fabrics
which we make—(hear, hear)—who will not look upon it with that

superstitious veneration and that abhorence of change with which landlords have been taught to regard their acres, but as something on which to give employment to the people, and which, by the application to it of increased intelligence, energy, and capital, may produce increased returns of wealth. (Cheers.) But we shall have another advantage from my committee. Recollect that hitherto you have never heard the two sides of the question in the committees which have sat to inquire into agricultural subjects; and I press this fact on the notice of the right hon. baronet opposite, as a strong appeal to him. I have looked back upon the evidence taken before these committees, and I find that in none of them were both sides of the question fairly stated. All the witnesses examined were protectionists—all the members of all the committees were protectionists. (Hear, hear.) We have never yet heard an enlightened agriculturist plead the opposite side of the question. (Hear, hear.) It is upon these grounds that I press this motion upon honourable gentlemen opposite. I want to have further evidence. I do not want a man to be examined who is not a farmer or landowner. I would respectfully ask the Earl of Ducie and Earl Spencer to be examined first. (Cheers from the Opposition.) And then, honourable gentlemen, you could send for the Dukes of Buckingham and Richmond. (Loud cheering, mingled with laughter from the Ministerial benches.) I would like nothing better than that—nothing better than to submit these four noblemen to a cross-examination. I would take your two witnesses and you would take mine, and the country should decide between us. (Renewed cheers and laughter.) Nothing would so much tend to diffuse sound views as such an examination."

Mr. Cobden went on to say that he asked for no advantages in the appointment of a committee. There was a sort of etiquette that the mover for a committee should be its chairman. He waived all pretension of the kind, and only asked to be present as an individual member. He told the landowners there that their boasted protection was not protection, but destruction to agriculture, and concluded by saying :—

" Let us have a committee, and see if we cannot elicit facts which may counteract the folly of those who are trying to persuade the farmer to prefer acts of Parliament to draining and subsoiling, and to be looking to the laws of this House when he should be studying the laws of nature. (Cheers.) I cannot imagine anything more demoralising— yes, that is the word—more demoralising than for you to tell the farmers that they cannot compete with foreigners. (Hear, hear.) You bring long rows of figures, of delusive accounts, showing that the cultivation of an acre of wheat costs £6 or £8 per year. You put every impediment in the way of the farmers trying to do what they ought to do. (Hear.) And can you think that that is the way to make people succeed? (Hear, hear.) How should we manufacturers get on, if, when we got a pattern as a specimen of the productions of a rival manufacturer, we brought all our people together, and said, 'It is quite clear that we cannot compete with this foreigner; it is quite useless our attempting to compete with Germany or America; why, we cannot produce goods at the price at which they do.' But how do we act in reality? We call our men together, and say, 'So-and-so is producing goods at such a price; but we are Englishmen, and what France or Germany can do, we can do also.' (Loud cheers.) I repeat that the opposite system, which you go upon, is demoralising the farmers. Nor have you any right to call out, with the noble lord the member for North Lancashire—you have no right to go down occasionally to your constituencies and tell the farmers, 'You must not plod on as your grandfathers did before you; you must not put your hands behind your backs, and drag one foot after the other in the old fashioned style of going to work.' I say you have no right to hold such language to the farmer. Who makes them plod on like their grandfathers? Who makes them put their hands behind their backs? (Loud cheers.) Why, the men who go to Lancashire and talk of the danger of the pouring in of foreign corn from a certain province in Russia, which shall be nameless—(loud cheers)—the men who tell the farmers to look to this House for protective acts instead of to their own energies—instead of to those capabilities which, were they properly brought out, would make the English farmer equal to—perhaps superior to—any in the world. (Loud cheers.) Because I believe that the existing system is worse for the farmer than for the manufacturer—because I believe that great good to both would result from an enquiry—because I believe that the present system robs the earth of its fertility and the labourer of his hire, deprives the people of subsistence, and the farmer of feelings of honest independence, I hope, Sir, that the House will accede to my motion for 'a select committee to enquire into the effects of protective duties on imports upon the interests of the tenant-farmers and farm-labourers of this country.'"

The debate is thus described in the *League* :—

"Mr. Gladstone replied; and paid a deserved compliment to Mr. Cobden for the temper which characterised his speech. But of Mr. Gladstone's own speech what can be said? The President of the Board of Trade is a very able man; but it requires great ability indeed to speak against one's own convictions, especially when there is a feeling of conscience and honour in the breast of the individual. The whole speech of Mr. Gladstone might be summed up in this way:—'You Mr. Cobden, and your friends, think so-and-so, but there are others who differ from you. No doubt, much of what you say is true, but there are other individuals in this House ready to question other parts of what you say; and seeing that is the case, it would be a very inconvenient thing to appoint a committee, to inquire whether what you say is true or not. Take the question of rent, which is very difficult and abstruse. The doctrine of rent is a crack subject with your Ricardo and your political economists. How hard, therefore, it would be to compel fifteen unfortunate gentlemen of the House of Commons to sit down and master the question of rent: they have enough to do to get in their rents as it is. Besides, Mr. Cobden confessed his willingness to allow a majority of protectionists on the committee—all he wanted was liberty to call his witnesses, and prove his case. But would it not be easy for these protectionists to protract the inquiry from session to session?—and would you adjourn the Anti-Corn-Law agitation, and suspend all your meetings until that report was made?' Mr. Bright called out that he for one was willing to do so. 'Yes,' says Mr. Gladstone, ' you may be willing to do so, but there are others who would not be willing to do so; and can you, therefore, think of pressing for this committee of inquiry? Country gentlemen would take it into their heads that there was to be another Corn Law and another sliding scale, and that would play the very mischief with us. It is all very well for honourable gentlemen to wish to bring differences of opinion to the test of argument and reason, based on a searching inquiry into the facts of the case; but such an inquiry would disturb the progress of agricultural improvement. In every way it is much easier, much less troublesome, to go on *asserting* instead of *proving* that the farmer and the farm-labourer have a greater interest in the Corn-Law than the landlord; and, therefore, it was expedient that the motion should not be granted.'

" Well did Mr. Hawes ridicule the utter inanity of the arguments of Mr. Gladstone, than whom no man could make a better defence if he had a tolerable case. Lord Pollington, one of the members for Pontefract, seemed to feel this; for he got up and said, boldly enough, that though he would not tax bread for the sake of revenue, he would do so for the sake of independence of foreigners and protection to agriculture. If this, in plain English, means anything, it signifies that he would not tax bread for the purposes of the nation, but he would do so for the sake of the landlords. This was put a little clearer by Mr. Francis Scott, who represents Roxburghshire, and is a son of Lord Polwarth, the head of the Border family of Scott, of which Sir Walter Scott was one of the branches. This young man, in a scolding tone of voice, which even his own side of the House felt was very injudicious in him to assume, railed away at the manufacturers because, he said, they made such a deal of money. If they could contrive to get a handsome profit on their capital by the exertion of their industry and skill, how hard it was not to let the poor landlords try to turn a penny by means of an act of parliament. Besides, the duration of life was longer, on the average, in the rural than in the manufacturing districts—a strong reason for keeping out foreign corn. This sort of logic may perhaps answer amongst a majority of the landlords and even the farmers of Roxburghshire, where there is a strong objection to manufactures, even to paper mills; but what would the honourable and astute Mr. Francis Scott say to an act of parliament compelling the farmers and landlords of Roxburghshire to sell all their produce to *themselves!*

"Two whig agricultural protectionists spoke in the debate, Lord Worsley and Mr. Herbert Curteis. Lord Worsley is the eldest son of the Earl of Yarborough, whose property in Lincolnshire has become a princely one, by dint of spirited expenditure and improvement. But yet, in spite of the evidence before his own eyes, that, with capital and skill, British agriculture may defy the world, Lord Worsley clings to protection as if *it* had been the source and origin of Lincolnshire prosperity. Lord Worsley is a very respectable young nobleman, and is staunch to his party, except on the Corn Laws. The other whig who spoke, Mr. Herbert Curteis, is member for Rye, and a Sussex landlord. He is a very honourable, spirited, out-spoken man, though mistaken in his corn policy, for, while he would venture the length of a moderate fixed duty, he is so afraid of total repeal that, rather than have that, he would keep up the sliding scale, the pernicious influence of which he acknowledges. He confessed that Mr. Cobden had made so fair a speech that he would vote for the committee, if he were not afraid that his vote would be misconstrued by his agricultural friends and neighbours.

"Colonel Sibthorp spoke, of course; and he made one of those droll speeches which set everybody laughing, not *with* but *at* him. He professed great horror of the *League,* a paper which he would not tolerate on the table of his house. But how does he know what it contains, unless he sometimes reads it? There can be little doubt that the gallant colonel reads the *League;* and, if he does, its influence can hardly be very despicable, after all. It may be a consolation to him to know that its weekly circulation is about twenty thousand copies.

"Mr. Villiers took up the cudgels for Colonel Sibthorp, and told the Ministerial side of the House that it was both ungrateful and audacious to laugh at its own colonel, seeing that his speech was as good for *protection* as one with less fun in it. **Mr.** Villiers then, in his own nutshell-cracking way, stripped the pretences bare by which the motion of Mr. Cobden was resisted. Were not the very contradictions of Mr. Cobden's allegations all so many additional reasons why the committee should be granted, in order that the facts might be sifted? The same question was put by Mr. Bright, who, in doing so, made one of the best points during the whole evening. He told the House, that *if the majority thought that the justice of the Corn Law could be proved, they would grant the committee at once?* The very force of contrast made this a most striking illustration.

"Of the entire discussion we may remark, that it evinces most strikingly the progress of public opinion. During the whole evening there was a full attendance of members. There was no emptying of the benches at seven o'clock—the hour of dinner. There was no skulking, no evasion; it was felt that the question must be met. But the most remarkable thing in the debate was the way in which the Ministerial side of the House treated Mr. Newdegate. That young man got up at a late hour, when the House was crowded, and charged the Anti-Corn-Law League with fomenting disturbances in the manufacturing districts, and with having objects ulterior to the repeal of the Corn Laws. But even those around him refused to listen. The general feeling evidently was—'Oh, that game won't do now—we must give it up!' A loud noise of conversation drowned his voice; there was an intense anxiety for a division. To prolong the debate was clearly felt to be but a strengthening of justice, reason, truth. All the argument was on one side—all the moral weakness on the other. So they pushed to a division; and at one o'clock in the morning 153 friends of justice and fair play voted for the proposed committee, but were opposed by 244 fearful monopolists; the majority being *ninety-one*, exactly the same that installed the present Ministry in office."

There was still much to be done, and much was done in the period between Mr. Cobden's motion for inquiry, and Mr. Villiers' for total repeal. The lecturers were each addressing three or four audiences every week; the distribution of tracts went on actively; and numerous meetings were held all over the country, the few meetings under the auspices of the agricultural association, or Anti-League League as it was called, most of them grievous failures, only stimulating the free-trade agitation into increased energy;

and on one day in every week, almost every newspaper in
London had a page of report of spirited and admirable
discussion in Covent Garden Theatre, spreading free-trade
argument throughout the kingdom and wherever a London
paper found its way; while the diversity of eloquence and
argument crowded the theatre with attentive audiences.
I must content myself with giving a mere catalogue of
those meetings.

March 20th, 1844.—The Earl of Radnor in the chair.
Speakers: Mr. Lattimore, of Bride Hall, Hertfordshire, a
tenant farmer; Mr. Hunt, another tenant farmer; and
Mr. Cobden. The fallacies of the monopolists with regard
to the benefit of the Corn Laws to farmers and farm
labourers were most triumphantly demolished. March
27th.—Mr. Milner Gibson, M.P., in the chair. Speakers:
Mr. Gisborne, M.P.; Mr. Bright; and Mr. W. J Fox.
April 17th.—Mr. Cobden in the chair. Speakers: Col.
Thompson, and Mr. George Thompson. Mr. Cobden
announced that the council had determined on holding a
great Bazaar, or Art Exhibition in that theatre. April 24th.
—Mr. Villiers, M.P., in the chair. Speakers: Mr. W.
Ewart, M.P.; Mr. Howard Elphinstone, M.P.; and Mr.
R. R. Moore. May 1st.—Lord Kinnaird in the chair.
Speakers: Mr. Ricardo, M.P.; Mr. Jas. Somers, a farmer
from Somersetshire; and Mr. Cobden. May 8th.—Mr.
Warburton, M.P. for Kendal, in the chair. Speakers:
Mr. Villiers; Mr. Gibbs, of Aylesbury, a farmer; and
Mr. W. J. Fox. May 15th.—Mr. Bright in the chair.
Speakers: Mr. Jas. Wilson of the *Economist;* Mr. Turner,
a tenant farmer from Somersetshire; and the Rev. John
Burnet, of Camberwell. May 22nd.—Major General Briggs
in the chair. Speakers: the Rev. Saml. Greene; Mr. Geo.
Thompson; and Mr. W. J. Fox. May 29th.—Earl Ducie
in the chair. Speakers: Mr. Edward Holland, of Dum-
bleton, a practical agriculturist; Mr. Cobden, who was
introduced to the meeting by his lordship as *their own*

Cobden; and Mr. Bright. June 5th.—Mr. Geo. Wilson
in the chair. Speakers; Mr. E. Bouverie (son of the Earl
of Radnor), who a few days before had been elected for
Kilmarnock; Mr. Milner Gibson; and Mr. R. R. Moore.
June 19th.—Mr. G. Wilson in the chair. Speakers: Mr.
Cobden; the Rev. Thomas Spencer; and Mr. W. J. Fox.

The death of Mr. R. B. Wilbraham, a conservative and
protectionist, had occasioned a vacancy for South Lancashire. It was felt by the free traders that to gain a seat
for that most important division of the county was of still
greater consequence than to retain, in spite of the undis-
guised and active exercise of ministerial influence, a seat
for London. Conferences were held of the leading reformers of Liverpool and Manchester, and it was resolved
to invite a free-trade candidate. On the 12th May an
address to the electors was published by Mr. Wm. Brown,
a merchant of Liverpool, and an extensive landed proprietor, the head of a firm whose mercantile transactions
influenced not only the commerce of Lancashire but of
the world. In his address he said that in South Lancashire, if anywhere, the cause of free trade ought to triumph,
and that he offered himself as its most strenuous advocate.
The tories did not think it prudent to put forward a
thorough obstructive, believing that they would be safer
with Mr. Entwisle, a conservative of the Peel school, who
would support Peel's tariff reforms while they continued to
exclude corn. A vigorous contest ensued, and at the close
of the poll the numbers were :—

For Entwisle 7,571
For Brown   6,963

The conservatives and monopolists professed greatly to
exult in the result—professed, for they must have felt a
strong conviction that at the next election they would be
defeated. The free traders were not depressed—on the
contrary, they rejoiced in the experiment because it promised the certainty of success at the next trial. At the

election in 1837, which was a contest between whigs and tories, two tories were returned. At the election for 1841, no whig candidate could be found, and the free traders did not think themselves strong enough to contest the county without whig aid. In 1837 the whig candidates had majorities in only two out of the ten polling districts. In 1844 the free traders had majorities in six of the ten districts. In 1841 the free traders knew that they would be out-numbered by 2,000 votes; now, so much had their principles spread, they were within 500 or 600 of their opponents. They saw victory before them. It came, and South Lancashire was represented neither by nominees of the great whig nor the great tory aristocratic families, but by one of the greatest of the Liverpool and one of the greatest of the Manchester merchants, both representing faithfully the best interests of commercial and manufacturing Lancashire. Mr. Brown was one of several who, at this period, were not so desirous to be in the House of Commons themselves, for the gratification of a selfish ambition, as to excite such a spirit, in the places where they were candidates, as would make free trade principles victorious at the next contest. Would that more frequently candidates could, with equal sincerity, say, " Not me, but the cause ! "

CHAPTER XI.

MR. VILLIERS' MOTION, 1844.

On Tuesday, June 25th, Mr. Villiers moved—That this House do resolve itself into a Committee, for the purpose of considering the following Resolutions :—

" That it appears by a recent census that the people of this country are rapidly increasing in number.

" That it is in evidence before this House that a large proportion of Her Majesty's subjects are insufficiently provided with the first necessaries of life.

" That, nevertheless, a Corn Law is in force which restricts the supply of food, and thereby lessens its abundance.

" That any such restriction having for its object to impede the free purchase of an article upon which depends the subsistence of the community, is indefensible in principle, injurious in operation, and ought to be abolished.

" That it is therefore expedient that the Act 5 and 6 Vic., c. 14, shall be repealed forthwith."

The subjects of his speech were :—

1. Continued discussion inspires hope; the protection societies were but an exhibition that theirs was a losing, while that of the Anti-Corn-Law League was essentially a gaining cause; and public opinion will ultimately carry that which is based on truth and justice.

2. All the arguments adduced in support of the Corn Law had been sifted, and found wanting; the most plausible of them all, that of " independence of foreigners,"

had turned out the most foolish, inasmuch as returns showed our habitual dependence on foreigners for the bread we eat; and, while the Corn Law was unequivocally injurious to commerce, the interest of the farmer and the agricultural labourer in it had been shown to be an utter fallacy.

3. Not only were the farmers in continual distress under this Corn Law, but the agricultural labouring population were lower in the scale of civilization than almost any other class of human beings. On this fact, incendiary fires shed an awful light.

4. The allegations of land being thrown out of cultiva- tion, and labourers out of employment, were disproved by the minute calculations of such men as Earl Ducie, who, combining science with practice, showed that land would pay rent, and therefore be cultivated, under any pressure from foreign competition. While they were talking about the danger of displacing agricultural labour, no less than 360,000 agricultural labourers had passed into and been absorbed in the manufacturing districts.

5. The people of this country were admitted to toil too long and to have too little to eat; they were better off with a good than with a bad harvest; yet there was no difference in principle whether food was rendered scarce by a bad harvest, or by limiting the supply from other countries.

6. A copious exhibition of statistics showed that abun- dance or scarcity in the supply of the essential food of the people had an intimate connexion between the increase or diminution of pauperism, crime, poor rates, disease, emi- gration, deficient nourishment, typhus fever. War prices and rent being the parents of want, disease, crime, and death.

7. The united cry of the more enlightened agriculturists was—Improvement: yet, if there were truth in protection principles, improvement ought to be as injurious as im- portation. Nor, while protection remained, would im-

provement be so carried out as to develop all the resources of the soil, with security to the farmer, comfort to the labourer, and benefit to all, including even the mistaken landlord himself.

Having given the subjects of Mr. Villiers' speech, I subjoin detached portions.

Independence of foreigners :—

" The difficulty with hon. gentlemen opposite in arguing this question was, that they were unable to defend the law on its real ground, and it was inconvenient to assign any other; for as soon as it was attempted to place it upon any public ground, that instantly became the subject of the closest inquiry : it was sifted and tested in every way to examine if the plea was hollow or true; and there was no one ground which he had heard since he came into that House that had not now been thus thoroughly examined, and as completely exposed. (Hear.) He was curious, therefore, to hear what fresh ground was to be alleged this time. The ground upon which it was placed when first introduced was the most plausible, before it was tested by experience, when it proved to be the most foolish on which it could stand—which was, that it was dangerous for this country to be dependent for its supply of food on other countries, and that, therefore, the landowners should be protected from competition. It was assumed that we might depend upon other countries for our revenue, for the material of manufactures, and for the means of employment to millions of our people, whereby they should obtain bread, but not be dependent upon them for the bread itself. (Hear.) That was the plea set forth for the enactment of the law—one which, at the time, all thinking men derided, and which has since become contemptible by the failure of the experiment. The returns laid before the House during the last twenty years, showed that since the law was passed we had been dependent on other countries for large supplies of corn, and in the last five years to the amount of 17,000,000 quarters of corn (hear); and that, too, a supply not raised with a view to this country, but obtained under circumstances the most disadvantageous to us. (Hear, hear, hear.) During the thirteen years of the duration of the law passed in 1828, there was imported from foreign countries no less than 30,000,000 quarters of grain actually necessary for the consumption of the people of this country. The advocates for monopoly in the home market would hardly then allege a sufficiency of home supply as an excuse—at least, he would not expect such an excuse from any man having regard for his character and truth. Whether this soil would or could not produce enough to support the people of Great

Britain, he could not pretend to say; but the fact stood upon record, that it had not produced enough, and that we had been obliged to import 30,000,000 quarters of grain from foreign countries."

Condition of farmers and farm labourers :—

" He had heard from honourable gentlemen opposite, on previous occasions, when the subject was discussed, that those connected with the ownership of lands had no interest in their continuance, but they supported the Corn Laws because those who were dependent on them (the landowners) had all their interest involved in their continuance. It was now, however, ascertained beyond a doubt, that neither the farmer, nor the farmer's labourer, nor any other class in the community, derived any benefit from these laws except the landowners themselves. (' Hear,' from the opposition.) No member of any agricultural county would to-night, he thought, venture to urge this flimsy pretext, so demonstrably untrue, as a reason for the continuance of the Corn Laws; no honourable member would here stand up and say, I can prove that the farmers or their labourers benefit by this law. (Cries of ' Hear, hear.') The interest of these classes in these laws had been fully and fairly inquired into by those leagued together for the purpose, and so far from the Corn Laws being of any service to them, nothing appeared to be more identified with the permanent interest of both the farmer and the agricultural labourer than their total repeal. Every person is now familiar with the fact that the distress of no class had been more prominently or more frequently obtruded upon the public than that of the farmers. He (Mr. Villiers) would undertake to bring before the bar of that House, or before a committee, such a body of evidence as would leave no doubt that, for the last thirty years, the farmers had been, of all men, the most embarrassed, and that their distress had been more obtruded upon the attention of this House than that of any other class of persons. In fact, it is now matter of notoriety that they had derived no benefit from the Corn Laws. (Hear.) The farmer had been duped and deceived by the promise of parliament as to the effects of these laws. (Hear, hear.) The landlords had told him that they would ensure him a certain price for his corn; and what had been the result? Why, that he had been deluded into the payment of higher rent. The same had occurred with regard to all the exemptions that had been procured for the farmer in the payment of taxes; there was not a landlord in the House who did not know that they contributed only to swell the rent of the landowner. (Hear, hear, hear.) The members of the House dare not call a single farmer before them, and ask him whether what they had done in his behalf, as they said, had been at all to his benefit?

Whatever relief they had procured for the farmer through parliament had been for the advantage alone of landowners. (Hear, hear, hear.) He would venture to say that not an honourable member in that House would repeat again to-night that the Corn Laws were enacted for the benefit of the farmers He defied honourable members to repeat that the law was upheld for such purpose. The farmers were not only the most distressed class in the whole community, but they held their lands under circumstances the most disadvantageous for the purpose of agriculture. The assertion that these laws were for the benefit of the labourer was equally absurd and unfounded. No one would now venture to say that it was to the advantage of the labourer that the prices of food should be kept up, and that high prices ensured high wages. There was a volume before them, produced by the labours of a commission of the Crown, which effectually disproved that assertion. No man in the face of that volume could rise and say that these laws were for the advantage of the labourers. Their mouths were closed by the evidence of their own commission. This was an authority which they did not venture to dispute. That evidence proved that no one could be lower in the scale of civilization than the agricultural labourer ; so much so, indeed, as almost to place him out of its pale. Scarcely a day passed but the papers were full of accounts of what were called the crimes of the labouring classes, which were, in fact, only the results of their necessitous condition. The honourable member for Stockport had asked for inquiry upon this subject ; he had made a motion to that effect, but the landowners in this House could not assent to it ; they felt that they dared not call upon a single farmer or labourer to give evidence with respect to their condition, and their experience of the operation of these laws. The motion of his honourable friend was a perfectly fair one, and one quite in point ; but the landowners were afraid to call upon their own tenants, and to ask them whether, in their opinion, the Corn Laws did not chiefly operate to raise their rents ; and upon the poor labourers, to say whether their case was not made more desperate by high prices Sure he was that the landowners would not bring forward either farmers or labourers to speak of their experience of the operation of these laws. He saw in the *Times* newspaper a statement, that in some parts of the country, where there had been once a great deal of disaffection, wherever the farmer allowed the labourer an opportunity of procuring provisions cheap, thus virtually repealing the Corn Laws, they became better affected, and property was safe. He would ask the landowners to answer this question, how it was that the labourer was always found to be contented and well affected when prices were low, but that they were always disaffected, and the property of the country endangered, when prices were high ? He asked the honourable

member for Knaresborough, who had thought it decent to give notice of
an amendment on the present occasion, to meet and answer this point."

Effect on the demand for agricultural labour :—

" With respect to the notion of the repeal of the Corn Laws displacing
agricultural labour, the right honourable gentleman gave the House none
of the data upon which that fancy was founded. He supposed, of course,
that the right hon. gentleman calculated upon agricultural labour being
displaced, as the consequence of certain lands being thrown out of cultivation. Now, looking at what had been said by agriculturists themselves,
he was at a loss to understand that the neccessary consequence of a
reduction of prices would be to throw any considerable quantity of land
out of cultivation. The fact, he believed, was that, if a little science and
economy were applied to the cultivation of the land, a low price might
pay the labour of cultivation, and yield a good profit. A nobleman, distinguished for his knowledge of agriculture, Lord Ducie, declared
publicly, that all apprehension upon this score was a fallacy, and that
without paying rent they could produce wheat on almost any land at
lower prices than those quoted at any port. (Hear.) Now, it was
obvious, that before land could be thrown out of cultivation, it must
have given up paying rent; and before it ceased to support the labourer,
it must go to waste. The right hon. gentleman ought to have shown at
what prices land could not be cultivated with a prospect of profit; and
he would have to show that it would not be worth the mere application
of industry required for cultivation, before he declared that the lowering
of prices in the market would be followed by the displacement of labour.
He (Mr. Villiers) thought it probable that the right hon. gentleman
would not repeat this argument again to-night. Since he had formerly
used it, he had possibly read what had been said by men who
knew something about the subject, and he had doubtless profited by it.
But there was another argument which the right hon. gentleman had
since advanced ; it was to this effect:—that we should be careful how
far we risked the reduction of rent, lest owners of land should themselves
become farmers. The right hon. gentleman was afraid that the farmers
themselves would be ousted from their tenancies, and the landowners,
by cultivating their own land, become useful members of society.
(' Hear, hear,' and a laugh.) Now, he did not think that the right hon.
gentleman need labour under any very serious apprehension on this
score. He did not think that the firstborn of the land would be very
likely to take to a very industrious and laborious pursuit as long as they
could be more agreeably employed in doing nothing. Let him not be
alarmed—let him rest satisfied that, during his time at least, those who

were born to inherit the land, would continue to be trained up in idleness, as they had heretofore been (a laugh), and be chiefly qualified for consuming the fortunes they possessed. (Hear, hear.) But whilst the right hon. gentleman was dreading the displacement of agricultural labourers let him reflect upon the alternative of injuring trade, which would result in the displacement of a considerable number of manufacturing labourers. It appeared that in ten years, upwards of 360,000 agricultural labourers had gone from their villages to the manufacturing districts, as a means of living. Did not the right hon. gentleman perceive that, by the returning of any considerable portion of that number to the agricultural districts in consequence of the want of employment in manufactures, there would be just as great a displacement of agricultural labour as he apprehended would result from the introduction of foreign corn, and the consequent lowering of prices. (Hear, hear.) But the landowners themselves were now convinced that increased production and low prices did not displace labour; on the contrary, they went to their farmers and told them that the principle to go upon was, by the application of more labour, and increased skill and new improvemens, to produce the largest possible quantity of corn, and at the lowest possible price. And if this argument against low prices was good, it was just as much so against improvement as against free trade; increased supply and reduced price was the result of both."

Increase of poor rates :—

"Those Corn Laws which the honourable member for Knaresborough (Mr. Ferrand) looked upon as essential to the protection of industry, the right hon. baronet at the head of the Government had himself altered, alleging as his reason that, as it was absolutely necessary that the price of food to the people should be reduced, those laws, the tendency of which was to keep up prices, must be altered. At last, however, they found the Queen congratulating the country on its improved condition —but when was this? When the harvest had been ascertained to be good, and when supplies from abroad had been introduced, and when the food of the people was to be cheap and abundant. And when was it that the Secretary of State announced to the country that he was happy to say that the rate of mortality had diminished? It was in 1843, when food was more plentiful, and importation had increased. (Hear.) Great God! the rate of mortality was diminishing! Then the people had been actually dying of want, starving to death, for that was what the admission of the right hon. gentleman amounted to. (Hear, hear.) The suffering of the people did not depend upon surmise; they had, unfortunately, official evidence of it, to which he was anxious to call the attention of the House. In the first place, he would refer to the increase of pauperism; and he found that, in 1837, the rates levied in England and Wales for the relief of the poor amounted to £4,044,741; and in 1843, they amounted to £5,200,000. The number of paupers chargeable upon the rates, when the period of distress commenced, was 1,000,000; and when the Minister announced that there were indications of the distress having subsided, the number was 1,500,000. What was the number of able-bodied adult paupers at the same period, unable to obtain employment, and depending upon the poor rates for relief? At the period when the distress commenced, the number was under 200,000, that was in 1836; and in 1842 the number was 407,570. Then, observe in particular places the increase in the amount expended in relieving the poor in dear years, as compared with cheap years. He found that the amount expended—

	In 1836.	In 1841.	Increase.
At Stockport	£2,628	£7,120	134 per cent.
Manchester	25,669	38,938	52 „
Bolton	1,558	6,268	304 „
Oldham	3,968	7,682	159 „
Hinckley	2,040	4,200	97 „
Sheffield	11,400	23,800	109 „

Throughout the manufacturing districts there was great increase, but it was not confined to these districts. The increase was hardly less in the agricultural districts. In the fifteen chief agricultural counties he found the increase in the amount of poor rates between 1836 and 1842 was 21 per cent., while in the twelve principal manufacturing counties the increase had been 30½ per cent. This surely was sufficient to show the injurious effect of high prices of food on the labouring population."

Effect of deficiency of food on health :—

" There was a most important report by Dr. Alison, in which it was stated 23,000 persons existed in Edinburgh in an entirely destitute state, and completely dependent upon casual charity. He said:—' As the botanist can tell the quality of the soil from the flowers that spontaneously arise upon it, the physician knows the state of a people from the epidemics that mow it down. It is not asserted that destitution is a cause adequate to the production of fever (although in some circumstances I believe it may become such), nor that it is the sole cause of its extension. What we are sure of is, that it is a cause of the rapid diffusion of contagious fever, and one of such peculiar power and efficacy that its existence may always be presumed when we see fever prevailing in a large community to an unusual extent. The manner in which deficient nourishment, want of employment, and privations of all kinds, favour the diffusion of fever, may be matter of dispute ; but that they have that effect in a much greater degree than any cause external to the human body itself, is a fact confirmed by the experience of all physicians who have seen much of the disease.' Then, again, there was the evidence of Dr. Grattan, in Ireland, whom he found writing as follows:—' Next to contagion, I consider a distressed state of the general population of any particular district the most common and extensive source of typhoid fever. The present epidemic (that of Ireland in 1818) is principally to be referred to the miserable condition of the poorer classes in this kingdom; and so long as their state shall continue unimproved, so long fever will prevail, probably not to its present extent, but certainly to an extent sufficient to render it at all times a national affliction.' He had lately applied to a medical gentleman, practising in a populous district of London, Dr. Hunter, of Bloomsbury, whose experience quite confirmed all the information he had received upon the point. This gentleman wrote as follows:—' An extensive practice for more than twenty years, almost in the very focus of typhus localities, has given me an opportunity of seeing that disease in all its various degrees of malignity. There are numerous predisposing causes; such as impure air, crowded neighbourhoods, want of cleanliness, and so on; but all these sink into insignificance and unimportance when compared with the great monster predisposing agent—I mean a scarcity of nutritious food. And it may be said, if other causes have slain their thousands, this alone has slain its tens of thousands. My experience justifies and warrants me in affirming that, where the people have insufficient nourishment, there typhus fever manifests itself with all the horrors of a depopulating plague. Witness Ireland. No sooner does a year of scarcity appear but this fell destroyer of the human race shows itself, carrying off thousands; and this affirmation will, I am sure, be confirmed by any medical practitioner who has had the misfortune to see, as I have, whole families carried to their weary bourne by this scourge of the human family, brought into existence and activity by the physical wants of the people. I happened to know a family of nine persons, seven of whom died in one short month, and all by the fell destroyer, typhus; and this too in an agricultural district, where the air was as pure as the morning breath of heaven, and where contagion was impossible, as the farm houses were at a considerable distance from each other. But in the same district, where the families had sufficient food, and of a good quality, fever was wholly unknown.' He had a great amount of evidence of the same kind, relating to France, Belgium, and Germany. All medical men seemed to come to the unanimous conclusion that the well-being of the people varied with the quantity of food with which they were supplied. (Hear.) Now, he might be asked, what all this had to do with the Corn Laws. They would say that these laws were intended to protect native industry, and keep up the supply of food—at least something of the sort was implied in the amendment of the honourable member for Knaresborough. But what was really the purpose of the Corn Laws? If it was not to produce scarcity, he wished to know what its purpose was? He wished to know why the opposite intention had never been avowed? He wished to know if any person who had spoken in defence of the Corn Laws had ever said or implied anything other than that scarcity was their end and object? If their object was to produce plenty, why were those who maintained these laws dissatisfied whenever there was abundance in the country? How was it that when the people were well fed and well off, that it was precisely that moment at which the agriculturists came forward with complaints? (Hear, hear.) They had evidence to show that it was always the case that, when the people were in a comparatively comfortable state, the complaints of the agriculturists were loudest. If plenty was the object of the law, why, at that moment, its supporters should be most satisfied." (Hear, hear.)

Mr. Villiers concluded a very able speech by saying: "Considering the misery which had been produced by the Corn Laws, the irreparable injury which they had inflicted on commerce, and the millions they had for ever morally and physically ruined, he, for one, could not, for the sake of conciliating a few great men, abandon a great principle, which had for its object a great public advantage, and the removal from the people of an enormous wrong."

" Mr. Ferrand, after descanting on a variety of topics (all urged in his old tone, his old manner, accompanied with his old stories, unredeemed by a spark of novelty, and his whole conduct manifesting that fools are not always taught by experience), moved an amendment, the terms of which were a copy, or rather parody, of the motion of Mr. Villiers, with the variation that machinery, not the Corn Law, was the cause of distress, and protection and encouragement to native industry its cure. This amendment found with difficulty a seconder; in answer to the repeated call of the Speaker, 'Who seconds this amendment?' Mr. Borthwick slowly and reluctantly raised his hat; but as it was scouted on both sides, scarcely even alluded to, and finally withdrawn, we shall take no farther notice of it.

" Captain Berkeley lauded the landed aristocracy, whose hospitality at home and courage abroad were conspicuous in peace and war. The Protection Societies should take the title of Anti-Tamworth or Anti-Peel Associations; and the Anti-Corn-Law League, by its interference with constituencies with which it had no concern, only prolonged a contest which was one merely of time. He condemned all these associations as mischievous; but, acting on principle, he should vote as hitherto, with Mr. Villiers, and in repudiation of the sliding scale.

"Mr. Gladstone said it would be his duty to meet the motion of Mr. Villiers with a direct negative; and he hoped, therefore, that Mr. Ferrand would not place his amendment in the way of a direct 'ay' or 'no,' on a subject of so much importance as the Corn Laws. He was not an advocate of extreme protection, but confidence in the stability of a law was essential to the complete working of a measure which, so far as it had been tested by the experience of two peculiar and unusual years, had realized the most sanguine expectations. In 1842 they had spent eighteen nights in fair hard discussion on the Corn Laws; they could not renew it every year; and he claimed something like stability for the decision of parliament. Sir Robert Peel was accused of having promised a particular price to the farmer for his grain. He had done no such thing, he had merely indicated that it would be desirable, if it were possible, to keep the price between 54s. and 58s.; and in the three seasons from 1842 to 1844 these limits were not exceeded, and the minimum, during the last year, had not been reached. Even Mr. Villiers was obliged to confess that, under this Corn Law, a foreign trade was maintained, not so extensive or so steady as he might desire, but sufficiently so for the supporters of the measure, which, in addition to its other merits, had realized a revenue, during the present year, of so much as 17s. the quarter. The existing law had obviated the objections which applied to its predecessor. The motion was directed, not so much against it as against the whole protective system sanctioned by the policy of the country; and there was, therefore, but one course for parliament to adopt, in putting a check to an agitation mischievous in its effects, by creating an impression of the instability of a law which ought to be considered as a settlement of the question.

"Lord John Russell found himself, like Sir Robert Peel a few evenings ago, in 'no very enviable position.' He was not prepared, either to say that the Corn Laws should be at once abolished, or that the existing law should be maintained. There were inherent vices in the present system, which indicated its premature decay; and when Mr. Gladstone appealed to the two last years, he merely proved that the present government, instead of being wiser, had only enjoyed much better weather than their predecessors. Would the existing Corn Law stand two successive bad harvests? It violated the commercial principle; while a fixed duty—whatever might be its amount, six, eight, or ten shillings—enabled the merchant to make his calculations with certainty. But he apprehended that a sudden repeal of the Corn Laws would cause panic, affect the employment of capital in agriculture, and lead to a greater importation than was consistent either with the profits of the importing merchant, or the security of the home cultivator. The only portion of the proposition of the Anti-Corn-Law League which had the slightest claim to originality- was the *immediate* abolition; all their other arguments had been anticipated by the masters of the science, Adam Smith, Ricardo, or such statesmen as Mr. Huskisson or Lord Grenville, who, however, guarded their views by great caution as to the mode of arriving at their accomplishment. He regretted that he could take no part in the present motion, and heartily wished that some compromise could be effected which might have the effect of subduing agitation; if trade and commerce flourished, the landed interest need not be afraid of decay. The better way would be to revise the whole system of our protective duties, instead of dealing in perpetual harangues against the Corn Law, the maintenance of which was more desired by the farmers than by the landlords themselves. But he could see no end to agitation so long as the government were determined to maintain the existing law.

"Mr. Miles commiserated the position of Lord John Russell, thanked Mr. Gladstone for his straightforward honest speech, and called on the country gentlemen to listen to no compromise at all. The Anti-League was merely a defensive, the Anti-Corn-Law League an aggressive, association, whose interference, however, at elections had proved anything but a successful experiment. The working population were well aware that the object of the League was to cheapen bread in order to lower wages—a conclusion which none of their speeches, pamphlets, or papers attempted to meet; while the prices at which foreign grain can be imported showed that utter ruin awaited the farmer if free importation were immediately permitted. He adduced a statement, signed by three practical farmers, contradicting Lord Ducie's statement as to the expense of growing wheat on the Cotswold Hills, and denied, through the medium of figures, that the Corn Laws constituted a landlord's question."

Viscount Howick had long entertained a preference for the plan advocated by the noble member for London; but when it became a matter of necessity to choose between the existing system and a free trade, he did not hesitate to follow up his avowed principles, and to advocate a practical and immediate application of them, in preference to countenancing either actively or passively the present "*unreasonable and unwise*" state of the law. In a speech replete with sound principles, and confidence in their practical and immediate application, he gave the following warning to the House :—" He would ask the House to beware how they persevered in the present system. The honourable gentleman who had just sat down seemed to treat with some derision the notion that this was a question of rent in which the farmers and the labourers had no stake. He (Lord Howick) told him that it was a question of rent, and of nothing else. He (Lord Howick) could not do otherwise than wish well to the land, because all his interests were involved in it; but he said that, if those who were connected with the land looked well into the matter, they would see that even upon the narrow ground of self-interest they ought to put an end to restrictions. Let them look at the continued succession of disappointed hopes of agricultural prosperity which had mocked their expectations, and the repeated series of agricultural distress with which they had been afflicted. He was persuaded that their own interests required an alteration of those laws ; but, whatever might be their own interests, he was persuaded it was their solemn duty not to maintain them. We knew that by divine authority there was a malediction on those who withheld from the labourer his hire, and his persuasion was that the guilt was as great in the legislator who should maintain these laws as upon the private and individual extortioner, who deprived the labourer of his wages. In that guilt he, for one, would not take a share, and he called upon the House to beware how they lent themselves to it. All experience proved, that if justice were too long withheld, more than justice would be demanded, and he thought there were significant symptoms that we were now not far from that end. It was true the government was all-powerful in that House, and in the constituency by which that House was returned ; but he was a friend to the political institutions of the country, and should look with alarm at any sudden or violent disturbance of those institutions,

and he warned the House that their foundations were
sapped from the moment when the persuasion became
general that those in whose hands power was placed per-
verted that power to their own benefit, to the oppression
of the rest of the community."

On the conclusion of Lord Howick's speech, the debate
was adjourned, although there had been loud cries for a
division from those who felt that discussion was dangerous
to the cause of protection.

CHAPTER XII.

ADJOURNED DEBATE.

The debate in the Commons was resumed on Wednesday, by

"Mr. Stafford O'Brien, who read copious extracts from speeches, newspaper articles, pamphlets, &c., in order to give an historical view of the proceedings of the Anti-Corn-Law League, whose conduct and operations he ridiculed and condemned. Captain Layard amused the House by observations of Mr. Disraeli, and by relating his pleasure on having seen Sir Robert Peel relaxing himself at the Opera, witnessing the ballet of 'Ondine,' the 'shadow-dance' in which he compared to free-trade flitting before the mental vision of the premier. The motion of Mr. Villiers had his support. Colonel Rushbrooke spoke shortly on the condition of the agricultural peasantry of Suffolk, which was much better than had been represented, and to which the incendiary fires had been wrongly attributed. Lord Rendlesham reminded the House that there were two parties to the letting of a farm, and that the landlord, like the manufacturer, could only command the market price. In his part of the country—and he believed that it was general—three rents were calculated on: one for the landlord; a second for the farmer, to recompense his outlay of capital; and a third was appropriated to the labourer, being spent in the shape of wages. But repeal the Corn Laws, reduce the price of grain to the continental level, and the farmer would be unable to compete with his lighter-taxed foreign rival, while wages, regulated by the price of provisions, would fall. He hoped that Sir Robert Peel would boldly avow his determination to maintain that system of protection which this country had so long enjoyed."

Mr. Ward, after ridiculing the pretensions and the doings of the Pro-Corn-Law Association, answering some of the fallacies of the protectionists, characterising Lord

John Russell as standing with a dogged pertinacity, the
type, in that House, of a fixed duty which no one wanted,
and Sir Robert Peel as combining very good principles
with very bad practice, concluded by saying :—" I am
perfectly certain that, if at this moment there were, from
any overruling circumstances, a change of opinion in this
House ; if gentlemen were to say to their tenants, ' We
are prepared to meet you on fair terms ; you have not the
interest which you fancy you have in these laws; and we
are quite prepared to enter upon the question of leases
with you, with a view to an alteration ; we are quite prepared to provide against that confusion ; ' for I will not
mince the matter : I know there must be confusion for a
certain period (hear) ;—' we are quite willing to assist you
for two or three years after your protection is withdrawn,
and we will then let you hold your land on terms which
will be advantageous to all parties.' I venture to say that
there is not a tenant farmer in this country who would not
gladly close with his landlord on such terms. I say, then,
that the question being one in the settlement of which not
merely the landlords but the whole population of this
country have a direct interest, and one which has so close
a connexion with the discontent of large classes of the
community, it would be a much wiser, a much more
honourable, a much more straightforward, and a much
more profitable course for honourable gentlemen opposite
to look at this question manfully, instead of staving off the
evil hour, as they will do to-night, by a large majority of
votes, without convincing any human being that they have
one single argument in their justification." Sir John
Trollope vindicated the protection societies, and made a
short speech in defence of the Corn Laws.

Mr. Milner Gibson spoke indignantly of the insinuation
that the incendiarism in some of the agricultural districts
had been occasioned by anti-corn-law agitation. He said :
" I must say we have a right to ask the right honourable

gentleman the Home Secretary, that we should be allowed
to live in peace without danger of our property being burnt
or our lives endangered. I utterly repel those insinuations
which have been thrown out, I must say, in a manner unworthy of him, by the President of the Board of Trade,
that this incendiarism must be the result of agitation
against the Corn Laws. (Hear, hear.) Sir, I say that that
insinuation is unworthy of the right honourable gentleman.
(Hear, hear.) I defy him to produce the smallest atom of
proof that any incentive to crime has been thrown out in
those counties by any of the advocates of freedom of trade.
I should think it unworthy of myself if I had attributed to
the society for maintaining a scarcity any such effect (hear,
hear), although that society has agitated those counties far
more than the Anti-Corn-Law League. (Hear, hear.) For
one placard which the Anti-Corn-Law League has stuck on
the gable ends of houses, the society for maintaining a
high price of corn has circulated, I venture to say, six or
even ten ; but at the same time, although you have been
agitating the country—although you have been telling the
labourers and the farmers that the interest of the community depends on the high price of corn—I should be
ashamed of myself if I could insinuate for one moment
that its members had incited any person to set fire to
property, with a view of promoting their own ends. It
might, indeed, be said that the agitation of the Pro-Corn-
Law League Society had induced persons to destroy corn,
with a view of promoting their own interest; because your
doctrine is, that the less corn there is in the country the
more the labourer will get; that the less the whole the
greater the parts. That is the doctrine which we have
heard explained by the noble lord the member for East
Suffolk, because he says the dearer corn is, and the less
there is of it in the country, the more the labourer will get
for his share." After a speech which showed that he had
a thorough grasp of the subject both in its commercial

and political aspects, he asked :—" What does the Duke
of Wellington, who does not say what he does not mean,
assert to be the object of the Corn Laws? The maintenance of the landed aristocracy in their present social
position in this country. The right honourable gentleman
the Paymaster of the Forces made a similar declaration not
long ago. (Hear, hear.) When the right honourable baronet
(Sir R. Peel) comes down to the House, and reads tables
of corn imported, and manufactured goods exported, I
assert that it savours of the same spirit. It seems to say,
' You have so much trade; are you not satisfied? See
what we have permitted you to have in reward for your
exertions and industry.' The real question is as to the
amount of trade which these laws have prevented; not
what the manufacturers now enjoy, but what they might
enjoy under a free trade. (Hear, hear.) Then the noble
lord the member for North Lancashire got up a scene
yesterday evening, about a petition from the landowners,
manufacturers, and farmers of North Lancashire, with
16,000 signatures :"

" Lord Stanley : No, no.

" Mr. Gibson : Were they farmers or manufacturers ?

" Lord Stanley : There were half the manufacturers of Preston and
Blackburn.

" Mr. Gibson : There might be; but I want to know what proportion
of the whole 16,000 were manufacturers. I very much doubt, if these
persons had known that the petition was for the maintenance of the
graduated scale, whether they would have signed the petition. If the
noble lord was so confident that protection would benefit the manufacturers, I wish the noble lord, as member for North Lancashire, would
rise in his place, and say that he was convinced he conferred a great
benefit on his constituents by supporting the right honourable baronet's Corn Law. Will the noble lord undertake to rise in his place,
and say that that was his conscientious belief?

" Lord Stanley : Yes, I say so.

" Mr. Gibson : Upon the manufacturers?

" Lord Stanley : I represent agriculturists and manufacturers, and I
believe I am conferring a benefit on the manufacturers by doing so.

" Mr. Gibson : I hope the noble lord does not suppose that they will
be contented with that explanation. (' Hear, hear,' from the Opposition.)
I should like to hear from the noble lord the grounds on which he
thought so. (Cheers and laughter.) Honourable members may laugh
if they please, but the noble lord did state the grounds once. Why ?
That they might be enabled to keep grooms and gardeners. (Cheers.)
Considering the position held by the noble lord in this house, we have
heard very little from him as to the effect of the Corn Law upon the
trading and manufacturing interest. It is true that he did once frighten
the agriculturists by his description of Tamboff ; but he has never
satisfied the manufacturers that the keeping out of corn is for their
benefit. I think some are treating this question in a way which amounts
to little short of insult. When gentlemen get up, they do not speak to
the question. (Hear, hear.) Honourable gentlemen on the ministerial
side are responsible in this matter, for they can alter the law, whilst
the opposition cannot. The right honourable baronet is their leader,
because they cannot form an administration out of the Central Society
for the Protection of Agriculture. (A laugh, and a voice, .' Can you
form one out of the League.') The right hon. baronet is nearer to
the League than he is to the Central Society for the Protection of
Agriculture, for he has acknowledged the principles of the former to be
right in the abstract, and has professed his belief that they must
eventually prevail. The right honourable baronet is responsible for
the Corn Law ; he imposed it, and he ought to give a distinct explanation of the benefit which it has conferred upon my constituents.
The right honourable baronet cannot legislate for a portion only of the
community. (Cheers.)

" Mr. Bankes dwelt upon the opposite side of the question, denying
that the agricultural labourers of Dorsetshire were so badly off as they
had been described, and somewhat discursively supporting the protective system.

" Mr. Hutt would support the motion of Mr. Villiers, though preferring
a moderate fixed duty to total repeal."

Mr. Cobden followed, having been loudly called for.
He ridiculed the notion of protecting " native industry," as
whatever advance of price was obtained by the producer
was a tax upon the consumer ; telling the House that they
were losing sight of the community at large who were
neither manufacturers nor farmers. He also exposed the
absurdity of protection on the ground that the protected
might be enabled to pay their taxes, and showed that

revenue rose as the price of corn fell. "It is," said he,
"a very remarkable fact that the price of corn is just a
barometer of the state of your taxation; that your revenue
declines just as your corn rises in price; and the revenue
flows over just as the value of corn falls: so much so, that
it is a perfect barometer as to the state of the revenue.
Now, I will take the first four years, from 1815 to 1820,
during which period the average price of wheat was 81s. 4d.,
and the farmers and landlords were glorying in scarcity
and high prices. What was the effect upon the revenue at
that time? Why, there was an annual taxation of £2,400,000
additional, imposed upon the country for the necessities of
the state. The next four years the average price of wheat
was 54s. 6d., being more than 25s. a quarter less than in
the previous period; then came 'unparalleled agricultural
distress;' and yet you had taxes repealed during those
four years to the amount of £8,100,000. I come to the
next period of an exceedingly low price of corn, and that
was in 1833, 1834, 1835, and 1836, when the average price
for those years was 46s. 9d.; lower than it had been for
forty years. Taxes were repealed during those four years to
the amount of 4,500,000 per annum. I now come to the
late period of dear years, from 1838 to 1842, during which
five years the average price of wheat was 64s. 7d. a quarter,
being higher than it had been for twenty years previous.
During that five years you had, first of all, 5 per cent. additional imposed on your general taxes, and 10 per cent.
on your assessed taxes that fell short; and then you had
an income-tax, a tax on coal, and other taxes; and the
whole amount of additional taxation then laid upon the
shoulders of the people of this country during the above
five years was £8,000,000 sterling per annum. Thus the
revenue of this country—at a time when the rent was
rising, when the landowners were laying on extra rents,
and when, if we may believe you, farmers were in a state
of prosperity—was in a state of depression. Now, during

the last year, and up to the present time, when the price
of corn has been rather lower, we have again had a season
of the remission of taxation ; and if prices continue low,
we may possibly get rid of the income tax, and have as
good a revenue as before.   I want to ask the right hon.
baronet, who, I presume, will favour the house with his
opinion on this question, where is the difficulty in carrying out the principle of Free Trade in everything?   I
wish to state most honestly and emphatically that I stand
here as an advocate for *Free Trade in everything;* and if
you will go into committee on the subject of corn, and the
rules of the house will permit me to add the repeal of the
duties upon every other article that is protected, I will
undertake to move its insertion."   Mr. Cobden, adverting
to protective duties, said that the whole amount of duty on
foreign manufactures imported did not exceed £300,000,
and that such protection the home manufacturers did not
ask for and would rather be without; and after referring
to Mr. Deacon Hume's evidence before the Import Duties
Committee as to the injury done to the revenue by protecting duties, he concluded an able speech by saying :—

"Now, sir, on the authority of Mr. Deacon Hume, and on the facts
which I have stated, I take my stand against all protection.   If you
cannot make the advantage equal, it is unjust to some portion of the
community; and if it is thus oppressive to any portion of the people,
that portion never ought, if they have the spirit of Englishmen, to submit quietly to such an injustice.   If you can make the system general,
then general protection cannot be special protection, and you can do no
good to anybody by its adoption.   Abandon this system—it is unsound;
it cannot be defended upon any principle of justice or sound policy;
and therefore I ask you now to give your decision against the principle.
You may say, 'We are strong in power, we have the constituencies with
us.'   Yes, you have the constituencies.   (Cheers from the ministerial
benches.)   How long will you stand on that pinnacle of power if the
foundation of the pedestal on which you are resting gives way?   You
must show that you have a just footing before you can hope to maintain
your present law.   I have never heard one expression—I have never
heard the question urged by honourable gentlemen upon any side of

the house—how this system benefits the farmer or farm-labourer; nor
have they attempted to show how it can benefit the other classes of the
community. You stand up and say, 'I do this for the benefit of the
farmer and farm-labourer;' but my honourable friend the member for
Wolverhampton did not ask you to say whether you would support the
Corn Law for that purpose or not; but he requested you to come here
and show *how you have* benefited them. Have you done that? Have
you proved the benefit which you confer upon them? No! Immediately
you rise you begin talking in the future tense, as you do in all your
arguments; you tell us what you imagine the opposite system *would*
do to injure the farmer and farm-labourer; but you have never attempted to show how the present system can possibly benefit them.
My honourable friend the member for Wolverhampton has brought
this matter fairly before the house. This is not a motion sanctioned
by the leading benches on this side of the house, I admit (' Hear, hear,'
from the ministerial benches); but it is the sole question of controversy
out of doors—there the point to be determined is entirely between protection and no protection—and when the honourable gentleman on this
side of the house, who has so large an amount of public confidence as
my honourable friend the member for Wolverhampton has (Loud cries
of 'Oh, oh,' and laughter, from the ministerial benches, met by counter
cheers from the opposition), brings forward a motion against protection,
I say the government is not treating him with due respect, nor the
public with justice, unless they meet the arguments which he has
brought forward on this occasion. The right honourable gentleman the
President of the Board of Trade has told us that he will not argue this
question, because protection is a principle which is recognised by this
country; we come here to deny the justice of that principle, we call on
you to justify that principle of protection. Is it not sophistry—I can
call it no less—to meet us by saying, 'The principle is admitted, and,
therefore, we will not answer your arguments unless you give some
special ground against this mode of taxing corn?' *We take exception
to the principle itself*, and I ask the right honourable baronet to meet the
arguments of my honourable friend by showing how this principle of
protection can be beneficial to the country at large. Gentlemen upon
the treasury bench have shown a disposition to evade this question.
There is, for instance, the noble lord the member for North Lancashire;
nobody can deny but that he possesses talent for debate. He came up
to this house pledged to defend the Corn Law, and he has never yet
opened his mouth upon the subject. I challenge him to give us his
opinion on this point—I defy him to justify this law to the manufacturers
of Preston and Blackburn, not to the minority, whom he says have pe-
titioned this house, but to the majority who are opposed to this system.

I ask him to show on public grounds the justice of this law. I do not ask him to do that which he is so competent to do as a mere slashing debater—to engage in personal skirmishes in this House —but I demand of him to show on public grounds the justice and policy of this system of protection. If he and the right honourable baronet, or either of them, will rise in this House to defend this system, then it will go forth to the country, and the people of England will see whether the arguments of my honourable friend the member for Wolverhampton are sound and supported by reason and facts, or whether those principles on which you are going to vote on the other side are so founded. But I appeal to you on this occasion not to go to a division until you have given us some argument to show the justice and soundness of the views you profess to entertain."

Sir Robert Peel commenced his speech with a bad joke :

" Sir Robert Peel said they had been engaged that night for the benefit of the company which usually performed at Covent Garden Theatre. During the greater portion of the performance, the front rank of the Opposition benches had been deserted, their usual occupants absent, perhaps, from a lively recollection of the assistance given by the members of the Anti-Corn-Law League the other night ' at my benefit.' Mr. Cobden complained of the habit of calling names—a bad practice, but one of which the Anti-Corn-Law League had set a prominent example, and, by attributing selfish motives to honourable men, had raised up that feeling of indignation which had greatly diminished their own power and influence. The moderate tone adopted in the present discussion was an indication that they felt the recoil of the weapons they had abused. The agriculture of this country was entitled to protection from reasons both of justice and policy ; there were peculiar and special burdens borne by the agriculturists; and there were not ten reflecting men out of the Anti-Corn-Law League who did not believe that a sudden withdrawal of protection, whether it were given to domestic or colonial produce, would cause great confusion and embarrassment. In the artificial state of society in which we lived, we could not act on mere abstract, philosophical maxims, which, isolated, he could not contest ; they must look to the circumstances under which we have grown up, and the interests involved. Ireland dependent on England for a market for her agricultural produce was a case in point. He was not prepared to alter the Corn Law of 1842, and did not contemplate it. Seeing that Lord John Russell had avowed himself a consistent friend to protection, and was opposed to total repeal, he thought he was somewhat squeamish in flying from his difficulty and declining to vote against the motion.

The noble lord, however, in arguing for a fixed duty, had adduced a powerful reason for a graduated scale, when he expressed his fears that a total repeal would lead to a glut without cheapness, and ruin to the agriculturist without advantage to the community. Adverting to the alleged promise of a price from 54s. to 58s., as the result of the Corn Law of 1842, he read the passage of his speech, to show that it bore no such construction. They were taunted with their 'predictions;' but Mr. Cobden and his friends had uttered predictions of impending ruin to trade and commerce, which no modification of the sliding scale could avert or protract. Yet, since the passing of the law of 1842, there had been a great increase and improvement in all the leading branches of our manufacturing industry. Lord Howick affirmed the right of the working man to expect ' a fair day's wages for a fair day's work,' from the legislature—a benefit which no legislature can secure, and no state of society—as witness the United States—could permanently afford. He therefore deprecated the holding out expectations which could not be realised, and the disappointment of which might lead to dangerous results. As to the Corn Law, the Government did not intend to alter it, or diminish the amount of protection afforded to agriculture."

Mr. Bright followed Sir Robert Peel, in a very telling speech :—

" Mr. Bright said :—I would not willingly occupy any of the time of the House at this late hour, did I not feel that my duty requires me to make some observations on the important question before the House, and especially after the speech which the right honourable baronet has just delivered. It is generally advantageous to have a speech from the right honourable baronet on this question; he narrows the ground upon which he is willing to defend the Corn Law. Three years ago, at the celebrated Tamworth dinner, the plea of special burdens was used as making it needful to give a higher protection than 8s. per quarter to agriculture. The special burdens were not pointed out. We could not get at them; but now the right honourable gentleman has summed them up in the imposition of the rate for the relief of the poor. (No, no.) I have no wish to misrepresent the right honourable gentleman, but this I understood him to say. Now, the noble lord the Secretary for the Colonies comes from a county where the landed interest are not quite so all-powerful as in some other counties—where there is other property than that which consists in acres—and he might have informed his honourable colleague that in that county there are poor's rates to pay as well as in the counties where agriculture is the chief pursuit. The manfacturer who has a mill pays the poor's rate on the building, steam-engine, and on everything which is considered by law to appertain to the freehold; but he does not pay the rate on his machinery, on his raw material or manufactured article, nor on his floating capital. How is the farmer served? Is he more hardly used? He pays on his farm and farm buildings so much in the pound on the amount of his rent, but he does not pay on his ploughs and harrows, on his stacks or growing crops, or on the money he may have in the bank to pay his rent. (Hear, hear.) Where, then, is the difference in the two cases? Is there any distinction which gives the farmer a claim upon the public to pay his poor's rate from an extra charge upon his wheat? Has not the manufacturer just as good a right to come to this House for a law to enable him to pay his poor's rate as the farmer has? (Cheers.) But how does the right honourable gentleman make it out that the poor's rate is a burden on the farmer? If the poor's rate were off altogether the simple result would be that the rent would be so much the higher. If the right honourable baronet will cross the Tweed, and ask the first farmer he meets why he can afford to pay so much higher rent than the farmer south of the river, he will be told that, as the Scotch farmer pays almost no poor's rate and no tithes, an amount equal to those imposts is added to the rent. (Cheers.) Some forty years ago the late Lord Eldon said that remission of taxes was of no use to the farmers; for, whilst great competition existed for farms, the amount remitted must of necessity be swallowed up in rent. (Cheers.) The right hon. baronet had also spoken of the capital invested in the soil; if he mean the value that is on the land, I cannot understand how the fact of a man's possessing property in land can give him any claim to an extra price for the produce of the land at the expense of the community. (Hear, hear.) If it is meant that the farmers have invested great capital in the soil, why, is it not the constant complaint that agriculture suffers more than all from a want of capital? and is it not evident that, under this protection of the Corn Law, capital may be said positively to shun the soil? (Hear.) The right honourable baronet has spoken of the predictions of my honourable friend, the member for Stockport. That honourable gentleman is precisely the man of all others who has avoided hazarding predictions. He said, and every one who thoroughly understands the Corn Law said, that this country never could rise from the depression which so lately existed, except through the repeal of the Corn Law, or that, through the bounty of Providence, we were again to be favoured with good harvests. The right honourable baronet owes his safety, as does the country, to the change in the seasons. What was the condition of the right honourable baronet some two years ago? How did he bear the weight of the responsibility of his office then? Was not his mind almost pressed down by the difficulties which surrounded him? and were not all the power and all the honours of his high office but a poor compensation for the cares which then pressed upon him? The condition of the country was such as to excite the liveliest apprehensions; and I am sure there is not a man in this kingdom more thankful for the change of seasons than is the right hon. baronet. It is said we have found no fault with the present law. Is there a feature about the old law which is not discoverable in this? And when the same circumstances come round, the same results will assuredly be produced. (Cheers.) During fair weather the Corn Law is partially in operation; its hideous features are to a great extent disguised; but good harvests will not always be granted us; and, when the unfortunate seasons come round again, then again will come disaster and distress. Must we wait for justice till events compel you to grant it? (Cheers.) Why not abolish restriction now, whilst we have a respite? (Cheers.) You may shuffle and evade the question, you may use sophistry, you may deny our facts and disregard our arguments, but this you will never disprove, that this Corn Law which you cherish is a law to make a scarcity of food in this country, that your own rents may be increased. The noble lord the member for North Lancashire himself acknowledged that the Corn Law raised prices and raised rents, and did not raise wages. It leaves all other classes to bear the effects of the fiercest competition, whilst it shelters the landlords altogether from competition. (Cheers.) I am convinced that, whatever may be the feelings of confidence now entertained by the right hon. baronet, whenever bad harvests again occur, he will either abolish this law or his Government will be overthrown, as was the Government he succeeded by the bad harvests we have lately suffered from. I do not wish this law to be repealed in times of excitement, nor do I wish its destruction to be achieved as a great party victory; I would rather it were for ever abolished by the unanimous verdict of the honest and intelligent classes of the country. We should regard it as a question of great national interest, not as one affecting our own profits or property; we should legislate upon it in such a manner that, laying our hands upon our hearts, we may say that we have dealt with it on great and just principles, with an honest regard to the common good, and not merely with regard to the claims of a particular interest." (Loud cheers.)

Colonel Sibthorpe followed in his usual style, after which Mr. Villiers briefly replied. On division the numbers were :—

$$
\begin{array}{lr}
\text{For the motion} \dots \quad \dots \quad \dots \quad \dots & 124 \\
\text{Against it} \quad \dots \quad \dots \quad \dots \quad \dots \quad \dots & 330 \\
\hline
\text{Majority against the motion} \quad \dots & 206
\end{array}
$$

The following is a list of the members who voted in the minority:—

Aglionby, Henry A.
Aldam, William
Amstrong, Sir Andrew
Bannerman, Alexander
Barclay, David
Barnard, Edward George
Berkeley, Hon. Capt. (Glo'st. C.)
Berkeley, Hon. Hy. F. (Bristol)
Bernal, Captain (Wycombe)
Blake, Mark (Mayo Co.)
Bouverie, Hon. Edw. Pleydell
Bowring Dr.
Bright, John
Brotherton, Joseph
Browne, R. Dillon (Mayo Co.)
Buller, Edward (Staffordshire)
Busfeild, William
Byng, Rt. Hon. George Stevens
Chapman, Benjamin (W. M'th.)
Childers, John Walbanke
Clay, Sir William
Clive Edward Bolton (Hereford.)
Cobden, Richard
Colebrooke, Sir Thomas Edward
Collett, John (Athlone)
Collins, William
Craig, William Gibson
Dalmeny, Lord
Dashwood, George H.
Dennistoun, John
D'Eyncourt, Rt. Hon. C. T.
Duncan, Viscount
Duncan, George
Duncannon, Viscount
Duncombe, Thomas (Finsbury)
Dundas, Frederick (Orkney)
Dundas, David (Sutherlandshire)
Dundas, Hon. J. C. (Richmond)
Easthorpe, Sir John
Ellice, Right Hon. Ed. (Coventry)

Ellis, Wynn (Leicester)
Elphinstone, Howard
Ewart, William
Fielden, John (Oldham)
Ferguson, Colonel (Kirkaldy)
Fitzroy, Lord Charles
Fitzwilliam, Hon. G. (Wentworth)
Forster, Matthew
Gisborne, Thomas
Granger, Thomas Colpitts
Grey, Right Hon. Sir George
Grosvenor, Lord Robert
Guest, Sir John
Hall, Sir Benjamin
Hastie, Archibald
Hawes, Benjamin
Hayter, William G.
Hindley, Charles
Hollond, Robert
Horsman, Edward
Howick, Viscount
Humphery, Mr. Alderamn
Hutt, William
Johnson, General (Oldham)
Langston, James Haughton
Layard, Captain
Leader, John Temple
Leveson, Lord
Macaulay, Right Hon. Thomas B.
Marjoribanks, Stewart
Marshall, William
Marsland, Henry
Mitchell, Thomas Alexander
Morison, General (Clackman)
Muntz, George Frederick
Murphy, Francis Stack
Napier, Sir Charles
O'Connell, Maurice (Tralee)
O'Connell, M.J. (Kerry)
Ord, William

Paget, Lord Alfred (Lichfield)
Parker, John
Pattison, James
Pechell, Captain
Philips, George R. (Poole)
Philips, Mark (Manchester)
Plumridge, Captain
Ponsonby, Honourable C.F.A.C.
Protheroe, Edward
Pulsford, Edward
Ramsbottom, John
Rawdon, Colonel
Ricardo, John Lewis
Roebuck, John Arthur
Ross, David Robert
Russell, Lord Edward (Tavistock)
Rutherfurd, Andrew
Scrope, George Poulett
Shelburne, Earl of
Smith, Benjamin (Norwich)
Smith, John Abel (Chichester)
Standish, Charles

Stansfield, W. R. Crompton
Stanton, William Henry
Stuart, Lord James (Ayr)
Stuart, W. Villiers (Waterford C.)
Strickland, Sir George
Strutt, Edward
Tancred, Henry William
Thornely, Thomas
Towneley, John
Trelawny, John Salusbury
Troubridge, Sir Edward Thomas
Tufnell, Henry
Wakley, Thomas
Walker, Richard
Wallace, Robert
Warburton, Henry
Ward, Henry George
Wawn, John Twizell
Williams, William (Coventry).
Wood, Charles (Halifax)
Wrightson, William Battie
Yorke, Henry Redhead (York)

Tellers—Mr. Villiers and Mr. Milner Gibson.

The progress made was marked rather by the decrease of the majority than by the increase of the minority. In 1842, when Mr. Villiers first put the question of total repeal on issue before the House, he had 92 votes, and 395 against him. In 1843, he had 125 votes, and 381 against him. In 1844, he had 124 votes, and 330 against him. He was out-voted in 1842, by 303; in 1843, by 256; and in 1844, by 206. There had not been many converts between the motion of 1843 and 1844; but there were many ashamed of a contest where there was scarcely a shred of argument on the numerically strongest side, and they staid away. A reduction of that numerical strength from 395 to 330, and the increase of the opponent force from 92 to 124, was something hopeful in a Peel-parliament, strongly pledged, and elected on that pledge, to support the Corn Laws without mitigation. Fifty votes from the protec-

tionist side, and fifty added to the side of free traders,
would not, in another session, give a numerical majority,
but would indicate such certainty of the triumph of free-
trade principles as would induce the majority to yield
before it became a minority. How was that change to be
effected, and when? A leaf must be taken from the
enemy's book. The battle, as Peel had said when the
tories recovered from the panic into which they were
thrown by the reform bill—" the battle must be fought in
the registration courts "—and the League directed its
energies in that course, confident that, if it were not possible to obtain repeal under a Peel-parliament, the triumph
would come at the next general election, come when that
might.

It was not expected that before the prorogation of parliament there would be any further discussion ; but on
Friday, August 9th, Lord John Russell raised a debate on
the condition of the country in which that question had its
share of notice. His lordship said :—

" There is another topic upon which I wish to say a few words, because I think it must force itself upon our attention in some shape or
other before a very long period elapses—I mean the condition of the
people of England. (Hear, hear, hear.) You cannot help, from day
to day, and from time to time, observing the state of the people of this
country—the inadequate means which the labouring people have to
supply their families with the comforts of life (hear, hear, hear) with
the extreme labour which, in the manufacturing districts, is undergone,
and with the discontent which, both in our agricultural counties and in
our manufacturing districts, is at short intervals excited ; and I think,
if we take a general view of this subject, *it is impossible not to see
whether it be the fault of our legislature or not, that the labouring classes
have not advanced in comfort and welfare in proportion to the other orders
of the community.* If we compare the condition of this country with
what it was a century ago—with what it was in 1740, for instance—it is
impossible not to see that while the higher classes have advanced in
luxury beyond measure—while the means available for the diffusion of
comfort and the enjoyment of life have prodigiously increased—that, if
we look again at the middle classes and their means of procuring comfort, of travelling from one place to another, the quickness with which

intelligence is conveyed, and the increase in the consumption of foreign articles of luxury—these classes have made a very great advance. *If we look to the labouring classes—if we look to the men who either till the soil or labour in the factories—if we look to the quantity of necessaries which their wages would buy in the middle of the last century, and that which they can buy now—if we go into the details with which I shall not now trouble the house, but which have been exhibited in the reports of the commissioners sent forth—some by the late government, and some by the present—I think we must be convinced that they have not participated in an equal degree in the advantages which civilisation and improved knowledge have conferred upon us.* (Hear, hear.)"

His lordship said he thought it would be necessary to revise the whole subject of the import duties, to ascertain their amount on articles of food and general consumption, and to see how small an amount of duty should be paid upon them ; but he took care to assure the agriculturists that he did not propose to deprive them of protection. He still adhered to his fixed-duty, desperately, for the question elsewhere had become one of total repeal or the continuance of the existing law. He said :—" In regard to what is due to the mitigation of burdens imposed upon the consumers of this country, I think we should likewise consider what is due to the agricultural interest of this country. I think you should consider, with respect to many subjects, whether that unequal taxation, which now presses upon us, cannot be remedied. I remember, at the commencement of the session, that some expressions I used on this subject were misunderstood by some members of the house, when I declared that I thought it would not be wise at once to abolish all laws restricting the importation of corn, without taking into consideration the increase of duties and taxes to which the producers of corn had been subjected since the commencement of the present century. I will mention but two of them. One, the very great increase in the *county rates* since the beginning of the war of 1793—another, the very large augmentation of the *malt tax*. It appears to me that now, when the government have the leisure of the recess before them, they might very well consider whether some relief might not be given to the agricultural interest—(hear, hear)—and whether, in giving that relief, they might not frame measures more in accordance with those principles of trade which the present government, as well as the late, uphold."

Mr. Villiers protested strongly against the assumption that there were any peculiar burthens upon land :—

" He had not risen to enter upon a discussion of these topics, or refer generally to those matters which had been touched upon by the leaders of the two great parties, and on which they appeared to differ, but only to refer to that point on which they seemed to agree, but on which he did so entirely differ, that he never would hear what had fallen from them without rising to express his utter and unqualified dissent. He referred to the assertion that had been made to-night, that agriculture bore any peculiar burdens, and afforded thereby an excuse for monopoly. (Hear, hear,) He did not hesitate to say, that this was not borne out by the fact; he gave it an unqualified denial, and in the most confident way in which he could. He defied those who asserted it to prove it. (Hear, hear.) Inquiry into this point had time after time been demanded by this house, and had been refused; and it literally stood before the country now as a bare assertion, unsupported by evidence, for which proof was refused, and used only as a pretext for the continuance of the Corn Law. (Hear, hear, hear.) He repeated, as he had done so often before, that there was not one single charge that could be termed peculiar or exclusive on the land. (Hear, hear.) Whatever local taxes were imposed were borne by property other than land in its due proportion, in some parishes and in some counties the property other than land bearing a much larger share than the land itself. (Hear, hear.) His noble friend had alluded to those that he thought were the most severe, and they were the county rate and the malt tax (hear, hear), and these had been assented to by the right honourable baronet. Now, he really wondered how they could keep their countenance in urging such an argument. (A laugh.) The county rate an excuse for the Corn Laws! Look at its amount, in the first place, compared with what the Corn Laws cost. (Hear.) Look to the property liable to it in the next, the owners of which suffered as much from the Corn Law as any other individual; and look again to the fact that, within a very few years, a very considerable portion of that which used to exist before the Corn Laws were passed has since been placed on the Consolidated Fund. (Hear hear.) Can this be gravely believed to be

an excuse for limiting the supply of food to the whole community?
(Hear, hear.)   Then, again, the malt tax, which is a tax on the beer of
the community, and which, if it injures the agriculturists at all, is, of
course, by first injuring the consumer, by limiting his power of consumption. (Hear, hear.) And after this injury being inflicted upon him,
he is to be told that on this account he is to be visited by another tax
on his bread (hear, hear) ; and because by his poverty he cannot consume beer enough to suit the landlord, therefore he is to be taxed for
his bread for the benefit of this seller of corn. (' Hear, hear,' and
laughter.)   That, certainly, is very just and rational, and these are the
grounds for continuing the Corn Law. (Hear, hear.)"

A faint attempt was made by Mr. Cochrane to link the
poor-rates to the list of burdens named by Lord John
Russell, but which was instantly answered by a few words
from Mr. Villiers :—

" Mr. Cochrane: The poor-rate?
" Mr. Villiers: The poor-rate? Why, really, he thought that this
notion had been abandoned, by its not having been mentioned with the
others that night, and because it was too silly to talk of. (Hear, hear.)
What ! make food scarce, make employment difficult, reduce the working
man to pauperism, and then complain of the cost of relieving him—
(hear, hear)—and call this self-inflicted burden a peculiar charge for
which you are to have indemnity. Very just, very consistent indeed.
(Cheers.) No, sir, those things can hardly be said earnestly ; they
will certainly not be treated so out of doors. (Hear, hear.) He was
glad, however, that they were mentioned at the close of the session,
when so many persons were giving thought to the subject, for they
would doubtless be well sifted and considered during the recess, and
they should be fully prepared for discussion next session. (Hear, hear.)
He was obliged to the noble lord for having raised the question upon
this occasion."

CHAPTER XIII.

INCENDIARISM.

In the mean time, the farm labourers, for whose benefit, and that of the farmers, legislative protection had been so long continued, were ungratefully burning the ricks of their employers. "There are now," says *The League*, of July 6th, 1844, "tens of thousands of men working for 7s., 6s., and 5s. a week, and from whose miserable pittances deductions are made whenever the weather or the farmers' arrangements may render their services for a day or a half day of little use. This fact is clearly established. Such a state of things is proved to exist in the east of England by the evidence of the *Times* reporter, and the reports of other newspapers, by the admissions of the landowners, the magistrates, and the residents of that side of our island; in the west of England the labourers themselves have assembled in public meetings, and in simple and pathetic language have proclaimed the existence of the same evils there. This is enough to account for incendiarism, or any other of the dreadful crimes ignorant men commit when they are rendered criminal by the extremity of suffering and despair. We stop not now to inquire whether the particular way in which legal charity is afforded under the actual poor law be an immediate cause of some, or all, or any of the incendiary fires in Suffolk and Norfolk, as the *Times* asserts and the *Chronicle* denies; but we know that the condition of the great mass of the farm-labourers is so

destitute, and apparently so utterly hopeless, that we seek
for no secondary or subsidiary cause.   And what aggravates
this evil is the fact, that all this misery—this, for the
present, hopeless misery—is the gratuitous infliction of our
dominant landed aristocracy."

A League meeting was held in Covent Garden Theatre,
July 3rd, the assembly being numerous to overflowing.
Mr. G. Wilson occupied the chair, and the Hon. Mr. Villiers,
Mr. Cobden, and Mr. Bright were the speakers.   Mr. Villiers
narrated the history of opposition to monopoly for the last
fifteen years, and, arguing from past progress, anticipated
final success.   Mr. Cobden addressed himself particularly
to the question of how far the farmers were with the
League:—" He was not so jealous of any of these arguments as he was of one employed in the House of Lords
by the Duke of Richmond.   That noble duke was always
repeating that the tenant farmers of this country had risen
as one man against the League.   *   *   Why did these
lords and dukes keep continually repeating that the farmers
were with them ?   Their conduct must have arisen from
doubts as to whether the farmers really were beguiled
and hoodwinked by the professions of attachment of the
landowners.   But when they affirmed that the farmers
spontaneously got up the Anti-League associations, he told
them that what they said was not the truth ; and they knew
that it was not the truth.   He would prove his assertion by
facts.   Take the meeting at Steyning, in Sussex.   It was
got up by the aristocracy and squirarchy, and if they did not
go round and entreat and canvass the farmers to attend,
their land agents and law agents did so ; and the tenant
farmers were urged, and pressed, and canvassed, with the
same diligence as was manifested at a general election.   Nay,
more ; carriages, horses, vehicles of all kinds, even the
deer carts were put at the disposal of the farmers, to carry
them to Steyning.   And what he said of the Sussex meeting
equally applied to any other meeting purporting to be the

spontaneous work of the tenant farmers. What he was
telling them was known to the whole community. There
was not a man from the counties, where these meetings
were got up, who would not corroborate what he was stating.
The land agent had the finger of the landlord. He had but
to point it, and the farmer did the bidding, knowing that
it was the bidding of the landlord at second-hand. *   *
He was jealous of their taking the tenant farmers' name in
vain. The League was told that its members had been
abusive to the farmers, and therefore that the farmers had
turned against them. Now, if there was a champion who
had more consistently than another stood up for the
farmers' rights and interests, he was that man. *   *   *
If he was a farmers' enemy, he had not been afraid to
trust himself amongst the farmers. But the landlords
would not meet him there. He had often asked them to
choose what county they liked to call a public meeting, and
to take the vote of the farmers for or against the Corn
Laws. But no! they never would consent, because they
knew that they would be outvoted if they did." Mr. Cobden enlarged on the fact that the Corn Laws were injurious to the farmers and all classes alike. He excepted the
clergy. "If there was a class which did benefit by the
Corn Law, it was the clergy. The Tithe Commutation
Act fixed their income at a certain number of quarters of
corn per annum. If a clergyman got 200 quarters of corn
for tithe, and the price was 40s., he received four hundred
pounds; and if the price was 50s., he received five hundred
pounds per annum. Was that a right position for the
clergy to be placed in? That they who prayed for plenty
should have an interest in the maintenance of scarcity?
He put it to the clergy whether, with this one fact glaring
forth to the world, they could, in consistency with their
own character, be seen going about to Anti-League meetings declaring for the maintenance of the Corn Law? They
would not be fit to sit as jurors upon the Corn Law; they

would be challenged as interested parties. All he asked
of the clergy was to maintain a strictly neutral position."
In conclusion, he announced the determination of the
League to persevere in their present course, unconnected
with party; and by attention to the registries for two years,
they relied with confidence on success. Mr. Bright followed in a long and able address; after which, the chairman
announced that the League would not meet again until
Wednesday, the 7th of August, which would be the last
night of their re-assembling for the present season. Before
breaking up, he called on them to give three cheers for
Mr. Villiers, Mr. Cobden, Lord Ducie, Lord Howick, and
the other noblemen and gentlemen who had taken part in
their proceedings. The call was loudly responded to.

   The last metropolitan meeting of the Anti-Corn-Law
League, for the season, was held in Covent Garden Theatre,
on the Wednesday appointed. Half an hour before the
chair was taken, every available seat was occupied: and
many failed to gain admission. Mr. George Wilson, chairman; T. Milner Gibson, Esq., Richard Cobden, Esq., and
Mr. W. J. Fox, were the speakers. Mr. Wilson, in alluding
to the diminished number of public meetings, held and to
be held, intimated that the energies of the League were
now to be spent principally in seeing to the registration of
voters. During the last few weeks they had, he said,
proceeded like men of business to the consideration of
the best mode of attending to the registration of electors
residing in boroughs throughout the kingdom. "We selected 140 boroughs, upon which we thought, with reasonable exertions, an impression might be made. We selected
for our visiting agents to such boroughs men fully acquainted with the subject of registration in all its parts;
men fully qualified to undertake the business in as work-
manlike a manner as any men in the kingdom; and they
had reported to the council of the League the result of
their inquiries. In some instances they found the regis-

tration had been totally neglected—in many partially attended to, whilst in others it had been entirely in the hands of legal agents—or rather in the hands and power of victorious bribers; but in a very few instances did they find that the matter had been properly attended to. They then formed committees where none existed, and exacted a pledge from the free traders in many boroughs, that the subject should be fully attended to hereafter; and although the work is a very great one, and it cannot be brought to perfection in a single day, yet I believe now that the first stimulus, the first great impulse, has been given, to put in full array and order the constituted body who have in their hands the fate of this country, and who can determine the fate of the Corn Laws and all other monopolies. Whenever, therefore, you hear it asked by anybody, what is the League doing? let it be clearly understood, that the whole of their attention is being given to the subject of registration in all its branches. The consequences of this assiduity was already seen. In the city of London you have a Registration Association, which has made unparalleled efforts on this occasion, and which has effectually, I believe, provided against the return hereafter of any monopolist to parliament for the metropolis. In South Lancashire, if I were to go into the interesting particulars, the result would be equally satisfactory; and I firmly believe, do what they will in the shape of objections hereafter in that county, that it has now been wrested from the hands of the monopolists; and, with ordinary attention, no monopolist will be again returned for that county." But though the registration occupied thus much of their time it must not be supposed that meetings were given up. They were being held, from time to time, as occasion required, all over the country. Mr. Wilson added:

"This is the 24th and last meeting of the League; and I venture to say the League is very differently estimated now to what it was at the time of our holding our first meeting in Drury Lane. (Cheers.) Where is the man now who will charge us with being the abettors of assassination? and yet the Prime Minister scrupled not to insinuate as much. (Groans and hisses.) Where are the organs of public opinion that would support him to do so now? and above all, where are the people who would believe either him or the press, if they so charged us? (Loud cheers.) It is true that this year we were threatened with an opposition which was to extinguish the League, in the shape of the protection societies? (Laughter.) We may fairly ask, where are they now? (Much laughter.) Have they accomplished all for which they were established? Have they increased the wages of the labourer? Have they made him satisfied with his 8s. a week, and protection to agriculture? (Cheers and laughter.) Do the incendiary fires of Suffolk show that he is so satisfied? If these societies possess the power which they profess to possess, there never was a field yet in which the leading members of such societies could exercise that power so advantageously as in endeavouring to arrest the fearful spirit which is abroad in that county and check the incendiarism which has been lately exhibited there. (Cheers.) But they could not do it; they have no hold upon the affections of the working class. The poor labourers know that whatever marriage portions and mortgages may be paid out of the proceeds of the Corn Laws, they have nothing to expect but the greatest penury and want. It will require greater strength than the protection societies possess to put down the discontent which prevails among the working classes. We have gone on from day to day and from year to year gaining strength, sometimes in victory, sometimes in defeat, and we are proceeding now to that great point which must surely end in victory. (Cheers.) This question, under the management of the League, has obtained a position which no other question ever did in the same length of time, and it occupies a position too, which no other question ever did occupy in the public mind, without becoming successful and triumphant."

Mr. Gibson intimated that, while he approved of the course of the League, he was not, indeed, one of those who was very confident as to the result of our present electoral institutions. He was aware that they could not hope for those full and generous fruits which they might have looked for from a more liberal representation of the people; but this he did believe, that the great body of the electors in this country were an intelligent, and, when once awakened, an independent class—that they had the power, and could, if they pleased, return a majority to the

House of Commons opposed to monopoly; and he trusted in God that they would do so, and thereby promote the happiness, virtue, and welfare of this great community; that they would throw aside all partial interests, and stand forward in support of independent principles, and return a majority, not of a particular set of partisans—not persons looking to the sweets of office—but of men who are determined to support great principles, and great principles' alone. He sketched the declining career of the protection societies, and amused his audience very much with some commentaries on the principles promulgated in the *Morning Post*, particularly its views as to the utter uselessness of all trade and commerce except trade in guano; and blamed the landed interest, "the provision dealers," and the clergy, for wishing for a war rather than that we should have free trade.

Mr. Cobden, alluding to the assertion, renewed from day to day, of the League being extinct, said the League was not extinct, nor anything like it. When it set about its great work—the overthrow of a monopoly, greater and more strongly fortified than the world ever before saw—it knew perfectly well that so mighty a task could only be accomplished by the most strenuous exertions, extending over a long period of time. It had to teach two generations—that which was passing away, and that which was rising up; and it had to teach them, not merely by arguments and general facts, but by their own experience; and this was necessarily a work of time. Much experience of a most valuable kind those whom they sought to teach had already had; and, if the present abundant harvest should be, by the blessing of God, safely garnered in, the next six months would complete the lesson which the farmers had for the three last years been learning, and which showed them that what they had hitherto credulously believed to be protection, was utter destruction to them. There were crops now on the surface of the country which, let them once be safely housed, might, in less than six months, bring down the price of corn lower than it would be under a perfectly free trade. Would the farmers be consoled by the landlords telling them to wait a year or two and all would be well again? Not they; for the landlords would by no means reduce the rents, according to the low price of corn, in the same way that they had raised the rents according to the high price of the article four or five years back. He relied much upon what the next six months would do to teach farmers the delusion that had been practised on them:

"He believed the farmers were everywhere beginning to entertain the strongest possible doubts as to this so-called protection. (Hear, hear.) In the agricultural districts, supposing the present crops to be got in, the farmers would be selling their wheat in their own country markets at from 40s. to 45s., and there would be a universal cry amongst them of unparalleled distress; and not unnaturally, for they would have to pay rents calculated on 64s. prices, out of from 40s. to 45s. And all this because they had trusted to a law which, no doubt, could for a time cause a high scarcity price for corn, but which could not, in the nature of things, maintain that high price for any permanency. * * * * He had no doubt that with respect to the question of free trade there would be a great progress made in the right direction during the next six months in the agricultural districts, but they could not expect that their cause could make greater progress than the nature of things would permit. He was sorry to see that the false doctrines of the monopolists had a greater influence on some than was desirable. Amongst others upon whom those doctrines had produced their results was a man in Suffolk, named James Lankester, who had doubtless read in the *Morning Post* the peculiar doctrines of the monopolists respecting cheap corn. He was a man who could read, but could not write; just the sort of man to be influenced by the doctrines of the *Morning Post*; and having read in that paper that wages rose as corn rose, and that abundance of corn made the price of corn low, and, consequently, made wages low, he drew a very natural deduction. The man was evidently naturally of a logical mind, but it was evident that he devoted himself to the study of the *Morning Post*, and the result of that study was, that he took it into his head to carry out practically those doctrines which had been laid down in that eminent public journal. (A laugh.) It was stated by the *Morning Post* that wages depended upon the price of corn, and that when corn was dear wages were high, and of course it naturally struck James Lankester that the best way to raise the price of wages was to raise the price of corn, and the best way to raise the price of corn was to make it scarce; and, acting upon that view, he went out and set fire to Farmer Hobb's stacks. (Laughter.) Let them not suppose that he (Mr. Cobden) was making up a story for the occasion. There was not in his account any addition of facts to those which appeared in the papers; and Baron Alderson, before whom the case was tried, stated, with his wig on (a laugh), and with all the gravity of a judge, that it was a most strange and extraordinary application of the doctrines of political economy. This man had evidently drawn that deduction from the philosophy of the *Morning Post;* for Lankester had no malice against Farmer Hobbs, and he, therefore, did not touch his cart horses or his saddle horses, or his dairy, but he went to his stacks and set fire to them, to make corn dear, and, of course, in his opinion, to raise wages. That was the effect of carrying out practically the doctrines of the *Morning Post;* so that, from such a result, they might in future call the philosophy of that journal, the logic of the lucifer match. (Laughter and loud cheers.) But James Lankester was sentenced to be transported for the term of his natural life, to propagate the doctrines of the *Morning Post* in Australia. (Laughter.) Now, he (Mr. Cobden) wanted to know the difference in principle (for he knew there was a difference in law) between creating an artificial scarcity of that corn which the Almighty gave to all the nations of the earth—he wished to know what was the difference between making an artificial scarcity of corn by preventing us from getting a supply from abroad, and making it scarce by setting fire to the stacks of Farmer Hobbs? (Cheers.) The plea in both cases was exactly the same, for Lankester's profession of faith was heard by the gaoler, who pretended to be asleep. Lankester stated to other prisoners in gaol, that the motive which induced him to burn the stacks was in order that he might make corn dear, and so raise wages; and what then, he would ask, was the difference in principle? (Hear, hear.) Where was the difference between those who made corn dear by artificial means, and Lankester, who took his own mode of making it dear? He much feared that half those who supported the present Corn Laws would stand less acquitted in the eyes of heaven than James Lankester, the unfortunate man who set fire to those stacks. (Hear, hear.) He repeated, that men who knew what they were doing, and notwithstanding that knowledge supported the Corn Laws for their own selfish purposes, were more to blame than the wretch who burned that corn, if in doing so he did not know how really guilty he was in the sight of heaven."

Mr. Fox delivered a brilliant address, continued to a

late period of the evening, which was principally a recital of the effects everywhere produced, from successive ministries down to the poorest classes of the community, by the free-trade agitation.   He said :—

" Rick-burning was only Richmondism in theory. (Immense cheering.) There never was a parallel more complete than that between the Richmondites and rick-burning; for if one wantonly destroyed property so did the other ; if one endangered human life, so did the other endanger it wholesale; if in the rick-burner's case the innocent suffered, who suffered in the other case? The innocent and the helpless, who suffered more the more helpless they were. If one destroyed the good gifts of heaven to man, so did the other; and probably a larger quantity of corn was destroyed in the course of the year by rotting in bond than had ever been destroyed by rick-burners, and at last was shovelled out into a river or harbour, as at Hull, when it was no longer useful. Where was the difference, unless in the elements of destruction ? Why was that villainous which destroyed corn by fire, and that virtuous which destroyed it by water? (Cheers.) But if the rick-burner was transported, the others would not escape punishment, for it would go hard if the honest historian did not gibbet their memories in his page to all posterity. There was another advantage which the League conferred. They had elicited the virtues and stimulated the philanthropy of the monopolists, and now they saw every day some question brought forward by those advocates of monopoly, with a view to serve the poor. They had even established societies for their advantage, and amongst them there was a society for the protection of the poor needlewomen; and those who attended the meetings of that society expressed their astonishment that persons should increase the sufferings of the needlewomen by purchasing cheap shirts. But they did not consider that with those who purchased those cheap shirts, it was their only chance of having a shirt at all. (A laugh.) They even had compassion on the poor for working too long, and they were desirous that the machinery in mills should not work too much, so that the workmen had time to go home and meditate on what they would do with more wages if they got it. (Laughter.) They even took care that the poor should be enabled to recreate themselves by travelling on the railways, and they proposed to have third-class trains for the purpose; and here the philanthropy of the bishops was brought into practice, for they could not think of the poor travelling on railways, unless their enjoyment was complete, and they proposed that they should be compelled to go in a comfortable first or second class carriage when they travelled by the railway. They looked everywhere for a means of indicating their philanthropy, but to the poor man's cupboard,

where they might see the reduced loaf, which they had sliced away by
their monopoly. Wheat had been 53s. last year, and they were still
told that they had not protection enough. (Laughter.) We paid 9s.
a quarter more for wheat than our fellow subjects in Guernsey ; thus we
paid 53s. a quarter for wheat, because we had never been conquered
from France, and prided ourselves on our own glorious British constitution. (A laugh.) But the overflowing benevolence of the monopolists
had not only regarded the physical condition of the people, it also
looked to their morals, reminding him of the words of the poet :—

> 'In pious as in impious works,
> Like water, still he found his level ;
> And having cheated all mankind,
> He built a church to cheat the devil '

(Laughter.) The *Morning Herald* said that Mr. Cobden and Mr.
Bright were inclined to back out of this agitation; but the writer did
not understand how impossible it was for them to back out of it. There
was a moral as well as a physical impossibility which prevented a man
of clear mind and true heart from looking back, when once he put his
hand to the plough, until he had achieved success. (Cheers.) The
monopolists had enormous influence—they had large possessions—they
had a portion of the press to support them—they had the use of the
Post-office—(a laugh)—they had the army and navy, and the appointments in the church; but those who opposed their monopoly had an
influence stronger than all these together, namely, the sense of justice
in the human heart. There was a power which they knew not how to
deal with, but which would teach others how to deal with them—a power
which was more ancient than their oldest ancestry, which existed before
their castles and cathedrals—before church and state—which was as
old, yea, older than the creation—it was Justice, that sacred power
which existed before the pillars of the earth were laid. It dwelt with
Wisdom in the Eternal Mind before the mountains were formed. It was
breathed into man with the first breath of life, and it would only perish
on earth when the days of mankind were over. (Great cheering.) It
was as vain to oppose it as to strive with the stars of heaven ; it would
yet be the witness as well as the agent of destruction of all wrong in
political and social institutions, and he hoped that soon might Providence send that blessed day. (Great cheering.)"

As I have only incidentally noticed the attempts made
by a certain portion of the chartists to obstruct the free-
trade movement, I copy the following report of a meeting
held at Northampton, as a specimen of their readiness to
do the monopolists' work :—

" On Monday, Aug. 5, an important meeting of the inhabitants of the town and county of Northampton was held at that place, pursuant to advertisement.

" Some short time back a requisition was forwarded to Messrs. Cobden and Bright, signed by 1,200 agriculturists, manufacturers, and others, inviting them to attend a meeting at Northampton, for the purpose of discussing the great question of free trade, a request with which those honourable gentlemen immediately complied. A second requisition, signed by ninety-one supporters of the Corn Laws, was subsequently despatched to Mr. Stafford O'Brien, one of the members for the county, and chairman of the Publishing Committee of the Agricultural Protection Society, calling upon him to meet and refute the arguments of the members for Stockport and Durham. An answer was received from that gentleman declining to be present; on the ground that the requisitionists were quite able to form their own opinions without calling in the aid of strangers.

" The Northampton branch of the Ishmaelite section of chartists also despatched a third requisition, which was accepted, to Mr. Feargus O'Connor, who, it was intended, should act in concert with the honourable member for the county, whose presence was confidently anticipated, from the important situation he was known to hold in the great Central Society for the maintenance of the Corn Laws. Lord Fitzwilliam, the Mayor, and several of the most respectable inhabitants of Northampton, were severally proposed by the free traders as chairman of the meeting, all of whom were successively objected to by the chartists, who intimated their determination to allow no person to fill that office except Mr. Grundy, a retired tradesman of the town, who is held in great estimation by them. Notwithstanding the palpable unfairness of this dictation, the free traders, knowing Mr. Grundy to be a gentleman of integrity and high respectability, acceded to the proposition, and the meeting was accordingly presided over most impartially and honourably by that gentleman. Commodious hustings were erected in the noble market-square—a space capable of accommodating with ease 50,000 persons. At the commencement of the proceedings the numbers present amounted to about 5,000, which was soon augmented to 6,000. A great number of the most influential tradesmen and gentlemen of the town and surrounding districts were present, including many farmers, several of whom held up their hands in favour of a repeal of the Corn Laws.

" Mr. Cobden, contrary to his usual practice, submitted to the meeting a resolution in favour of free trade, which having been seconded by Mr. Alderman Cotton, Mr. Feargus O'Connor came forward and proposed a long and desultory amendment, recognising the great evils of the Corn

Laws, but declaring their repeal to be inexpedient and injurious, unless preceded by the charter. It is a singular fact, of which probably no parallel is to be found among the numerous and flagrant derelictions of principle too often met with in the history of political parties, that this amendment was supported by the votes of nearly all the conservatives of Northampton, including most of their distinguished leaders, notwithstanding it recommended two propositions—the charter and the ultimate repeal of the Corn Laws—to both of which measures they have repeatedly avowed hostility, in the hope that by the combination of these two extreme, and, in principle, utter antagonistic bodies, they should be enabled to overthrow the free-traders. Bodies of chartists had been brought in from the surrounding districts, and every exertion was made to secure the defeat of the Anti-Corn-Law League.

" Mr. Grundy having been voted to the chair, read the requisition convening the meeting, and called upon

" Mr. Cobden, who was received with loud cheers. The honourable gentleman called upon the meeting to discuss the question in the terms of the requisition, with reference to the interest of the farmers, the labourers, and the community in general. He then proceeded, in his usual lucid manner, to show that the Corn Law had been positively injurious to all those classes. With reference to the interests of the farmer in the Corn Law, as securing high prices, if the present harvest were well got in, wheat, which is now as low as 47s., would, before next Christmas, be down to 42s. Mr. Cobden then alluded to the efforts made by the working classes in 1815, to prevent the passing of the law, and in subsequent years to procure its repeal. It might be asked, why had not the masters then united with the men for that purpose? The reason was, that there was not that union which ought to have existed between the two bodies; but that was no argument against the present generation acting more wisely than their fathers then did, especially as we have had thirty years' experience of its injurious working. He (Mr. Cobden) was at school at that period, and therefore could not be blamed for any sins of omission or commission which were made at that time. Whenever bread had been low, wages had risen in the manufacturing districts, and poor rates and deaths had diminished in an equal proportion. If the Corn Law had thus injured England, would any Irishman stand forward on that platform and maintain that it had benefited Ireland? If so, he would appeal to the highest authority with reference to that country—Mr. O'Connell himself, who always voted in Parliament for the repeal of the Corn Laws, and had attended all the League annual meetings at Manchester. The Corn Laws were only maintained for the benefit of the landlords. (A voice, ' And the cotton lords.') It could not be for the ' cotton lords,' for there were only some fifteen of

them in Parliament out of 658 members. After referring to the reduction of the duty on wool, Mr. Cobden reverted to the case of hides,
leather being an article with which the inhabitants of Northampton
were well acquainted. The effect of prohibiting the importation of
hides would be the same as the prohibition upon wheat—there would
not be half enough for general consumption. People would be compelled to wear wooden shoes, or go without, and the trade at Northampton
would be ruined. It had been said that there were important interests
connected with the Corn Law, and, therefore, that it should not be immediately abolished. That point had been well settled at a public
meeting by a man in fustian, who asked, ' Why do you dispute about
doing away with the Corn Law all at once ? Did they not put it on all
of a ruck ?' There was a certain duty imposed on French shoes; but
the smugglers brought them into this country at half the money; but
wheat was a more bulky article, and could not be so dealt with, and the
landlords had, therefore, the best of the bargain. Let them, then, have
free trade in corn, for they had already done their worst with shoes.
There were other questions, no doubt, of very great importance to the
country; but let them not endeavour to carry those important points
by frustrating the achievement of that which they acknowledge to be a
great good. The League would not go out of their way to interfere
with any other agitation, but, in any work where the road was long and
the journey arduous, a man would not be worse off by having plenty of
bread procured for him by the way He himself had voted for the
motions of Mr. Duncombe and Mr. Sharman Crawford. With regard
to the sugar question, his (Mr. Cobden's) object had always been to
get the people as much as possible, and at as cheap a rate ; and, for
aught he cared for mere political parties, he would sell either whig or
tory, provided he could gain for the people a reduction of 1d. per lb. in
sugar. Mr. Cobden concluded by proposing the following resolution :—
' That the Corn Law and all other laws restricting trade for the benefit
of a class, are unjust, and ought to be forthwith abolished.' The hon.
gentleman concluded amidst loud cheers.

" Mr. Alderman Cotton seconded the resolution.

" Mr. Feargus O'Connor then came forward amidst loud cheers from
the chartists, and addressed the meeting for upwards of an hour, chiefly
vituperating the manufacturers and the Anti-Corn-Law League. He
said that the requisition, in pursuance of which he attended the meeting,
contained 153 signatures more than that to Mr. Cobden. He denied in
their presence, and that of the Great Ruler of events, upon his honour
as a gentleman, and his oath as a man, that he had ever received a
farthing, or the fraction of a farthing, from man, woman, or child, whig,
tory, or chartist, corporation, or individual, in the whole course of his

existence, or had ever travelled one mile, or had eaten one meal, at the expense of anybody. When the poor men met at Peterloo to petition for the repeal of the Corn Laws, it was the Manchester manufacturers who came upon them and cut them down. What had caused the change in the spirit of their dream? They were then in political power, and now they wanted to regain their lost influence. Mr. O'Connor then proceeded to read extracts from the prize essays published by the Anti-Corn-Law League, which he alleged contained great contradictions, one set of arguments being for town and another for country—in the former representing that the manufacturers would get cheaper bread, and in the latter that the farmer would get higher prices. The League were only for pruning the rotton tree; he was for laying the mattock and the axe to its root. He was for free trade all over the world, but not for being monkeys or tame cats to any party; his object being to secure the poor man a share in the benefit which the manufacturers wanted to deprive him of. Mr. Cobden had spoken of the operatives being possibly reduced to wear wooden shoes, but they actually wear them at this time, and were glad to get them. Where was now (Mr. O'Connor asked) a working man's clock, feather bed, chest of drawers, and other things which he used to have? They had all gone; while the manufacturers boasted of possessing as much wealth as would pay the national debt. He did not charge the fault upon Mr. Cobden, but it was nevertheless true that a workman had been discharged from that gentleman's employ for reading the *Northern Star*.

"Mr. Cobden emphatically denied the assertion.

"Mr. O'Connor proceeded to read some extracts from 'Almack's Character and Proceedings of the Anti-Corn-Law League,' but the purport of them, save for abusing the League, and thereby avoiding the question of the expediency of the Corn Laws, no one could discover. After uttering a great quantity of irrelevant matter, he concluded by moving the following amendment:—'Resolved, That we, the inhabitants of the county and town of Northampton, in public meeting assembled, are of opinion that the repeal of the Corn Laws, unaccompanied by a fair and equitable adjustment of the several interests that would be affected by the change, must lead to a confiscation of the properties of the most weak and unprotected, and to the centralization of all manufacturing operations in the hands of those who would be most capable, from the possession of large capital, and most ready, by the possession of a large amount of inanimate machinery, to take advantage of the change. That, while we declare ourselves hostile and opposed to the principle of restricting commerce by interfering with the rights of exchange, we nevertheless feel assured that the question of free trade is one which must be dealt with as a whole, and not upon mere party grounds. And as we feel convinced that the whole question cannot be justly, equitably, or satisfactorily discussed, arranged, and finally settled by any other tribunal than that constituted by the whole people, or by representatives fully, fairly, and freely elected by them; and inasmuch as such full, free, and fair representation cannot by possibility be accomplished through other principles than those contained in the document entitled *The People's Charter*, we hereby pledge ourselves, in spite of all opposition, to continue our glorious struggle until the people's charter is made the basis of the British constitution.'

" M'Grath, the chartist orator, then followed his leader in a similar style of incoherency, and concluded by seconding the amendment.

" Mr. Bright then came forward amidst loud cheers, and spoke as follows:—I have listened with the utmost attention to the two speeches that have been made by the mover and seconder of the amendment which is now before you; and I confess that, with respect to the speech of the mover of that amendment, I am unable at this moment to discover any very clear ground for forming an opinion as to his views on the question of the Corn Laws; he spoke against and for them in about an equal quantity; but, if I had been under any difficulty with respect to his speech, that of his seconder has wholly cleared up that difficulty, for I have perceived during the progress of that speech a repetition of the arguments in favour of the Corn Laws which are poured forth to a small portion of the readers of the public newspapers in the columns of the *Morning Post*, the *Herald*, and the *Standard*. (Cheers and laughter.) That gentleman might, without any impropriety, be the writer of those articles, so clear is the resemblance, so entire the identity between his views on this question and those of the high protectionist paper, the *Morning Post*. I address this meeting with the impression that if there be one class in this country more deeply interested than another in the discovery and adoption of truth, that class is the great mass of the people who live by their industry. (Hear.) It may be that the aristocracy and the clergy benefit by a law which is unjust in principle and injurious to the rest of the people; but there can be no injustice practised in this country by the legislature under which we live which can be advantageous to the millions of the people, who have no property but their labour, and no income but their wages. Being, then, impressed with this opinion, I am conscious of no anxiety on the subject but that of discovering the truth. I am willing to and do assume that in your minds also there is an entire wish to perceive the truth. and act upon it. I shall, therefore, go into no extraneous matter that I can possibly avoid. I shall not heap obloquy upon this or that man (hear, hear), but I will ask you as a class of intelligent men, the thousands here assembled to hear the arguments fairly on this momentous question, to

judge impartially, and help by your voices to swell the cry which is
hastening the glad time when the worst brand which ever tyranny
inflicted on a people shall be swept away, and your industry and mine
shall be free. (Cheers.) But, before I go to that, there is just one
point with respect to Mr. O'Connor that I must be permitted to allude
to, and I am sure he will not object to it. I said I was unable to discover from his speech what were his views on this question, and if I
leave to-day out of consideration, and look back to former periods, I am
equally unable to discover anything like a clear course which he has
pursued on this question. Mr. O'Connor was a member of the House
of Commons in the year 1834. In that year, immediately after the
passing of the Reform Bill, Mr. Hume, a gentleman whom the last
speaker has thought fit to place before you in terms neither fair nor
complimentary, moved for a committee of the whole house, for the purpose of abolishing the then existing Corn Law, and substituting for a
time a much lower fixed duty, with a view of ultimately coming to the
principle of total free trade. Mr. O'Connor was in Parliament then,
and what said he on that motion? Did he then say that he was in
favour of free trade with all the world, but that he would not have free
trade because the working people were not represented? No; he did
nothing of the kind. Mr. O'Connor got up in his place in Parliament,
and there and then defended the Corn Laws, and not upon any of those
grounds which he has advanced here to-day, but upon grounds totally
different. Mr. O'Connor may not be to blame in this matter, he may
have changed his mind from conviction since.

" Mr. O'Connor: Not a bit of it.

" Mr. Bright continued: It will not be amiss if I give you a portion,
or, if he please and you have no objection, the whole, of his speech on
that occasion. It is taken from Hansard's publication of the debates;
it has been before quoted in Mr. O'Connor's presence, and he has never
disputed the accuracy of it :—

" 'Mr. Feargus O'Connor: My honourable and gallant friend the
member for Bolton has appealed to the Irish members upon this subject, and has called upon me more especially, as being the representative
of the largest agricultural county in Ireland, to give him my support.
Sir, I am going to give him my support, but it will be in the spirit of a
guardian angel, to protect him from sacrificing his interest and his happiness upon the shrine of that block called political economy. The
hon. member for Middlesex has said that this question is now at rest.
I agree with him, and it is the only part of his speech with which I do
agree. It is high time that this question, which, at present, not only
agitates the manufacturing and agricultural interests of England, but
also the agricultural interests of Ireland, should be set at rest. It is

due to this house that I should point out certain fallacies into which those who support the present motion have fallen, and lay before it the different situation of Ireland, as contrasted with the situation of this country.   The situation of Ireland is this: we are a great agricultural country without manufactures, and we depend, as a vent for our produce, on the markets of England.   If, then, you admit the importation of foreign corn, duty free, you will throw us completely out of the English market; agriculture in Ireland will be neglected; and not only will you sacrifice the only interest existing in that country, but also the landed interest of England, for the benefit of the continental growers of corn.   When we shall have ceased to cultivate our land at home, and when foreign nations find that we have so ceased, they will take advantage of our want of home production, and raise the price of their own corn at pleasure; and thus we should be left at the mercy or the whim and caprice of the foreign market.   It has been said that the Irish members are unanimous in their determination to oppose it.   I think I speak the sentiments of a large majority of those members, when I state that the agitation of this question will do considerable mischief in Ireland, and that mischief will be increased, if a determination to put it aside for some time is not manifested by a very large majority of this house.   This is the only question, as it appears to me, in which the interests of the two countries are completely united and identical.   The honourable member for Middlesex says that this is a question of justice against injustice—of the many against the few.   But what is the reason that we have not heard of any manifestations of public opinion against the Corn Law?   It is this—that while those persons who oppose the present system reside in large towns, and are easily called together in order to express their wishes to this house, the great agricultural population, who are interested in the continuance of the system, are spread thickly over the face of the country, and have not the same facilities for meeting together to declare their opinions upon the subject.   It is said that the repeal of the Corn Laws will make bread cheap, without reducing the value of the land.   This is a doctrine I cannot comprehend.   If you reduce the price of the produce, rent must fall; if you keep up the standard of rent, you cannot reduce prices; and if not, how can you give the people cheap bread?   I rose with a determination not to mix up any extraneous matter with the subject of this debate.   I appeal again to the house not to allow itself to be led away by the absurdities or assertions of the honourable member for Middlesex.   Without troubling the house any farther, I conclude by imploring the members from Ireland to consider this as a neutral question, threatening in its consequences, if carried, the annihilation of the liberty, rights, and protection of the poor man, and unanimously to resist the motion.'

" Mr. Bright proceeded at considerable length, with great force and eloquence, to refute the calumnies and fallacies of Mr. O'Connor, and to demonstrate the benefits which would accrue to all classes from the adoption of free-trade principles.

" The Chairman then took the sense of the meeting, when there appeared a decided majority in favour of the original resolution of Mr. Cobden.—Mr. O'Connor came forward, and questioned the accuracy of the chairman's conclusion, and requested a division.—The Chairman replied that there could by no possibility be a doubt upon the subject.— Notwithstanding the indecency of impugning the decision of a chairman appointed by themselves, the chartists separated from the rest of the meeting, when their minority, had there been any previous doubt, became still more apparent.—Mr. Cobden moved, and Mr. Bright seconded, a vote of thanks to the chairman.—The Chairman briefly returned thanks, and declared the meeting dissolved; notwithstanding which, after the departure of the free-trade party, Mr. O'Connor remained and harangued the meeting.—Clarke, one of the colleagues of Mr. O'Connor, then proposed a vote of confidence in that gentleman, which, as a matter of course, was carried."

CHAPTER XIV.

DUDLEY ELECTION.

A seat for Dudley was vacant. There was little chance of success for any but a monopolist candidate; and few men will fight without success being probable, the desire, "the laudable ambition," as it is called, to be in the House being generally stronger than the desire to spread right principles. Dudley is a manufacturing town, containing about 30,000 inhabitants, who are chiefly employed in iron, glass, and nail manufactures. A part of the town and the principal part of the surrounding mining district belongs to Lord Ward. From the possession of this immense property, great numbers of the voters were in his employ; and it was always a condition that they should vote for his nominee. At every election a note was sent to each elector, under the *direct* influence of his lordship, couched in the most courteous terms, respectfully requesting the vote and influence of such elector in favour of his lordship's candidate. This request was understood; and if not complied with, the offender was visited with the summary punishment of discharge from employment, or notice to quit land or premises, as the case might be. His lordship, in addition to his direct, exercised perhaps a still more powerful influence *indirectly;* the mines chiefly belonged to him, and were let on leases to the ironmasters. These leases, however, afforded no security for independence on their part. There were so

many conditions attached to them that they were exposed
to constant loss and annoyance from an ill-natured and
unfriendly agent; and, therefore, on occasions of election
contests, it was always the interest of the ironmasters not
to offend his lordship by opposing his nominee.   The
ironmasters gave employment to large numbers of the
electors, and many of the shopkeepers were dependent on
them.   The same influences which were exercised by Lord
Ward over his dependents were exercised by the ironmasters over theirs, and these influences were united to
return whomsoever Lord Ward pleased to appoint.   Under
these circumstances, there would be no contest, unless a
candidate could be found who cared less about his own
success than to avail himself of the opportunity for promulgating the principles of free trade.

A deputation from the Council of the League, on the 3rd
of August, 1844, visited Dudley, to consult with the free-
trade electors as to the state of the borough, and the candidate to be proposed.   No one connected with the town
could be induced to stand, from the very prevalent feeling
that the influence of Lord Ward, and of the ironmasters
under his control, was too potent to be successfully resisted.   Several gentlemen were called upon, and urged to
offer themselves, but without obtaining the consent of any
of them.   It then became a matter of discussion whether
the election should be uncontested, or one of the League
deputation should offer himself, to give the electors an
opportunity of recording their votes.   It was hoped that
Mr. W. A. Smith the brother of the honourable member
for Norwich, and candidate at the last election, would
arrive and offer himself.   Mr. Smith was, unfortunately,
in France, and could not return in time for the election ;
this hope was, therefore, at an end, and no resource was
left but that one of the deputation should stand.   Mr. W.
Rawson, of Manchester, treasurer of the League, therefore,
most reluctantly issued an address to the electors, and

proceedings were immediately taken to canvass the borough. The following is a copy of Mr. Rawson's address :—

" GENTLEMEN,—The resignation of Mr. Hawkes having caused a vacancy in the representation of your borough, I have, at the earnest request of the friends of free trade in Dudley, consented to offer myself as a candidate for your suffrages.

" Free trade I believe to be essential to the prosperity and happiness of all classes in this country. In this district the iron, nail, and glass trades have, until very lately, been in a state of great depression; the most skilled and hard-working men have scarcely been able to live by their labour.

" Every recurrence of insufficient harvests, and seasons of scarcity, must inevitably bring about periods of suffering, similar to those which you have just experienced, unless you can secure for the fruits of your industry a free exchange for the commodities of other countries.

" The repeal of the Corn Laws would increase your trade, and so find room for your ever-increasing population, by enabling you to sell your glass, iron, nails, and other manufactures, for the corn and provisions of foreign countries. There need never be want in England. The industry and skill of the people are unequalled, and yet the working men do not get a fair day's wages for a fair day's work; and never can, until they are at liberty to work for the whole world, and take in payment whatever the world can give.

" Should I be chosen to represent you in the House of Commons, my utmost efforts shall be used to carry the total repeal of the Corn Laws, and of all other laws made for the benefit of the few, to the injury of the great masses of the people.

" I have the honour to be,
" Gentlemen, your faithful servant,
" WILLIAM RAWSON.
" Manchester, August 3, 1844."

In the evening a very numerous public meeting was held in the large Lancasterian School-room, Stafford-street, which was addressed in a speech of much ability by R. R. Moore, Esq., and by Mr. Rawson, the free-trade candidate. A very excellent spirit pervaded the meeting, and a resolution to do all that could be done was manifested by those present. During Monday and Tuesday the canvass was prosecuted with zeal, and in all quarters where independence existed there was a most gratifying result. On

Tuesday, Mr. Bright, M.P., arrived, and attended a second
meeting held on the evening of that day in the Lancasterian School-room, which was crowded to excess. Mr.
Palmer was in the chair, and Mr. Bright spoke for about
two hours, on the great question of freedom of industry,
and on the solemn responsibility of electors. The arguments carried conviction to every mind, and the enthusiasm
of the meeting was extraordinary. Mr. Bright alluded to
the fact that ironmasters and manufacturers were acting
along with Lord Ward's agents in retarding the triumph of
free-trade principles. He felt a deep commiseration for
the electors, whose position and whose necessities almost
compelled them to submit to the dictation of the powerful
monopolists. He was not surprised that Lord Ward and
his order should work for "protection" whilst they believed
that their interests and rents were involved in the question
of its abolition; but he expressed the utter abhorrence he
felt that men employing their capital in trade and manufactures, and dependent on the industry of the operative
class, should combine with the lordly monopolist to ruin
their own order. He compared them to the wretches who,
whilst their town was surrounded by a hostile army,
panting for the spoliation of its inhabitants, should traitor-
ously throw open the gates and invite the spoilers to come
in and gorge themselves with their prey. He felt so deeply
the conduct of such men that he knew hardly how to speak
of them, but hoped they might be marked as traitors to
their order, and as men unworthy of all confidence, and
deserving of the scorn and contempt of every right-minded
citizen of a free country.

The nomination took place on Wednesday morning,
when about 5,000 persons assembled. Mr. Benbow, the
monopolist candidate, was proposed by Mr. Badger, a
glass and nail manufacturer, and seconded by Captain
Bennett; Mr. Rawson was proposed by Charles Twamley,
Esq., solicitor, and seconded by the Rev. J. Palmer. Mr.

Benbow's speech was not heard beyond the few who surrounded him on the hustings, but he agreed that free trade
was a good thing if other nations would become free
traders.   Mr. Rawson spoke with great freedom and effect.
He pointed out the hollowness of the plea that the Corn
Law protected the industry of the people, for by it the
price of their food was raised, and the value of their labour
depreciated.   He drew a picture of the terrible sufferings
which the population of that district had so recently endured, and proved its intimate connection with the high
price of food during the years 1839, 1840, and 1841; and
tracing the matter still further, he clearly showed how
reviving prosperity was the attendant on reduced prices of
food, the consequence of more abundant harvests.   These
points were loudly cheered, and were evidently well understood by the auditory.   He then stated his conviction that
two-thirds of the electors would vote for him if they dared ;
wherever he had gone they had wished him success, and
declared that he should have their support if they could
vote for him without the risk of losing their employment.
He asked his honourable opponent, on behalf of these
voters, to pledge himself before that meeting that no
unfair conduct would be pursued towards those who voted
according to their consciences at this election.   After this
appeal, Mr. Rawson, turning towards his opponent, said,
" I pause, sir, for a reply ; " but the monopolist candidate
remained silent amidst the shouts of the people, " *Let us
vote as we like.*"

Mr. Bolton, the returning officer, then called for a show
of hands, when certainly two-thirds of the immense multitude raised their hands in favour of Mr. Rawson.   The
decision of the returning officer was at once given in his
favour, amidst the most deafening cheers from the assembled thousands, and the countenances of the poor
colliers who had been brought against him bore evidences
of no less pleasure from the decision than did those of the

great majority of the assemblage. After the nomination, Mr. Godson, M.P., addressed a crowd from a window of the hotel. He denounced all the League deputation as paid to agitate the free-trade question. He heaped slanders upon the manufacturers of the north of England, and declared that in the best of times the cotton spinners and millowners had never paid wages sufficient to buy good wheaten bread for their workmen. He did not show how this, if it were true, could justify a law to make bread dear, whilst there was no law to raise the wages of the workmen.

On Thursday, the election terminated in the return of the nominee of the old castle influence. " No one expected anything else," said the *Morning Chronicle*, " and there is, consequently, no disappointment experienced. The League came here merely to disseminate the principles of free trade, and not to win the election. That they knew they could not do, but they also well know that had they the ballot they would have won. There is not a man, woman, or child in Dudley, having arrived at the use of reason, and uninfluenced by the terror of their superiors, who would not vote for cheap bread, and plenty of it. At present, however, the greater part of the people have no will, and were obliged to vote as they were compelled."

FINAL CLOSE OF THE POLL :—

Mr. Rawson 175
Mr. Benbow 388

Monopolist majority 213

Amongst the few who had been candidates—not so much for the " honour," such as it is—an honour shared by such men as Sibthorp and Ferrand—of securing for themselves a seat in parliament, as for the opportunity of making emphatic declarations of principle, and of paving the way for its triumph, was Mr. John Benjamin Smith, who in 1841, at an emergency when it was necessary to show that a protectionist whig stood in the same relationship to the League as a protectionist tory, stood a manly contest at Walsall. In that borough, in this 1844 represented by a free trader, there remained a deep feeling of gratitude for the services which had led to its independence; and the ladies, who had taken a deep interest in the effort to return Mr. Smith, had subscribed to present him, in the shape of a handsome silver salver, with a testimony of their esteem, A tea party was considered the most appropriate medium through which the compliment could be conveyed. An evening of September was selected for having the *soirée* in the large assembly-room. At five o'clock, the appointed hour, the room was filled to excess by a highly respectable company of ladies and gentlemen. Robert Scott, Esq., the member for the borough, presided at the head of the table, supported by John Bright, Esq., M.P., Charles Greatrex, Esq., Thomas Brittle, Esq., Samuel Cox, Esq., Charles Wilkinson, Esq., and Messrs. Grafton, Mason, Swift, Standley, Westwood, &c. At the same table sat a number of highly respectable ladies, amongst whom were Mrs. Cox, Mrs. Whitney, Mrs. Grafton, Mrs. Bartram, Mrs. Myring, Mrs. Griffiths, Miss Mall, Miss Creswell, and Mrs. Standley.

The chairman said he well remembered when, in the year 1841, they were called upon to come forward as the champions of free trade in England. That was the first borough in which the question was fairly tried, and nobly indeed did they respond to the call. They had then a whig candidate who did not come up to the mark; they tested him and found him wanting; upon which, with great prudence, he retired from the contest; and the conservative candidate was actively engaged in his canvass, and his friends busily employed bringing to bear upon the electors every possible interest which they possessed. Many incautiously had given in their promises without considering that the trust which had been reposed in them was not one given for their own exclusive benefit, but one for which they were answerable to the non-electors who were not so favoured. He well knew the anxiety which the friends of free trade had felt at that period, and the difficulties they had in procuring a candidate to stand forth as the uncompromising advocate of the great principles which they were desirous of testing in that borough. It was at that moment of difficulty and struggle that Mr. Smith—a gentleman of great station, of well-known character, of extensive commercial knowledge, and considerable talents —unhesitatingly consented to become a candidate, and make an effort to rescue the borough from the thraldom in which it had been held. Mr. Smith was then the president of the Chamber of Commerce in Manchester, chairman of the Anti-Corn-Law League, and universally known and respected throughout the country. He came to Walsall at their request, and conducted the contest in such a manner as to merit not only the applause and esteem of his friends, but the approval of even his opponents. There was not a person in Walsall who could be found to utter a single word against Mr. Smith during that memorable contest. They were, however, borne down by the influence to which he had already adverted, but not until they had reduced the majority of their opponents to that point which proved the impossibility of his or any other monopolist again successfully contesting the borough. The ladies of Walsall felt grateful to Mr. Smith for his invaluable services, and they were resolved that at some future time they would prove the estimation in which they held him, by the presentation of a substantial token of respect.

Mrs. Cox then rose, and, taking up a very splendid silver salver which was on the table, presented it to Mr. Smith, saying, "I have great honour in handing you this piece of plate." The honourable gentleman accepted the

plate, which was a specimen of exquisite workmanship. It
bears the following inscription :—

" Presented to J. B. Smith, Esq.,

" By the ladies of Walsall, as a testimonial of their gratitude and esteem for the patriotic and spirited manner in which he stood forward in
February, 1841, to contest the representation of the borough against a
monopolist and bread-taxer; for his upright and independent conduct
and urbane demeanour during the struggle; for his general and unwearied advocacy of the rights of labour and happiness of all, in opposition to the selfish interests and usurped domination of a class. May
he live to enjoy the reward of his exertions, in beholding truth triumphant and his country happy."

Mr. Smith then rose and said, that after so long an absence they would not be surprised that he felt some embarrassment at coming before them, and inadequate to express himself upon the reception of that beautiful testimony of their kind esteem and regard. It was delightful
to see so many then around him who had cheered him on
in his contest, and many of whom had made great sacrifices for the advancement of those principles which he and
they deemed essential to the welfare of their country.
When he first came to Walsall, he had not the most distant
idea of becoming a candidate, and it was nothing but a
deep sense of the importance of the struggle in which
they were then engaged that could have induced him to
engage in so arduous a contest. It was the first struggle
for free trade which they had had in the kingdom. It
was nobly fought, and, though they were defeated, they
were greatly indebted to the generous enthusiasm of the
ladies for the favourable struggle they had made. When
he commenced the canvass, his opponent boasted that he
could command 700 votes, and that he (Mr. Smith) could
not raise 500 supporters. He believed there was some
truth in the calculation which was then made; and if he
had come forward upon any other grounds than those
which he had adopted, he never could have succeeded to
the extent he did against such great odds. He did not

come before them as the advocate of any faction, nor the
tool of any party, but he preached a new doctrine which
found a response in the heart of every man, woman, and
child in the borough ; he contended for the right of every
man who could make any description of goods to exchange
them for any other description of articles in which he
might stand in need. He contended for perfect freedom
of trade, independent of any paltry party consideration ;
and having submitted the arguments in favour of this principle to the people of Walsall, they at once saw the reasonableness and justice of them. They saw how inti-
mately their own immediate interests were bound up in the
question. And what was the consequence ? Why, the
election came on, and, instead of having 300 majority
against him (Mr. Smith), the monopolist got only 27 votes
above him. To those who knew the circumstances under
which that contest was fought, the result would be surprising, and nothing less than a great amount of enthusiasm could have effected such wonders. In five months
after, however, the contest was renewed ; and in place of
a majority of 27 in favour of the monopolist, they had a
majority of 23 in favour of his honourable, excellent
friend, Mr. Scott, and free trade. He believed there was
a spirit planted in the borough at that time which would
never die until they got freedom of trade established
throughout the whole world. Mr. Smith went on to say
that the monopolists were boasting of the present prosperity, but there was none that had not been occasioned by
two comparatively good harvests, which had somewhat revived trade ; but if they had free imports of food, they
would always have good trade. He defied any man to
show him where prosperity reigned among the people
without there being an abundance of food in the land.
It was impossible that prosperity could exist in this country unless that the people were in the enjoyment of plenty.
When corn was scarce and dear, all the money the working

men of Walsall could get for their labour was insufficient to buy enough of bread for themselves and families ; therefore, they had no money to expend upon clothes or other necessaries, the consumption of which was essential to the well-being of other parts of the community.

The chairman, in highly complimentary terms, next proposed the health of John Bright, Esq., M.P. for Durham. The announcement of this gentleman's name was received with loud and continued cheering, waving of handkerchiefs, &c. Silence having been restored, Mr. Bright rose, and was again received with renewed applause; after which he delivered one of those powerful and patriotic addresses in favour of free trade, for which he had already obtained, both in the House of Commons and out of it, so much applause. He appealed to facts in proof of the doctrine of free trade, and most forcibly elucidated the advantages which all classes in the community would derive from an entire free trade in corn. His address throughout was listened to with great attention, and made a deep and lasting impression upon all who heard it. He regretted the absence of Mr. Cobden, who was detained at home in consequence of the temporary illness of his lady at the time when he was about to leave for Walsall. The healths of the Rev. W. Mackean, the committee of 1841, who assisted in the contest of Mr. Smith, and subsequently of Mr. Scott, were given, and the company soon afterwards separated.

After this period, tea parties, at which ladies might attend, became an important part of the agitation.

In the course of this autumn was published an abstract of the answers and returns obtained in 1841, relative to the occupations of the people, and was read with great interest, as it settled a mooted question as to the relative proportion between agricultural and manufacturing labour. By those returns it was ascertained that between the years 1831 and 1841 the amount of employment afforded by the agriculture of Great Britain *remained nearly stationary,* notwithstanding the enormous increase in the population. The multitude of additional hands had been obliged to find work in other departments. The total male population of Great Britain, twenty years of age and upwards, was, in 1831, 3,199,984 ; and in 1841, 3,829,668, showing an increase in ten years of about 630,000 adult males. *Hardly one of these additional men had been able to find employment in agriculture.* The agricultural occupiers and labourers were, in 1831, 980,750, and in 1841, only 961,585. Allowing here for a correction pointed out by the enumerators, it still appeared that at the end of the decennial period, there was either no increase, or a very small one, in the number of adult males employed in agriculture. The numbers employed in commerce, trade, and manufactures were, in 1831, 1,278,283, and in 1841 they amounted to 1,682,044, showing that those branches of industry had found employment for *more than* 400,000 *additional persons of the class before mentioned.* The preface to the abstract contains the following observations :—

" In columns 28 and 29 are given proportional tables of the two great classes of occupations, viz., agricultural and commercial (or trade and manufactures). In the former are included all farmers, graziers, nurserymen, &c., together with the whole number of persons returned as agricultural labourers; in the latter, all shopkeepers and manufacturers, with those working under them; while from both classes are excluded those returned as domestic servants or general labourers, together with all professional persons. It will be seen that for all England *trade and manufacture include rather more than double the numbers included under the head of agriculture.*

" The altered proportion which the agricultural bears to the com-mercial classes for Great Britain generally, will at first, perhaps, excite surprise. The proportions which the agricultural, the commercial, and the miscellaneous classes bore to each other were in

	Agricultural.	Commercial.	Miscellaneous.
1811	35	44	21
1821	33	46	21
1831	28	42	30

While they were respectively in

1841	22	46	32

"It should be noticed that these comparative statements refer in the three first decennial periods to families, but upon the present occasion to individuals. The latter mode gives a more accurate view of the amount of employment afforded in each division of labour; but inasmuch as there are rather more of the younger branches of a family employed in trade and manufactures than in agriculture, it may have slightly augmented the difference here exhibited. The other facts shown by these returns are, however, so much in accordance with these results as to confirm their accuracy."

"Thus," said the *Morning Chronicle*, "the agricultural class comprises less than one-fourth of the people, and it is stationary in point of numbers, while the other sections of the population are rapidly increasing from year to year. Can anything more clearly demonstrate the folly of legis-lation which checks the development of the only kind of industry which is found to be capable of expanding with the multiplication of labourers? Is this to go on for ever? The foundation of that vast system of manufactures and commerce by which so many millions are maintained, is the interchange of manufactured goods for raw products. The great check upon our prosperity is the increasing difficulty of obtaining those raw products. With respect to the essential article food, we deliberately enhance the difficulty for the sake, professedly, of this agricultural class, which is every year losing some portion of its rela-tive importance. Is it possible, when the numbers on the one side and on the other are now authoritatively stated, that this grievous injustice can be suffered to continue? The injustice would be palpable, even if all those engaged in agriculture could be said to benefit by what is called agricultural protection; but when we know that they, like every other class, are interested in having the chief article of consumption abundant, we can hardly use language strong enough to condemn the nefarious policy which so openly sacrifices the many to the few."

There was a cessation for several weeks of public mani-festations on the part of the League. The harvest had been plentiful, and the price of bread was comparatively low. Trade had considerably revived; for even one good harvest has a great effect on the internal trade of the country. A great portion of the community, after supplying themselves with food, had something over to expend in clothing, and the demand for manufactures began to revive. Prognostications began to be uttered that the League would not be able, under such circumstances, to keep up its agitation; but the belief had now become general, that if one good harvest was almost invariably followed by prosperity, it would be well to have a regular share of the good harvests in all parts of the world; and instead of there being only a few far-sighted persons, as was the case in 1822 and 1835, saying, " would that it were always thus," there were millions who said, " if there was always the permission to share in the abundance of other lands, the multitude at home would have their share in it." The League only seemed to have lessened the activity of its labours. It had only turned them into another direction. The work of instruction had, in a great measure, been done. Opinion had been rapidly becoming right; the great object now, was to make it productive of action. The register of voters was defective. Tens of thousands were on the lists who had no right to be there, and tens of thousands were omitted who ought to have been there. To reform the registration was now the business of the League, and it set itself to effect this reformation, very quietly, but very vigorously. From July to October, it had been engaged, in all its wide-spread ramifications, in this useful and necessary labour. On the 24th of the latter month, a great meeting was held in the Manchester Free Trade Hall. The monopolists beheld, with no slight apprehensions of danger, that the League had not been asleep, as they believed, or affected to believe; but very earnestly at work, and in a direction to influence the legislature whenever a general election took place;

for, as yet, there was little hope of a change there before
another election.   Mr. Wilson was in the chair, and gave
a detailed account of the great gains to the free-trade
parties in the registration for every borough in Lancashire,
and stated that in sixty-eight boroughs, in other parts of
the kingdom, there had been similar gains.   He then
came to the county of Lancaster :—

" We all know the position of South Lancashire.   On the one hand,
you have evidence of the greatest amount—I may say the gigantic
amount—of energy, of industry, of capital, and wealth, ever seen ; and
on the other you have a landed proprietary, with a territory almost unknown in any other county.   At the last election—the first contest on
free trade principles—we all know the trifling majority which graced
the victory of the monopolist candidate.   It has been no secret that the
work of registration has been going on ever since that time ; the monopolists placarded the walls immediately the contest was over inviting
their friends to come and claim to be on the register, and the League
gave them due notice to ' put their house in order,' and hold themselves
ready against another election. (Applause.)   And if they have not
done so, it is for the best of all reasons—that they could not. _(Hear,
hear.)   Well, the first reports from the monopolists of what we were
doing was our index to what would be the result—for they began to cry
out against the shameful number of objections made by the free traders.
(Laughter.)   We admit that there was a great number ; and why ?   We
took the register—and every one knows that it was in a most shameful
state—the properties giving qualifications were described in the most
vague manner—we took the registration upon our own hands—and,
with the greatest anxiety to place it in the best possible, state, we induced 2,600 of our friends to reclaim, in order that they might give, as
they were bound to do, the best and fairest description they could of the
property for which they claimed to vote. (Hear.)   Then we objected
to our opponents, finding they had not done so, on that ground ; and I
am sure no man here will feel sympathy for men wishing to remain on
the register with a wrong description while they had it in their power to
amend such description. (Hear.)   We had not the means of striking
off these votes if they attended before the barrister ; but we considered
ourselves justified, in order that we might have the descriptions cor-
rected and given in accordance with the law.   Most of you are probably
aware of the result of the last election for South Lancashire.   There
were 14,544 votes given for the two candidates together ; being for
Entwisle 7571, and for Brown 6973, leaving a majority for Entwisle of

598. On the objections against those 7571 voters who polled for
Entwisle, we struck off 878 at the revision. (Loud and repeated
rounds of applause.) And of the 6973 who voted for Brown our opponents have struck off 422—we striking off more than two to their one,
thus having a majority, or gain, on the objections over them of 456,
and within 142 of the whole majority by which Mr. Brown was defeated
at the late contest. (Loud applause.) Then the register has gained at
this revision by the new claims. There were 4982 new claims; of
these the free traders made 3141, and established 2821 (loud applause),
being a failure of only 320 of the whole of the claims made. So much
for the reports propagated week after week that the free traders were
filling the register with spurious claims! The number of claims made
by the monopolists was 1841, of which they established 1357, being a
failure in 484 cases, and giving us a majority on the claims of 1464
votes. (Cheers.) Well, then, there are 169 new claims, belonging to
parties whose opinions we have not yet had time to ascertain; but we
will give the monopolists the whole of them, and we shall still have a
gain on this revision, taking claims and objections together, of 1751
votes. (Great and prolonged cheering.) Now, it is quite right that we
should see in what district this great gain has been accomplished. In
the first place, in the polling district of Ashton we have 40 of the 1751;
in Bolton 142, in the district of Bury 75, in that of Wigan 11, in that
of Ormskirk 17, in that of Oldham 102 (applause), in that of Newton
106 (bravo!) in that of Rochdale 233 (applause), at Liverpool 490, and
in the district of Manchester 704. (Loud cheering.) This makes a
total of 1920, from which deduct the 169 unascertained ones, and that
leaves us a gain of 1761. Then take from these 1920 the 598 majority
of Entwisle at the last election, and the 169 unascertained, making altogether 767, and we have a working majority upon this register of 1153
votes. (Loud cheers.) An analysis of the new register, therefore, shows,
of old electors (free traders) 6551, new electors (free traders) 2821;
total free traders on the registers 9372. Of the old electors being monopolists 6693, ditto new electors 1357; neutrals 169; leaving a total of
8219, or a working majority, as already stated, of 1153. (Applause.)
And now, gentlemen, we come to the Northern Division. We have
not done much there, but we have done something. We have attained
a gain there upon the revision, with comparatively little exertion, of
533. (Applause.) The result has been, then, to give us a gain of 533
votes for North Lancashire, to give us a seat for South Lancashire,
(cheers), and to leave the monopolists three seats in the boroughs, or
five out of the whole 26 members for the entire county. I think, then,
that you will agree with me that there never was, in the history of the
registration, so complete a sweep of a county as this has been. (Hear,

and loud cheers.) I have also in my hand a list of returns for 70 out of the 140 boroughs over which the League has exercised some influence, and of these there are 68 in which there has been a clear gain upon the registration—in some a great gain, but less or more in all. (Applause.) Well, now we will leave these results to speak for themselves; they are here, before the country. Our opponents may gather from them whether the League has been dead or slumbering, and they will accordingly derive what consolation they may from them. (Applause.) We have concentrated our energies on these points. We thought it was where, for the season, our efforts were most required; and although I may say we have done much, I believe the League is but yet in its infancy, that it is opening up new fields of labour, is occupying ground not before occupied, and that the exertions before made will afford no parallel to its future efforts."

Something more was wanted than the reformation of the registers. There was an opening for a great increase in the number of forty-shilling freeholds. Mr. Cobden came forward after Mr. Wilson had concluded, and pointed out this as the means of gaining many of the counties. He said :—

"Mr. Chairman, ladies, and gentlemen, I congratulate you upon this magnificent meeting. I was thinking, as I sat here, that probably there never had been so many persons assembled under a roof in England, or in Europe, as we have at this great League meeting; and the occasion and the circumstances under which we meet afford the most encouraging symptoms,—(hear)—encouraging, inasmuch as they prove that it is from no transient motive that you have joined together in this great cause—(hear)—that it is not from the pressure of distress, temporary distress, that you have banded yourselves together—that the cause of free trade is, in your minds, something more than a remedy for present evils—that you look at it, under all circumstances, as a great and absorbing truth—and that your minds crave for it with an intellectual and moral craving, which has made it almost a part of the religion of your souls. ('Hear, hear,' and applause.) I venture to say that this meeting, held under these circumstances, with no pressure or excitement to call you together, will have more weight, more effect, upon public opinion than a score of those assemblies we used to hold, when we were driven together, as it were, under the pressure of local and temporary distress. (Hear, hear.) And quiet as has been those statistical tables that you have heard by our chairman, I venture to say that they will strike more terror into the ranks of the monopolists than the loudest demonstrations or the most brilliant declamation with which we have ever tried to interest you. (Cheers.) Upon the subject of this registration there is one thought that occurred to me as our chairman was giving you an account of the proceedings in the county revision. It is this, that the counties are more vulnerable than the small pocket boroughs, if we can rouse the free traders of the country into a systematic effort such as we have exercised in the case of South Lancashire. (Hear, hear.) In many of the small boroughs there is no increase in the numbers; there is no extension of houses; the whole property belongs to a neighbouring noble, and you can no more touch the votes which he holds, through the property, than you can touch the balance in his banker's hands. ('Hear, hear,' and a laugh.) Now, the county constituency may be increased indefinitely. It requires a qualification of forty shillings a year in a freehold property to give a man a vote for a county. I think our landlords made a great mistake when they retained the forty-shilling freehold qualification; and, mark my words, it is a rod in pickle for them. (A laugh, and cheers.) I should not be surprised if it does for us what it did for Catholic Emancipation, and what it did for the Reform Bill—give us the means of carrying free trade; and if it should, the landlords will very likely try to serve us as they did the forty-shillings freeholders in Ireland, when we have done the work. ('Hear, hear,' and 'Oh, oh.') The forty-shilling franchise for the county was established five or six centuries ago. At that time a man, in the constitutional phraseology of the time, was deemed to be a 'yeoman,' and entitled to political rights, provided he had forty shillings a year clear to spend. That was at that time a subsistence for a man; probably it was equal to the rental of one hundred acres of land. What is it now? With the vast diffusion of wealth among the middle classes, which then did not exist, and among a large portion, I am happy to say, in this district, of the superior class of operatives, too, that forty-shilling franchise is become merely nominal, and is within the reach of every man who has the spirit to acquire it. ('Hear, hear,' and cheers.) I say, then, every county where there is a large town population, as in Lancashire, the West Riding of Yorkshire, South Staffordshire, North Cheshire, Middlesex, Surrey, Kent, and many other counties I could name—in fact, every other county bordering upon the sea coast, or having manufactures in it—may be won, and easily won, if the people can be roused to a systematic effort to qualify themselves for the vote in the way in which the South Lancashire people have reached to the qualification. We find counties can be won by that means and no other. (Cheers.) It is the custom sometimes for many to put their savings into the savings' banks. I believe there are fourteen or fifteen millions or more so deposited. I would not say a word

to lessen the confidence in that security, but I say there is no investment so secure as the freehold of the earth, and it is the only investment that gives a vote along with the property. (Hear, hear.) We
come then to this: it costs a man nothing to have a vote for the county.
('Hear,' and applause.) He buys his property; sixty pounds for a
cottage is given—thirty or forty pounds in many of the neighbouring
towns will do it; he has then the interest of his money, he has the
property to sell when he wants it, and he has his vote in the bargain.
(Loud cheers, and cries of 'hear.') Sometimes a parent, wishing to
teach a son to be economical and saving, gives him a set of nest-eggs in
a savings' bank; I say to such a parent, 'Make your son, at twenty-
one, a freeholder; it is an act of duty, for you make him thereby an
independent freeman, and put it in his power to defend himself and
his children from political oppression—(loud cheers)—and you make
that man with £60 an equal in the polling-booth to Mr. Scarisbrick,
with his eleven miles in extent of territory, or to Mr. Egerton. (Renewed cheers.) This must be done. In order to be on the next year's
register, it requires only that you should be in possession of a freehold
before the 31st of next January.' We shall probably be told that 'this
is very indiscreet—what is the use of coming out in public, and an-
nouncing such a plan as this, when your enemies can take advantage of
it as well as you?' My first answer to that is, that our opponents, the
monopolists, cannot take advantage of it as well as we. (Hear, hear.)
In the first place, very few men are, from connexion or prejudice,
monopolists, unless their capacity for inquiry or their sympathies have
been blunted by already possessing an undue share of wealth. (Hear,
hear.) In the next place, if they wish to urge upon others of a rank
below them to qualify for a vote, they cannot trust them with the use of
the vote when they have got it. ('Hear,' and cheers.) But, apart
from that, I would answer those people who cavil at this public appeal,
and say, 'You will not put salt upon your enemy's tail—it is much too
wise a bird. They have been at this work long ago,' and they have the
worst of it now. (Hear, hear, hear.) What has been the conduct of
the landlords of the country? Why, they have been long engaged in
multiplying voters upon their estates, making the farmers take their
sons, brothers, nephews, to the register; making them qualify as many
as the rent of the land will cover; they have been making their land a
kind of political capital ever since the passing of the Reform Bill.
(Cheers and a laugh.) You have, then, a new ground opened to you
which has never yet been entered upon, and from which I expect, in
the course of not more than three years from this time, that every
county (if we persevere as we have in South Lancashire) possessing a
large town population may carry free traders as their representatives to

parliament. (Cheers.) Now, gentlemen, with just these preliminary remarks, I was going to notice a common objection made to us during the last two or three months—that the League has been very quiet of late—that we have been doing nothing. (Hear, hear.) Many people have said to me, ' When are you going out into the agricultural districts again? I think they will be quite ripe for you now, for most of your predictions have fallen true, and the farmers will come and listen.' (Hear.) My answer has been, ' We are better employed at present at home, and the landlords are doing our work very well for us at their agricultural meetings.' "

Mr. Cobden then adverted to the great improvements that had been effected in agriculture since the League had pointed out the wretched system of farming that had prevailed over England, and concluded a most effective speech by saying :—

" I believe, when the future historian comes to write the history of agriculture, he will have to state :—' In such a year, there was a stringent Corn Law passed for the protection of agriculture. From that time agriculture slumbered in England, and it was not until, by the aid of the aid of the Anti-Corn-Law League the Corn Law was utterly abolished, that agriculture sprang up to the full vigour of existence in England to become what it now is, like her manufactures, unrivalled in the world.' (Loud cheers.) It is a gloomy and most discouraging thought, that whilst this system of Corn Laws alternately starves the people in the manufacturing districts and then ruins the farmers, it really, in the end, confers no permanent benefit on any class. (Hear.) I told you in the beginning I did not believe the agricultural labourer was now so badly off as he was when corn was 70s. a quarter; but I will tell you where distress in the agricultural districts is now. It is among the tenant farmers themselves. (Hear.) They are paying rents with wheat at 45s. a quarter, which they have bargained for at a calculation of wheat being 56s., and in many cases 60s. a quarter. It is owing to this discrepancy in the prices that the tenant farmers are now paying rent out of capital; they are discharging their labourers, unable to employ them; and theirs is the real distress now existing in the agricultural districts. This state of things will not continue either here or in the agricultural districts. What is the language that drops from the landlords at some of their meetings? It is, ' We shall not very likely have higher prices for corn this year; we must wait for better times; we will give you back ten per cent. this year.' No permanent reduction, and why? Because they know that, by the certain operation of this system, in less than five years from this time this wheel of fortune, or rather misfortune. will go round again; you will be at the bottom and the farmers at the top, and you will have wheat again at 70s. or 80s. a quarter, causing thus a pretended prosperity among the farmers. As sure as you have had this revolution before, so sure will you have it again. There is nothing in Sir Robert Peel's Corn Law to prevent the recurrence of similar disasters. The law is as complete a bar to legitimate trade as the old law was. I speak in the presence of merchants shipping to every quarter of the globe, men who bring back the produce of every quarter of the globe, and I put it to them whether, with this sliding scale, they dare to order from a foreign country a single cargo of wheat in exchange for the manufactures which they sell? This being the case—and it is the whole case—you are not stimulating other countries to provide for your future wants, you are laying up no store here or stores abroad, and there will again be a recurrence of the disasters we have passed through."

Mr. Bright then addressed the meeting in a spirit-stirring speech. He warned the country against the belief that the then comparative prosperity was likely to be permanent :—

" The Providence which has given us two or three good harvests may give us one, or two, or three more; but we must bear in mind that the course of the seasons cannot be changed, will not be changed, to suit the caprice, the folly, or the criminality of human legislation. (Applause.) As we have had before, so we shall have again a change of seasons; and when that change shall come, and if the people of this country have not, in the meantime, bestirred themselves and shaken off this iniquitous impost, I ask you whom will you blame but yourselves, and where can you run for refuge? for your own folly will have led you into danger, and by your own neglect alone will you have allowed these evils again to come upon you. You will again have to suffer those evils which arise from the price of bread rising all over the country. The consumption by the great mass of the people of all kinds of manufactured goods will be greatly crippled; you will have again a great exportation of gold, and a great derangement of the monetary affairs of the country; you will again have numbers of merchants and manufacturers going rapidly, week after week, into the *Gazette;* you will again have your shopkeepers impoverished; and, worst of all, you will again have the labourers of this district, our honest and industrious artizans plunged into all that distress which we have lately witnessed; and arising from that distress, discontent, and disaffection, and a brutalizing and barbarizing of the minds of the people, such as they have suffered from for the last half-a-dozen years, and which they are now only partially getting rid of. (Applause.) It is impossible to draw a picture too gloomy of that which we have already seen in this district, and it is much less possible to draw a picture of that which must come if we neglect the power that we have in our hands to wipe away these infamous laws. I am sure we have the power; the statements made by our chairman to-night prove that we have the power. (Applause.) The Reform Bill never has been worked by either the liberal or free trade party in this country. (Applause.) It may be a bad bill; it has flaws enough we all know; it has pitfalls many for us, and it has privileges far too many for our opponents. Applause.) But for all that, if we will only work it, I am persuaded there is within it enough of the popular principle to enable us to amend it, if need be (applause), and to do many other things which we may think necessary for our welfare."

Mr. Bazley, President of the Chamber of Commerce, moved a vote of thanks to Mr. Cobden and Mr. Bright, and the meeting, after giving three enthusiastic cheers, separated. The report of the proceedings spread everywhere the desire to increase the free-trade influence in counties, by the purchase of forty-shilling freeholds, much to the alarm of the monopolists, who had regarded these as their impregnable strongholds.

CHAPTER XV.

THE REGISTRATION AND FREEHOLD MOVEMENT.

On the 20th of November, Mr. George Wilson, Mr. Cobden, and Mr. Bright, visited Rochdale, where, at a very numerous meeting, they inculcated the duty of attending closely to the registration and obtaining freehold qualifications. Mr. Wm. Brown, afterwards member for South Lancashire, and Mr. Sharman Crawford, member of the borough, enforced the recommendations. On the 22nd, a meeting was held at Halifax, where Mr. Bright and Mr. G. Wilson showed how the West Riding might be won. At Hebden Bridge, and at a great meeting at Leeds, Mr. Cobden and Mr. Bright convinced thousands of the certainty of winning that most important of the three Ridings. The same gentlemen visited Huddersfield, with a similar result. In the metropolis, also, effective meetings were held to secure the independence of the county of Middlesex. In that gloomy month of November, 1844, it became evident that there was to be energetic action in 1845, and Sir Robert Peel, no doubt, felt deep apprehensions, in reference to his recommendation of doing battle in the registration courts, that his tactics would be turned against himself and the monopolists who supported him because they believed that he would continue to support their exactions.

The course adopted by the League was fully explained at an excessively crowded meeting, held in Covent Garden

Theatre, on Wednesday, December 12th. Mr. Wilson, the chairman, detailed, at considerable length, the operations during the last three months. Mr. Villiers followed in a tone of confidence that victory was not far distant, and said :—

"With regard to the end, we are all agreed : it is to give force to the free-trade party. The means, I presume, are most legitimate, for they are those of our first ministers. (Laughter.) When Sir Robert Peel was out, and wished to be in, he called his friends together, and explained to them the rights they possessed, and how they could use them for him (laughter), and told them to go, each man, and register a vote ; and they went and did as he bid them, and Sir Robert Peel came in in consequence (laughter) ; and if Sir Robert Peel had not told them they would not have attended to the register, and he would not have come in. (Hear.) Well, then, is not this the advice which the League tenders to its friends, whom they advise to profit by the privilege which the constitution gives them, to register their votes ; and with this difrerence only in the end, that the League does not want to turn anybody out or anybody in, but to compel whoever is there to do what is just to the people (cheers) ; and Sir Robert can hardly say—Register, register, to put me in power ; but do not register, register, to make me use that power justly and wisely. (Hear.) I see no reason why the League should not succeed in adding greatly to the strength of their means ; and one thing is sure, that nothing will be gained unless something is attempted. The League is trying what they have reason to believe will succeed. They are not standing still, or, as our opponents say, dying, but they are trying something new, and which, from what I have heard my honourable friend the chairman say, is not unlikely to succeed. (Cheers.) It is gratifying to hear what he has told us of the rescue of one important county, which has always heretofore been in the hands of the monopolists, and would have remained so but for the efforts the League have made. (Cheers.) That is a proof that it is worth making some attempt to improve our position. We were beaten at the last election in that county, perhaps, from not having attended to the register. I believe that the monopolists of Lancashire have given up that county now in consequence of their having attended to it. (Hear.) I see no reason why that which has happened in Lancashire should not occur in Yorkshire ; and if that which happened in Lancashire and will do so in Yorkshire is the result of the intelligence, numbers, and property of the commercial and productive classes, I ask why should not that happen in Middlesex which has been accomplished in the other two ?"

Mr. Cobden, reviewing the proceedings of the League, and adverting to the change of opinion that had already taken place amongst the agriculturists, spoke in the same hopeful tone :—

"Our worthy chairman has told you something of our late proceedings. Some of our cavilling friends—and there are a good many of that class, men who seem to be a little bilious at times, and are rather disposed to criticise—individuals who do not move on themselves, and, not being gregarious animals, are incapable of helping other people to move on, and therefore they have nothing to do but to sit by and quarrel with others—these men say, ' This is a new move of the League, attacking the landlords in their counties ; it is a change in their tactics.' But we are altering nothing, and we have not changed a single thing. I believe every step we have taken has been necessary, in order to arrive at the present stage of our movement. (Hear.) We began by lecturing and distributing tracts, in order to create an enlightened public opinion ; we did that for two or three years necessarily. We then commenced operations in the boroughs ; and never at any time was there so much sytematic attention, labour, and expense devoted to the boroughs of this country in the way of registration as at the present time. (Hear, hear.) As regards our lectures, why, we continue them still, only that, instead of having small rooms, up three pair of stairs back, as we used to do, we have magnificent assemblies, as that now before me. (Cheers.) We distribute our tracts, but in another form ; we have our own organ, the *League* paper, twenty thousand copies of which have gone out every week for the last twelve months. I have no doubt that that journal penetrates into every parish of the United Kingdom, and goes the round of the district. Now, in addition to what we proposed before, we think we have had a new light ; we rather expect that we can disturb the monopolists in their own counties. (Cheers.) The first objection that is made to that plan is, that it is a game which two can play at ; that the monopolists can adopt the move as well as we can. I have answered that objection before, by saying that we are in the very fortunate predicament of sitting down to play a game at a table where our opponents have possession of all the stakes, and we have nothing to lose. (Hear, hear.) They have played at it for a long time, and won all the counties ; my friend Mr. Villiers had not a single county voter the last time he brought forward his motion. There are 152 English and Welsh county members, and I really think it would baffle the arithmetic of my friend the member for Wolverhampton to make out clearly that he could carry a majority of the house without having some of them. We are going to try if we cannot get him a few. We have obtained him one already—the largest county in the kingdom; we have secured South Lancashire, and that is the most populous district in the whole kingdom."

Mr. Cobden described the counties that might be won, and concluded by saying :—

" We look to the more populous districts first; we say it will not be necessary to gain the whole of them; if we obtain North and South Lancashire, the West Riding of Yorkshire, and Middlesex, the landed monopolists will give up corn in order to save a great deal more. (Cheers and laughter.) There is one other point. Many people may say, ' this is something not quite legitimate ; you cannot go on manufacturing these votes.' We reply, the law and the constitution prescribe it, and we have no alternative. It may be a very bad system, that men should be required to have £40 or £50 laid out on the surface of the earth, in order that they should be represented; but the law prescribes that plan, and there is no other. And we say, do not violate the law ; conform to it in spirit and in fact , and do so by thousands and tens of thousands, if you can. (Cheers.) There is nothing savouring of trick or finesse of any kind in it; you must have a *bonâ fide* qualification. It will not do now, as it did under the old system, to create fictitious votes ; there is now a register, there was none formerly. That is where we will stop them; we will put them through a fine sieve at the registration. No, no ; under the old system, when the Lowthers contested Westmorland against Brougham—the Henry Brougham that was, you know —(cheers and laughter)—the contest lasted for 14 days, and they went on manufacturing collusive and fictitious votes during the whole period, making them as fast as they could poll. The voters went up with their papers, and the day after the polling put them into the fire, or treated them as waste paper. (Hear.) But things are altered now; you must be twelve months on the register, and be hung up at the church doors for a certain period, before you can vote. Therefore we do not intend to win by tricks, for we are quite sure the enemy can beat us at that. Gentlemen, there is one other objection ; they will say you should not tell this, it is very bad tactics. I say you have nothing to gain by secresy. (Hear.) There are tens and hundreds of thousands in this country whose hearts will beat when they see the report of this meeting, and who will read every word of it. Those are our friends. Our opponents will turn their heads away, and will not read what we say. We speak to the sympathising multitude, whose feelings and hearts are with us ; and we make an appeal to them, not only to you in Middlesex, but to those who are unqualified throughout the length and breadth of the

land. Scotland expects it of you; they say in that country, ' Oh! that
we had the 40s. franchise here; we could then clear them out of twelve
counties in twelve months.' (Hear.) Ireland looks to you, with her £10
franchise, the same as Scotland. England, wealthy England, with nothing
but her nominal franchise of 40s. a-year, with such a weapon as this in
her hand, and not to be able to beat down this miserable, unintelligent,
incapable oligarchy, that is misgoverning her. (Loud cheers.) No; I
will not believe it; we will cry aloud, not here only, but on every pedestal on which we can be placed throughout the country, though there
is no pinnacle like this to speak from—we will raise our voice everywhere. ' Qualify, qualify, qualify.' Do it, not only for the sake of the
toiling millions, and the good of the industrious middle classes, but for
the benefit of the aristocracy themselves. Yes, do it especially for their
sake, and for that of their dependent, miserable serfs, the agricultural
labourers. Do it, I say, especially for the welfare of the landed interest,
who, if left to their own thoughtless and misguided ignorance, will bring
this country down to what Spain or Sicily is now; and with it they will
reduce themselves to the same beggary that the Spanish grandees have
been brought to. To avert this calamity from them, the ignorant and
besotted few, I say again, ' Qualify, qualify, qualify."

Mr. Bright, always effective in exciting to action after
conviction, having described the position of their opponents
and their vulnerability, said :—

" My hope is brighter than ever; my faith is undimmed by the
smallest shadow of a doubt. There is everything throughout the whole
country which betokens the speedy and final triumph of this great
question. And why should it not triumph? We seek only that which
the good and the just in all ages have sought; we are seeking for freedom and justice. This is a struggle which has been going on upon the
earth for thousands of years. Our forefathers have carried it on, and
they are gone to their rest; we are working out the same object in our
day and generation. Many of us will live to see the accomplishment of
this great work, and those who come after us will have something else
to do. And I trust that in all this labour we shall leave them an example of steady determination and unflinching perseverance on behalf
of that which we believe to be right and just. (Loud applause.) In a
great struggle, in the long run, the just always wins. He must have
read very little of history who does not know that liberty is triumphing.
There is more freedom and justice in the world now by far than there
ever was at any former period. There are more men having a love of
what is right and just; the oppresser is cowed and abashed; he does

not come amongst us with force and violence, but he works insidiously and treacherously; he wraps his chain in chaplets of flowers, and thus he tyrannises over his countrymen. (Cheers.) Yes, freedom is Heaven's first gift to man. It is his heritage; he has it by charter from Heaven; and although it has struggled so long, this principle is still living, breathing, growing, and every day increasing in strength. (Cheers.) The infant of our father's day has become the giant of our own time. An American poet, speaking of liberty and its struggles, says,—

> ' Power at thee has launched
> His bolts, and with his lightnings smitten thee;
> They could not quench the life thou hast from Heaven.
> Merciless power has dug thy dungeon deep
> And his swart armourers, by a thousand fires,
> Have forged thy chain.'

But liberty still survives, is indestructible, and man shall yet enjoy its blessings. But, bear in mind that, precious and excellent as this liberty is, there are certain conditions upon which alone it can be obtained and secured. You must rely upon yourselves for it. Liberty is too precious and sacred a thing ever to be entrusted to the keeping of another man. Be the guardians of your own rights and liberties. If you be not, you will have no protectors but spoilers of all that you possess. (Hear.) You can only hold it on the condition of perpetual vigilance. You must work at it as though it were a matter of business; you must consider this question of defending your rights as a concern no less important than that of providing for your family. What is it but this, if we come to look narrowly into it? This freedom for which you struggle is the freedom to live; it is the right to ' eat your bread by the sweat of your brow.' It is the freedom which was given to you even in the primeval curse; and shall man make that curse more bitter to his fellow-man? (Immense applause.) No; instead of despairing, I have more confidence and faith than ever. I believe that those old delusions and superstitions which, like verminous and polluted rags, have disfigured the fair form of this country's greatness, are now fast dropping away. I think I behold the dawn of a brighter day; all around are the elements of a mighty movement. We stand as on the very threshold of a new career; and may we not say that this League—this great and growing confederacy of those who love justice and hate oppression—has scattered, broadcast throughout the land, seed from which shall spring forth ere long an abundant, a glorious harvest of true greatness for our country, and of permanent happiness for mankind."

Before the separation of this great meeting, Mr. Wilson

announced that the Council of the League had resolved that the Bazaar, in aid of the funds, would be held in London, on the following May.

Before the close of the year, meetings were held in Liverpool, Bradford, Sheffield, Rotherham, Wakefield, Barnsley, Bolton, Keighley, Pontefract, and other towns, attended by deputations from the League; and everywhere the proposal to increase the number of forty-shilling free-holds was hailed as a constitutional and effective means of rescuing counties from the thraldom of the landowners.

A number of letters had appeared in *The League* paper, with the signature, "A Norwich Weaver Boy," written by Mr. W. J. Fox, which had been read with deep interest; and I think I may appropriately close my notice of the proceedings in 1844 by copying his fourteenth letter:—

"TO THE RIGHT HON. SIR ROBERT PEEL, BART., M.P., FIRST LORD OF THE TREASURY, ETC., ETC.

" Sir,—Any attempt to prove to you the truth of free-trade principles or the importance of their practical application, would be a superfluous procedure. You have made repeated profession of those principles. In various ways you have applied them, although it may be but par-tially. From the proposition of your tariff to the recent admission of Venezuelan sugar at the reduced duty, there has been a slow and cautious, but a distinctly perceptible, advance in the measures of your government towards free trade. The question to be argued with you is not one of principle but of policy; not one of object, but of time, mode, and degree. You are afraid of injuring existing interests by sudden changes. And you are also not unobservant of the influence of your measures on the strength of your political position. This wariness has marked your whole public career, and is deeply inwrought into your personal character. The danger is, lest you should be too wary, and pass the point at which boldness is the safest caution. Did such peril only affect yourself, with yourself its consideration might be left; but it involves the condition and prospects of millions. Those who participate in your connexion as to principles; who are thankful for every step, however small, which you have taken in their application; and who are anxious for that immensity of national good which would arise from their consistent and complete adoption, have claims on your attention, however different from your own may be their political sympathies and antipathies. The topic is paramount to all party demarcation.

"How much further can you go towards the introduction of a consistent free-trade policy without fairly grappling with the food monopoly? Are you not all but brought to a stand-still already? The landowners are alarmed and vigilant. You had a taste of their quality on the sugar question. They will not again help you in the demolition even of the minutest monopoly. You will no more be able to persuade them that they are the safer for the sacrifice of others. It will be impossible for you to open your mouth on import duties, but they will look down at your feet and think they see more than your boot covers. You are crippled for what you know to be the only sound commercial policy. Suspicion will track you through every speech and bill with the scent of a bloodhound. You will rise in the House with the vindictive monopolist in your rear, the whig partisan in your front, and that magnetic telegraph at work between them which ensures co-operation without coalition. What a helpless and pitiable condition! Can you endure it for the sake of office? Or can you long secure office by enduring it?

"On the other hand, imagine the corn-law question disposed of, what ulterior division need you apprehend in your majority? In all remaining applications of your commercial principles they would be a band of ready helpers. None so decided as they to raze every remaining fortress of monopoly, and not leave one stone upon another. There would no longer be any apprehension from your measures. The threatening aspect would change to one of promise. In each new move they would foresee increasing profit instead of impending peril. The spell of 'protection' in his own case once broken, not a landowner but would cheer you on in your progress towards its utter demolition. The country would breathe freely, in the grateful perception of each successive benefit. Controversy would give place to congratulation. The din of the old warfare of agriculture and manufactures would die away into the remoteness of historic distance. A career of useful statesmanship would open before you, limited only by the capacity of your own intellect, wherein classes might be harmonised, misery abated, the labouring many raised, and the truest glory, that of peaceful aggrandizement, be achieved for our country.

"But the intermediate step—' there's the rub.' True, you peril office by attempting it, and might very likely be for a while unseated. What then? Are you satisfied *never* to apply your free-trade principles to corn? Or do you anticipate a better time by delay?

"Never! Why, then, as I have already shown, you submit to be obstructed in *all* your commercial legislation. You consent to live the manacled and maimed slave of a suspicion. You forego the noblest prize that remains to recompense the toils of office. You will neither do good nor win credit. Much too deeply is the thought of your ultimate purposes rooted in the minds of the landed monopolists for either forgiveness or forgetfulness to enter there. Years will not eradicate their suspicion. It will outlive your power, and be planted on your grave.

"A better time? What can bring it? The whig leaders are still too infatuated to pre-occupy the ground. With that renowned ingenuity which builds a wall to knock their heads against, they hold themselves pledged to their fixed duty, and you unpledged as the free air. They stick to their stand by the wayside, where you may pass on and welcome. As to them, delay only provides against you the chance of their having a lucid interval. The chance may be remote; it is not an absolute impossibility.

"You have brought in a bill so lately—Psha! Sir Robert; you are too much of a man to mind that. It is a good deal longer since the enactment of your bill than that enactment was from the time of your declaration against any change. Besides, how stands your bill as to the different parties interested?

"To the agriculturists, who reckoned upon its keeping up the price of wheat to 56s. the quarter, it is a complete failure. Nothing has been kept up but rents, unless it be agitation. At meetings of protection societies, the farm tenantry are declared to be posting rapidly on the road to ruin. Do not think of reading your history in *their* eyes, or hearing it from their lips. You can lose no popularity at their meetings. Even with the landlords, your law is a forlorn hope. They merely think,

'Better to bear the ills [or bills] we have,
Than fly to others which we know not of.'

You have no clinging attachment on their parts to overcome. They are in no state to offer stout resistance to a bold onset. Moreover, can they govern the country? Were they to turn you out, there is only one other thing in the wide world which they could do, and that is, to let you in again.

"Wheat at 45s. is a good repeal price. No great shock would be given by the change. It would simply render more clear what people were to do. Any great fall or rise will breed confusion and entanglement; desolation in the south or commotion in the north. It is a price to take advantage of for action, as you would the conversion of a stock in the funds. The moment is a golden one. Old Time bends his brow for the forelock to be seized. There is utter destruction to the small farmers, in the perspective one way; and in the other, the well-remembered horrors of Paisley, with many a scene of kindred misery.

"Although the cheapness resulting from abundant harvests has

baffled your bill in its understood promise to the agriculturists, and
stimulated a degree of manufacturing prosperity which could not have
existed had that promise been realized, yet the condition of great
masses of the people continues to be such as demands attention and
amelioration. The agricultural labourers are unhelped. The swarms
of our city population are unhelped. Every daily paper records some
death by destitution. Every charitable society testifies to the necessity
for change. Not a near-sighted philanthropist but has his nostrum.
But they all obtain more credit for the fact of the disease than for the
efficacy of the alleged specific. They are all witnesses that the poor
' come off shorts' in the distribution of the food and wealth which their
labour is the agency of creating. And for that the poor will take their
testimony. The rest they set down as quackery. You, Sir Robert,
know it to be quackery. You are aware, if not of the means of absolute
cure, yet of the best remedy in the stores of legislation. Till that be
produced, the mischief grows. Your bill can do no more for it.

"I have spoken, in general terms, of the ' landowners' as the lion in
your path. Really, it is only a landowning clique. With such men as
the Duke of Wellington and Lord Stanley, the money worth of the
Corn Laws to their class is altogether subordinate to political or party
considerations. With the Dukes of Richmond and Buckingham the
case may be different. The landlords whom *they* represent make a
great noise, and with the help of stewards, jobbers, and a host of syco-
phants and hangers-on, they muster their troops of dependent tenantry,
and put on a big face of hostility. Is it much more formidable than
what you so suddenly and virtuously confronted for Catholic Emancipation? And is there any comparison in the results to be anticipated?

"Do not fancy that the writer dreams of persuading you. I deem
persuasion as unlikely as conviction is unnecessary. You are making
a blunder, and I am exposing the blunder; that is all. To be the
greatest of those who lead, has never been the praise or the ambition of
your statesmanship; but you have commonly won the humbler fame of
being the expertest of those who follow. In the present case, even
this glory is likely soon, by over-caution and prolonged delay, to be in
danger of forfeiture. This is a great pity on your own account; a yet
greater on that of the industrious millions who must endure the
consequences.

                                        "A NORWICH WEAVER BOY."

On the 8th of January, 1845, a splendid and spirited
meeting was held in the Free Trade Hall; Mr. Wilson
was in the chair, and spoke briefly on the progress of the

registrations.   Mr. Mark Philips, M.P., spoke briefly also, but effectively.   Mr. W. Brown followed.   He had been selected by the free-traders as a candidate for the representation of South Lancashire, with a certainty of success. He took a comprehensive view of the effects of the Corn Laws on the trade with various nations, and convinced his large audience of his fitness to represent their county. He was followed by Mr. Cobden, who successfully disposed of some charges of intolerance which had been brought against the League.   If that body quarrelled with the projects of others, it was, he said—

"Because they had been ostentatious projects, brought forward to divert public attention, and not, as they believed, with the real intention of serving the object professed by the propounders Who could say that the League had ever found fault with private benevolence, or had ever stopped to quarrel with men going about to do good, and not seeking to proclaim trumpet-tongued their own good works? But it was when men who supported the Corn Laws were found ostentatiously propounding other schemes to meet a great political evil, it was then that they had a right to criticise and question the intelligence, at least of those parties, and to ask how they could profess to serve the people, and at the same time, by their votes, they were trying to starve and impoverish the people.   He must confess that, having been let a little behind the scenes in the conduct of these parties, he did suspect that a great number of those who had got a reputation of being benevolent-minded in public matters, were trying to start these false scents, with the view of leading the people off from the question of the Corn Laws.   Ordinary intelligence might teach them the utter futility of trying to benefit the people, who, by their own legislation, were kept short of the necessaries of life.   *   *   *   He received a letter the other day from an old friend of his, and a fellow-labourer in those efforts they made six or seven years ago in the cause of education—he meant Mr. James Simpson, of Edinburgh, in which he spoke in somewhat a tone of complaint of the remarks which were made in Covent Garden Theatre upon the subject of public baths.   Now he should be anxious to pay the tribute of his highest admiration to the conduct Mr. Simpson had pursued.   He had not prominently advocated free trade in corn; but he had been a silent contributor to the League, and they knew that they had his good wishes. But if he or any one else thought they could promote the benefit of mankind, by giving their attention to other questions, why, God speed them, and he wished them well in their labours."

Mr. Cobden was urgent and eloquent on the subject of registration. He threw a generous halo around the question :—

" Every age, every generation, had some distinguishing struggle that marked its history. In one century we had the contest for religious freedom—another century marks the era of political freedom—another century comes, and the great battle of commercial freedom has to be fought; and Manchester, and those free cotton districts around it (he called it a free district, because the cotton trade had never been dandled by protection, and never owned its devotion to monopoly), were pledged to take the lead in this great contest—a contest that had already become historical; for it was marked upon our parliamentary annals as one of the greatest of modern combinations. They could not draw back from this contest, but they must bring not merely disgrace upon themselves, but disgrace upon the nation, and prove themselves recreant from the very race from which they sprung. It was not a mere contest for a few more pigs, a few more sheep, or a little more corn. If the mere physical, the material gain to which we were looking, was all that we had to hope from the trial of our principles, why it would be a sordid and mercenary conflict after all. No; the triumph of free trade was the triumph of pacific principles between all the nations of the earth. (Cheers.) It was a blow, and a death-blow to the old system of diplomatic intrigue between the governments of countries. It was making them, as the industrious fabricators of this district, and their friend Mr. Brown, and such as him, the ambassadors and merchants of this country, it was giving to them the title-deeds, by which they would secure to themselves and to all nations the blessings of peace for all times. He saw in the distance—he might perhaps be dreaming—but he saw in the distance a world's revolution involved in the triumphs of free-trade principles. The very motives which had led governments and ambitious rulers to rear up great empires, and to aggrandise the world's territory—those motives would be gone, and gone for ever, when they had taught people that they could better profit by the prosperity and freedom of other nations, through the peaceful paths of industry, than they could triumph through the force of war or military conquest. (Cheers.) He might be dreaming, but he thought he saw in the distance that great empires, and vast and powerful military and naval establishments, would be no longer necessary in the governments of the world when they had established free trade throughout it. If what he said was founded in reason, and not the dreams of the imagination, then he said this was a cause which was worth contending for; one that not merely the merchant and the manufacturer, but the philanthropist and the Christian might well lay hold of, and glory that he had lived in an age when he might take a share in the conquest over selfishness and monopoly. (Loud cheers.)"

Mr. Cobden was followed by Mr. Bright, who spoke of the activity that prevailed in the West Riding of Yorkshire, which promised triumph in that important division of the county.

Other meetings were also held; at Warrington, attended by Mr. Cobden and Mr. Bright; at Preston, by the same gentlemen; at Oldham, by Mr. Cobden, Mr. J. Brooks, and Mr. Edward Watkin; at Chorley, by Mr. Bright and myself; at Macclesfield, by Mr. Cobden; at Blackburn, by Mr. Cobden and Mr. H. Ashworth; and at Durham, by Mr. Bright. There were also numerous meetings held in other towns, not attended by any deputation from the League.

CHAPTER XVI.

PREPARING FOR PARLIAMENT, 1845.

As a prelude to the opening of parliament, there was a great gathering in Covent Garden Theatre on the 15th of January, and the crowded attendance proved that the subject was as interesting as it had been when the first meeting was held there. Mr. Wilson was in the chair, and called attention to registration, and the purchase of freeholds :—

" Since the idea was broached we have had forty meetings in Lancashire and Yorkshire, for the purpose of inducing our friends in those counties to qualify as voters. All these have been thorough business meetings. We have had some experience in public meetings during the course of this agitation ; but never since the League commenced its operations have there been such large assemblages convened for business objects as those to which I am now referring. (Cheers.) We want our friends in the counties of Yorkshire, Lancashire, and Middlesex, to run side by side—not in a spirit of jealousy, but with a feeling of honest rivalry—so that each county may present a proper return at the next election. The counties I have now enumerated are such as any man may well be proud of becoming a freeholder of : they are leading districts of this country, but they have not been made so by the influence of the aristocracy of the land. (Cheers.) Their inhabitants have not been raised to their present high position by the efforts of the aristocracy, nor have they attained their present standing by anything which mere rank or station may have contributed to their welfare ; but it is attributable to the muscle and sinew, skill and intellect, of their operatives and capitalists, manufacturers, masters, and merchants. (Cheers.) It never can be long the destiny of these counties to be held in the thraldom of an aristocracy, or to be misrepresented by men who are hostile to the very principles upon which their prosperity is founded. (Cheers.)"

Mr. Milner Gibson, after alluding to the failure of the agricultural associations, said of the Anti-Corn-Law League:—

" There are in this society men who have enlightened the agriculturists upon husbandry, and the different modes by which the produce of the earth may be increased. I venture to say that there is not in any part of this kingdom an individual to be found more anxious to improve the agriculture of the country, or to see two blades of grass grow where one only is now produced, than our excellent leader, Mr. Cobden. (Cheers.) His speeches have been replete with sound advice to the agriculturists. They have also, I believe, led to a practical improvement in agriculture. (Hear, hear.) In different parts of the kingdom where they have been delivered, they have turned the attention of the agriculturist to the improvement of his art, and have withdrawn him from that fatal reliance upon what Parliament can do for him, which has hitherto been the bane of the farming body. (Hear, hear.) We are no enemies, I say, to agriculture. It has been stated also that we are opposed to the British farmer. When the Anti-League meetings have been held, we have been told that ' the British lion'—meaning, by the expression, the British farmer—' was shaking his mane at us.' (Laughter.) The British farmer is beginning to think, at least in that part of the country where I reside, namely, the county of Suffolk, that perhaps the League will turn out to be his best friend. (Hear, hear.) We are not foes to the farmer. We desire to see him prosper: but we know that there can be no permanent stability in his calling until every vestige of protection is swept away; when he relies on Corn Laws we know that he is building his prosperity upon an unsound basis; raising his house upon a sand, which will not stand the shocks with which it will have to contend. Experience has proved that no class in this kingdom has suffered more severely from the operation of the Corn Laws than the British farmer. (Hear, hear.) Then it is said that we are opposed to the landowner. We are not hostile to men merely because they own land. We are enemies to the principle which is laid down by the landowners of this country—or at least by many of them— that the possession of land entitles a man to go to the legislature, and ask it to prevent persons from buying food of any one but himself. (Cheers.) If a shoemaker made the demand that the inhabitants of this metropolis should buy all their shoes of him, and we objected to such a monopoly, could it be said on that account that we were opposed to the body of shoemakers? (' Hear, hear,' and great cheering.) We are opposed, undoubtedly, to the unjust demands of the landowners. We do object to the principle which is laid down by them, that trade is to be a secondary consideration in this country; that the merchant, manufacturer, all other classes, are to be deemed in the eye of the legislature of minor importance to the landowner. We hold, on the contrary, that all are equally worthy of the regard of the legislature. The landowners have legislated for England on the principle that they themselves constitute the country, and that the rest of the community are only to enjoy just so much of the comforts, trade, and conveniences of life as may suit the pecuniary interests of the dominant class. This has been the constant principle of landowners' legislation. You cannot look through our statute-book without discovering it in nearly every page. Can there be a more conclusive instance of the favouritism of such legislation than the statement which appeared in the *Times* newspaper the other day, in reference to the legacy duty? What could be more striking than that law, as one small instance of the way in which the landed proprietors of this country have used their power in the legislature? (Hear, hear.) When personal property passes, after the death of its holder, to another, it pays a heavy duty to the government. Landed property, however, is exempt from any such tax. (Hear, hear.)"

In the course of his speech, Mr. Gibson referred to the wages question as affected by the price of food :—

" Now, it is said, ' If you reduce the price of corn, you will lower the wages of the labourer.' It is stated that the Anti-Corn-Law League is totally indifferent to the welfare of the labourer; that this question is a mere contest between the manufacturers on the one hand, and the landowners on the other; and that the interest of the labourer is completely lost sight of in the matter. It is alleged that the interest of the labourer would be even injured by reducing the price of corn, and making food more abundant. Now, I should not have much difficulty in convicting our opponents, from their own proceedings, of uttering what they do not believe. What do I read in the papers? Why, even within the last two or three days I have seen, in the *Morning Post* and other journals, a statement that certain philanthropic gentlemen are about to establish a society for the purpose of grinding flour and baking bread for the poor. (Laughter.) They propose to raise a large sum of money, and to erect mills, offices, and bakehouses, in order to undersell the present millers and bakers, who, they tell us, are extracting too high a price for their bread from the pockets of the poor. But how does this tally with the oft-repeated statement, that if you reduce the price of bread to the poor, you will bring down their wages? What is it to me who raises the price of bread, whether it be the miller, the landowner, or the baker? If the raising of the price be a benefit to me, I say, ' Do not lower it.' Hear, hear.) The labourer does not buy his loaf in Mark-lane; we

do not purchase our corn and food by the averages which are published
in the *Gazette*. No, we buy our bread from the bakers. They tell us
that if we make bread cheaper in price we shall reduce wages. ' Well,
then,' we reply, ' if you make it cheaper by baking or grinding more
cheaply, you will cause wages to be lower than they are at present.' So
that these philanthropic gentlemen are convicted from their own course
of conduct, of not really entertaining the belief that the wages of the
labourer will be reduced by lowering the price of bread. (Cheers.) These
worthies seem determined that nobody shall rob the poor except the
landlords. (Great laughter.) Oh! it is a shocking thing for millers
and bakers to be getting this large profit out of the hard earnings of the
poor man, and it is a dreadful thing for people to take such advantage
of the labourer; but yet my lord duke is entitled to increase the price
of flour by an act of the legislature, and he has a right to call men fools
who do not believe that to do it in that way is a benefit, though in all
other modes he admits that it is a curse. (Hear, hear.) However,
the day is not far distant when this great delusion will be thoroughly
exposed and understood. I am convinced that we are approaching the
time when the Corn-Law repeal and the question of free trade must
have a practical issue. (Hear, hear.) The *Morning Post* is an honest
paper, after all. (Laughter.) What did that journal tell the agriculturists but the other day ? It said that the only difference between the
policy which even Sir Robert Peel is prepared to pursue, and that of
the League, is this, that Sir Robert's is a slow decay of gradual poverty
saddened by disappointed hopes, while the policy of the other, namely,
of the League, is prompt as the guillotine; but he says they are both
forms of extinction—both are going in the same direction to a certain
extent. I believe this is true. I am sure, from all that I have heard
Sir Robert Peel say in Parliament, that he is, in his own mind, firmly
convinced of the truth of the principles of free trade—(hear, hear)—but
that he is prevented from doing all he would do by the power of the
aristocracy of this country, which rules not only Sir Robert Peel, but
the Queen upon her throne. (Cheers.)

Mr. Cobden was received with great enthusiasm. After
referring to other questions analogous to the cause in which
they were contending, he said :—

" What I wish to guard ourselves against is this—that Sir Robert
Peel shall not mix up our question of Free Trade with his dexterity in
finance. (Hear, hear.) If he likes to shift the cards, and make an
interchange between tea, cotton, tobacco, malt, and the income-tax, and
ply one interest against the other, it is all very well; let him do so; it

may suit his purpose as a feat in the jugglery of statesmanship. (Cheers.) But let it be understood that we have nothing to do with all this mystification and shuffling. Ours is a very simple and plain proposition. We say to the right honourable baronet, ' Abolish the monopolies which go to enrich that majority which placed you in power and keeps you there.' We know he will not attempt it; but we are quite certain that he will make great professions of being a free-trader notwithstanding. Oh! I am more afraid of our friends being taken in by plausibilities and mystifications, than anything else. I wish we had the Duke of Richmond or his Grace of Buckingham in power for twelvemonths, that they might be compelled to avow what they really want, and let us have a perfect understanding upon the matter. We should not then be long before we achieved the object of our organization. Ladies and gentlemen, Sir Robert Peel will meet Parliament under circumstances which may perhaps call for congratulation in the Queen's speech. Manufactures and commerce are thriving, and the revenue is flourishing. Was that ever known when corn was at an immoderately high price? (Hear.) Why the present state of our finances and manufactures is an illustration of the truth of the free-trade doctrines. As the chairman has told you, I have been, during the last two months, paying a visit to nearly all the principal towns in Lancashire and Yorkshire, and have seen much prosperity prevailing in those places where, four years ago, the people were plunged in the greatest distress; and I am glad to tell you that I have everywhere met larger and more enthusiastic meetings than I did in the time of the greatest crisis of distress. We have passed through that trying ordeal which I had always dreaded as the real and difficult test of this agitation; I mean the period when the manufactures of this country regained a temporary prosperity. We are proof against that trial; we have had larger, more enthusiastic, and more influential meetings than ever we had before; and I am happy to tell you, that, so far as the north of England goes, the present state of prosperity in business is merely having the effect of recruiting the funds of the Anti-Corn-Law League. (Cheers.) There is not a working man in the manufacturing districts who has not his eyes opened to the enormous falsehoods which have been told by the monopolists during the last four or five years. You know that the operatives do not deal learnedly in books: they are not all of them great theorists, or philosophers; but they have, nevertheless, a lively faith in what passes under their own noses. ('Hear,' and laughter.) These men have seen the prices of provisions high, and they have then found pauperism and starvation in their streets; they have seen them low, and have found the demand for labour immediately increase, and wages rising in every district of Lancashire and Yorkshire, and a state of things prevailing the very opposite

of that which was told them by the monopolists. (Cheers.) In fact, in
some businesses the men now have their employers so completely at
their mercy that they can dictate their own terms to them. We have
heard of one gentleman in the north—not one of the Leaguers, but a
large employer of labour—who remarked, ' Why, my hands will only
work four days a-week now; if we have free-trade in corn, and business
is as prosperous as you say it would then be, I should not be able to
manage them at all.' (Cheers.)"

Mr. Cobden concluded with an earnest recommendation
to purchase freeholds. South Lancashire, he said, had
been already secured, and he would guarantee the West
Riding of Yorkshire. " Will you do the same for Middlesex ? " he asked, and he was answered by loud cries of
" We will."

Mr. Fox followed, and his eloquence excited great enthusiasm in the assemblage. In reference to the purchase
of freeholds, so earnestly recommended by Mr. Cobden,
he said :—

" In this plan there is a moral good, beyond, perhaps, what in its
original conception was thought of. It tends to act upon the character
of the entire labouring population of the country,—the working classes,
—the more toilsome section of the middle classes ; it holds out to them
a hope, promise, and incitement of the most desirable and elevating description. It says to them, ' Become proprietors of a portion, however
small, of this our England; have a stake in the country ; be something
here.' It was thought a wise thing, when, by the measure introduced
by the late George Rose, the savings bank funds were connected with
the public funds of the country ; it was deemed judicious in this way to
link those who could amass but very small sums with national institutions and public interests ; and, if it was wise and good to endeavour
to make all who could save their pittance become fundholders, it must
be at least as prudent and just to induce them, according to their proportion, to become landowners also, joint shareholders in this lovely,
and fruitful, and beautiful country—and their country as much as that
of the wealthiest nobleman whose lands cover half a county. (Cheers.)
It gives them a tangible bond of connexion with society; a feeling of
independence and honest pride. They are put in the position which
was deemed necessary to citizenships in the republics of ancient days ;
and this is adapted to cherish in them the emotions which best accord

with consistency, propriety, and dignity of character. The poet Campbell has described the feelings of the outcast when he wanders through
the village ; how he looks wistfully at the cottage with its little garden ;
leans on the gate, and says to himself :—

> ' Oh ! that for me some home like this might smile,
> Some hamlet's shade, to shield my sickly form—
> Health in the breeze, and shelter from the storm !'

To those whose lives are spent in toilsome exertion and constant endurance, but who can take time so far by the forelock as to accumulate
a little sum, such hope and promise as this, does the present plan hold
out and offer as an excitement. May their spirit arise to aspire towards
and seize it ; and obtaining it, I think we shall be on the high-road
towards a better choice of legislators, a more complete identification of
the interests of those who toil with the advantages of those who think,
—a better identification of the different classes that extend themselves
through the demarcations of society ; and our House of Commons will
then be in a fair way to show what it is to have a full, fair, and free
representation of the Commons of England.   (Great cheering.)"

From this time there were thousands of free traders who
purchased freeholds, at an expense of several hundred
thousand pounds; a practical kind of movement, promising
a practical result, and a proof of earnestness and determination which led many influential landowners to give more
consideration to the free-trade question than they had ever
given before.

The third annual aggregate meeting of the Liverpool
Anti-Monopoly Association was held in the Music Hall, on
Monday, January 20th. The chair on the occasion was
filled by Thomas Thornely, Esq., who was supported by
William Brown, Esq., Thomas Blackburn, Esq., &c. The
chairman, in the course of the remarks with which he
opened the meeting, alluded to the subject of sugar in the
following terms :—" There was one new point in the sugar
bill of last year, which was, that foreign sugars from certain
countries named in the act of parliament—it being considered in this country that the labour was the labour of
freemen—should be admitted at certain protecting duties ;
that wherever we had a treaty with a foreign power,

provided that the duty in the two countries should be alike, whether on British or foreign vessels, the duty should be the same.   Now, he was glad to find that there had been two importations of Venezuelan sugar into Liverpool, at 34s. per cwt.   He understood that next month, or the month of March, they would have importations of sugar from Manilla, and they would also have some from the United States of America.   But although so little sugar, almost none, had come in under this new regulation, yet he begged to be allowed to say, that the apprehension of increased supplies had done what the laws should have done—it had checked the price of sugar in the market, and they now had sugar at a much lower price, from the apprehension that foreign sugars would be imported and would interfere with the sugar of the monopolists."   Mr. Rawlins, secretary to the association, read the report, which was a very able and interesting document.   It canvassed, among other subjects, the state of trade, the state of the representation, the chances of success; on which subject it was said, " The association had never looked with so much confidence to the ultimate and not far distant success of the free-trade cause as at the present moment.   Aid had sprung up from the most unexpected quarters, and the ministry now in power, after deliberately giving in their adhesion to the truth of their principles, were gradually applying them to the destruction of the monopoly they were raised up by the monopolists to support.   But the people demanded, not a free trade in principle, but a free trade in practice."   " Nor is it altogether," proceeds the report, " to the efforts of the free-trade party that we are to attribute this rapid progress of our cause.   Compared with former years, those efforts have been somewhat abated. But it is rather owing to the fact, that added experience is daily proving the truth of our principles.   Events have, indeed, spoken trumpet-tongued in our favour.   Every fallacy which a selfish policy endeavoured to impress on the public mind is at this moment in process of refutation. Cheaper food was to lower wages ! We have had cheaper food, and, in a great number of trades, even money wages have been actually increased ; in some cases voluntarily, by the employers in others at the demand of the operatives, and the combinations of the latter have, in almost every instance, been successful. Everywhere real wages—the amount of comforts for which money wages stand as only the representative—have advanced ; and we believe that the working classes are becoming more and more convinced that the only permanent and true protection for the labourer is in the active demand for his labour. Our late distress was said to be owing to over-production of manufactures and the use of machinery ! Returning prosperity has been accompanied by increased production, while an unexampled extension of machinery has led to a like extension in the employment of manual labour. Cheaper food was to injure the revenue ! The revenue, which had declined in years of scarcity, has flourished in seasons of abundance." The report also went at length into a discussion of the sugar, coffee, and other duties. It was well received, and the meeting altogether was very satisfactory.

The annual aggregate meeting of the League was held in the Free Trade Hall on Wednesday, January 22nd. The report of the council and the treasurer's statement of accounts were first read. The report detailed the operations of the League during the past year, being particularly minute as to what had been done with respect to registration. It appears that " 160 boroughs in England and Wales have been visited during the past year, and the council have obtained a mass of information which will enable them to direct their future efforts with greater efficiency ; while the returns already in their possession show an undoubted gain in 112 of the boroughs thus acted upon, and in many of these the improvement on the register is such as to ensure the return of free traders in the place of

monopolists, in the event of an election.   *   *   Hitherto
the county registration has been almost entirely neglected
by the commercial, trading, and industrious classes, and the
council resolved to invite their friends everywhere to acquire that political influence to which they are so justly
entitled, by taking up their enfranchisement for the counties.   The appeal has been received and acted upon with
a promptitude and an enthusiasm surpassing their most
sanguine expectations.   The council have reason to believe
that, within the last three months, a sufficient number of
persons have purchased freehold qualifications in North
Cheshire, South Lancashire, and the West Riding of York,
to secure to those important constituencies a free-trade majority : whilst a large addition to our ranks has been made
in Middlesex, North Lancashire, and several other populous counties."   Simultaneously with these electoral movements, the communications between the council of the
League and every portion of the kingdom had, by means
of correspondence and deputations, been not only maintained, but greatly increased during the past year.   " More
than 200 meetings, attended by a deputation from the
council, have been held in England and Scotland since
October, 1843.   Of these meetings, more than 150 have
been held in parliamentary boroughs, and the increased
numbers by which they have been in all cases attended,
and the zeal and enthusiasm manifested, prove the extent
and the depth of the public conviction in favour of free
trade.   Besides these, the great meetings held in Covent
Garden Theatre, London, and in the Free Trade Hall,
Manchester, show that the question has lost none of its
hold on the public mind in the metropolis, or in Manchester, the birth-place of the League.   The lecturers of the
League have visited and lectured in 36 out of 40 counties
of England, and in nearly all the Welsh counties.   The
demand for this mode of instruction has been much greater
than the council have been able to supply, the desire for

lecturers having been especially manifested in the agricultural districts. More than 2,000,000 of stamped and
other publications have been distributed. In addition to
these, there has been an average weekly publication of
20,000 copies of the *League* paper, 15,000 to the subscribers
to the League fund, besides a sale of 5,000 copies weekly,
amounting in sixty-seven weeks to 1,340,000 copies, making
the total distribution of publications nearly 3½ millions.
The correspondence, since the last report, has more than
doubled, the number of letters received at the League
offices in London and Manchester being about 25,600,
while the numbers despatched from the two offices have
been about 300,000." The report concludes thus:—"The
council have now entered upon the seventh year of their
labours. Of the past they can speak with satisfaction.
They have seen public opinion gradually, but surely, becoming more and more settled in favour of free trade; the
public press, the organ of that opinion, uniting more
earnestly and cordially with the exertions of the League;
the cabinet chosen by the monopolists, moving slowly it
may be, but still moving on in the direction of free trade;
whilst, throughout the manufacturing districts, the return
of active and prosperous commerce has not only done
nothing to abate the enthusiasm and determination of
their friends, but has given them enlarged means of advancing the object they have so greatly at heart. The
League is emphatically the representation of the classes
that live by industry; it is an embodiment of the spirit
and energy of trade which is struggling to be free; it seeks
no private, no partial good, but the true and permanent
interests of the whole people; hitherto it has received a
degree of support unknown to any other organization in
this country; it has sought, by a faithful discharge of its
duties, to deserve the confidence reposed in it; its success
is to be seen wherever the opinion of the people is freely
manifested, and its complete and not distant triumph is as

certain as its determination is firm and its principles are impregnable." By the treasurer's accounts, which were afterwards read, it appeared that the sum of £82,735 3s. 5d. of the fund of £100,000 proposed to be raised, had already been received, and the chairman explained, that when the proposal of levying the sum of £100,000 during the past year was first launched, they had it in contemplation to raise a large portion of that amount by a bazaar, to be held in Covent Garden Theatre, but that bazaar had not yet been held. The amount received, therefore, he said, was quite as much as they had anticipated; they proposed still to hold the bazaar, and he had no doubt the amount then received would carry them far beyond the sum originally expected. The announcement made, that as the funds stood, after deducting all the expenses of the leviathan agitation, there was yet a balance in hand of £26,675 19s. 9d. "was received with loud and reiterated bursts of cheering." Afterwards Mr. Milner Gibson, Mr. Bright, Mr. Edward Baines, jun. of Leeds, and Mr. Lawrence Heyworth, of Liverpool, addressed the meeting on the cheering prospects of the cause, when the proceedings terminated.

The Agriculturists also had their meetings, and were very valiant—after dinner. On Thursday, January 23rd, the first dinner of the Sussex Agricultural Protection Society took place at Brighton. At an early period of the day a private meeting of the members of the society was held in the Town Hall for the purpose of receiving the annual report, and appointing a committee for the ensuing year. Mr. W. Burrell, the secretary, read the report, after which the usual routine of business of such meetings was despatched, and the members separated. Afterwards, about 300 persons, members of the society, sat down to dinner in the Ship Hotel. The duke of Richmond presided, and the Duke of Norfolk acted as vice-president. Amongst some of the most distinguished persons present, were noticed, the Earl of Egmont, Earl of Sheffield, Earl of March, Lord A. Hervey, Sir C. Burrell, M.P., Colonel Wyndham, M.P., G. Darby, Esq., M.P., Stafford O'Brien, Esq., M.P., Sir H. D. Goring, J. Sheppard, Esq., M.P., &c., &c. Such was the fervour against free trade pervading the meeting, that even the usual formal toasts were not allowed to pass without its displaying itself. Thus, in reply to the toast of "The army and navy," the Earl of Egmont said (and he said nothing else,) that, "he did not wish to obtrude himself, but when he read the speeches which were delivered at the Anti-Corn-Law League, he could not sit still, but felt it his duty to come forward and express the opinions which he entertained with respect to them. Could any man read those speeches and not believe that the whole foundation of their proceedings was revolution? For his part, he was happy to have that opportunity of identifying himself in the most public manner possible with the Agriculture Protection Society, which he was sure must succeed against the League. They had hoisted the flag of protection to agriculture, and they would bid defiance to the Anti-Corn-Law League." The noble chairman deputed Mr. Stafford O'Brien to give the toast of the evening, "Prosperity to the Sussex Agricultural Society," in doing which the honourable gentleman thus described to the farmers what would be the effect of free trade :— "They would, then, indeed, see England in a different condition from that in which she is at present; they would see whole districts thrown out of cultivation, families deserted, estates brought to the hammer, and though such a state of things might offer a good investment to the monied leaguer, yet he would find that the convulsion which had been produced would ill satisfy him; that he, too, would be a loser by the proceedings which would have already broken the hearts and the fortunes of the farmers that had cultivated the soil, and would be under other circumstances the best support of the landowner." This statement was received with loud cries of "hear, hear," and loud cheers.

Mr. Ellman returned thanks, who, alluding to the protection agitation, said, "they had not commenced this—they had been bearded in their own dens. In the town of Lewes a meeting was held by the Anti-Corn-Law emissaries, at which their itinerant orators invited the farmers to attend, and after much consideration, it was resolved not to attend, in order to prevent a breach of the peace, which would have taken place if the young farmers of Sussex had attended. It was on mature deliberation judged to be more prudent to refrain from attending. The meeting was held in the vicinity of a stream, and it was highly probable that some of the orators might have experienced an involuntary ablution if the young farmers of Sussex attended."

After this compliment to the taste, talents, and virtues of his neighbours, Mr. Ellman proposed the health of the Duke of Richmond, eulogizing his conduct as a soldier and civilian. In reply, the Duke, among other things, said, "I may be permitted to say, gentlemen, as an old soldier, in a few words, that in my humble career in military life I took a share in the battles, in the victories which took place; and I can state that I always found the private soldier anxious to save my life, because he looked up to me as his officer, as being the person to lead him to victory. * * * I knew that the soldiers were recruited from the ranks of our labouring classes; I saw that they were always inclined to preserve the life of their officer, for they knew that he was the man who was capable of rightly directing them, and leading them to victory." Passing from the soldiery and himself, the Duke went on to speak of agriculture and himself, and his famous fish, as follows. He said :—"So long as I have blood in my veins I will stand for the agricultural interest; and I will do so, gentlemen, from my firm conviction that if the agricultural interest be further attacked—and it has been too much attacked already—this nation, as an independent nation, cannot continue to exist. I came here as a freeman to express my opinion—I appear as a landowner, as a farmer, and as a member of the aristocracy—and I maintain that I have a right to express my opinions (whatever newspapers may say) as well as any other man. Is a manufacturer to get up a large meeting whenever he pleases, and is not a landowner to be allowed to address the farmers, whose interest he has at heart? Ask the labourers of the county who are their best friends, and they will tell you the farmers; and if you poll the farmers, I do not think they will abuse the landlords. The Anti-Corn-Law League says that the Anti-Corn-Law League is everywhere; that when the Earl of Radnor speaks in the House of Lords it is there. Well then, when I get up in the House of Lords am I not entitled to say that the Protection Society is there? The Anti-Corn Law League took a great deal of pains to distribute their tracts; they distributed them in the Town Hall to-day; and in one of those tracts they have done me the honour to call me the 'Coronetted Fish-monger.' I inherit large fisheries in the north of Scotland, and I can assure you that I have suffered very much by free trade; but I am obliged to those who distribute that tract amongst you, for they have given my portrait, and I hope you will all take it home; cut the nonsensical writing away, but keep the portrait, and tell your neighbours and friends, and instil it into the minds of your children, that the 'Coronetted Fishmonger' never forgot his duty to the farmers." The Duke, in conclusion, paid the following compliment to himself and his class:—"If you do not wish to act with your landlords against them: but let me assure you that you will find your landlords your best friends. There is one great good which has resulted from this society, namely, that it enables us to state in parliament that the landlord, the tenant, and the labourer feel they have the same interest and are united in their opinions."

The Parliamentary Session for 1845 was opened by the Queen in person, on Tuesday, February 4th. The speech put into her Majesty's hands concluded thus:—" The prospect of continued peace, and the general state of domestic prosperity and tranquillity, afford a favourable opportunity for the consideration of the important matters to which I have directed your attention; and I commit them to your deliberation, with the earnest prayer that you may be enabled, under the superintending care and protection of Divine Providence, to strengthen the feelings of mutual confidence and good-will between different classes of my subjects, and to improve the condition of my people." The prayer was not from the Queen, but her ministers. *They* prayed for the superintending care and protection of Divine Providence—they who, when Divine Providence had sent abundance upon the earth for the sustenance of the whole brotherhood of mankind, had the daring impiety to enact that the superabundance of one part of the globe should not go to supply the deficiencies of the other!

In the House of Lords, the Lord Chancellor having read over her majesty's speech, the Marquis of Camden moved the address in reply, which was, as usual, an echo of the speech, and Lord Glenlyon, who was dressed in the costume of a Highland chieftain, seconded it. In the discussion which ensued, and which was shared in by the Marquis of Normanby, the Duke of Richmond, Lord Wharncliffe, Lord Brougham, the Earl of Hardwicke, the Marquis of Lansdowne, the Earl of Malmesbury, the Earl of Aberdeen, Lord Campbell, and the Lord Chancellor, the various topics of the speech were canvassed at some length, but the address was subsequently agreed to *nem. con.*, and a committee was appointed to draw it up. The Duke of Richmond objected to the expressions in the address which signified that the condition of the country was improved. " The farmers," he said, " were in a bad way. Was there any man in this house who would say that there was not considerable distress among the tenantry of the country? Was there an individual in this house who could say that the tenantry had not this year lost a great deal of capital? He rose now to call their lordships' attention to that fact. He blamed not the government. because he never saw a government that troubled themselves much about agriculture. One of the misfortunes of this country was that as soon as ever a government got into office, they appeared to forget altogether that there was any such thing as agriculture. The state of manufactures and commerce was well known to them through the Board of Trade; but there was no board of agriculture, and therefore the government were not aware of the fact which he had mentioned. But he could state from his own knowledge that there was great distress among the tenantry, and upon that ground he thought it should have been referred to in the speech. One recommendation contained in her majesty's speech was, that the income tax should be continued for a further period. Now, he merely wished to remark that he hoped, if the income tax were re-enacted, as far as the tenantry were concerned, they would charge them according to their profits; for at present, whilst other trades paid the tax upon £150 profits, the farmer had to pay the tax on £150 if his rents amounted to £300 a-year, when it was clear that, with the existing low prices, it was impossible he could realise that amount of profit. He would not, however, provoke a Corn Law speech; he only rose in order to protest against the omission from the royal speech of all reference to the subject of agriculture, and to inform her Majesty's government that what he had stated was the truth, and that there was very considerable distress in many parts of the country."

In the House of Commons the address was moved by Mr. Charteris, seconded by Mr. Baring. Lord J. Russell, referring to the present flourishing condition of trade and manufactures, thought steps ought to be taken to make them more permanently so. "No man," his lordship said, "can expect the course of things to continue unaltered, or that we shall have in this country every year a recurrence of those bounteous harvests with which we have of late been blessed. If, then, we cannot expect that—the reflection occurs—can men do anything to remedy the evils which deficient harvests bring along with them? I think we can; not, indeed, by attempting to interfere with the course of Providence, but by looking at another dispensation of Providence which enables man to exchange the products of his own country with other and distant regions. Let us, then, as I hope we shall, consider in the course of the present year whether we have not the power to ward off the storm which at some future period of deficient harvests may fall upon us, by giving to those productions of other nations which we can best use and employ, a more favourable inlet into this country than they have at present. By so doing, you would be only acting in consonance with the principles of the present government, and of the great majority of this House. They do not hold with that great society which met yesterday, that protection to British industry is the true way to ensure a permanent flourishing condition for the people of this country. On the contrary, with respect to many articles of great value, they have declared that principles opposed to those of protection, and which, if not entirely free trade, are known by the name of free-trade principles, are those by which the intercourse of nations should be regulated. If they continue in these opinions—if they differ from those great authorities which maintain that protection is for the benefit of the people— let us have the advantage of the practical working out of those opinions. I know that those who propose this are called the enemies of agriculture, but *I am convinced that protection is not the support but the bane of agriculture.* I will not say, for this would not be the time if even I were prepared to say it, what particular measures should be, or what the right honourable gentleman himself would think

the best way to get rid of that which encumbers a great
part of the commercial policy of the country. But this
much I may say, that there is not the smallest doubt upon
my mind upon the question as to whether you should do
that which you intend to do, calmly, considerately, in a
season of prosperity, and with the dignity becoming legislators; or whether you should do it hurriedly, inconsider-
ately, under the pressure of popular uproar, and in the
dread that you cannot deny that which still you fear to
grant. I think, both with respect to Ireland and to the
question of free trade, you ought to take advantage of the
present time. You say Ireland is tranquil—you say trade
is prosperous. Shall we, then, lose this opportunity? I
think almost every man will admit, if you were forced by
foreign war or internal commotion, you would give to
Ireland everything she asks, excepting repeal; and also
that, if similarly operated upon, you would not hesitate
long about a change in your Corn Laws. If that be so,
then, I would say, take advantage of the time before you,
and consider yourselves most happy in being able to show
yourselves indeed worthy of that great nation you are called
upon to govern." Sir Robert Peel considered Lord John
Russell's speech a mere party speech, and defended, at
great length, the foreign policy of government. And, referring to promised financial changes and legislation, the
right honourable baronet said :—" It being foreseen that
alterations are to be made affecting certain branches of
commerce, I believe an early declaration of the intentions
of Her Majesty's government is by far the wisest course,
although it may be a departure from the general rule.
Next week will not, therefore, elapse before that outline
shall be given. * * * I will not anticipate discussions
which must hereafter come on. The House will judge
whether the statement made by Her Majesty's ministers
to-day in respect to the condition of trade, in respect to
the state of the revenue, and in respect to the general

condition of the country, its tranquility, and the total absence
of all political excitement in Great Britain is borne out,
and whether there were any of these indications of improvement upon which Her Majesty has congratulated you.
I shall shortly have a measure of great importance to
propose to the House, when the House will have an opportunity of declaring whether in their opinion the administration of affairs has been misconducted by us, and the
condition of the country has been deteriorated—whether
they will continue to us that confidence without which no
government can conduct the public affairs well, and without
which, the noble lord will permit me to say, no government
ought to remain in office. The other speakers were Mr.
Mills, Sir C. Napier, Mr. Plumptre, Mr. Wyse, Mr. Bellew, Mr. Villiers, Mr. Sheil, Sir J. Graham, Mr. Shaw,
Lord Palmerston, Sir R. Inglis, Lord Sandon, and Lord
Howick. Of these the first named said "he hoped that
in any intended reduction of taxation the agricultural interest should not be forgot." Mr. Wyse, Mr. Bellew, Mr.
Sheil, and Lord Sandon spoke in favour of the proposed
legislation for Ireland; Mr. Plumptre, Mr. Shaw, and Sir
Robert Inglis were not pleased with it. Mr. Villiers said
that it was now clear that all the objects of the protective
system had been defeated, and that in consequence of the
relaxation of that system the present prosperity of the
country had been produced. "He did not hesitate to
assert that it was owing to everything having occurred
which it was the prime object of protection to prevent—
cheapness of produce, and abundance of food, arising
chiefly from a most singularly abundant harvest, aided by
certain relaxations of the protective system. Those things
had occurred—there has been plenty, and they were, thank
God, gathering its fruits. The means of the community
had been increased, and consumption was extended. This
was the promise of free trade; this had occurred in spite
of the gentlemen opposite, and the country had to thank

Providence rather than the ministry for it. The country
at this moment was prospering, and the discontented and
disappointed were those who supported protection. They
have legislated, and have failed; they have been thwarted
in their object by Providence; and the poor, the people, the
trade, and the revenue, have all profited by the result. So
far as the right honourable gentleman has relaxed the protective system, he has reason to be satisfied; it has contributed to the prosperity of the country, and he has
nothing to regret as regards revenue, or any other circumstance. The right honourable gentleman cannot point to
any duty that he has reduced, with the view to relax protection, that he has not reason to be satisfied with and for
advancing farther in the same direction. It ought to be
his object, as it is that of all wise men, that this country
should continue in its present state, so far as it is prosperous. What vast importance then is it to settle this
question of protection, and determine whether it is not for
the liberation of trade, that the great mass of the people
are enabled to possess the great essentials as well as the
comforts of life. The system of protection is opposed to
this. It has no object if it is not." He rejoiced in the
declaration of Lord John Russell, that protection was the
bane, and not the support of agriculture, and called upon
the House to watch with the closest attention the new
financial measures of government—to support them if they
abandoned, and to oppose them if they were based on, the
protective principle. The address was ultimately put from
the chair, and unanimously agreed to, when the House
adjourned.

How stood the question now? Sir Robert Peel had
avowed that the principles of free trade were those which
ought to regulate the interests of nations, and that we
ought to buy in the cheapest market and sell in the
dearest; Sir James Graham had declared that they were the
principles of common sense; and Lord John Russell had

denounced protection as the bane and not the support of agriculture, and had prophecied that two or three bad harvests would cause such popular excitement as would force a change in spite of all resistance.   When there was such an agreement between the leaders of parties as to the general principle, why did they not unite, and at once repeal the Corn Laws?   Sir Robert Peel had modified them, and his modification must have a fair trial.   Lord John Russell still clung to his shibboleth of a small fixed duty for revenue.   And thus the two factions, at variance on almost everything else, each struggling to drive the other out of office, combined to sacrifice the interests of the public, which both professed to be most anxious to promote!

CHAPTER XVII.

THE BUDGET.

The Budget, brought forward by Sir Robert on the 13th February, would have been regarded on the whole as the production of a statesman, had it not left the landowners' monopoly untouched, and that of the West India planters unmitigated, and continued the income tax, bearing as heavily on precarious earnings as on income derived from realized property. Sir R. Peel had computed the saving, which the reduction on sugar proposed would make to the consumer, to be about 1¼d. per lb.; and, including the numerous indirect charges which would also be saved, he estimated an advantage of at least 1½d. per lb. from the present price. The largest quantity of sugar which had hitherto been consumed in any one year was 207,000 tons, and under the new duties, Sir Robert Peel calculated on a consumption of 250,000 tons, and which he estimated would give revenue as follows :—

160,000 Tons	Colonial Muscovado at ..	14s.	..	£2,240,000
70,000 „	Ditto Clayed	16s. 4d.	...	1,140,000
5,000 „	Free labour Muscovado ..	23s. 4d.	...	116,000
15,000 „	Ditto Clayed......	28s.	..	420,000
250,000 „	Estimated revenue with new duties ..			3,916,000
	The gross revenue last year was			5,216,000
	Showing a loss on new duties of ..			£1,300,000

The minister next proceeded to refer to a list of articles, *four hundred and thirty* in number, which yielded but trifling amounts of revenue, and many of which are raw materials used in the various manufactures of the country —including silk, hemp, flax, and yarn or thread (except worsted yarn)—all woods used in cabinet making, animal and vegetable oils, iron and zinc in the first stages, ores and minerals, (except copper ore, to which the last act will still apply,) dye stuffs of all kinds, and all drugs, with very few exceptions; on the whole of these articles he proposed to repeal the duties altogether, not even leaving a nominal rate for registration, but retaining the power of examination. The timber duties generally he proposed to remain as they were, with the one exception of staves, which, as the raw material of the extensive manufacture of casks, he proposed to include with the 430 articles, and to take off the duty altogether. On these articles the loss amounted to £320,000.

The next, and the most important, relief in the whole proposition was the article of cotton wool, on which the minister proposed also to reduce the duty altogether; and on which he estimated the loss at £680,000; and these constituted the whole of the proposed reductions of the *import* duties—that is, sugar, cotton wool, and the numerous small articles in the tariff.

The next items of reduction proposed were the few remaining duties on our exports, such as china stone, and other trifling things, but including the most important article of coals, on which the duty was placed by the present government, and of the result of which Sir Robert Peel candidly avowed his disappointment. The duties he estimated at £118,000.

Sir Robert Peel then passed on to the excise duties, among which he had selected two items of great importance for entire repeal—the auction duty and the glass duties. By a repeal of the auction duty he estimated a loss of £300,000 ; but as he proposed, at the same time, to increase the auctioneer's license, uniformly from £5 to £15 (making one license answer for all purposes, whereas, at that time, several licenses were often necessary to the same party), he expected from *four thousand* auctioneers an increased income, to reduce this loss to £250,000.

On the important article of glass he gave up £642,000. These constituted the whole of his proposals ; and the surplus of £2,409,000 was thus proposed to be disposed of :

	£.
Estimated loss on sugar	1,300,000
Duty on cotton repealed	680,000
Ditto on 430 articles in tariff	320,000
Export duty on coal	118,000
Auction duty	250,000
Glass	642,000
	£3,310,000

The inconsistencies of the budget were thus described by the *Leeds Mercury :—*

" Sir Robert Peel has combined in his measures some of the most glaring inconsistencies that ever disfigured the policy of any minister. The following specimens, arranged in parallel columns, illustrate the assertion :—

A Tariff, whose express object is declared to be to *cheapen* the necessaries of life.

Corn and Provision Laws, whose sole object is to make the chief necessaries of life *dear.*

Great concern professed to *relieve* trade and commerce, for the sake of which a *Property* Tax is imposed.

A still greater concern to uphold the *Rent* of land, for the sake of which trade and commerce are *loaded* with a *Bread* Tax.

The repeal of duties on *raw materials.*

The taxation of the greatest of all raw materials, namely, that of *labour.*

Total and Immediate Repeal of small taxes.

A *Sliding Scale* for the heaviest tax of all.

Taxes for the mere purpose of *Revenue.*

Taxes for the mere purpose of *Protection.*

Repeal of the Duty on Slave-grown *Cotton.*

Prohibitory Duties on Slave-grown *Sugar.*

Encouragement of Brazilian *Coffee* and *Cotton.*	*Refusal* of Brazilian *Sugar.*
Admission of cheap Slave-grown Sugar, to be refined in England and supplied to the *Continental* nations.	*Prohibition* of the selfsame cheap Sugar to *our own working people.*
Encouragement of the *United States* Slave Trade.	Discouragement of the *Brazilian* Slave Trade."

The Budget excited great interest among the free traders. An aggregate meeting of the League was held in Covent Garden Theatre on the evening of February 19th. Wm. Brown, Esq., of Liverpool, occupied the chair, and introduced the proceedings by a short commendatory notice of those parts of the new ministerial measures of finance which were founded on free-trade principles. The speakers were Messrs. James Wilson, George Thompson, and Jno. Bright. The speech of Mr. J. Wilson was principally on the proposed new sugar duties, and the wrong that would be inflicted by them on the consumer and the revenue in consequence of the increased amount of protection given to the West Indian interests. He said :—" In order to illustrate the effect of a differential duty, I would take the proposal of the right honourable baronet (Sir R. Peel) on Friday night. The right honourable gentleman seeks to establish four different rates on the quantity of sugar which it is supposed will be imported in the course of the year. He has one rate for 160,000 tons, another for 70,000 tons colonial, another for 5,000 tons foreign, and another for 15,000 tons foreign. On the 15,000 tons there is a duty of 28s. per cwt. It is clear, that before this class comes into consumption, 28s. per cwt. will be added to the first cost ; and being sugar which is used equally in all continental Europe, and fetching the same price of 24s. per cwt. at Hamburgh and Antwerp as it does here, our consumer would have to pay, with the duty, 52s. per cwt. It is equally clear, that any sugar of the same quality is worth the same price. Therefore, if any sugar is brought in at a lower rate of duty, the difference would go towards enhancing the price for the importing merchant. He then calculates on a supply of a second class of foreign sugar, at 5,000 tons, paying a duty of 23s. 4d. The importing merchant will, therefore, get as much more in price as the difference between the duties. Instead of 24s., the price of the first class, he will get 28s. 8d., which, with the lower rate of duty, will reach 52s. On one class of colonial sugars he charges 16s. 4d. duty. He calculates the amount imported will be 70,000 tons. The merchant would charge 33s. 8d. as the price of the article which the first importer got for 24s. There is a fourth class of sugars. He calculates the produce of this, coming from the West Indies, at 160,000 tons. But on this a duty so low as 14s. is fixed, which will give the merchant a price of 38s. instead of the original price of 24s. In all this process he is not lowering the price to the consumer, but increasing the price to the importer. You see, therefore, that on these four rates the importer pays 21s. for one, 28s. for another, 35s. for a third, and 38s. for a fourth, while the consumer pays the same price of 52s. for all. Suppose the minister said, I will charge the highest rate of duty on all sugars, it is clear he would not raise the price a fraction to the consumer. He makes a sacrifice of nearly £2,000,000 of revenue, and he asks the country to make it up by the imposition of an income tax. Now, if he imposed the same rate of duty on all the sugars, he would realise a revenue of £7,000,000, and the community would not have to pay a farthing more for their sugar.

Mr. Bright, after a racy and cutting description of those members of both houses of parliament who called themselves farmers' friends, gave the following account of their own great association, for promoting liberty of trade and perfect freedom of industry :—" They had no alliance with lords nor dukes. The prominent men of the League were men from the ranks. They had not embarked in the agitation

to gain wealth, or power, or rank—but if they conceived
any one rank to be more honourable than another, it was
to be placed among those who had done something in their
generation to shake off the trammels which hampered the
honest industry of their fellow men.   From their weak beginning to their present strength they placed no reliance
but on the omnipotence of truth and the intelligence and
virtue of their countrymen.   To them they had again and
again appealed, and nobly had that appeal been responded
to.   In 1839 they first asked for subscriptions, and £5,000
was given.   In 1840 they asked for more, and between
£7,000 and £8,000 was subscribed.   In 1841 they held the
great conference at Manchester, at which upwards of 700
ministers of religion attended.   In 1842 they had their
grand bazaar in Manchester, from which £10,000 was realised.   In 1843 they asked for £50,000, and got it.   In
1844 they called for £100,000, and between £80,000 and
£90,000 had been paid in besides what would be received
from the bazaar, to be held in May.   This year was yet
young, but they had not been idle.   They had asked their
free-trade friends in the northern counties to invest some
of their property so as to be able to defend their rights
and liberties at the hustings.   This had been done, and it
now appeared that, at the recommendation of the council
of the League, their friends in Lancashire, Cheshire, and
Yorkshire, had invested a sum of not less than £250,000
in the purchase of county qualifications.   Besides all this,
they would have their grand bazaar next May.   Committees
were already actively at work making the necessary preparations.   A great deal was being done, and a great deal
more would and could be done before the time, in order to
produce a display which he hoped would be so remarkable
as to be worth a visit from the highest personage in the
realm."

In the debates on the Income Tax and the Sugar Duties,
the free traders in the House distinguished themselves by

the clearness with which they treated the principles which ought to regulate taxation. On Monday, February 24th, Mr. Milner Gibson moved :—" That no arrangement will be satisfactory and permanent, which does not involve an equalization of duty on foreign and colonial sugar." The argument on the part of the free traders was unanswerable. The *Nonconformist* which, fearing that free trade in corn was not to be obtained without " complete suffrage," was not very apt to praise the Leaguers, said that Mr. Gibson's speech was " crowded with evidence to prove that, by the present discriminating duty, the people of this country are annually taxed to the tune of some £2,800,000, not to enrich her Majesty's exchequer, but to enable non-resident proprietors of colonial estates to maintain a lazy and improvident system of agriculture, the whole profits of which are eaten up by attornies, bailiffs, and overseers. The West Indian proprietors affected to treat the question as an abstract one; but, as Mr. Bright well reminded them, the eagerness they displayed to be present—the earnestness with which they spoke—and the solemnity with which the matter was viewed by the Chancellor of the Exchequer, proved clearly that, in their estimation, the subject was practical enough. The debate was not a lively one, but the speeches of Lord Howick, of Mr. Cobden, and of Mr. Bright, were able, convincing, and thoroughly out-spoken. The whigs who deemed protection as the bane of agriculture, shunned the House, and ministers entrusted their defence to Sir George Clerk and Mr. Cardwell." The indifference of the late whig ministers and their adherents to the real principles of free trade which they professed to advocate, was shown by the division, the numbers being :—

Against the motion 217

For it 84

The importance of the debates in the House of Commons rather increased than diminished the interest which

attached to every movement of the League.   The attendance at the meeting in the Manchester Free Trade Hall
on Wednesday, March 5th, was shown, by the number of
tickets taken at the door, to have exceeded six thousand.
The gallery was filled with ladies, and there were six hundred influential gentlemen of the town and neighbourhood
upon the platform.   Mr. Wilson, the chairman, gave a
gratifying account of the progress of preparation for the
great bazaar, and said that the Messrs. Darby, of Colebrookdale, would furnish a stall with beautiful articles of
their own manufacture, which, at cost price, would be £500;
that thirty towns had already promised to supply a stall
each, and seventy others had promised if they did not supply a stall each, to furnish a portion, and that Mr. Moore
and Col. Thompson were then in Scotland in promotion
of the object of the bazaar.   The meeting was addressed
by Mr. W. J. Fox and Mr. George Thompson, both of
whom spoke at great length, and with an eloquence which
excited the utmost enthusiasm of the meeting.

On the 7th March, Mr. Cobden brought forward the
motion of which he had given notice, for a "Select Committee" to inquire into the causes and extent of the alleged
existing agricultural distress, and into the effects of legislative protection upon the interests of landowners, tenant
farmers, and farm labourers.   The distress of the farmers
had been declared by the protectionist landowners in their
interview with the prime minister, and he thought it was
from them rather than from him that his motion should
have come.   The farmers were distressed, but whence did
the distress arise?   It was for want of capital for one
thing.   A capital of £10 an acre would be required for
arable land, and he did not believe that on an average
farmers had one half that sum for each acre.   Capital was
seeking employment everywhere but in farming, because
capitalists would not invest upon it without the security of
equitable leases.   No man would lay out a farthing on a

tenancy-at-will. Speaking further on this subject, Mr. Cobden said :—

" Even when you have leases in England—where you have leases or agreements—I doubt whether they are not in many cases worse tenures than where there is no lease at all; the clauses being of such an obsolete and preposterous character as to defy any man to carry on the business of farming under them profitably. I do not know whether the honourable member for Cheshire is here, but if so I will read him a passage from an actual Cheshire lease, showing what kind of covenants farmers are called on to perform :—

" ' To pay the landlord £20 for every statute acre of ground, and so in proportion for a less quantity, that shall be converted into tillage, or used contrary to the appointment before made ; and £5 for every cwt. of hay, thrave of straw, load of potatoes, or cartload of manure, that shall be sold or taken from the premises during the term; and £10 for every tree fallen, cut down, or destroyed, cropped, lopped, topped, or willingly suffered so to be ; and £20 for any servant or other person so hired or admitted so as to gain a settlement in the township ; and £10 per statute acre, and so in proportion for a less quantity of the said land, which the tenant shall let off or underlet. (' Hear, hear,' from the Ministerial side.) Such sums to be paid on demand after every breach, and in default of payment to be considered as reserved rent, and levied by distress and sale as rent in arrear may be levied and raised. And to do six days' boon team work whenever called upon ; and to keep for the landlord one dog, and one cock or hen ; and to make no marlpit without the landlord's consent first obtained in writing, after which the same is to be properly filled in ; nor to allow any inmate to remain on the premises after six days' notice ; nor to keep or feed any sheep, except such as are used for the consumption of the family.'

" Now, what is such an instrument as that ? I will tell you. It is a trap for the unwary man, it is a barrier against men of intelligence and capital, and it is a fetter to the mind of any free man. No man could farm under such a lease as that, or under such clauses as it contains. (Hear, hear.) I perceive that the honourable member for the rape of Bramber (Shoreham) is cheering. I will by-and-by allude to one of the honourable member's own leases. You will find in your own leases, though there may not be a stipulation for cocks and hens and dogs, and probably team work, yet there are almost as great absurdities in every lease and agreement you have. (' Hear, hear,' and laughter.) What are those leases ? Why, they are generally some old antediluvian dusty remains, which some lawyer's clerk takes out of a pigeon-hole, and merely writes out for every fresh incoming tenant:—a thing which

seems to have been in existence for a hundred years. You tie them
down by the most absurd restrictions; you do not give men credit for
being able to discover any improvement next year and the year after,
but you go upon the assumption that men are not able to improve, and
you do your best to prevent them doing so. (Hear.) Now, I do not
know why we should not in this country have leases for land upon similar
terms to the leases of manufactories, or any 'plant' or premises. I do
not think that farming will ever be carried on as it ought to be until
you have leases drawn in the same way as a man takes a manufactory,
and pays perhaps £1,000 a-year for it. I know people who pay £4,000
a-year for manufactories to carry on their business, and at fair rents
There is an honourable gentleman near me who pays more than £4,000
a-year for the rent of his manufactory. What covenants do you think
he has in his lease? What would he think if it stated how many revo-
lutions there should be in a minute of the spindles, or if they prescribed
the construction of the straps or the gearing of his machinery. Why,
he takes his manufactory with a schedule of its present state—bricks,
mortar, and machinery—and when the lease is over, he must leave it in
the same state, or else pay a compensation for the dilapidation. (Hear,
hear.) The right honourable gentleman the Chancellor of the Exchequer
cheers that statement. I want to ask his opinion respecting a similar
lease for a farm. I am rather disposed to think that the Anti-Corn-Law
leaguers will very likely form a joint stock association, and have none
but free-traders in the body, that we may purchase a joint-stock estate,
and have a model-farm ('hear, hear,' and laughter); taking care that
it shall be in one of the rural counties, one of the most purely agricultural parts of the country, where we think there is the greatest need of
improvement—perhaps in Buckinghamshire (laughter); and there shall
be a model farm, homestead, and cottages; and I may tell the noble
lord the member for Newark, that we shall have a model garden, and we
will not make any boast or outcry about it. But the great object will
be to have a model lease. (Cheers and laughter.) We will have as
the farmer a man of intelligence and capital. I am not so unreasonable
as to tell you that you ought to let your land to men who have not a
competent capital, or are not sufficiently intelligent; but I say, select
such a man as that; let him know his business and have sufficient
capital, and you cannot give him too wide a scope. We will find such a
man, and we will let him our farm; there shall be a lease precisely
such as that upon which my honourable friend takes his factory. There
shall be no single clause inserted in it to dictate to him how he shall
cultivate his farm; he shall do what he likes with the old pasture. If
he can make more by ploughing it up he shall do so; if he can grow
white crops every year—which I know there are people doing at this

moment in more places than one in this country—(hear, hear)—or if
he can make any other improvement or discovery, he shall be free to do
so. We will let him the land, with a shedule of the state of tillage and
the condition of the homestead, and all we will bind him to will be this,
' You shall leave the land as good as when you entered upon it. (' Hear,
hear,' from both sides of the house. If it is in an inferior state it shall
be valued again, and you shall compensate us ; but if it is in an improved state it shall be valued, and we, the landlords, shall compensate
you.' (Hear, hear.) You think there must be something very difficult
about this, and that it will be impossible to be done ; but it is not. We
will give possession of every thing but the land, whether it be wild or
tame animals ; he shall have the absolute control. There shall be no
game, and no one to sport over his property. Take as stringent precautions as you please to compel the punctual payment of the rent ;
take the right of re-entry as summarily as you please if the rent is not
duly paid ; but let the payment of rent duly be the sole test as to the
well-doing of the tenant ; and so long as he can pay the rent, and do it
promptly, that is the only test you need have that the farmer is doing
well ; and if he is a man of capital, you have the strongest possible
security that he will not waste your property while he has possession
of it. (Hear.)"

When such was the condition of farmers, the condition
of labourers could be nothing else than deplorable ; and
that it was deplorable there was abundant evidence. Mr.
Cobden proceeded to show that both tenants and labourers
would profit by the free importation of food for man and
for cattle, and asserted that restricted importation was far
more likely to throw land out of cultivation than unrestricted commerce. What were landowners doing now ?

" We have heard of great absurdities in legislation in commercial
matters of late. We know that there has been such a case as sending
coffee from Cuba to the Cape of Good Hope in order to bring it back to
England under the law ; but I venture to say that in less than ten years
from this time people will look back with more amazement in their
minds at the fact that, while you are sending ships to Ichaboe to bring
back the guano, you are passing a law to exclude Indian corn, beans,
oats, peas, and everything else that gives nourishment to your cattle,
which would give you a thousand times more production than all the
guano of Ichaboe. (Loud cheers.) Upon the last occasion when I
spoke upon this subject, I was answered by the right honourable

gentleman the President of the Board of Trade. He talked about throwing poor lands out of cultivation, and converting arable lands into pasture. I hope that we men of the Anti-Corn-Law League may not be reproached again with seeking to cause any such disasters. My belief is —and the conviction is founded upon a most extensive inquiry among the most intelligent farmers, without stint of trouble and pains—that the course you are pursuing tends every hour to throw land out of cultivation, and make poor lands unproductive. (Hear.) Do not let us be told again that we desire to draw the labourers from the land in order that we may reduce the wages of the workpeople employed in factories. I tell you that, if you bestow capital on the soil, and cultivate it with the same skill as manufacturers bestow upon their business, you have not population enough in the rural districts for the purpose. (Hear.) I yesterday received a letter from Lord Ducie, in which he gives precisely the same opinion. He says, if we had the land properly cultivated there are not sufficient labourers to till it. What is the fact? You are chasing your labourers from village to village, passing laws to compel people to support paupers, devising every means to smuggle them abroad to the antipodes if you can get them there; why, you would have to chase after them, and bring them back again, if you had your land properly cultivated. I tell you honestly my conviction, that it is by these means, and these only, that you can avert very great and serious troubles and disasters in your agricultural districts. Sir, I remember on the last occasion when this subject was discussed, there was a great deal said about disturbing an interest. It was said that this inquiry could not be gone into because we were disturbing and unsettling a great interest. I have no desire to undervalue the agricultural interest. I have heard it said that they are the greatest consumers of manufactured goods in this country; that they are such large consumers of our goods that we had better look after the home trade and not think of destroying it. But what sort of consumers of manufactures think you the labourers can be with the wages they are now getting in agricultural districts? Understand me: I am arguing for a principle that I solemnly believe would raise the wages of the labourers in the agricultural districts. I believe you would have no men starving upon 7s. a week if you had abundant capital and competent skill employed upon the soil; but I ask what is this consumption of manufactured goods that we have heard so much about? I have taken some pains, and made large inquiries as to the amount laid out in the average of cases by agricultural labourers and their families for clothing; I probably may startle you by telling you that we have exported in one year more goods of our manufactures to Brazil than have been consumed in a similar period by the whole of your agricultural peasantry and their families. You have

960,000 agricultural labourers in England and Wales, according to the last census. I undertake to say they do not expend on an average 30s. a year on their families, supposing every one of them to be in employ. I say manufactured goods, excluding shoes. I assert that the whole of the agricultural peasantry and their families in England and Wales do not spend a million and a half per annum for manufactured goods, in clothing and bedding. And, with regard to your exciseable and duty-paying articles, what can the poor wretch lay out upon them, who out of 8s. or 9s. a week has a wife and family to support? (Hear.) I undertake to prove to your satisfaction—and you may do it yourselves if you will but dare to look the figures in the face (loud cheers)—I will undertake to prove to you that they do not pay upon an average each family 15s. per annum, that the whole of their contributions to the revenue do not amount to £700,000. Now, is not this a mighty interest to be disturbed? I would keep that interest as justly as though it were one of the most important; but I say, when you have by your present system brought down your agricultural peasantry to that state, have you anything to offer for bettering their condition, or at all events to justify resisting an inquiry?

He maintained that, at least in the manufacturing districts, whenever provisions were dear wages were low, and whenever food was cheap wages were high, and said that the recent strikes in Lancashire for advance of wages was the consequence of the fall of wheat below 50s. What was the plan of the agriculturists to raise the condition of tenants and farm labourers? Mr. Cobden concluded by saying :—

" With mere politicians I have no right to expect to succeed in this motion. But I have no hesitation in telling you, that, if you give me a committee of this house, I will explode the delusion of agricultural protection. (Cheers.) I will bring forward such a mass of evidence, and give you such a preponderance of talent and of authority, that when the blue book is published and sent forth to the world, as we can now send it by our vehicles of information, your system of protection shall not live in public opinion for two years afterwards. (Hear, hear.) Politicians do not want that. This cry of protection has been a very convenient handle for politicians. The cry of protection carried the counties at the last election, and politicians gained honours, emoluments, and place by it; you cannot set up for any such. Now, is that old tattered flag of protection, tarnished and torn as it is already, to be kept hoisted still in the counties for the benefit of politicians, or will you come forward honestly and fairly to inquire into this question ? Why, I cannot believe that the gentry of England will be made mere drumheads to be sounded upon by others to give forth unmeaning and empty sounds, and to have no articulate voice of their own. (' Hear, hear,' and cheers.) No. You are the gentry of England who represent the counties. You are the aristocracy of England. Your fathers led our fathers : you may lead us, if you go the right way. But, although you have retained your influence with this country longer than any other aristocracy, it has not been by opposing popular opinion, or by setting yourselves against the spirit of the age. In other days, when the battle and the hunting-fields were the tests of manly vigour, why, your fathers were first and foremost there. The aristocracy of England were not like the aristocracy of France, the mere minions of a court; nor were they like the hidalgos of Madrid, who dwindled into pigmies. You have been Englishmen. You have not shown a want of courage and firmness when any call has been made upon you. This is a new era. It is the age of improvement, it is the age of social advancement, not the age for war or for feudal sports. You live in a mercantile age, when the whole wealth of the world is poured into your lap. You cannot have the advantage of commercial rents and feudal privileges (hear, hear) ; but you may be what you always have been if you will identify yourselves with the spirit of the age. The English people look to the gentry and aristocracy of their country as their leaders. (Hear, hear.) I, who am not one of you, have no hesitation in telling you, that there is a deep-rooted, a hereditary prejudice, if I may so call it, in your favour in this country. But you never got it, and you will not keep it, by obstructing the spirit of the age. If you are indifferent to enlightened means of finding employment for your own peasantry ; if you are found obstructing that advance which is calculated to knit nations more together in the bonds of peace by means of commercial intercourse; if you are found fighting against the discoveries which have almost given breath and life to material nature, and setting up yourselves as obstructives of that which the community at large has decreed shall go on, why, then, you will be the gentry of England no longer, and others will be found to take your place. (Hear, hear.) And I have no hesitation in saying that you stand just now in a very critical position. There is a wide spread suspicion that you have been tampering with the best feelings and with the honest confidence of your own country in this cause. Everywhere you are doubted and suspected. Read your own organs, and you will see that this is the case. (Hear, hear.) Well, now is the time to show that you are not the mere party politicians which you are said to be. I have said that we shall be opposed in this measure by politicians; they do not want inquiry. But I ask you to go into this committee with me. I will give you a majority of country members. You shall have a majority of the Central Society in that committee : I ask you only to go into a fair inquiry as to the causes of the distress of your own population. (Hear.) I only ask that this matter may be fairly examined. Whether you establish my principle or yours, good will come out of the inquiry ; and I do, therefore, beg and entreat the honourable, independent, country gentlemen of this house that they will not refuse, on this occasion, to go into a fair, a full, and an impartial inquiry. (Cheers.)"

The motion was opposed, on the part of government, by Mr. Sydney Herbert. He said former committees on the same subject had not given reports that led to any good. No doubt the honourable member's object was a legitimate one; but he (Mr. Herbert) hardly saw why the House should consent to save the Anti-Corn-Law League the expense of publishing its pamphlets, by printing them in a blue book, at the expense of the country. He hoped that nobody would be taken in by the sympathy which Mr. Cobden had professed, first for the distress of the agricultural peasantry, and afterwards for that of the farmers and their landlords. It had soon evaporated, and given way to his real feeling—" Give me this committee, and I'll blow up your protective system." But the fact was, the report would be dependent on who was on the committee ; and it was not, in his opinion, necessary to appoint a committee on a subject which had been so often before them, and to go up stairs in order to inquire into a mass of well-known facts. The matter could be fully debated there, without appointing a committee of fifteen gentlemen to inquire into it up stairs—a committee of gentlemen with preconceived opinions, necessarily so formed, from the frequency of inquiry and discussion on the subject, that if he (Mr. S. Herbert) could only ascertain on which side the majority of members was in the committee, he could anticipate the report. He dissuaded agricultural members from voting for the committee, which advice Messrs. Stafford O'Brien, Wodehouse, Bankes, and Lord Worsley,

speaking for themselves and others, intimated that they
would take. Lord Howick, Mr. Bright, and Mr. Villiers
—the latter being particularly happy in his jokes about
" the agricultural mind," which Mr. O'Brien had said
would be " soothed by inquiry," but which inquiry. Mr.
O'Brien would not go into—were the speakers on the
other side. Mr. Cobden complained, in his reply, first,
that a cabinet minister had intercepted two or three agricultural members on the opposition benches, and had given
them their cues ; and next, that the agricultural members
had been too happy to take it. They were going, he said,
on a future night to oppose the ministers on the auction
duties—he told them frankly that their opposition was a
mere sham. The House then divided, when there appeared :—

For the motion 121
Against it............................... 213
                                          ——
Majority against it 92

On Monday, March 17th, Mr. Miles brought forward· a
motion, of which he had given notice, " That it is the
opinion of this house, that, in the application of surplus
revenue towards relieving the burthens of the country by
reduction or remission of taxation, due regard should be
had to the necessity of affording relief to the agricultural
iuterest." The following description of the debate is from
the *League ;* and it is followed by a curious discussion on
GREASE and LARD, in which certain of the agriculturists,
escaping from the control which Sir Robert Peel had
exercised over them in the debate on Mr. Cobden's motion,
made an exhibition of themselves, much to the amusement
of the country :—

" In support of his views, Mr. Miles went into an extensive series of
figures, comparing the annual importations of foreign grain, and the
average prices in low-priced years, under the Corn Act of 1828, with the
average prices and the importations under the act of 1842. The present

low prices of cattle and corn he traced to the measures of the government—an opinion which coincided with that of the farmers, who were
able now to draw accurate conclusions as to the causes of their distress.
In 1842 the harvest was good, but a heavy importation of foreign and
colonial corn, suddenly thrown on the market in the autumn, threw
down prices ruinously low.   In 1843 there was a deficient harvest, and
prices which, measuring the deficiency, should have been 63s., were
only 48s.   In 1844 the harvest was above an average, and there was no
chance of the market recovering.   The fall in prices, both in meat and
corn, was not attributable to any panic, as he showed, by quoting the
rates, evincing a gradual though steady declension.   Having stated his
case, and expressed a wish that there were a department of the government specially devoted to the statistics of agriculture, he proceeded to
develop his propositions for relief.   This he did by going into the de
tails of the poor-rates and the county-rates, both as to the amount of
their collection and the purposes to which they are applied, which he
contended pressed unequally on the agricultural community, as compared with other classes, from which they should be relieved, and
urging that the expense of criminal prosecutions should be borne by
the state, instead of by each separate county.   He confessed that, in
bringing forward his motion, it was not in concurrence with the whole
of the agricultural body, but in justice to his own feelings and opinions.

"The Earl of March, eldest son of the Duke of Richmond, having
seconded the motion,

"Sir James Graham rose and made a speech, many parts of which
told well for free trade.   He was strongly of opinion that, looking to the
interests of the whole community, protection should still be afforded to
the agricultural interest.   But the question was not as to its principle,
but its amount.   The efforts made by the late government to check the
accumulating deficiency in the revenue showed that we had reached the
limits of taxation on consumption, as evinced by the failure of the
additional ten per cent. in the Customs and Excise.   The present
government were, therefore, obliged to resort to great experiments, by
which, in three years, they remitted between six and seven millions in
indirect taxation, of which the agricultural interest would receive its
share.   Take the wool duties, which he considered to be a boon to the
landed interest three or four times the value of the proposition made by
Mr. Miles, the price of wool being now higher than ever.   When complaint was made of the large quantity of foreign corn imported in the
three years following the act of 1842, as compared with the three years
following the act of 1828, it was forgotten how largely the population
had been and was increasing.   Without larger facilities for the admission
of foreign corn, *we ran the risk of some frightful convulsion*, as during our

recent commercial distresses. He looked upon the Canadian Corn Bill
as a useful subsidiary measure to the act of 1842. The great defect of
the sliding scale was its tendency to encourage speculation, with a view
to raise prices immediately before the harvest was reaped. This the
Canadian Corn Act kept in check, as the opening of the St. Lawrence
in the spring enabled cargoes to arrive here during summer. Ridiculing
the idea of the importation of foreign cattle causing the fall in prices,
looking to the small number brought over, he told the agriculturists
that there was another thing which they ought to fear much more—*low
wages in the manufacturing districts, thereby contracting the ability to
consume agricultural produce.* As to Mr. Miles's proposition, never had
there been so small a demand made by so great an interest. In 1813,
with a population of 10,500,000, the poor and county rates were
£8,600,000; in 1845, with a population of 16,500,000, they amounted
to £6,800,000, or, in other words, while the population had increased
one-third, the rates had diminished one-third; at the former being a
charge of 16s. 3d. on each head of the population, at the latter, of only
8s. 4d. Arguing generally against the proposition for shifting the
the burden of the county-rates, which was not now in that house, he sat
down by intimating the determination of the government to oppose the
motion.

" After Mr. Newdegate had made a complaining speech,

" Lord John Russell (in a speech which was spoken with great spirit,
and in the progress of which he paid a marked compliment to the
ability of Mr. Cobden) addressed the house with vigour and effect on
the free-trade part of the question. He remarked that the proceedings
of that night were an additional evidence that ' protection *was* the bane
of agriculture.' Mr. Miles, instead of proposing the repeal of the tariff
and the Canadian Corn Bill, asked for a pitiful boon of some two or
three hundred thousand pounds on the county-rates ; and the ' consola-
tory' speech of Sir James Graham was neither more nor less than a
declaration that protection must be gradually abandoned. Restriction
and monopoly was every way unfavourable to that energy which competition inspires. Holland once protected spices and silks : these were
luxuries; but corn was a necessary which could not be unnaturally en-
hanced without injury to the community. When in power, he had
proposed a moderate fixed duty; but those then in opposition declared
that they would not throw the Corn Law into the ' lottery of legislation.'
Coming into power, they had commenced breaking down that protection
which they had been placed in office to maintain, and which, so long as
it continued to exist, gave the farmer a false reliance and checked his
use of capital, science, and skill. He had been accused by Sir Robert
Peel of ' oscillating' between protection and free trade. He preferred a

'cautious' (to use Ricardo's phrase) abandonment of monopoly, but then he would never disguise the ultimate end. Quoting from a pamphlet by Lord Ashburton, when Mr. Alexander Baring, in support of a gradual abolition of monopoly, he said that there was one thing they could do for the farmers—not to inspire them with false hopes. How ungracious it was to come forward with a complaint that the working man did not pay more for his meat and his bread. Such a complaint tended to diminish all regard for that landed interest which he had every reason to respect. (A loud cheer from Colonel Sibthorpe.) That cheer compelled him to state what he otherwise would have abstained from. His connexions were deeply interested in the progress of agriculture; it was the delight of his uncle and his father to gather around them farmers, in order to exhibit the most recent scientific improvements, and to interest them in the advancement of agriculture; and he had, therefore, some ground for urging the landed interest to evince to the people at large that, being the most powerful, they were also the most generous interest in the state.

"Mr. Disraeli would not, he said, then enter on the great question of how far, not free *trade* but free *imports* would, with hostile tariffs, affect our power of production, the distribution of the precious metals, and our ability to maintain a standard—he would leave that for a time when it might receive a profounder treatment. There was a budget and a surplus; and the agriculturists thought then, as they do now, that *they* might be considered. After dwelling sarcastically on the consistencies of the Prime Minister and his adherents, he told the agriculturists that they must not contrast too nicely the hours of courtship with the moments of possession. Sir Robert Peel had avowed that he was prouder of being the leader of the gentlemen of England than of being intrusted with the confidence of sovereigns. There was little said now about the gentlemen of England; when the beloved object has ceased to charm, it is in vain to appeal to the feelings. Instead of listening to their complaints, he sends down his valet, a well-behaved person, to make it known that we are to have no 'whining' here. (This allusion to Mr. S. Herbert's expression in the debate last week was received with vociferous cheering and loud laughter from the Opposition.) Such is the fate of the great agricultural interest; that beauty which everybody wooed and one deluded. (Cheers and laughter.) There is a fatality in such charms, and we now seem to approach to the catastrophe of her career. Protection appears to be in about the same condition that Protestantism was in 1828. (Loud cheers from the Opposition.) The country will draw its moral. For my part, if we are to have free trade, I, who honour genius, prefer that such measures should be proposed by the honourable member for Stockport, than by one who though skilful in parliamentary manœuvres, has tampered with the generous confidence of a great people and a great party. (Loud cheers.) For myself, I care not what will be the result. Dissolve, if you like, the Parliament you have betrayed, and appeal to the people, who, I believe, mistrust you. For me there remains this, at least—the opportunity of expressing thus publicly my belief that a conservative government is an organized hypocrisy. (The honourable gentleman sat down amid cheers which lasted several minutes.)

The debate was shared in by a number of members; amongst them was Sir Robert Peel, who said that to encourage the idea that a mere transference of a portion of the county-rate to the consolidated fund would be any benefit, would be to practise a delusion on the agricultural interest. But support for Mr. Miles's motion had been sought on other grounds than a mere transference of a sum of £250,000, which would involve the additional charge of £400,000 on the consolidated fund. Reading a circular from a local protection society, he drew the conclusion that the object of the motion, in general, was to censure the financial policy of the government, and to stop their measures. He did not repent of the course he had adopted since he assumed office. He remembered Sheffield, with its unlet houses; the tales of people living on the putrid bodies of animals; of Paisley, with its thousands who rose daily without food; and when he assumed office, he had done so, not for the sake of favouring any one class, but of consulting the interests of the entire community. The house had given its assent to the income-tax, which it would not have done if the country did not approve of their measures. Compare the present state of commerce and trade with 1842, and, whatever may be said of the effects of good harvests, the influence of commercial reforms could not be denied, which, by promoting consumption, benefited agriculture. Thinking extreme protection and prohibition wrong, he defended *moderate protection* as necessary, not on principles of commercial policy, but as essential to a state of things where great interests had grown up, and whose injury would be that of the community at large.

The house went to a division, when there appeared :—

For Mr. Miles's motion 78
Against it.. 213
                                                ———
Majority 135

" On Wednesday the house was again in committee on the Customs Acts; and the question was again put that ' grease ' be admitted duty free. It seems that Mr. Miles was absent, owing to a domestic affliction; and on the intimation of that fact, both sides of the house testified audibly their sense of the sufficiency of the excuse. But his place was taken by Mr. Bramston, one of the members for South Essex, and a deputy-lieutenant of the county, who ' objected to the removal of the duty on *grease*, as he dreaded that it would lead to a great importation of foreign butter.' Sir George Clerk replied that foreign butter, mixed with tar, and so rendered unfit for human food, was used for smearing sheep, and its free admission was, therefore, *a boon to the agricultural interest*. The precautions taken at the Custom-house would prevent any fraudulent introduction of foreign butter fit for food. Mr. Ward, as one connected with land, begged to be excused the humiliation of such arguments. There was something grand in a comprehensive monopoly, but these dirty, petty, contemptible monopolies reduced the bold barons and aristocracy of England to a level with ' area sneaks.' The advocates of free trade desired nothing better than the continuance of these discussions. After some remarks from Sir J. Tyrrell, Mr. Bright, and Mr. M. Milnes, Mr. Aglionby said he was aware of the importance of the remission of duty on grease, as in the north it was extensively used by sheep farmers. Mr. Villiers remarked that the protectionists were only agreed when united in one object of plundering the public. But they occasionally quarrelled when one county asked for protection against another. Here it was Northumberland against Essex—one had sheep to smear, the other grease to sell; and while the one asked admission for foreign grease, the other sought protection for the domestic article. Mr. Bramston would not press his opposition to a division. Mr. Cobden thought he should, as it would test, and doubtless satisfy, sundry honourable members. The suggestion was not adopted, and therefore it was resolved that *grease* should be admitted duty free.

" Mr. Grogan moved the omission of lard, on which a discussion arose, during which Colonel Wyndham said he was sorry to see his agricultural friends imitating the example of the representatives of the manufacturing interest, ever jumping up, like jacks-in-the-box, preferring their claims, to the disgust of the country. The agriculturists would share in the reductions proposed by the government; and he was surprised and sorry at their clamours. Lord A. Lennox, as a constituent of Colonel Wyndham's, did not think that such sentiments were likely to lead to his re-election. Mr. Ward thanked Colonel Wyndham for the good humour, good sense, and impartiality which marked his speech. He repeated his feeling of contempt for the paltry, peddling, opposition of the agriculturists. Mr. Stafford O'Brien treated free trade as a system to reduce commodities to the lowest price—its only principle was cheapness. Mr. Cobden replied that they sought abundance, which was not always synonymous with mere cheapness. In the Prayer Book they were used as convertible terms. The monopolists, on the contrary, wished for dearness and scarcity. (Being met by repeated cries of

' No,' he asked, ' What is it then you do want?') What a plight had
the landed interest placed themselves in by their recent conduct in that
house! He was going down to Lancashire, and he was sure that he
would be stopped at the corner of every street with exclamations as to
the pitiable exhibition of the great landed interest. He besought them
to look at it themselves: all their whining and entreaties could not induce the Prime Minister to get up and defend them; and surely it was
not worth their while to endure all this obloquy for any benefit they
reaped from it. For his part, nothing could bribe him to submit to
similar taunts and obloquy. After some remarks from Mr. Darby, Sir
Robert Peel regretted to see personal feeling mixing itself in the discussion. He defended members on his side of the house in making
motions respecting matters in which their constituents were interested.
Good arose from all these discussions, as they brought out explanations.
Lord John Russell admitted the propriety of this, but what was applicable to lard was equally applicable to every other article of protected
agricultural produce. If the representatives of the agricultural interest
wished to act honestly, they should either surrender the principle of
protection to native industry, or resolutely stand by it in and out of
Parliament. Mr. Gladstone would not worry the agricultural interest
with nibbling changes in order to obtain infinitesimal degrees of cheapness in articles of food. But he looked on lard as a raw material in
trade and manufactures, as it might be made a substitute for sperm oil,
the supply of which was diminishing, as well as other oils used for
machinery, in the manufacture of soap, and so forth. Mr. Grogan withdrew his opposition, and lard was added to the articles to be admitted
duty free."

CHAPTER XVIII.

THE BAZAAR.

A meeting of the Manchester Ladies' Committee, for forwarding the preparations for the bazaar about to be held in Covent Garden Theatre, was held in the Council Room of the League, Newall's Buildings, on Tuesday morning, the 11th of March, when upwards of sixty ladies were present. Mrs. Woolley took the chair. Mr. George Wilson addressed the committee, and explained at considerable length the arrangements already made by the Council. Mr. Leadbetter then presented £5 on behalf of Mrs. Leadbetter, who was unable to render personal services. Mrs. Woolley addressed the committee with the view of ascertaining their opinions on the best means of furnishing the Manchester stalls at the bazaar, and suggested that the town should be divided into districts, and that the ladies of the committee should undertake to canvass for contributions for the bazaar. Mrs. Massie and other ladies approved of the suggestion, which was ultimately adopted. Mr. Prentice addressed the committee, offering various suggestions to the ladies. He suggested the getting of contributions of other articles besides ladies' work,—such as models, minerals, old coins, fossils, and vegetable remains, &c. A conversation afterwards arose, in which the question was considered : " What was to be done with money donations ?" The opinion come to was that on no account should such sums be spent in articles for furnishing the stalls, but that it should be kept entire and separate.

On the morning of Thursday, March 20th, Sir Thomas Potter expired at his residence, Buile Hill, near Manchester. The *League*, of the following Saturday, said of him, " He has gone down to the grave full of years and of honours, respected by the wise, mourned by the good, and eulogized by the honest. A new generation in Manchester enjoys the fruits of his toils, for to him that town is mainly indebted for the best part of its municipal institutions." I trust I may be excused in inserting here the more extended notice which appeared in my newspaper at the time :—

" Sir Thomas Potter was the son of a farmer, near Tadcaster, whose industry, intelligence, and skill in agriculture, enabled his sons, about the year 1800, to establish themselves in Manchester, with a capital of £14,000, a very considerable sum in those days; and this they had employed so judiciously, that in 1815, when we first knew them, and when the eldest brother, the subject of our notice, was forty-one years of age, they were recognised as amongst the first houses in Manchester. They had then acquired the character, which they sustained throughout life, of deep sympathy for the sufferings of the poor, and an earnest desire to elevate the condition of their fellow citizens and their fellow subjects. Since then we have been close observers of their career; but as a history of the exertions of their public spirit, and their private benevolence, would lead us into a detail too wide for our present purpose, we shall notice only a few of the points which tend to illustrate their public position.

" Few men of the present comparatively tolerent days can conceive the bitterness of party spirit prevailing at the period to which we refer. After a long war, in which British blood had been shed as if it had been water, and British treasure had been squandered as if it had been dross, a peace was concluded without a single stipulation for the security of commerce; and this was followed by the enactment of the Corn Law, that landlords might continue to draw, in the time of peace, the rents they had exacted during the war. Deep distress followed. The working classes, driven almost to desperation, met in great numbers, and demanded parliamentary reform and the repeal of the Corn Law. In 1817, the ministers of the time, on the pretence of disaffection in Lancashire, obtained the suspension of the *Habeas Corpus* act, and proceeded to put into prison, without any intention of bringing them to trial, the persons who were prominent in the agitation; but, cowardly as they were cruel, they incarcerated only those whom they supposed to be friendless, and with whom, as they thought, the middle classes would have no sympathy. Regardless of the odium which their neighbours attached to every one who showed any commisseration for the sufferings of the distressed multitudes, the Messrs. Potters, at a time when probably not more than twenty men, of the class of merchants and manufacturers, could be found to act with them, stood forward and raised the means to obtain for the incarcerated a fair trial, and to support their families during their imprisonment.

In 1819 a deep tragedy was enacted in Manchester, to which we can now only allude, but which cannot be, and ought never to be forgotten. The Messrs. Potters zealously assisted in raising a large subscription, not only for the relief of the sufferers, but to secure that which every British subject claims as his right, but which, at that time, was of difficult attainment, a fair trial. We well remember, at one of the numerous meetings then held, not to sanction the proceedings of the ' radicals,' as they were then called, but to obtain justice for the falsely accused, Mr. Thomas Potter saying: ' Gentlemen, I have not the talent for public business possessed by my brother Richard, but I promise you that I will work in our business, that he may devote himself freely to the protection of the oppressed.'

" In 1826, a meeting, mainly promoted by the Messrs. Potters, was held in the Manor Court Room, to petition for a reduction of taxes and the repeal of the Corn Law, at which Mr. Mark Philips appeared for the first time before the public. That assemblage is memorable, as about the first movement amongst the middle classes for free trade in the food of the people, now advocated by the highest intellect of the country, and the agitation of which has contributed, more than anything else, to throw distrust on all party contests, and to direct men's attention, regardless of the old names and claims of whig and tory, to the only true object of legislation, the benefit of the whole community.

" In 1828, the then ruling party in the management of the municipal affairs of the town, applied for an act of parliament, by which it was proposed that no person should be eligible as a police commissioner, unless he was assessed at a rental of £40 a-year, and that no person should vote in the election of a commissioner who was not assessed in a rental of £25 a-year. The Messrs. Potters entered, with their usual earnestness, into the opposition, and after a hard contest for extending the right of voting to all ratepayers, and then to all who were assessed on a £10 rental, the respective qualifications were fixed, by parliament, at £16 and £28. Public dissatisfaction with the act ultimately led to the demand for that liberal charter of incorporation, for which the

community of this borough is mainly indebted to the great exertions of
Mr. Thomas Potter, and of which, as a testimony to his well-merited
pre-eminence, he was elected the first mayor.

"In 1830 commenced the great struggle for parliamentary reform,
which ended in the passing of that great, but as experience has proved,
still defective measure—so much has corruption done the work of bad
government — the Reform Bill.   Previously to that agitation, Mr.
Thomas Potter had always said, ' I will do Richard's work, while he
works for the public ;' but the agitation was for a great object, to put
down the rotten-borough system, under which the people had only a
shadow of representation, and to make way for those great practical
reforms that were required to secure the civil, religious, and commercial
liberties of the country ; and Mr. Potter threw himself into the movement with an energy, the inspiring effects of which were felt not only in
his own locality, but throughout the kingdom.   From that time forward,
in the absence of his brother Richard, who had become the member for
Wigan, there was not a single movement in Manchester, for general or
local reform, for the promotion of education, for the relief of the poor,
or for the improved administration of the town's affairs, in which Mr.
Potter did not stand in the first rank, aiding with his always-open
purse, but more by his characteristic energy, we may almost say im-
petuosity, of character, which saw no obstacles, and permitted none to
be seen, to the fulfilment of any really good object, and which communicated itself to all with whom he had to act, stimulating the faint-
hearted to hope, and rousing the phlegmatic to exertion.

" The reform of the ancient municipal corporations having followed
the amendment of national representation, Mr. Potter, along with Mr.
Cobden, Mr. William Nield, and other friends of popularly constituted
local government, applied for a charter of incorporation, in which the
right of voting should extend to all resident householders actually paying rates.   A fierce opposition was organised, but it was defeated, and
the charter was obtained.   Long litigation followed, and the rates
necessary to carry on the business of the corporation were refused, in
the hope that the want of funds might break it down.   But the opponents of popular institutions had under-calculated the effect of that
determined purpose which Thomas Potter could infuse into a public
body.   A guarantee fund of more than £30,000 was instantly subscribed,
and the corporation ultimately triumphed over all. opposition.   As the
leader amongst our reformers he was chosen the first mayor of the
borough, and his discharge of its then very arduous and responsible
duties was so admirable, as to secure his unanimous re-election to a
second term of office.

"Sir Thomas, from the time of the imposition of the Corn Law in

1815, had never ceased to protest against it as a measure most injurious to commerce, and most unjust and cruel to the working classes, whose wages it diminished while it raised the price of food. With this strong and just feeling on the subject, he was amongst the very first of those who enrolled themselves as members of the League, and throughout its course, from its origination in Manchester till it became a great national institution and made its power felt in Parliament, he gave it his most strenuous and influential support.

" In the election contests for Manchester and Salford, and the neighbouring counties and boroughs, Sir Thomas always took an exceedingly active part, communicating his own ardour to all around him ; and it is not too much to say, that, in a great degree, the stability and power of the reform interest throughout this important and vast district of the empire, is mainly owing to his indefatigable exertions in organising and directing what might otherwise have been the inert strength of the constituencies. He was equally active and equally influential at the last election for South Lancashire, and assisted in laying the foundation of that new movement which promises to rescue several of the counties from the deadening control of the landowners.

" He was ever ready to promote education amongst the people, both by the liberal expenditure of his own money, and by assisting in obtaining the reform of educational institutions. The Grammar School of Manchester, with funds to the amount of £4,000 a-year, had long given instruction to only about two hundred boys, and that not gratuitously, for every branch of education, beyond what in the old parlence was called grammar, was charged for, and at a high rate. Sir Thomas and Mr. Mark Philips, *at their sole expense*, made application to Chancery, and obtained an order, under which the number of pupils has been more than doubled ; and they are taught, *without charge*, not only ' grammar,' but writing, arithmetic, mathematics, drawing, and several of the modern languages.

" There had long been exacted from the parishioners of Manchester more than £4,000 a-year under the name of Church Rates. For many years the meetings held to impose the rate had been very stormy, and the exposures of the manner in which its proceeds were expended had become exceedingly distasteful to the clergy ; but still the rate was clung to, as if the Church could not exist without it. At length the opposition, headed by Sir Thomas and Mr. George Hadfield, became so exceedingly formidable that the rate was abandoned altogether, and the amount required is now raised by a sort of subscription, which is denominated an ' *optional* ' rate.

" Hand-in-hand with his exertion of public spirit went his works of private beneficence, and he did not wait for the applications of poverty, but earnestly sought it out, and administered relief. In this respect, ' a warmer heart death ne'er made cold.' "

The final metropolitan meeting of the League before the opening of the great bazaar was held in Covent Garden Theatre, on the 10th April, Mr. Geo. Wilson in the chair; who, after alluding to the preparations for the Bazaar which would make it a very brilliant affair, even as a spectacle, said : " I am free to confess that, if the promotion of a collection for the fund was the mere object we had in view, a greater amount of money might be easily procured by a general subscription than we are likely to receive from this exhibition ; but we want a more generally implied co-opera· tion than the mere amount of money alone would imply. We want to see assembled in this theatre our friends from all parts of the kingdom, in order that they may converse together; that they may confer together; that they may become known to each other ; that they may derive from such meetings and from what they will see here a new impetus, and carry to the extremities of the country a redoubled resolution to assist us in promoting the great object which we have in view. And then we have the pleasing satisfaction of knowing that the bazaar will not in the slightest degree interfere with any of those useful operations in which the League is employed. The lecturing in the agricultural districts will go on just as usual; the daily meetings of the council, in all probability, will be held just as usual; the attention to the registration will be proceeded with as usual. Our registration agents will visit the boroughs and counties just as they would if no such exhibition was taking place here. There is not a single wheel or pinion in the machinery of the League which will not be in the most perfect order, as much as if the supervision of the council were constantly directed to it, without the interruption—the supposed interruption—which will take place here. And then we shall see that for a fortnight successively we can sustain an interest in the free-trade

question in this theatre ; and at the termination our friends
will have the satisfaction of knowing that, although but
seven years ago a few individuals—men unknown to fame
—associated themselves together to form a society, the
greatest ever recorded in this country—the anticipation of
those who originally suggested it will be tenfold more than
realized."

Colonel Thompson was then introduced to the meeting,
and was received with loud applause. After alluding to
his recent tour in Scotland, the gallant veteran said :—

" This is an ill time for any man to slacken when we seem to be
moving so rapidly on towards the point which we wish to attain.
Friends are multiplying everywhere, and enemies falling before us ;
they are doing a better thing still, they are joining us. (Cheers.) Look
at your Premier. (Hear.) How much is he worth? A tribe or two,
I suppose, at least. (Laughter.) He cannot help coming over to you ;
the commercial blood that is in him stirs him to take our side ; and
more than that, he sees that opposition is so foolish and hopeless, that a
man who would maintain that character for good sense and prudence
which he possesses, must be looking out for a safe port in time. With
him will come whole shoals of those waiters upon Providence (laughter)
who consider him their god, their Æolus ; and whichever wind he blows
they are ready to sail before it. (Cheers and laughter.) Your adversaries—what have they done for you? All that men could ; and nobody
could do more. Had you paid them to let down their cause, and told
them how, you could not have done half so well as they have for you.
You have all, I dare say, looked to the recent debates. Grease, lard,
and butter,—these are what occupy the attention of the statesmen upon
the other side of the question. The great subjects of national interest
are dwindled, sunk, to such greasy things as these. (Laughter.) Shall
I tell you what I recently amused your solemn brethren of Scotland
with ? I told them that when they had formed their schools in all their
factory districts, and had taught the little boys to answer to the questions, ' Who was the wisest man? and who was the strongest man?'
they should ask them, ' What is a government for?' and then the little
ones should pipe out, ' To put tar into our butter.' (Laughter and
cheers.) Our immediate mission to Scotland was to invite contributions
to the Bazaar ; and when some have said to me, ' What may be your
particular concern with that matter ? How came you into that line, of
all others?' I replied to them, ' This is a foraging party ; why should

I not take charge of a foraging party, if asked, as well as of any other?'
Cheers and laughter.) Strange things have been proposed for our
foraging party; singular figures should we have made had we been
obliged to appear here bringing them all tacked to our horses' quarters.
Some promised linen, some yarn, some bedticking, some minerals—by
which at Newcastle they meant coals, and we engaged that they should
be sold by sample, and that tickets should be provided bearing this inscription, 'Pay to the bearer 10 chaldrons of coals.' (Cheers.) Why
a lady should not sell those tickets at a stall is more than I can understand. Depend upon it our genius shall go along with any thing they
will bestow upon us. One merchant at Leith stated, he had sent to
Shetland for a horse only forty inches high; and we promised he should
appear at the Bazaar, and over him there should be written: 'This is
what man and horse come to, when they cannot get corn.' (Loud
cheers.) But there is more than jest hangs by that horse and his
country. You know, or might have known, that the inhabitants of the
Shetland Islands maintain themselves principally by the produce of
their fisheries, which they convey to Spain and Portugal; and, if they
were permitted to bring home corn in return, their families might eat
bread during the winter season, and they might sell it to their countrymen who would enjoy the same. Now that case is deemed so pre-
eminently hard, that it has been suggested that it might be possible, if
the thing were gone about quietly, to obtain for the Shetland Islands,
being small, the same privileges as the Channel Islands possess; or, as
in some degree, I believe, through the interference of our friend and
your friend, Dr. Bowring (cheers), have been obtained for the Isle of
Man. But what I want to invite the attention of the citizens of London
to is, the consideration whether the case of the Shetlanders be in reality
one whit harder than their own? Are not the interests of such of you
as are engaged in mercantile and maritime pursuits just as much destroyed by the existence of these restrictions, as the interests of the
inhabitants of Shetland? Does it not tell as bitterly in London as in
Lerwick; at Manchester where 500 pairs of hands are crowded perhaps
in one factory, as in the Shetland cottage where the fisherman's wife
knits solitarily the shawl which may not be sold abroad to procure her
family bread? It is only the difference between a large case and a
small one. You then, being the larger, use your greater strength, and
take advantage of the opportunity offered to you to make your contributions in the way which for the moment is most useful. Aid the Bazaar
to be held in your own metropolis: make foreigners go away and say,
that never before was there such an exposition of British products, industry, and genius. You that are here, know these things well; but we
have not yet succeeded in persuading all the outside barbarians that

they are interested upon this point. (Laughter.) You then, when you go forth from this house and return among them, make yourselves, each man and woman, a missionary for the truth; and see how long it is before you combine such a force as friends and enemies shall equally admit to be irresistible. (Cheers.) It has been intimated to me that we have some unexpected aid to-night; I, therefore, who am old in your service, will not detain you, but will make way in order to afford you a taste of what is new. (Loud cheers.)"

The gentleman who was to give "unexpected aid," was introduced to the meeting by Mr. Cobden, who said:— "I find myself unexpectedly sitting beside a gentleman who, in times past, has been a consistent, but, I hope, an amicable opponent of our good cause—a gentleman largely connected with agriculture; one who himself farms, I believe, 3,000 and odd acres of land; one who, as an agent, in connexion with many of the largest landed proprietors in the kingdom, has upwards of 200,000 acres under his charge; and who is also, in his own person, a landed proprietor. I allude to Mr. Houghton, who was examined before the Parliamentary Committee in 1836; and who has been since, I believe, an active opponent of free trade. Now, I am happy to say, that Mr. Houghton has maturely reconsidered the question, and that he is prepared to-night to address a few words to this meeting; and to explain to us, and, what is of far more importance, to the country, the grounds upon which he has seen reason to alter his views in reference to the Corn Laws. Allow me now to introduce Mr. Houghton, for the purpose of making a few remarks."

Mr. Houghton, on coming forward, was received with enthusiastic plaudits. After the cheering had subsided, he said:—" Mr. Chairman, ladies, and gentlemen, it has been said by one of our greatest men—

' All the world's a stage,
And all the men and women merely players.'

But little did I ever expect that it would fall to my lot to

be a performer upon these boards, and to address you
upon a subject of such great importance.   I have, for
twenty years of my life, been an upholder of the system of
protection.   I have been so conscientiously, and conscientiously am I now opposed to it.   It will be necessary for
me to take a review, not of the session, as opposition
members generally do at its close, but of the system of
protection which has extended over a period of thirty
years ; and I will, as briefly as I can, give you my reason
for abandoning the ship, because I have found that, do
what we will, we cannot make her seaworthy.   I have no
fear that any other man will address you who is so greatly
interested in agriculture, who is so large a landowner, or
who has so much property under his charge; but feeling
the strongest conviction that it is my duty as a citizen to
state the views which I have formed, although all I have
in the world is in land, yet I have no hesitation in coming
forward and saying that I think it is the duty and the
interest of all to join in bringing about the consummation
of this great struggle :

"I shall first of all ask my brother farmers, if there be any present :
Have the laws of protection been of any service to you ? (Cries of ' No,
no.')   In the year 1815 the Corn Law was passed.   You were then told
that 80s. would be the price of wheat: that amount being guaranteed to
us in terms as strong as any that could possibly be used.   But in the
year 1822 we found that not 80s., but 40s.—half that price—was all that
we could obtain.   Then, in 1825, we were told that it would be impossible to carry out the law—that if it were carried out there would be
a famine ; and Mr. Canning then considered it his duty to go down to
the House of Commons, and propose to let all the wheat out of bond
without paying any duty at all.   Gentlemen, it was then said that the
law would not do; but in 1827 or 1828 a new law was introduced,
founded on what was termed the sliding scale ; and that law was to
ensure us 64s.   In 1836 I was one of the parties who were called up to
be examined before the committee of the House of Commons ; and on
that occasion it was clearly shown that 35s. was all that we could get.
That was the whole amount which it was possible for us to obtain,
although 64s. was the sum which had been promised, and in the expectation of getting which all our contracts as farmers had been entered

into. (Hear, hear.) It was then found that that law would not do. In 1841, a different state of things was brought about. Sir Robert Peel came into power, and he said, or at least implied, ' If you will be led by me, if you will allow me to adopt a fresh scale, I will make the price 56s.' (Laughter.) But I need hardly add that what he then told us has not been brought to pass, for we are now obliged to sell wheat for 45s. (Hear, hear.) The contracts we have entered into, however, remain the same—(hear, hear)—our expenses remain the same. (Hear, hear.) After the number of years' experience that I have now had, I say that it is impossible for any man, however clever he may be, to control the seasons (hear, hear), or to say what shall be the price of the bread of man. (Cheers.) Gentlemen, that being the case, and it is clearly proved to be so,—for while 56s. is the price which we were to receive, we actually sell at 45s.,—it is no longer of any use, I say, to stick to the system of protection; but I trust that, instead of that, we shall extend our commercial enterprise, and see if we cannot, by increasing our trade, grow more, and get you more to eat Gentlemen, I have only this to say : I tell you that it is necessary that we should all come forward upon this question—landlord, tenant, and labourer; and, when I look at the immense mass of people who take an interest in this cause, I have no doubt of its being triumphant. (Cheers.) Gentlemen, I say it is to the interest of the landlord that this question should be settled ; and I do trust he will let it be seen by his consideration, by his liberality, and by joining with his tenant in carrying out improvements, that it is the interest of the tenant to use his best endeavours, by increasing the production of the soil, to fill the mouths of the vast and increasing population. (Cheers.) We know that it is not in the power of any man to control the seasons. It has been shown to us over and over again, that they go in cycles; that while, on the one hand, the bountiful Giver of every good may be showering down his blessings, and giving crops in abundance in another part of the world, our own, unfortunately, may not be so favoured. Not only may this happen, but it has happened that we have been burned up with a scorching sun, or drowned with a drenching rain. Then, I say, let us, whose country is the mistress of the sea, send our ships into deep waters. (Cheers.) Let those who are living at the uttermost parts of the globe know that we will send our vessels to them for food; carry to them things necessary for a life of civilisation; plant there our flag; teach them to cultivate the fruits of the earth ; carry them the things necessary to do so ; and be, as we ever must be, the workshop of the world. (Loud cheers.) Gentlemen, I say that it is necessary to do this ; and I do not doubt that the landowners, tenants, and all classes, will join hand-in-hand in carrying out so great a cause ; that, like the

Phœnix springing fröm its ashes, shall we the landowners of England, and we the tenants of England, arise and show, by our determination and by our skill, our desire to do all we can to procure for the people of this country what is necessary for them to eat. (Cheers.) I am more than ever satisfied that the more we extend commerce the better will our produce sell. (Hear, hear.) If you will allow me, I will repeat an anecdote which I heard the other day in Ireland, which will illustrate the fact of which I am speaking; and I hope it will be the means of convincing my brother farmers that they have not that which they think they have under this system. It had a great effect upon my mind, as showing that the more we extend the hand of fellowship to trade, the better will be our own condition. (Hear, hear.) Three years ago, the Irish butter, as it appears, could not be sold. It could not be turned into money; not because there were none to eat it, but because the people of Glasgow, who were the principal purchasers, had nothing to do. (Hear, hear.) But within the last month, when I left the shores of Ireland, butter could not be got for money. Glasgow is the consuming place; and the people of Glasgow say, 'Butter we must have; and as long as there is employment for us we will be your customers.' In that country, mark you, I met a manufacturer from Glasgow; and these are the words which he stated to have taken place between himself and a person to whom he was selling his goods : 'Pray, don't give us too great an order.' The woman said, ' A large order I must give ; for, since you give us such prices for our butters, all our farmers' wives want new shawls.' (Cheers and laughter.) Now, if we only carry out that principle, by letting other nations send us corn, while we try to grow it also, and at the same time are manufacturing for them; if, I say, we go to them to purchase, they will be like the farmers' wives in Ireland, they will want shawls too. ('Hear, hear,' and cheers.) You need not fear the result, if you can only obtain customers. This has been proved over and over again. In any part of the country where we find manufactures flourishing, and population increasing, there we find land and produce the most valuable. (Hear, hear.) I am sorry for having detained you so long. (Cries of ' No, no,' ' Go on.') If it is necessary for me to say more, I can only declare that I am at your service. (Cheers.) Gentlemen, I told you that I had just left the shores of Ireland; I have been told again and again that this Corn Law was made expressly for that country. And now I ask any of you who may be acquainted with it, what is its condition at this moment? (Hear, hear.) Has it there had the desired effect? (Hear, hear.) Has it there made the farmers rich? (Cries of ' No, no.') Has it there increased the happiness and comfort of the people? (Cries of 'No, no.') I tell you that it has not; a gentleman in Ireland said to me the other day, when I was speaking of the Corn Laws, 'Never keep them on on our account; I can only say, it is impossible to make this country worse, or to bring it into a state of greater degredation.' (Hear, hear.) It has not, therefore, answered their purpose; and, if I am to believe what I hear from the mouths of British farmers, it has not answered their purpose either. When I look at the farmers in this country, when I look at the condition in which they are placed at this moment, I say it is necessary, when you talk of an experiment being tried, to ask upon whom are you to try it? Not upon a party that is whole, but upon one that is sick. And when I look to what we are brought at this moment—for we are glad even of lard—I ask, is this the state of things after thirty years' protection? (Hear, hear.) If it is, I for one am willing to give up that protection. (Loud cheers.) I say this conscientiously. All I have in the world is in the land and on the land (hear, hear); but I have this consolation, let the wind blow high or blow low, I have acted conscientiously. I have made this declaration, because I am a party deeply interested. I have taken an active part against free trade, and, now that I have changed my opinions, I am not ashamed to own it. (Loud cheers.) I have done this conscientiously; I have done it because I believe free trade to be right; and, mark you, I do not mean free trade only in corn, but in sugar and timber too. (Hear, hear.) And one reason why I come forward to espouse this cause is, because I cannot ask for free trade in sugar while corn is protected. I know well, that, if I want to build a house, I must build it with timber which will soon decay, because I cannot go to the market to buy better. Therefore, I think it is for the interest of every class that this cause should triumph; and I have come forward in its behalf, as I have told you, conscientiously, because, I believe, it will secure the safety of the crown, the upholding of the aristocracy, and the increase of the happiness and comforts of the people. (Immense cheering.)"

Mr. Cobden and Mr. W. J. Fox followed, and delivered spirit-stirring and hope-inspiring speeches, exciting the utmost enthusiasm in the meeting.

The opening of the Bazaar in Covent Garden Theatre, May 8th, created an interest scarcely inferior to that which was felt at a later and happier period at the opening of the Crystal Palace, in Hyde Park. The London newspapers, whether of protectionist or free-trade principles, vied with each other in describing the interior of the theatre, the extensive contributions, and the daily proceedings. The

following is from the *Morning Herald*, the organ of the ultra-
monopolists :—

" Notwithstanding the very unfavourable state of the
weather, and the high price of the tickets of admission, the
attendance at the doors was very numerous, and the staircase, saloons, and lobbies—even the body of the house
itself—was soon full to overflowing. The arrangements
to prevent confusion appeared, however, to be very excellent, and to be well carried out by the stewards, so that,
although visitors were almost subjected to the *peine forte et
dure* during their transit, there was no complaint, but each
appeared content to bear it. The public were only admitted through the chief entrance in Bow-street, from
whence they ascended, as during the dramatic exhibitions
at the theatre, up the grand staircase to the Shakspere
saloon, now fitted up with tapestry, carpets, shawls, &c. so
as greatly to resemble the show room of a mercer. In this
place also is a magnificent mirror, one such as giants only
should survey themselves in, also an interesting stall of
chemical preparations ; and a box from Darlestone, in
Staffordshire, containing coal and iron, the latter in its
various stages from the rudest ore to the most polished
and tempered metal, which is capable of being wrought by
human ingenuity. In the box lobby on the left is a stall
for Miller's glass works, containing many remarkable
curiosities, and also the apparatus at work by which they
are produced, and glass thread is woven into soft and beautiful fabrics. Passing on to the centre of the lobby we find
two boxes are removed, and come suddenly upon a scene
so novel and romantic, so incongruous and grotesque, that
for a moment we could fancy ourselves transported to the
east, and about to deal with Turks and Mussulmans. Certainly, in its palmiest days, no visitor to Covent Garden
ever witnessed on its stage a more complete transformation.

" The whole area of the pit and stage is boarded over,
and transformed into a ' Norman Gothic Hall,' with an

arched roof, gaily decorated, and supported on each side
by rows of ornamental pillars. The sides are covered with
imitation panelling, with grotesque ornaments and devices,
and numerous free-trade mottoes. At the extreme end is
a large Gothic window so prepared and lit up as to resemble stained glass ; there are also similar windows at the
sides, and from the roof are suspended rows of illuminated
lamps, which cast a rich but subdued light over the hall,
and add very much to the beauty of the spectacle. We
understand the whole of these arrangements were devised
by Mr. Sloman, the machinist of the theatre, and Mr.
Grieve, the well-known scenic painter, and carried into
effect, under their superintendence, by Mr. Edwards, of
Manchester. Descending a few steps we find ourselves in
the body of the hall, which is 150 feet long by 50 feet wide,
and is occupied by four rows of stalls, each about a yard
in width, but divided into various lengths, in proportion to
the wants of the occupants, and the value of their mer-
chandise. Upon the stage, where the hall is wider, and in
the refreshment room, there are additional stalls. The
length of the counters is said to be 900 feet, and the whole
appears to have been used to the best advantage. The
stalls are not numbered, nor are the holders' names affixed
to them, but they appear to have been allotted according
to certain localities, the names of which are hung over
them. Thus, on passing the slips in the centre boxes, we
find the boxes on each side converted into stalls, the one
being allotted to Northampton, and the other to Dunstable,
and respectively filled with the staple commodities of these
places—shoes and bonnets. Upon entering the hall we
saw the stalls on the right allotted to Rochdale, Halifax,
Leeds, and Bradford. These, as they are first in order,
appeared to us also to be first in merit, both as to the
quality of the articles displayed, and the taste shown in
their arrangement. They contained chiefly fancy articles
of needlework, toys of various descriptions, carpets, shawls,

materials of various kinds for ladies' dresses, and curiosities, among which may be mentioned a piece of muslin, printed by the late Sir Robert Peel, and a pen-and ink portrait of the Queen, the lines of which, instead of being blank, are written words, and comprise the whole contents of a book which is attached to, and descriptive of, it. This singular specimen of ingenuity is to be raffled for at 2s. 6d. a head, and, strange to say, we saw several Quaker ladies pressing forward to have their names set down as gamblers for it. Opposite these stalls, and on the right centre of the hall, are the stalls allotted to Northampton, Stockport, Swansea, Carlisle, York, Stockton, Hull, Beverley, and Bristol. Then comes, at right angles, the Newcastle stall, followed by those of Huddersfield, Barnsley, Wakefield, and Bloomsbury, and the Kentish-town stalls. Opposite these, and on this side the stage, are the stalls appropriated to the metropolitan districts, which are described as Peckham, Islington, City, Kensington, Camden-town, Sussex, Norwood, Pentonville, Hoxton, St. Martin's, and the Savoy. The stalls in the curved line at the top, which unites the two central lines of stalls, are allotted to Sheffield.

"The refreshment room is appropriately allotted to refreshment stalls, with the single exception of a book stall, and is much resorted to by visitors, who really need some refreshment after their toilsome and tedious passage to it. But, next to the creams and ices vended there, the chief object of attraction is a huge plum cake—a cake, the idea of which could, we think, have occurred in a dream only to some imaginative schoolboy—so vast in its expanse, so ponderous its size, so rich its ingredients, so delicious its fragrance. It is a Bury Simnel, and measures, we should think, some five feet in diameter, weighs 280 lbs., and bears upon its broad surface a sheet of iced sugar so large as to have inscribed upon it nearly all the maxims which embody the religion of the League, and so sweet and richly ornamented as to almost induce the visitor to swallow them. We hear that it is to be cut up and distributed on the last day of the exhibition; but let the League beware how they previously admit a school to their Bazaar, for to resist the combined temptation of this cake and its free-trade inscriptions is, we think, beyond the possibility of schoolboy nature. In this room is also the 'post office,' an ingenious device for (among other purposes) raising money, and disseminating free-trade doctrines. It is suggested to the visitor to knock and inquire if they have a letter for him, and upon his supplying them with his name and address, he is himself, in due time, supplied with a packet (not pre-paid), which, on receiving, he finds filled with League tracts and other free-trade publications. The scheme was so successful that the arrival of a 'foreign mail' was soon notified, and of course it brought with it a despatch for every applicant, and at the foreign rate of postage.

"Leaving the refreshment room, but not before examining at the book stall an ancient mass-book, printed at Madrid, with the music on the old system of notation, we return to the stage, and see before us on the right centre the stalls of Gloucester, Norwich, Exeter, Dudley, Warrington, Preston, and Lancaster. At the Dudley stall were some interesting fossils and mineral specimens from that place. The Lancaster stall, among other articles of interest, exhibited a miniature bedstead in mahogany, of very elegant construction; and the chief object of interest at the Preston stall was a model carriage made for the Preston Guild, which was certainly a pleasing exhibition of the taste and ingenuity of our countrymen. It was complete in all its appointments, and was offered for £35. Near to these was the Liverpool stall, at which was exhibited, together with miscellaneous fancy articles, as baskets, lace collars, book-markers, &c., 'a lock of Sir Walter Scott's hair,' price £3. 3s.; and a wax medallion 'Portrait of R. R. Moore, Esq., with autograph,' price 15s. Of the latter there was a large supply at many of the stalls, but we are unable to speak as to the demand for them. There were also autographs, *ad libitum*, of Mr. H. Smith's 'Stanzas on the Bazaar,' and of the most renowned free-traders. Near these, and returning on the right, are the six stalls assigned to Manchester, three of which are in recesses illuminated by transparencies representing stained glass windows. These stalls contain a very elegant assortment of fancy articles, chiefly made by ladies. Among others, we particularly noticed some elegant painted satin and velvet cushions. One or two magnificent chairs, having backs and seats covered with beautiful needlework, some elegant shawls, and children's fancy dresses. There was also a nautilus cradle, in imitation of that made for the royal nursery, which excited general admiration. Opposite the Manchester stalls were those of Staleybridge, Ashton-under-Lyne, and Bury. At the Ashton stall were several curiosities, from an old black-letter volume of 1568, entitled 'The Dial of Princes,' price £6, to a prize shoe made without seam or stitch by some ingenious local artist. Bury, also, was not without its curiosities, for it contributed a huge bear's paw, with a goodly collection of children's frocks, carpeting, and paintings and engravings. Returning still, we have on either hand the Scotch stalls and those of the Midland Counties. The tributary towns in Scotland are Dundee, Edinburgh, Glasgow, Paisley, Shetland, and Dunfermline. Edinburgh sends chiefly miscellaneous toys, Paisley Shawls, and the other ladies' work, toys, shawls, and table-linen. On the other hand, the Midland Counties also send chiefly their staple manufactures, as Nottingham, lace; Leicester, lace and hosiery; Coventry, ribbons, and a newly-invented gimp for bonnets: Birmingham, a handsome collection of hardware and fancy goods, in every respect of very superior quality; Bolton supplies a number of handsome footstools, slippers, and articles of that description, with autograph letters of the 'Rev. J. Fletcher,' and other eminent personages.

"Having thus traversed the body of the hall, we again ascend the steps through the boxes, and, availing ourselves of the ample directions posted about, soon find our way through the lobby into the lower saloon, where we find collected the contributions of Sheffield, Colebrookdale, and the Potteries. And here, in our humble judgment, is to be seen the best portion of the Exhibition. The Sheffield department contains contributions of the staple manufactures of that place, and the specimens are in the highest degree creditable to the enterprise, ingenuity, and skill of our manufacturers and artisans. Here are instruments and tools of almost every description, both of material, and quality, and workmanship, from the revolving saw, which cuts through steel bars or gnarled oaks as easily as a knife divides a twig, to scissors, needles, and other things appurtenant to a lady's work-box, so minute, yet so highly finished and exquisitely modelled, that one might imagine them 'made to order' for *Titania* and her attendant fairies. There are also instruments of various kinds, so highly polished as to reflect the countenance like mirrors; and such a collection of knives, forks, shears, surgical instruments, and ingenious tools of all descriptions as are rarely seen in London. Many of these, too, were much admired for their admirable finish, and the beautiful execution of several ornaments and devices adapted to the occasion, among which we may particularly mention a large pair of shears, on which were exhibited excellent full-length portraits of Mr. Bright and Mr. Cobden. The exhibition from Colebrookdale, in the centre of this saloon, was no less attractive and no less worthy of attention. It consisted chiefly of ornamental iron works, in some of which our native artists appeared to have attained perfection. There were vases, fountains, bronzes, ornamental grates, fire-screens (on which were painted striking portraits of Messrs. Cobden, Bright, and Villiers). American rocking chairs, and iron chairs of several descriptions, garden seats, and similar articles in great profusion, almost every one of which had round it a knot of admirers, who were loud in their eulogiums. At the other end of the saloon were china and earthenware from the Potteries; but as these were only partially unpacked we saw but little of them.

"The upper saloon has been newly decorated for the occasion, having free trade mottoes enclosed in medallions, on the hangings, the effect of which is novel and interesting. Stepping from this saloon into the upper circle, to take a bird's-eye view of the whole exhibition before leaving it, the spectacle is very fine and animating. The effect produced by the softened light of the rows of illuminated lamps, both upon the splendid roof and pillars, and the busy scene below, was very beautiful. It was also amusing to see the diligence in business of the amateur shopkeepers, and the difficulty with which, from the pressure of the crowd, a customer maintained his ground until he could complete a bargain. The impression produced was that the place was much too small both for the satisfactory exhibition of the goods, and for the accommodation of visitors. Probably to this cause we should attribute the absence of much of that taste in the arrangements of the stalls that is customary on such occasions. As it was, the articles generally were rather heaped together than displayed, which made the counters more resemble those of the wholesale than the retail dealer. There was also a palpable want of variety in the articles exhibited, more than three-fourths of the stalls, consisting of miscellaneous articles of fancy needlework, which, however pretty in themselves, lost their interest when the view of them was so frequently repeated. As a Ladies' Bazaar, however, the experiment on the whole appeared to be successful. But as a great 'national exhibition' of our arts and manufactures by those of our manufacturers and artisans who are interested in free trade, which some of the free traders affect to call it, the affair must be pronounced a total failure. With the exceptions we have particularly noticed, even those exhibitions of staple manufactures that were made contained very little in them peculiarly worthy of remark; and we feel satisfied they would never have been sent to an exhibition of national industry had we one similar to that of France in this country.

"As to the attendance, it was, throughout the day, extremely numerous, a great number of the visitors being evidently from the country, brought up, probably, by the double inducement of the Bazaar and the May meetings. Among the persons present we noticed Sir J. C. Hobhouse, M.P., Sir De Lacy Evans, Mr. Pattison, M.P., Mr. Bright, M.P., Mr. M. Gibson, M.P., Mr. Brotherton, M.P., Mr. Hutt, M.P., Mr. Wilson, Mr. P. A. Taylor, and other noted Leaguers. The attendance of members of the Society of Friends, both male and female, was also very numerous. The prices of the various articles appeared to be quite as high as is customary on such occasions. We should add that a musical band was in attendance throughout the day, and played a number of popular airs very effectively."

We are now approaching the most stirring period in the history of the Anti-Corn-Law League, requiring an extent of notice which precludes further detail of the proceedings within the walls of Covent Garden, and I must content myself with giving the following extracts from some of the journals of the period :—

From *The League* :—

" The Bazaar, which for nearly three weeks continued to be the most attractive spectacle ever displayed in London, has finally closed; the decorations are taken down, and the goods removed. As all the accounts are not yet closed, we cannot state the results with perfect accuracy; but we have ascertained that rather more than £20,000 have been obtained for admissions and sales, independent of about £5,000 in money contributed from various localities, and of the unsold goods, which are reserved to stock the Bazaar that will be held at a later period of the year, in the Free-Trade Hall, in Manchester. There were aggregated those ladies who, for seventeen days, had devoted their time, their toil, and, we fear, their health, with unwearied assiduity, to advance the great cause of humanity and justice; ladies who had manifested an intelligence, tact, and spirit of self-sacrifice which cannot be too highly estimated, or too gratefully remembered. They were not conscious of the capabilities they possessed until they found them developed in action by the force of circumstances. Everybody was willing to concede to everybody; and there was no need for administrative functions when all minds were animated by the same feelings, guided by the same principles, and directed to the same obejct. Collected together from all parts of the British islands, those who had never seen or heard of each other in their lives found themselves encircled by friends though surrounded by strangers, community of feeling becoming the basis for community of affection. Never was there such a perfect illustration of the Sallustian rule, ·*Idem velle atque idem nolle, ea demum firma amicitia est*'—(To like the same thing, and to dislike the same thing, that indeed is firm friendship); for the best feelings of the heart were at once called into warm action by the mere force of association in the same glorious cause. No one could gaze, as we have done for hours together, on the continuous stream in which the crowd flowed through the Hall, without being deeply impressed by the order, the forbearance, and the conciliatory demeanour of every individual in the vast multitude; women went about fearless of insult, and children without danger of injury. It was a striking evidence of the improved culture and higher tone of moral feeling which the discussions and instructions of the League have infused into the public mind. It was a manifestation of the intellectual and ethical character which a great political movement assumes when kept free from the exacerbations of party. All who visited the hall, whatever their former opinions may have been, left it with a conviction that the objects of the League are neither selfish nor partial, but tend equally to raise the physical comfort and the spiritual character of the British nation. It has been officially announced that the artistic character of the Exhibition will be discussed in the Art-Union, by the gentleman who wrote the account of the Paris Exposition for that journal; and that two eminent artists have been engaged to prepare drawings, illustrating the most important articles of manufacture that have been displayed. We shall not interfere with this part of the subject further than to say that, if the Bazaar answered no other purpose than showing the great advance which British artists and artisans have made in design within the last few years, it would have been worth ten times the cost and trouble of its preparation. But it subserved higher purposes even in relation to art: it showed manufacturers how much they may learn from each other in relation both to beauty of form and taste of pattern. The worker in iron has found that he can study with profit the productions of the manufacturer of lace; the printer has received valuable hints from the weaver; and the artist for the loom has profited by the artist for the hammer. The Exhibition gave overwhelming evidence of the immense value of the industry which we seek to set free from the fetters of monopoly. To emancipate such powers of production as those which here gave proof of their existence and their importance would be to open a new field of greatness for the English nation, and to place Britain onward in that career of destiny to which our land has been specially called by Providence, as the great civiliser of the world, and the true benefactor of the human race. The voice of truth has declared that ' Glory to God in the highest' can only be promoted by ' Peace on earth, good will towards men;' but the common interests developed by free trade are the bonds of peace, and the common justice established by equal commerce is the firmest cement of good will."

From the *Morning Chronicle* :—

"We consider this Bazaar, taken in connexion with the singular political movement of which it forms so conspicuous a feature, as a sign of the times well worthy of the attention of our statesmen of every party. As an indication of the progress of opinion, as a pledge of earnestness and determination in the assertion of opinion, it is more impressive than any kind or quantity of what we ordinarily call 'agitation.' No amount of public meetings, parliamentary petitioning, or popular noise and excitement, could give so significant a demonstration of genuine power. The immense mass of contributions, even yet continuing to arrive in quantities that far exceed the ability of the most skilful management to find room for them in the over-crowded stalls; the number and variety of the contributors, from the wealthy manufacturing and commercial capitalist, who gives by wholesale, as he makes and trades by wholesale, to the artisan whose donation represents the toil of spare hours painfully saved out of laborious days and short nights; the completeness with which all branches of our national industry—agricultural, manufacturing, domestic, and literary — are represented in this extraordinary museum; the evidences that everywhere meet the eye, of the lively interest which the women of Great Britain feel in a question which even the well known contributions of their sex to the literature of political economy have scarcely yet withdrawn, in common estimation, from the category of the abstract sciences; the enormous expenditure of time, money, labour, and thought, which must have been devoted to this undertaking, for many months past, in every part of Great Britain;

—indicate a quiet earnestness and force of purpose, of a kind such as has never before been displayed on any public question. The destination of the large pecuniary proceeds of this enterprise—to the carrying on of that business of agitation in which its promoters have attained so exemplary a proficiency—is a consideration scarcely worth adverting to as an element of its political importance. Mere agitation, conducted with whatever talent, or sustained by whatever amount of money power, is not, in this country, by any means so formidable an agent of social and political change as many persons imagine. *Here* is the true 'agitation'—that which gives reality and potency to those external efforts to which the name is commonly restricted—in the settled purpose and conviction of the multitudes of whose zeal, union, and working power the Covent Garden Bazaar is the embodiment. The spirit which has animated all this mass of sustained and concentrated exertion is a spirit which no opposition can subdue, no failure dishearten, and no delay tire out. The writers and speakers of the League have laid much stress on the significance of this spectacle as an *exposition* of our national industry, and a practical appeal to society against the impolicy and injustice of laws that narrow the market of that industry, and abridge its earnings. It amply deserves to be thus characterised, and cannot fail of having, to a large extent, the intended effect on public opinion. If, during the first few days of the exhibition, there seemed something for a hypercriticism to object to on this head, in the predominance of those lighter wares which represent only the industry of the *boudoir*, the criticism has long since become inapplicable. From day to day the Bazaar has increasingly assumed its higher and more interesting character, as a display of the resources and capabilities of British industry."

From the *Art Union :*—

" Although it was the leading intention of the late Exhibition at Covent Garden Theatre—which opened on the 12th and closed on the 27th of May—to obtain a large sum of money to advance the object of ' the Anti-Corn-Law League, there can be no doubt that it has answered a purpose far more important and universal; for it has gone a long way to make the public acquainted with the capabilities of British commercial art—if so we may term that class of art which has immediate reference to trade. No circumstance has ever occurred in this country so directly tending to augment ' the Mercantile Value of the Fine Arts.' The occasion not only brought to London a large mass of wealthy and influential individuals—influential, as, in a great degree, guiding the tastes of hundreds of thousands of persons—but it brought them into intimate connexion with those whose opinions ought to have weight with the producers of manufactured articles; while, therefore, on the

one hand, there is largely increased information as to what is doing—
and what may be done—in the manufacturing districts, on the other
there is an advanced appreciation of excellence and added desire to
adopt the safest and surest means of attaining it. We deplore, indeed,
that the government of this country disdains, or at least delays, to do
that which has been so nobly, so effectually, and so profitably done in
France; but we are willing to accept so great a boon from any hand,
and are bound to consider that, be the motive what it may, this
'Bazaar' will have given a great impetus to British manufacture as
deriving value from British art. It was utterly impossible for any
visitor to move about the living mass which thronged the theatre without
encountering every now and then some proof that, after all, they do not
'manage matters so much better in France.' France, at its national
'Exposition,' fostered by the king, patronised by the nobility, and aided
by the people,' pour la gloire,' furnished no 'stalls' so unquestionably
excellent as some of those to which we refer."

From *Douglas Jerrold's Magazine :*—

"The scene which, during the last month, Covent Garden Theatre
exhibited, was a great demonstration—a great fact. The sight which it
exhibited to the country was one to make it think. Within a spacious
area were collected innumerable triumphs of industry and skill—a mute
parliament of labour. And these thousand objects imagined by ingenuity—created by toil—pleaded in all the eloquence of silence for the
rights of those who fashioned them. The workman was represented by
his handicraft; the toiling city was shadowed forth by rich stuffs, or
glancing metals; and the fabrics, gorgeous from the loom, or dazzling
from the forge, cried aloud, although they spoke not :—' Let us accomplish our mission; let us go forth over the earth, civilising, aiding,
comforting man; and bringing, in return, plenty to the board, and peace
to the hearth, of the toil-worn men and women who have fashioned us!'
A 'Bazaar'—'tis a trite word for a commonplace thing—often an idle
mart for children's trumpery—for foolish goods brought forth of laborious idleness. But an idea can ennoble anything. Nobility, in its true
sense, is an idea; and how grand is the idea which ennobles *our* Bazaar
—which, even apart from its claims as an industrial exposition, makes
it a great and holy thing. 'Free Trade.' These words form a spell by
which the world will yet be governed. They are the spirit of a dawning
creed—a creed which already has found altars and temples worthy of
its truth. The Anti-Corn-Law League Bazaar has raised thoughts in
the national mind which will not soon die. As a spectacle, it was
magnificent in the extreme; but not more grand materially than it was
morally. The crowd who saw it, thought as well as gazed. It was not

a mere huge shop for selling wares; but a great school for propagating an idea. And the pupils were not Londoners alone. From every part of the land monster trains hurried up their visitors. From the tracts where tall chimneys stand like forests—from the districts where the plough, not the engine, labours—where the farm-steading takes the place of the factory—where the 'mill' means not that weaving yarn, but that grinding 'corn—from town and country—shipping port and inland city—steam has whirled its tens of thousands to one common centre—to see a great demonstration—to take a great lesson, and then to narrate and teach what they have beheld and learned to others."

From the *Illuminated Magazine*:—

" It *is* a great public cause, and we never witnessed so much and such widely-spread conviction in any other. There has been a soul of devotion, a heroism in individuals of all classes, an amount of excitement no selfish feelings could have produced. Small tradesmen and trades-women in London have given away their goods out of their own shops to the Bazaar as a patriotic offering; giving away their stock and their trade at the same time—quiet, unostentatious offerings to the spirit of good, and with no hope of their names being published in the news-papers. Women have made presents of their jewels, toys, and trinkets, as well as their time; and we have no doubt that had such a proposal been made, and a free-trade use found for it, thousands of women would have been found to shear away the hair from their heads, as is recorded to have been done in one of the sieges of old to furnish cordage for the engines of death. We could almost wish that such a use had been found—not in the cause of war, but of peace—and we are sure that there are thousands of high-minded women who would have considered it a reproach to be seen adorned with the beautiful hair which might help to purchase freedom from misery to millions of their fellows. The distinctive mark of free trade would have been written on their brows in the unmistakeable character of self-sacrifice."

From the *Economist*:—

" The most important and stirring sensations, in the presence of this great national exhibition, will probably be viewed altogether apart from the place and its gorgeous display, though necessarily excited by them. We see stalls bearing the inscription of nearly every important town and neighbourhood in the kingdom, containing the richest specimens of all that art and ingenuity and taste can display, presided over by the votaries of a great principle, and by those who have been moved to a compassionate sympathy for the sufferings of the great masses of our fellow-countrymen in the recent years of scarcity and distress;—who, now that those clouds are passed, and a more happy and prosperous period accompanies a time of plenty, are still willing to make any personal effort or sacrifice to save their neighbours and their country from a recurrence of such scenes as have stricken with grief and sorrow the hearts of the stoutest during the late years of suffering. We see in all that there surrounds us a silent but eloquent proclamation of the will, the persevering and untiring determination of a people expressed in a way that no statesman can safely overlook. A visit to this scene, with a knowledge of all that has preceded its construction, and a knowledge of the objects and principles which it demands, is well calculated to pro- duce an impression and conviction on the mind of any reflecting man, whatever his previous opinions may have been."

From the *Patriot :—*

" Yes, the League is a great fact; but this Bazaar is a greater fact still : and it affords us no little satisfaction to have entered the lists in this grand rivalry of devotion to the cause of the people. Our fair friends have made contributions more ingenious and more beautiful, and our great manufacturers have presented offerings more splendid and more costly; but we confidently challenge the whole array of con- tributors to produce one which could be viewed with greater interest by any well-constituted mind, than that which we venture to claim as, in some sort, our own contribution. In some obscure corner of the theatre, probably where no eye can see them, or where, if seen, they will be passed by wholly unregarded, lie some huge bundles of flocks, sufficient to make 500 beds, together with sundry bales of quilts, blankets, and sheets ; the design of which is, to enable benevolent persons to purchase, at the nominal price of five shillings, a perfect bed-suit for gratuitous bestowment upon poor peasants in Oxfordshire and Dorsetshire. How came they there ? In the *Patriot*, of March 20th, there appeared, from that indefatigable friend of the poor, the Rev. W Ferguson, of Bicester, a letter addressed to Mr. Harcourt, one of the members for Oxfordshire, which we inserted at the writer's request. On turning to that letter, it will be found to convey a picture of misery in the midst of plenty not to be surpassed by the most destitute or squalid court or alley in the city of London, or any part of the empire. This harrowing description of utter destitution found its way from our columns into those of the *League* and the *Economist ;* and, whether owing to its original insertion in the *Patriot*, or to its transcription by our contemporaries, those inter- esting contributions to the League Bazaar which we have noticed are the gratifying result."

CHAPTER XIX.

LORD JOHN RUSSELL'S RESOLUTIONS.

We now return to parliament. There had been long debates on the Income Tax and upon the tariff; then came the Whitsuntide holidays, followed by long debates upon the Maynooth Grant. On the 26th May, Lord J. Russell brought before the House of Commons the following resolutions, of which he had given notice :—

" 1. That the present state of political tranquility, and the recent revival of trade, afford to this House a favourable opportunity to con - sider of such measures as may tend permanently to improve the condition of the labouring classes.

" 2. That those laws which impose duties usually called protective, tend to impair the efficiency of labour, to restrict the free interchange of commodities, and to impose on the people unnecessary taxation.

" 3. That the present Corn Law tends to check improvements in agriculture, produces uncertainty in all farming speculations, and holds out to the owners and occupiers of land prospects of special advantage which it fails to secure.

" 4. That this House will take the said laws into consideration, with a view to such cautious and deliberate arrangements as may be most beneficial to all classes of her Majesty's subjects.

" 5. That the freedom of industry would be promoted by a careful revision of the law of parochial settlement which now prevails in England and Wales.

" 6. That a systematic plan of colonization would partially relieve those districts of the country where the deficiency of employment has been most injurious to the labourers in husbandry.

" 7. That the improvements made of late years in the education of the people, as well as its more general diffusion, have been seen with satisfaction by this House.

" 8. That this House will be ready to give its support to measures, founded on liberal and comprehensive principles, which may be conducivè to the further extension of religious and moral instruction.

"9. That an humble address be presented to her Majesty, to lay the foregoing resolutions before her Majesty."

The country believed that with his lordship a fixed duty had become a fixed idea, and it looked with little interest to the debate ; and it was remarked that he did not attach much consequence to an expression of opinion upon the Corn Laws when he included education, colonization, and parochial settlements in his resolutions. His lordship began by vindicating the policy of bringing them forward together, as they referred to subjects inseparably connected with each other. His opinion was that the House ought to endeavour to free trade from restrictions, and to relieve industry from the trammels of legislation, but that in so doing it ought to accompany measures of relaxation with other measures of great importance. He maintained that the general subject of education and instruction should form part of the system to be adopted by government, and of the measures to be by government submitted to parliament ; for it could not be expected that any measure for the general education and instruction of the people would be effective unless their physical condition was essentially improved. He then took a retrospect of the condition of the country from the period of the French revolution down to the present time, and contended that during the course of the war, which commenced in 1793, many changes for the worse occurred, under which the nation was still suffering. Among these changes he enumerated the enormous increase of the debt, and of taxation to pay the interest upon it—the bank restriction act of 1797, which had degraded the labourer, diminished the value of his labour ; and had at the same time led to an extravagant mode of living, and a neglect of forethought and prudence among the employers, who suddenly found themselves in the enjoyment of high profits—and Sir R. Peel's act of 1819 and of last year for the resumption of cash payments—measures which, though they were founded on sound principles, from which it would be a great misfortune to depart materially, had still produced the evil which was generally the result of a contraction of the currency, and had injured the industrious classes to a considerable extent. He then adverted to the policy of restriction and monopoly, or, as it was sometimes called, the policy of giving protection to native industry, which had grown up during the war, and on which he contended that parliament might legislate with benefit by overturning altogether that erroneous system. He showed that the chief monopolies which now existed had been introduced by ministers who were still living, and that the policy which in Adam Smith's time was called the mercantile system, had been adopted, according to that high authority, by the country gentlemen from a wish to protect the interests and promote the welfare of the commercial classes. The experience of our times led us to form a very different conclusion from that formed by Adam Smith. Our manufacturers now saw that it was of no advantage to them to have restrictions imposed upon articles imported into this country ; and had adopted the theory of Adam Smith that the policy of restriction was mischievous, that it favoured one class at the expense of another, and that it injured the labouring classes more than any other. He proved that our manufacturers were correct in the views which they now entertained, by taking a retrospect of the history of the restrictions formerly imposed on timber and wool. He gave that history as a specimen of the mischief created by the high duties imposed during the war, and of the emptiness of the apprehensions entertained of the evils likely to accrue from the remission of those duties. He contended that history also showed that under protective duties the labourer was less able to educate his children, to live in comfort, and to become satisfied with his condition. Nevertheless, there was still a party of great weight in the legislature, which insisted that without protection certain branches of industry could not be maintained. To such persons he said, " Let us either protect all branches of industry, whether manufacturing or agricultural, or else let us abandon the system of protection as vicious and unsound." The tendency of this system was, in his opinion, to impair the efficiency of labour, and they had now arrived at that period when they must maintain the protection laws in their full power, or abandon them as vicious and unsound. Parliament had no right to interfere with the choice of a man as to the cheapest or dearest market for his labour or produce ; but, in removing restrictive laws, it was manifestly unjust to apply free-trade principles to one class and not to another :—

" Now, I must say that to introduce change and excite alarm among these men—even upon sound principles—is hardly fair, unless you introduce measures founded upon the same principles that shall be applicable to other classes—(cheers)—not making them applicable to men earning a guinea and five and twenty shillings a-week, but to men who are represented by peers of ancient descent—men of hereditary honours, of great wealth, and possessing vast power to resist your proposal. It is not just that, with regard to the first class—the labouring class—we should be called upon to be guided by the principles and authority of Adam Smith and Mr. Ricardo, while with regard to the second, the wealthy, the titled, and the powerful, we should be required to be governed by the principles of protection, and should be called upon to maintain for that class these protective laws. The right hon. gentleman who was last year the President of the Board of Trade (Mr. Gladstone) has shown the effect of these reductions in so far as manufactures are concerned."

The noble lord then referred to the origin of the Corn Laws, and the fluctuations that had taken place in the scale, and contended that the result of the system had been to create speculation and enhance the price to the consumers, without benefiting the revenue. Even at present, the owners and occupiers of land, with a protection

of 46 per cent. on the ordinary and common food of the
country, were not satisfied with their position. He maintained that the argument of the rate of wages being
dependent on the price of corn was entirely erroneous,
and he felt satisfied that the Corn Laws could not be continued in their present shape. The only suggestion he
could make would be for a low fixed duty, but he did not
think that corn should be taxed at all. At present he
should be in favour of *a fixed duty of 4s., 5s., or 6s., as
being preferable to a vanishing scale*, commencing at 10s.,
and abating annually, until they arrived at total repeal.
The noble lord then referred to the existing poor law, and
strongly urged the necessity of a more equitable adjustment of the law of settlement, and recommended a well-
considered scheme of emigration and a more general
diffusion of education. While pious men were in the
present month meeting day after day to send missionaries
to China and the South Seas, there were masses of our
own population utterly ignorant of the common elements
of the Christian faith; and suggested the voting a sum of
£150,000 in the present parliament to place our national
system of education on a more extended and effective
footing. The noble lord concluded by moving the first of
his series of resolutions.

Mr. S. Crawford moved an amendment to the effect that
the present time of tranquility afforded a favourable opportunity for giving immediate attention to the claims so
repeatedly urged in the petitions of the people for an
extension of parliamentary suffrage.

Sir James Graham admitted that Lord John Russell
had referred to the various matters comprised in his comprehensive speech with fairness and good temper, but he
complained of the unspecific nature of the resolutions.
The great object of Mr. Huskisson had been the substitution of protective for prohibitive legislation, and such
was the policy of the present government. He contended

that a fixed duty on corn would operate injuriously, and in times of scarcity could not be maintained ; while, under the present system, prices were equable, and the supply of corn steady and regular. Protection and improvement in agriculture had been coincident, and the increase in the produce of the soil had been commensurate with the increase of the population. By their recent measures for the reduction of protective duties, the present government *had gone to the verge of throwing land out of cultivation, and masses of the agricultural population out of employment !* He admitted that there were great difficulties in grappling with the question, as since the present government had come into power the population had increased one million and a half. The right honourable baronet then referred to various returns, for the purpose of showing that the labouring classes, in amount of wages and command over the necessaries of life, were in a very different position from what they were a few years since. Admitting the influence of a good harvest, he thought the government was entitled to some credit for the change. The right hon. baronet then referred to the improved position of our commercial affairs, and the large amount of capital invested in railway and other speculations. He disapproved of any government plan of emigration, inasmuch as voluntary emigration was at present going forward fully equal to the wants of our colonies. He believed the education of the people had been of late years materially improved, and that the means at present adopted for the purpose were carried out in the most efficient manner. After expressing the anxiety of the government to do everything in their power to promote the physical and moral welfare of the people, he concluded by meeting the proposition of the noble lord by moving the previous question.

After a few words from Sir C. Burrell, who contended that the labourers in his neighbourhood were *well paid and fed*, Mr. Labouchere said he regarded a great portion of

Sir J. Graham's speech as supplying powerful arguments in aid of Lord John Russell's proposition. Extended production, good seasons, enlarged supply, provisions cheaper, and wages higher, were all powerful encouragements to pursue a course of liberal and enlightened commercial policy. He urged on the government the necessity of availing themselves of the opportunity now afforded them of improving our commercial relations with foreign countries.

Sir J. Tyrell complained of the distressed state of the agricultural classes, and said he could no longer place any confidence in the present government. He feared that the agricultural interest would be in no better position if the noble lord opposite came into power.

Lord Pollington did not think there was any just ground for the alarm of the agricultural interest. He advocated an improved system of colonization rather than emigration, and thought a system of education without religion was worse than no education at all.

Mr. Villiers maintained that the government had given no answer whatever to the arguments of Lord J. Russell. On the contrary, the statements of Sir James Graham went to show that a more liberal system of commercial policy, and the low price of articles of general consumption, had materially benefited the working classes :—

" The right honourable baronet had shown them that crime had diminished since food had become cheap, and crime, he had stated truly, was necessarily connected with poverty, and he had shown them, also, that wages had increased, not only in the manufacturing, but also in the agricultural districts (loud opposition cheers) ; and he had shown them that in every village and in every parish the rate for the relief of the poor had diminished ; that there were fewer people receiving parish relief, fewer out of employment, and much less destitution in the country than when the price of food was high. The right honourable baronet actually proved the case of the advocates of free trade (cheers), and he gave them the prices of the various articles of consumption, namely, of wheat, flour, meat, and sugar, and had shown the reduction in the price of each, and how that reduction affected beneficially the condition of the labourer. And this was the argument by which the question, whether the total abolition of all protective duties was not the means of improving instead of deteriorating the condition of the people, was met. (Hear, hear.) The noble lord (Lord John Russell) had proved that the people were not advancing relatively with the wealth and prosperity of the country, and had told them that this was owing to their legislation, and it was in their power, by altering the system upon which they had legislated, to improve their condition. Now, this statement of the noble lord's was useful, for it came at a time when many from fear or benevolence were always talking in that House of the poor, and suggesting some crotchet or remedy for the distresses of one branch of industry or another; but the noble lord said, ' Away with all this pretence and affected sympathy for the poor, unless you relieve yourselves from the charge that for the purpose of promoting your own interests you are the cause of their deterioration.' (Hear, hear.) The noble lord told them fairly that they upheld the present system, because they believed it to be most conducive to their own interests. He said, ' You, the legislature, are the cause of the misery and distress of the poor, by passing laws to keep up the price of food.' (Hear, hear.) He (Mr. C. Villiers) did not defend the noble lord's conclusion, in one respect, but he thanked him for having advanced, and given the weight of his authority to the very measure which he (Mr. Villiers) would recommend for the benefit of the labouring classes, and of the people generally. (Hear.) The noble lord had shown that when they compelled the people to pay high prices for food, they were deprived of the comforts of life, and were rendered altogether incapable of providing education for their children. The noble lord said that by raising the price of food they injured and deteriorated the condition of the working classes, while on the other side no man upheld the price of food, he believed, except for the purposes of protection. (Hear, hear.) They raised the price of food by these protective duties; that was their purpose (hear, hear), and the right honourable baronet, the Home Secretary, had told them what was the consequence of success in that object. He had shown them, that if they had high prices they would return to the state of 1840 and 1841, and if they did not succeed by their legislation in raising prices—and that was their grievance—that they did not get so much for their wheat by 10s. a quarter, as the right honourable baronet had promised the present law would give—then they were disappointed, and complained of the government. Those who advocated high prices, and those who witnessed the results of low prices, were now together—let them solve the question as they would, the country would look on and judge between them. The advocates of high prices were now about to withdraw their confidence from the ministry, and why? Because they got 46s. a quarter for their wheat instead of 56s. (Hear, hear.) Did anybody doubt that that was the reason? (Hear, hear.) And what was the natural and only conclusion, that they would withdraw their confidence from a ministry because they had not produced misery enough, crime enough, disease enough, and death enough. (Loud cheers.)"

He did not expect the resolutions of his noble friend would meet with much favour from the House; but the discussion would form an appropriate preliminary one to his motion on the Corn Laws.

After a short address from Mr. Scott, on the motion or Mr. P. Howard, the debate was adjourned till Wednesday.

On Wednesday, Mr. Philip Howard resumed the debate on Lord John Russell's resolutions, condemning them. Mr. Escott followed on the same side, giving the protective system, however, some heavy blows as he went along :— " The fact was," he said, "that the system of protection was shattered and tottering, and every succeeding discussion served to knock out another stone from the ill-constructed arch. There was but one rational way to defend protection. If it could not be supported as the means of ensuring a certain domestic supply of corn, and thereby, on an average number of years, enabling the consumer to procure it cheaper, he thought it could not be defended at all. He thought no statesman could defend protection of one of the first necessaries of life upon the ground that it would put money into the pockets of the owners of land. He believed that all the arguments which had been made by those who had put themselves forward as the exclusive defenders of protection, had only tended to prove that such protection could not much longer be maintained. It might be injurious to his interests to make such an avowal, but although he had received favours from individuals who differed from him in that opinion, he felt that they were not favours which had been bought at any sacrifice of his own integrity, and they should not be preserved or continued if their preservation and continuance could not be secured consistently with what he conscientiously believed to be his duty to the House, the country, and the people who had sent him to parliament."

Captain Pechell having spoken in favour of, and Sir John Walsh against, the resolutions, Lord Howick defended the policy which Lord J. Russell had recommended to the adoption of the House in these resolutions, and contended that that policy had been met by arguments singularly inconclusive. He had expected that Sir Jas. Graham, when he rose to speak in behalf of her Majesty's government, would have said either that the condition of the labourer was satisfactory, and that the interference of parliament was therefore unnecessary, or that it fell short of what every man desired, but that any improvement of it was beyond the reach of the legislature, and that it was therefore better for parliament not to interfere, lest its interference should encourage hopes which must be ultimately disappointed. He had expected, he said, that Sir James Graham would have adopted one or other of these courses; but Sir James had come down to the House, and made a speech filled with details and arguments, not refuting, but confirming every statement of Lord John Russell, and had concluded it, to the surprise of everybody, by moving the previous question. That course amounted to nothing more nor less than that her Majesty's government would neither affirm nor deny that these were measures which were calculated to improve the state of the labouring population. He regretted that a question of this importance should be discussed in so thin a house; but still more the absence of Lord Ashley, who ought to have been present to support Lord J. Russell in his attempt to ameliorate the condition of the labouring population. All the grievances of which Lord Ashley complained, and which he wished to redress, arose from the inability of the labourer to command sufficient remuneration for his labour; and the object of the

present motion was to obtain from parliament a recognition
of the existence of a state of things in which its interference
was absolutely necessary. It had been said that these
resolutions embraced too wide a field; but in that opinion
he could not concur. They were important, not only for
the propositions which they included, but also for the
propositions which they excluded. They were also closely
and inseparably connected with each other; for the country
was suffering at present both from the moral effects of
mental ignorance, and from the physical effects of individual poverty. Poverty was too often the result of ignorance, and of the improvidence which ignorance created:
on the other hand, it was often the cause of ignorance
itself; for how could it be expected that a population
suffering from hunger and distress would ever think of
obtaining the blessings of education? Lord John Russell
had pointed out the measures which he thought would
prove the best combination for remedying the double evil
under which the country was now suffering. He was well
aware that any attempt to raise wages by parliamentary
interference would only tend to aggravate the evil which
he deplored. The measures which Lord J. Russell looked
forward to as the means of mitigating the distress of the
labourer were such as would free industry and labour from
the restrictions under which they were suffering at present.
He confessed that some of those restrictions—for instance,
those by which you prevented parties who produced clothes
by manufacture from exchanging their produce with those
who produced corn—appeared to him to have been framed
almost *with the intention of thwarting the designs of Providence.* The noble lord then proceeded at great length to
point out the impolicy of supporting the existing Corn Laws,
for the protection, as some asserted, but for the ultimate
destruction, as he contended, of the agricultural interest,
and to show that the repeal of those laws would increase
trade in every part of the country, and thus benefit all the

industrious classes of the community. Such were the views he entertained, and, entertaining them, he gave his cordial support to the resolutions on the subject of protective duties and of the Corn Laws; but he would not conceal from the House that he went far beyond Lord J. Russell in the conclusion which he drew from his facts. He thought that the time for compromise was gone by, and that the conclusion to which parliament ought now to come was, that the system of restriction which takes the bread out of the mouths of the labouring classes ought to be completely abandoned.

Sir J. Hanmer said he could not vote for the resolutions of the noble lord without evincing ingratitude towards the government, which, though it had not gone quite so far as he could have wished, had yet done a vast deal towards improving the condition and prospects of the whole community. He was, however, in favour of a low fixed duty on imported corn.

Sir Robert Peel denied that the thin attendance in the House during the greater part of the evening could be ascribed to any apathy on the part of its members with respect to the welfare of the labouring classes. On the contrary, he viewed it as an indication of the general impression which prevailed that the noble lord had not introduced his various resolutions in a manner which rendered it possible to act upon them with practical effect. He could not attempt to venture upon the discussion of topics so multifarious, many of them of great importance, and each of them sufficient to justify a long debate. It was far better to deal practically with these various subjects as they became ripe for legislation, instead of dealing in promises, which, however easily made, were sometimes very difficult, as they had very recently experienced, to be carried out in all their details. Government had already done much towards the advancement of education, and of other matters referred to in the resolutions of the noble lord; and they were ready to avail themselves of every opportunity as it arose, to propose practical measures for the improvement of the condition of the labouring classes. He had not by his measures hitherto gained the confidence of the opposition benches, while, if he was to believe the honourable baronet who represented Essex, he had lost the confidence of the great agricultural body. How that might be he knew not; but, *if that confidence could be re-purchased by a single expression of regret for the course pursued by his government, he would not consent to make it*, feeling as he did that the course was productive of essential benefit to every class of the community, and without inflicting the slightest injury upon the agricultural interest.

Lord John Russell replied principally with reference to the Corn Law question, which he earnestly impressed on the House should be settled in a time of tranquility and prosperity, and directed himself, in conclusion, to the subject of confidence in ministers :—

" That the measures of the right honourable baronet should have lost for him the confidence of honourable gentlemen on his own side of the House was not surprising, while they had not been of that character to secure for him that of his opponents. But though he agreed with the honourable member for Essex, that he had, considering the under-standing upon which he had supported the right honourable baronet in obtaining his present position, grounds for withdrawing his confidence, he disagreed with him, and those who thought with him, that the im-portation of foreign cattle and Canadian corn had injured the farmers of this country. He did not believe that those importations had been at all injurious; those importations he believed had had but little effect on the markets of this country, but if those imports were greater, he was of opinion it would be for the benefit rather than the injury of this country. The agricultural interest must look for their prosperity to the prosperity of the country generally. So far he differed from the hon. gentleman opposite. (Hear, hear.) But when they went on to say that they had been led to expect that the present government would be in favour of protection, and against free trade, he thought they were fully justified in that observation. (Cheers.) In fact, the truth of it was un-deniable. The speeches of the right honourable baronet (Sir Robert Peel) and his friends in 1839 and 1840 tended to produce, and no doubt did produce, an impression that they were the determined friends and advocates of what was understood as protection to the industry of this country (hear, hear, hear); and while he said that their subsequent measures had been in many respects useful and not pernicious, that was no ground of confidence in them on the part of any party, for it could not be denied that they had, by declaring against our course of policy, carried the election of 1841, and having thus obtained office, had proposed measures, which he admitted to be beneficial to the country, but at the same time opposed to those declarations. (Hear, hear.) As the right honourable baronet had raised this question of confidence, this was his (Lord John Russell's) answer. But if the honourable baronet, the member for Essex, after what he had said, should take the course of the honourable baronet the member for Devon (Sir J. Y. Buller) in 1841, and move a vote of want of confidence in the government, he (Lord J. Russell) should hesitate before he agreed with him in that motion (hear, hear); for what he had to consider now was how they were likely best to carry into effect those measures which were most favourable to their principles. He saw very well that if those who now sat on the opposition benches were in office, and were to propose liberal measures, they would be opposed by the honourable baronet, the member for Essex—very consistently, no doubt; for the honourable baronet had not intimated any change in his opinions—they would be opposed by the honourable baronet and his friends, and by those now in office, and be defeated. Therefore, desiring to see measures in conformity with those principles he had declared, and endeavoured to carry when in office, carried into effect, he felt that his better course was not to vote with the honourable baronet, the member for Essex, in favour of such a motion, if proposed, against the present government. These were his opinions, not only as to the general question of import duties and these resolutions, but as to that of confidence in the government. He thought if those whig principles he and his friends advocated were to be carried into effect, they would, under present circumstances, be more likely to be carried into effect by the present government than by their opponents. (Hear, hear.)"

When the House went to a division, there appeared :—

For Mr. S. Crawford's amendment 33
Against it 253
_____
Majority...................................... 220

The House again divided on the previous question, when the ministers' desire to prevent Lord John Russell's resolutious from being put to the House was gratified by 182 votes to 104, and the resolutions were consequently thrown overboard.

There was no longer any argument; Lord John Russell compared the Corn Law to an intoxicating stimulant, which could not safely be removed all at once, and his cure was to administer a smaller dose, not to become smaller by degrees, but to be fixed, unchangeable, not to "entail a change every year." Issachar was an ass, had long crouched between a heavy burthen on each side, and had grown accustomed to them. Issachar had indeed groaned under his burthens; but it would be dangerous to the constitution of Issachar, to take them off all at once, or even by degrees. The remedy was to make them less, but to "fix" them unchangeably. Argument was abandoned. Sir James Graham, who had formerly characterised the principles of free trade as the principles of common sense, now took refuge under the gabardine of Mr. Huskisson, who had said that prohibitory and protective duties should only be lowered in proportion to the increase of the population. The people had three loaves, when they could eat and required four. "When your numbers are increased by one-fourth," said Sir James, " we will add a fourth to the number of your loaves." Argument was abandoned. Sir Robert Peel was obliged to fall back on the maxim in Single-speech Hamilton's parliamentary logic, that when two men call for the redress of a grievance, and do not agree in all particulars as to the mode, the best way is to deny the existence of any grievance. Lord John Russell had argued for a 5s. duty; Lord Howick had argued that there should be no duty at all; and *therefore* Sir Robert Peel would adhere to his almost totally prohibitive sliding scale. Besides, Lord John had once been for an 8s. duty, and now would take one of 4s., 5s., or 6s.; and *therefore* things should remain as they were.

On the 3rd of June, the House of Commons came to

two rather contradictory decisions. Mr. Hume, not much accustomed to support pensions, moved, " That an humble address be presented to her Majesty, that she will be graciously pleased to grant such a pension as she shall think proper to the Right Honourable Sir Henry Pottinger, K.C.B., as a reward for his eminent public services, and especially for having, as her Majesty's Plenipotentiary in China, brought war in that country to a conclusion, by a peace alike honourable and advantageous, and to assure her Majesty that this House will make good the same." Mr. Hume, in speaking in support of his motion, said that " Sir H Pottinger had done that which no man had ever done : he had established a friendly intercourse, and had concluded a treaty of commerce with the Chinese on terms of liberty that had astonished all Europe ; a treaty which *opened trade to every nation*, not confining it to this country ; a treaty which he believed stood alone in the annals of diplomacy." The motion for a pension to one who had induced the Chinese government to adopt the principles of *free trade* with all nations was passed unanimously. The honourable House then proceeded to take into consideration Mr. Ward's motion for an inquiry into the peculiar burthens on land, these burthens being almost the only plea left for opposing a free trade in corn ; and the same House that had voted a pension to the man who had induced the Chinese to adopt the principles of free trade, refused, by a majority of 182 to 109, that there should be any inquiry which might lead to an adoption of the same principles at home. No, there should be no inquiry, for the sun was shining and there might be another good harvest to keep up the boasted " prosperity." I find the " State of Trade" thus recorded in my paper of that week :—" In the general description of both cloth and yarn adapted for the East a good business has been doing at very firm rates, particularly for yarns. The wonderful improvement in the weather has had a magical effect on vegetation, and, from present appearances, we shall have an ample harvest. This will enable Sir Robert Peel to hold out a little longer against his own convictions of the necessity of a free trade in corn." If the sun continued to shine, with occasional refreshing showers, until about the 12th of August, ministers could then prorogue parliament with a flourish about national prosperity, and retire to their country seats, and their country recreations, and wait there for about some five months, believing that the clamours for free trade in corn would cease ere they met parliament again. Was there any chance of success for the motion of which Mr. Villiers had given notice, in such genial weather, producing such magical effects on vegetation? There was the promise of an ample harvest—*if the weather would only continue to be fine for some six weeks more.* Would it be wise and prudent to legislate under such promise that legislation would be unnecessary? The nation, meanwhile, must look to the thermometer and the barometer, and not to the Lords and Commons.

CHAPTER XX.

MR. VILLIERS' MOTION.

On Tuesday, June 10th, Mr. Villiers moved for a committee of the whole House for the purpose of considering his resolutions for the abolition of all restrictions on the importation of foreign corn :—

"That the House resolve itself into a committee of the whole House, for the purpose of considering the following resolutions :—

"That the Corn Law restricts the supply of food, and prevents the free exchange of the products of labour.

"That it is, therefore, prejudicial to the welfare of the country, especially to that of the working classes, and has proved delusive to those for whose benefit the law was designed; and

"That it is expedient that all restrictions on corn should be now abolished."

After taking a review of the declarations made by Lord J. Russell, Sir James Graham, Colonel Wood, and many others on this important subject during the session, Mr. Villiers proceeded to congratulate himself on the improvement of his position in bringing forward these resolutions at present, as compared with that which he occupied on similar occasions in former sessions. There was now a general admission on the part of those on both sides of the House that it had become the duty of some member of parliament to test the opinions of the most influential parties in parliament on this question; and, therefore, he now came forward to contend that the Corn Laws were

wholly unsuited to the present condition of the country—
that they never had a laudable object in view—that at
times they had proved most injurious to the labouring
classes—and that the sooner they were abolished the
better. The object of them originally was to make land
dear ; and that object had been consistently pursued in all
the legislation which had been adopted since. The farmer
—who had been declared, on high agricultural authority,
to be a man of very contracted views—had been deluded
into the support of these laws by the fiction that price
meant profit. He had, therefore, given his vote in support
of those gentlemen who told him that high prices meant
high profits, and against those who told him that if he
trusted in such a fiction he would find himself wofully
disappointed :

" They had heard lately from the honourable and gallant member for
Sussex a description of the farmers of the country. That honourable
and gallant member had told the House that the farmer was a man of
narrow and contracted views, that his vision was singularly limited, and
that he was wholly engrossed with the vegetables he grew and the cattle
he fattened. (Hear, hear, and a laugh.) Further, that he judged of
the affairs of the world by the prices he got at market. The honourable
and gallant member had added that he would not be dictated to by
such men. Was it to be wondered at that such persons could be deceived into the notion that high prices meant high profits, and be induced
to support a law which secured them a high price ? Many members
now sat in that House through having persuaded the farmers that they
were farmers' friends. (Cheers and laughter.) His object in bringing
forward the present motion was to let the farmer see who were his
friends and who his enemies. The honourable member for Somerset
had lately stated that, thanks to the League, the farmer was now much
better informed than formerly. He (Mr. Villiers) hoped that was the
case ; perhaps his vision was now clearer that he had got his other eye
open. (Hear, hear, and a laugh.) He wished to hear what the Protection Society had to say on the subject. The farmer was now in a
sorry position; he wished to hear the honourable member for North
Northamptonshire, the chairman of the society, explain the causes of
that position. (Hear, hear.) He wanted to hear that honourable member define the farmer's relation with his landlord; and how, by giving

an exorbitant price for land, he placed himself on the high road to fortune. (Cheers.) He knew that the honourable member's only care
was for the farmer, and that he perfectly understood his case; and,
therefore he (Mr. Villiers) had brought forward this motion to meet the
honourable member's sentiments. He denied that the farmer's present
position was attributable to the measures of the right honourable
baronet's government. The farmer had long been subject to such
attacks. In 1836 he was as badly off as at present, and then he was
told it was all owing to the whig government. Prices were low, it was
said, because the enemies of agriculture were in office. (Cheers.) But
the farmer was equally badly off in 1822, when production was at its
maximum. (Hear, hear.) He (Mr. Villiers) should be glad to hear
from the chairman of the Protection Society what had been the matter
with the farmer on those occasions, and how it was that he was so often
indisposed? (Cheers.) It could hardly be said that he rowed in the
same boat with his landlord, seeing that the latter seemed to be as well
off as ever, and was equally profuse in his expenditure. He (Mr.
Villiers) had not heard of a landlord having discharged a footman or
groom in consequence of the low prices. (Cheers.) He believed there
was great distrust among the different classes of the agricultural
interest."

He then proceeded to ridicule the language used by
speakers at agricultural meetings in different parts of the
country, and to show that such meetings were now dividing themselves into two classes—one consisting of
landlords claiming from the government further legislative
protection, and the other of farmers claiming from their
landlords something very different from legislative protection. That fact had led Mr. Cobden to declare that protection was injurious to agriculture, and to move for an
inquiry to test the correctness of that declaration. That
motion was refused, and the House was told by Mr. S.
Herbert to trust to her Majesty's government, and to see
what would happen. Great improvements in our system
of agriculture were said to be required, but it unfortunately
happened that before they could be made, the landlords
required further protection from the government, and the
tenants further consideration from their landlords, and
neither the government nor the landlords would grant what

was required of them. Those who were anxious to provide
a further supply of food for the population were told to
wait, and therefore they were obliged to inquire whether
the improvements for which they were to wait had any
chance of being accomplished.   Mr. Villiers then entered
into a long argument to show, that so long as the present
system continued there was not the slightest chance of
those improvements being accomplished.   There. was,
therefore, no likelihood of providing from domestic sources
that adequate supply of food which the population required.
What, then, was the reason that precluded us from providing it from foreign sources ?

   " He (Mr. Villiers) had taken the trouble to look over all the publications of the Protection Society, and he found that the leading topic,
from beginning to end, was that if you made food cheap you would reduce the wages of the people, and that if you made it dear you would
increase their wages.   (Hear, hear, from some honourable members on
the ministerial side of the house.)   Was he to understand, then, that
there were still some persons in that house who maintained this doctrine ?   (Hear, hear.)   He considered that what he now stated ought to
be regarded as a very serious charge against an influential class in this
country.   (Hear, hear.)   The present Corn Law was maintained by a
great majority of both houses of the legislature, and they contended
that the people were not desirous of seeing it repealed.   Many persons,
both in that house and the House of Lords, had lent their names, carrying with them great authority, to maintain that notion.   In a publication
which was now in his possession, the charge was reiterated against
gentlemen on his (the opposition) side of the house, particularly against
the manufacturers, that their object in seeking the repeal of this law
was purely of a selfish nature.   They say (continued the honourable
member) that our object is to lower wages.   (Cheers.)   The honourable
members for Lincolnshire and Devonshire both cheer that sentiment ;
they will, therefore, have something to do to meet the statements of the
Home Secretary.   (Hear, hear.)   I suppose they are going to stand
forward to night, as they ought to have done the other night, to prove
that the right honourable baronet is wrong and fallacious; they do not
shrink from the task of charging us and him with the propagation of a
deception ; they are prepared to vindicate what they have said and done
—that the right honourable baronet is in error when he maintains that
when wages rise criminals decrease, and the happiness and comfort of

the lower orders is promoted according to the cheapness of food. They cheered me when I said that the publications of the Protective Society charge gentlemen on this side of the house with wishing to repeal the Corn Laws for the sake of lowering wages, and I shall be curious to hear them, and I shall listen to them with the greatest interest while they occupy the time of the house in proving what they assert. On the surface it is evident that when corn is dear wages fall, and when it is cheap they rise, and the honourable members for Lincolnshire and Devonshire will have something to do when they undertake to controvert this position. I did not think there had been a single member of this house who would adopt what is put forth by these writers. I fancied that they would say, ' These are no representatives of ours or our opinions. They are amusing themselves with inventing arguments, but they really have no connection with the landed interest, and you must not judge us by them.' The honourable members for Lincolnshire and Devonshire, however, identify themselves with the authors of these publications, who address themselves not merely to the uninformed, but to the unthinking and unreasoning, when they say that cheap bread makes low wages. What the honourable members may have to say I cannot conjecture; and I will not, therefore, state what I was inclined to say, that persons of great wealth and high station lower themselves by propagating what is so untrue and so delusive. (Cheers.)"

The fact was, that when they rendered the price of food high, they threw two-thirds of the labouring population of Great Britain out of employment. A scarcity was said to be a curse inflicted on a country by God; but ought we, when we create a scarcity by our faulty and imperfect legislation, to attribute it to the operations of Providence, who has "filled the earth with good things?" The existing Corn Laws and the Canadian Corn Bill had not been passed to increase the supply of food for the people, but for special reasons, and they had nothing to do with the present agricultural distress. Sir J. Graham had told the House that there was an annual increase of 380,000 souls in the population of Great Britain every year, and had admitted that some relaxation must be made in the Corn Laws in proportion to the future increase of the population. Sir J. Graham now said that he did not make that admission with that view. Be it so. Then he (Mr. Villiers) would say, that it was not the annual increase in our population, but the enormous amount of destitution and distress in the country—evinced by the fact mentioned by Sir J. Graham, that we had 1,500,000 paupers last year—which required the alteration he proposed in the Corn Laws. He showed that if an unfavourable harvest or a period of scarcity should recur, there were circumstances which would make the pressure of them more severely felt than it had ever been, inasmuch as the standard of living had been much exalted both at home and abroad; and as many countries, France and Belgium for instance, which had been exporters, were now importers of corn. Besides, their legislation had discouraged agriculture in every country in Europe, and there was not a grain of corn grown upon the continent at present with a view to the English market. Moreover, the recent alteration in our banking system would render the revulsion more severe on the manufacturing interest, whenever it should become necessary to export bullion; and whenever they were first compelled to send for corn, they must send bullion, or else submit to a most ruinous fall of prices in their manufactures. He was at a loss to know what plea would be urged by the government in reply to his demand, on behalf of the people, for free access to the means of subsistence. If the government should either plead the pressure of local taxation, or the peculiar burdens on land, he would reply, "Bring us in at once an account of what is paid on those scores, and we will show that it is far less than the loss which the people sustain every year owing to the restrictions on their supply of food." He called upon the government to indemnify the landlords in any way they pleased, except that of making the food of the people dear.

Mr. Oswald, one of the members for Glasgow, seconded the motion in a brief but excellent speech.

Mr. Christopher moved a direct negative to the motion. He did not think the working classes at all interested in the question :

" The hon. gentleman talked of the universal feeling in support of his views; whereas for a long time past there had been no petitions complaining of the price of food, or of any difficulty in purchasing it; and his (Mr. Christopher's) belief was, that the working classes, whom the honourable gentleman so ably put himself forward as the advocate of in this matter, would, if they were consulted, reply that they were perfectly satisfied with the Corn Law as it at present stood. (Hear, hear.) He should himself be the last man in the house to oppose the motion, did he conceive that it would produce the results which the honourable gentleman anticipated, but he entirely differed from the honourable gentleman in the matter. One object of the late Corn Law had been to prevent excessive fluctuations of prices, and the subsequent returns showed that, under the operation of the measure, there had been less fluctuations in price than at any former period."

The repeal of those laws, he said, would not be attended with the beneficial results which Mr. Villiers anticipated; for no reciprocity in foreign countries had followed any of the other relaxations which we had recently made in our tariff. There was no risk of our population suffering any privation, or of our manufacturers sustaining any loss from the want of exchange and intercourse with foreign states owing to the operation of these laws, as an immense amount of corn had been imported into the country during the last two years, under the existing duties, and a corresponding amount of manufactures had been exported to pay for it.

Mr. Mitchell expressed his intention of supporting the motion, although he had previously gone only the length of supporting a motion for fixed duty. He showed that the Zollverein had been instituted in consequence of our Corn Laws, and that, owing to the Zollverein, which operated almost as a prohibition on our manufactures, we could not get corn from Prussia unless we paid for it in bullion. That bullion was in consequence withdrawn from our circulation; and, as soon as that was done, the Bank was compelled to put on the screw for its own protection. That depressed the price of our manufactures, and aggravated the distress which was likely to prevail from other

causes during a time of scarcity. He had been told that
the crop of this year had already sustained considerable
injury; but, be that as it might, it was at any rate a backward crop, and a backward crop always subjected the
country to great risk. The object of those who advocated
the present Corn Laws was to make the country independent of any supply of foreign corn. But had they considered, supposing that our crop failed in the ensuing
autumn, where the requisite supply was to be got? Europe
was completely drained of corn. There was no chance of
obtaining it in the Mediterranean. In the northern parts
of Russia a famine was prevailing at present. In Odessa,
perhaps, you might procure a million of quarters; but no
one dared to send out an order for corn, either to Odessa
or to our more legitimate market, the United States, at
present, because nobody could say what the effect of the
duties would be before the corn ordered from those markets arrived in the harbours of England. It was, therefore,
possible that we might have such a price of corn next
autumn as we had not had for many years. Mr. Mitchell
then proceeded to explain the reasons which had converted
him from a partisan of a moderate fixed duty into an advocate of the total repeal of the Corn Laws. He recommended the house to legislate upon this subject at present,
when it could legislate calmly, and not to wait for a time
of destitution and distress, when it would have to yield
the repeal of these laws to clamour and intimidation.

Mr. Buck made a stout agricultural speech in favour of
the existing Corn Laws, and deprecated the constant but
ineffectual attempts of Mr. Villiers and his friends to
repeal them.

Mr. Mark Phillips supported the motion, and exhorted
the house to come to a speedy solution of this question,
which was at present keeping all the great interests of the
country in suspense.

Sir James Graham said, that notwithstanding the sneers

to which he had been exposed for the speech he had lately made, he would again declare, that the prosperity of agriculture must depend on the prosperity of the other branches of native industry, and that this prosperity would be most effectually promoted by giving an uninterrupted course to the natural flow of native industry. He would not deny that it was his opinion, that by a gradual and cautious policy it was expedient to bring our system of Corn Laws into a nearer approximation to those wholesome principles which governed our legislation with respect to other industrial departments. It was, however, his conviction that suddenly and at once to throw open the trade in corn would be inconsistent with the well-being of the community, and would give such a shock to the agricultural interest as would throw many other interests into a state of convulsion. The object of every government, without distinction of party, for the last twenty years, had been to substitute protecting for prohibitory duties, and to reduce gradually protecting duties where it had them to deal with. He approved this as a safe principle, and showed that it was the keystone of the policy of Sir Robert Peel. He asserted that the Corn Law of 1842 was expressly meant to lessen the protection then enjoyed by the agricultural interest. He also combated the doctrine of Mr. Villiers, that under a system of protection no improvement had taken place, nor could possibly take place, in the agriculture of the country. He showed that England, with a population the double of that which it possessed fifty years ago, now provided food for it with greater ease than it did formerly for half the number. If Mr. Villiers could show him that free trade with open ports would produce a more abundant supply to the labourer, he would make him a convert to the doctrine of free trade in corn. He confessed that he placed no value on the fixed duty of 4s. proposed by Lord John Russell; it would be of no avail as a protection, whilst it would be liable to all the obloquy of a protecting duty; and he therefore agreed with Mr. Mitchell, that if we got rid of the present Corn Law, we had better assent to a total repeal. He thought that the probable quantity of corn received with open ports was greatly under-rated, and argued that it would displace one-eighth of the produce of Ireland, and in England the clay land, which was most costly in cultivation, and throw agricultural labourers out of employment.

Mr. Bright said, that, from recent discussions both in that House and elsewhere, he could form but one conclusion as to the probability of the maintenance of protection. The right honourable baronet appeared, during the delivery of his speech, to have been endeavouring to say one thing at one part of it, and to unsay it at another part; so that it would have been impossible for any member of that House, if he were not acquainted with the right honourable baronet's opinions from former speeches and previous passages in his life, to ascertain to what side of the question he was most inclined to lean. He said that the change in the Corn Laws ought to be gradual and easy—that they ought gradually to diminish protection, and advance towards free trade, by bringing corn into a nearer relation with other articles which the government had already interfered with; and then he had proceeded to show that, if there were any further alterations made, it ought to be an entire repeal of the Corn Laws. He demonstrated that there existed no arguments in favour of a fixed duty; so that, having repudiated a fixed duty, and demonstrated that the next change in the Corn Laws should be repeal, he then fell back upon the fallacies of some of the supporters of the government in that House (with which fallacies the right honourable baronet notoriously did not agree); and he went on to speak as if he really thought that the statement of placing this country in dependance on foreigners for corn ought to have any weight in the discussions on this question. He encouraged

the agriculturists to be sensitive, to be shrinking, and
then he used that sensibility as an argument against the
advocates of free trade in corn, and stated, that in consequence the present system of Corn Laws was not to be
touched, although it starved thousands of the population
of the country. The right honourable baronet had asked
the advocates of free trade in that House for some proof
that free trade would give more food to the people ; and
he said that he felt with great force the responsibility of
the question put to him, whether he, as a minister of the
crown, would retain in existence a law which restricted the
supply of food to a population which was increasing at the
rate of 400,000 every year. Did the right honourable
baronet want any proof to convince him that the true
source of a certain and unfailing and abundant supply in
the article of corn was to permit the laws of nature to take
their course with respect to it, and to repeal at once those
restrictive laws which ignorant men had made in direct
contradiction to the laws of nature? If the right hon.
baronet did not know that, then he must have studied the
condition of this nation to little purpose indeed. How
were the people of this great city fed? Here was a population of two millions, and during the last few weeks there
was an addition of a hundred thousand or more persons to
it, and all those individuals were supplied with provisions
every day without the intervention of a secretary of state,
and without inconvenience or uncertainty. Corn was the
produce of most countries ; and how could he suppose
such a deficiency when we were enabled to have a stock
on hand of commodities, some of which were almost
entirely the produce of only one country, such as cotton.
There was at that time more than six months' stock of
cotton in Liverpool, although it was chiefly produced in
the United States ; and there was a similarly large stock
of everything which we required which the unhallowed
finger of protection had not touched. Of all the articles

which were not protected we had a large supply, and our experience on that head formed a conclusive argument as regarded the fears of the right honourable baronet—an argument which was a thousand times more conclusive than the prophecies of the right honourable baronet as to the dreadful effects which might be expected to follow the abolition of the monopoly in corn. The right honourable baronet spoke as if he believed that, in consequence of the abolition of the Corn Laws, there would be a suspension of labour. Did the right honourable baronet know that the whole number of persons who were engaged in producing the 2,000,000 quarters of corn, which he spoke of, was not as great as the number of persons who were thrown out of employment probably in one town in this country by the state of things caused by this monopoly, like Sheffield, Leeds, or Stockport? But he was certain he could name two towns at least in which a number of the population were thrown out of employment in 1841 and 1842, greater than the whole number of individuals who were directly employed in producing 2,000,000 quarters of corn. They could not find 25,000 persons in any part of England employed directly in the cultivation of 2,000,000 quarters of wheat, and yet that number of persons had been thrown out of employment in one or two towns in 1841. Mr. Bright then addressed himself to the agriculturists in the House, and adduced numerous instances of greatly increased importation of articles, the produce of the soil, which had not at all injured the interests of agriculture. He warned them that there was a strong feeling throughout the country against protection, and that it would not be safe to despise it. In allusion to the bazaar, and its success as an indication of public opinion and feeling, he said :—

" It was easy to sneer at these things, but there was one member opposite who would not sneer at them, and that was the right honourable baronet who led their party. He knew better than to sneer at the opinions of a vast body of the middle classes. He might not feel it right, with the responsibilities of his office, to do exactly that which he (Mr. Bright) or others wished; but coming from that county from which he derived his birth, and knowing the feelings, the wants, and the condition of the middle classes, he would be the last man to sneer at the efforts they were making for the abolition of this law. An honourable member opposite had lately given to the world a book in which he represented the monarch of this country as reigning over two nations—the rich and the poor; and there was a deal of truth in that. Others talked of the widening of the gulf which separates the very rich and the very poor. The Corn Law created nothing, it blighted almost everything. There was an abundance of capital, of labour, and of material in this country; but there wanted an honest distribution of it, and that honest distribution could only be given upon those just, true, and immutable principles which the great Creator had given for the regulation of the ordinary affairs of life. He knew that on going to a division his party would be in a minority; but he also knew that minorities in that House often became majorities; but if a man advocated a sound principle, and knew that millions out of doors supported it, let him not be deterred because the teller gave a majority against it, instead of in its favour. They had seen good principles growing and strengthening until everybody supported them, and bad principles fading away, and those who formerly adhered to them ashamed to recall them. If they wanted this law to be maintained, if it were resolved to continue a system so barbarous and unjust, their ancestors should have prevented Caxton from erecting his press in Westminster Abbey, they themselves should place an interdict upon the labours of William and Robert Chambers, proscribe Knight's Weekly Volume, and put down all newspapers, and, above all, put a stop to those locomotive engines which came up from Manchester to the metropolis in four hours and a half."

Mr. A. S. O'Brien observed, that although Mr. Villiers had challenged him to rise and defend the publications of the Protection Society, he was too old a fish to rise at that fly. He merely rose to show that he was not unwilling to do justice to the great taste and skill displayed by the manufacturing classes in the arrangement of the bazaar recently opened in Covent Garden. The agricultural legislation of her Majesty's government was not sufficiently popular with the farmers to induce a county member to stand up in its defence. The last person, however, whom the county members could blame 1or it was Sir R. Peel, whom they had placed and still kept in office.

Dr. Bowring, Mr. Cavendish, and Lord Ebrington all followed, speaking in favour of the motion.

Mr. Cobden rose and said, that the question mooted by Mr. Villiers had not been met, but had been systematically evaded during the whole of the present debate. The question was—first, had they a right to restrict the supply of food for the people ; secondly, was it true that they had a law to that effect; and, thirdly, if their Corn Law was not to that effect, what was its purpose? He asserted that the Corn Law did restrict the supply of the food of the people, and called upon the members for Dorsetshire and other agricultural counties to deny it if they could. If they denied it, then he called upon them to explain whether the labouring classes in their respective districts were sufficiently and wholesomely fed, and if they were not, why they were not. He then proceeded to prove that the present system of Corn Laws was not only injurious to the community at large, but also to every portion of it. He denounced it as rash and perilous, inasmuch as it had left us with no more than 200,000 quarters of corn in bond at a period when Europe was drained of corn, and we had the prospect of a backward, not to say a failing harvest.

" Was there ever such rashness, as for twenty-seven millions of people, who could grasp the produce of the world, and who could mortgage it before it was grown, to leave themselves in this dilemma? (Hear.) Under a different system, what would have been the position of the country? Instead of having 300,000 quarters of foreign wheat in the country, they might have what it would well hold—four or five millions. That would be brought in, not by the government, but by the application of capital; and could the country more legitimately apply its capital than for the purpose of supplying itself with food? (Hear, hear.) The Dutch, at one time, held 700,000 quarters of foreign corn in their granaries. That was probably sufficient for a year's consumption What were the Dutch as capitalists as compared with the capitalists of England? They might as easily hold 20,000,000 of quarters as the Dutch held 700,000 many years ago. Honourable gentlemen opposite might think that the stock at present in hand in this country was a terrible thing—might think that it might be sold for nothing, and that, by its invasion, they would receive no adequate price for their corn. But what had happened in the case of wool? Had foreign competition reduced the price of wool to the producers of that article in this country? They were then the rash men who interposed to prevent the adoption of the proposition which emanated from that side of the House. (Hear, hear, hear.) The artificial system which was fostered and bolstered up, had brought us, in this country, back to the barbarous position in which this country was placed five or six hundred years ago, with this sole difference, that then, from the bad state of the roads, and the want of the means of facile communication, counties used to suffer from famine; whereas now they were setting at defiance all the lights of science, all the discoveries of modern times, and all the improvements founded upon these discoveries, and were bringing us into the same peril as a nation, as we formerly had to encounter only by counties. (Hear, hear.) He did not ask them to store up their granaries for years. They were reluctant to interfere; but if they would not interfere, why then interfere to prevent others from storing up as capitalists? why prevent such a provision being thus made in the country as would guard against future famine? Was not this the time, of all others in which to do this? Why were they making these amazing strides in physical science, uniting nations together, as provinces had been united before? Why were they to have railways and steamboats? Why were they to go on, uniting nations together by all the discoveries of modern times, if legislation was to lag behind, and prevent them from availing themselves of those advantages which it was the interest and the birthright of the people to derive from these discoveries, and the consequences to which they led? (Hear, hear.) He would not allow the right honourable baronet, with his proverbial caution, to take from the honourable member for Wolverhampton what he considered his due. He was the man of cautious foresight; he was the man of prudence and forecast, who would make provision for future evils, and on the government and on those who led them, when they should lead their followers, on the government rested the responsibility of anything which might happen from the present absurd and anomalous state of our laws."

Mr. Bankes replied to the arguments of Mr. Villiers and Mr. Cobden, endeavouring to show that they had fallen into several historical errors, materially bearing on the question before the House.

Lord John Russell indulged in several pleasantries upon

the speech of Mr. Bankes, but commented with some
severity on his admission that the condition of the labourers of Dorsetshire was still most deplorable, and
deserving the commisseration of the House. He then
pointed out the inconsistencies of which Sir J. Graham
had been guilty in his speech of that evening. Sir James
had told them that industry ought to have its own course
—that what was true of manufacturing, was also true of
agricultural industry—and that protection was injurious
to the landowner. He had, therefore, expected that Sir
James Graham, if he did not go along with him in his
proposition for a moderate fixed duty, or with Mr. Villiers
for a total repeal of the Corn Laws, would, at any rate,
propose some scheme by which the existing protection
would be diminished, and by which some advances might
be made in that approach to free trade which all parties
deemed so desirable. There was nothing in Sir James
Graham's past conduct to render such a supposition unnatural, or such an alteration of his policy impracticable.
From that point, however, he suddenly started off, and
used against the motion all the arguments which had ever
been urged in behalf of Corn Law protection. With regard to the motion of Mr. Villiers, he had only to observe,
that his first two resolutions were in accordance with those
which he (Lord John Russell) had proposed a few nights
ago ; and as his honourable friend proposed to consider
in committee his third resolution : " That it is expedient
that all restrictions on corn should be now abolished," he
(Lord John Russell) felt himself at liberty to go into committee with him, and to consider in what way a relaxation
of the Corn Law should be made. The Corn Law, as it
now stood, was vicious in principle, and could not be long
maintained in its present condition. He saw its fall indicated not only by the vigour of the attacks made upon it,
but also by the feebleness of the defence offered for it ;
and he therefore warned the country gentlemen to pause

before they allowed an impression to be made to their disadvantage in the minds of their fellow countrymen, by the constant repetition of the remark that it was only kept up to enable them to keep up their rents.

Sir Robert Peel, after some remarks upon Lord John Russell's intended vote, proceeded to observe that experience proved that the high price of corn was not accompanied with a high rate of wages; for the rate of wages did not vary according to the price of corn. If he could believe in the predictions of Mr. Cobden, his objections to an immediate repeal of the Corn Law would be greatly alleviated; but he could not, and therefore he must proceed, in pursuance of his own policy, to reconcile the gradual approach of our legislation to sound principle on this subject with the interests which had grown up under a different state of things. He then proceeded to defend the existing Corn Law and Tariff, and to maintain that under their operation there had been a great revival of domestic industry and foreign commerce. He did not think that the existing Corn Law was liable to the objections urged against it. He did not think that the predictions of its failure had been verified, and therefore he was unwilling to accept the proposition of Mr. Villiers. He did not defend the Corn Law on the ground that it was a protection to any particular interest. He admitted that it would be impossible to maintain any law on the ground that it was intended to keep up rents; but looking to the obligations of the landlords, he thought that any such change as that which Mr. Villiers suggested, would, if suddenly produced, tell injuriously on them, and still more injuriously on the large and numerous class of the cultivators of the soil, and others connected with them.

Lord Howick called attention to the fact that not one word had been said that evening by the government in contradiction to the first two resolutions of Mr. Villiers, condemnatory of the principles and policy of the present

Corn Law. If the last resolution had been thus worded, "That it is expedient that all restrictions on corn should be gradually abolished," the speech of Sir Robert Peel would have been an admirable one in support of it.

After a brief reply from Mr. Villiers, the House divided, when there appeared :—

> For the motion 122
> Against it 254
>
> Majority against it......................... 132

It was clear from this debate, that the repeal of the Corn Law, or the substitution of revenue for protective duties, waited only for such an emergency as would be created by a depression of commerce sufficient to lessen materially the productiveness of the Customs and Excise; or for such a deficiency of harvest, with accompanying high prices of food, as would add popular clamour to the existing agitation for free trade; or for the expulsion of monopolists from the representation of a few of the large counties and the most important towns. The argument was brought to this :—" The nation is in comparative prosperity now; be quiet till calamity comes." The state physicians would not prescribe until the disease came to its height. Wait for bad trade; wait for a greatly falling revenue; wait for a bad harvest; wait for starvation prices; such were the suggestions made by men who called themselves statesmen !

It was gratifying to observe the steady, although not rapid increase of Mr. Villiers' supporters. The following shows the comparative strength of the free-trade party in 1844 and 1845 :—

> 1844—For Mr. Villiers' motion......... 126
> Paired 11
> Absent 28
>
> 165

1845—For Mr. Villiers' motion......... 124
      Paired 10
      Absent 56

                      190

And it was still more gratifying to see that the number of
those who were ashamed to be found amongst the supporters of a selfish monopoly was rapidly increasing. The
numbers voting in opposition to Mr. Villiers were :—

    In 1842............395
        1843............383......Decrease...... 12
        1844............330......   ,, ... 53
        1845............254......   ,, ... 76

      Total decrease 141

The proportion between monopolist and free-trade votes
was :—

    In 1842......17 monopolists to 4 free-traders.
        1843......12   ,,   4   ,,
        1844......11   ,,   4   ,,
        1845...... 8   ,,   4   ,,

Here was encouragement for those who were not disposed
to wait till the calamity came, but to do their best to avert it.
Some encouragement was also had from the hopeless tone
of certain organs of the agriculturists. The *Mark Lane
Express*, quoting the admissions of Sir James Graham,
said : " Here is a full concession of the principles of free
trade. The only ground for demur is that Mr. Villiers'
motion is too precipitate." The *Express* turned to the
premier, to see if there could be any help there ; but Sir
Robert had said of himself and his colleagues that " every
act which they have carried has been an act to establish
principles which I believe to be sound ones, namely, those
embodying the gradual abatement of purely protective
duties," and that he meant to abide by those principles,
whereupon the *Express* said : " We will not mar these

words by any remarks of ours ; we trust they will vibrate loud and long in the ears of our readers."

The *Farmers' Journal* equally despairing, after a seemingly hopeless appeal to the members of the Agricultural Protection Society, to exert themselves at the next election, said : " If this be not done, one hope, and one hope only, will remain to the English tiller of the soil. A perfectly free trade in corn, ruinous as it must prove in the first instance, will either *wipe off the national debt*, and all its necessary train of direct or indirect taxation, or, after a time, compel a return to a scale of duties amply protective of native industry in all its branches ; and, all things considered, *if we are doomed* to see the principles now adopted by ministers ultimately and fully carried into action, perhaps *the sooner the better* ought to be the cry of all concerned." These predictions did not lower the price of consols.

CHAPTER XXI.

HARVEST PROSPECTS.

The belief was general, for a month after this debate, that the harvest, upon which so much depended, would be an abundant one; but there then appeared indications of change, and people began to think that *three weeks' rain* would change the hope of abundance into gloomy prospects of starvation. The state of the weather excited as much attention in manufacturing and commercial towns as it usually did in the agricultural districts in the north of England, where hay had been cut for ten days without the chance of being safely put into the ricks. My paper of the 19th of July said :—" There is an universal conviction amongst us that the prosperity of manufactures depends mainly on the abundance of the necessaries of life; and while the produce of other lands is excluded from our ports, we look, earnestly and anxiously, to the circumstances which affect the amount of our home agricultural produce. Yesterday the weather was not merely fine but brilliant; and, at the time of our going to press, we have the prospect of its continuance, and of the fair ripening of the crops now promising to be unusually abundant. Would that the time were come, when, knowing that we could command the products of the Mississippi Valley, we should rejoice as much in the rain which gives luxuriant growth and the sun which ripens *there*, as we do now when such favourable circumstances present themselves *here!* As we have often said, there never was scarcity over all the earth at one time ; and it is only from the absurdity—the wickedness—of man's legislation, that the superfluity of one portion of the globe does not supply the deficiency of another."

Besides the loss by death of Sir Thomas Potter, the free traders had now to regret that of another munificent supporter of their cause, thus noticed in the *League* of June 14th :—" We have to announce, with sincere regret, the death of Mr. Marshall, of Leeds, whose eminence as a manufacturer was not more conspicuous than his energies as a patriot and his zeal as a philanthropist. By the honourable exertion of his industry and talents he acquired a princely fortune, and he employed it in establishments that have furnished comfort to thousands of operatives, and greatly added to the material wealth of the nation. Few manufacturers have more nobly illustrated the great importance of the capitalist to the labouring community ; his great resources enabled him to work his mills during seasons of depression, and thus to save his men from those alternations of stagnation and suffering which have produced so much of misery in the industrial districts of England. Mr. Marshall was a zealous free trader, and a member of the Council of the League. Though for some time in parliament, he did not take a very conspicuous part in political life ; but he was far from being an uninterested spectator of public events, and he was ever ready to aid largely and liberally in all efforts made to promote the cause of truth and justice. He has left behind him a large fortune, but, what is much more, he has left behind him an honoured memory and an unsullied reputation."

During this week a meeting was held in Wiltshire of a class of persons, for whose welfare, as well as for the benefit of the farmer, it was alleged that the Corn Laws were enacted and sustained. The *Wiltshire Independent* describes it as being "held at Upavon, a populous village in the fertile

' Bourne,' a district purely agricultural, and where, if anywhere, the farm labourers might be expected to be in
favour of that 'protection' which so many landowners and
farmers declare to have been devised for their especial
benefit. But even here, 'protection,' such as is afforded
by the Corn Laws, is sadly at a discount, and hundreds of
men, spite of the threats of the farmers, their masters, to
discharge them if they attended the meeting, wended their
way to it after a hard day's toil, to discuss their grievances
and to make them known to the public. Upwards of 1,000
persons, chiefly consisting of agricultural labourers, some
of them accompanied by their wives and elder children,
were present, and formed an imposing and interesting
scene, assembled, as they were, under a fine old tree on
the green. The meeting was conducted in the most
orderly manner, and the deepest interest was exhibited by
all present in the proceedings." The chairman and the
speakers all belonged to the class of farm-labourers, and
they described their grievances with a natural eloquence
which was clearly the result of a thorough conviction united
to plain common sense. David Keele, the chairman, declared that the labourers after a hard day's work could earn
no better subsistence than potatoes and salt, and his hearers responded, "We don't get half enough of that." His
illustration of the coercion used by the protectionists to
stifle the complaints of the labourers was equally clever
and characteristic :—" Our opponents, in my part of the
country, serve the people like as the carters used to do the
ploughboys when I was a boy. They would give the boys
the whip, and threaten that they would give it them again
if they told their parents ; and so it went on from day to
day. The case is the same with the labourers. Your
masters say, if you come forward to tell your case, you
shall be turned out of employment, and thus they keep
you in fear ; and you will never be better as long you are
kept down in this way. But if you come forward boldly

and tell your case, you can't make it worse. If the plough-boy had told his father of the carter, the carter would have been punished, and that was what he was afraid of. You are prevented coming forward by the arbitrary conduct of your opponents; but fear not their frowns, they are in the hands of the Lord, and can only go so far as He permits. Always remember, however, that, whatever law is issued by the legislature, we are bound to obey; 'whoever resists the powers that be resists the ordinance of God.' It is the arbitrary Corn Law that has done all the mischief, and we believe free trade will be beneficial to ourselves and families." Mr. Westell dwelt with great force on the injury inflicted on the farmers by affording an excuse for the ex-action of oppressive rents, and thus forcing tenants to stint the wages of labour. Abundant proof was given of the utter inadequacy of the wages of the farm-labourers to pro-cure sufficient sustenance, to say nothing of comforts. One man with five and another with eight children de-clared that their earnings were only seven shillings per week. The examples given of "the short and simple annals of the poor" were equally graphic and affecting :— " The children," said Ozias Lealey, " would jump across the house if they saw a couple of potatoes, and quarrel which should have them. It was enough to drive a man mad. When he came home at night, and found them crying for food, and he had none to give them, it almost drove him mad; he could not stand it another winter. What would the gentlemen think of this, filled as they were with their roast beef and sherry wine; when the poor man was happy in heaven he knew not where the rich would be." Several people exclaimed that every one with a family was in the same state, and many others would have come forward to speak, but were kept back by fear. At the conclusion of the meeting three cheers were given for the League, and three for the repeal of the Corn Laws. Would the condition of the children described by Ozias

Lealey be improved by a bad harvest and a failure of the potato crop? Would a lessening of the quantity of food in the kingdom give the children more to eat?

On the 18th of June the League held one of its great meetings in Covent Garden Theatre. The speakers, besides the chairman Mr. George Wilson, were Mr. Cobden, Mr. Bright, and Mr. W. J. Fox. From the statement of the chairman it appeared that £25,046 0s. 11d. was the exact sum realized from the late bazaar, while as many articles remained unsold as would enable them, in autumn, to hold a similar exhibition in Manchester. The contributions to the £100,000 Mr. Wilson said, were now closed, and exceeded that sum by nearly £17,000. A detailed account was read to the meeting. Mr. Cobden humorously exposed the "special burden" farce: "They, the inhabitants of London, knew very well what a dodge was; they often saw a man walking about the streets with his arm bound up; that was a special burthen, a grievance, and he made money by it. But when one of the mendicity officers went up to him, and wished to examine the arm, he found the *Artful Dodger* loth to comply." That was the case with the landlords, the protectionist landlords. They had been exciting public attention by the complaints of their heavy burthens, but when the mendicity officers came forward and offered to examine them, they refused to comply. The following is a summary of his observations on the aspect and prospects of the free-trade question:—

"They had now brought it to a mere question of time. (Cheers.) They had narrowed it down to one little word—When! Mr. Cobden then referred to a leader in the *Times* of Tuesday, calling upon the League to say why it was expedient to have immediate repeal. He (Mr. Cobden) did not object to answer that appeal. As Sir Robert Peel would say, there were three ways of deciding the question. Firstly, while you acknowledge the justice of the principle of total repeal, you may defer it until a time shall arise when circumstances will compel you to carry it out. Secondly, you may abolish the Corn Law by a small fixed duty of say eight shillings, to slide off one shilling a-year until the corn shall come entirely free. Thirdly, you may come to the principle of total and immediate repeal. (Cheers.) The policy of that principle the government had acknowledged, but they would not apply the principle at the present moment, nor would they say when they would do it. What were they thinking of then as a mode of repealing the Corn Laws? He knew very well. They were prepared in a time of scarcity and famine to repeal the Corn Laws. (Hear, hear.) Was that statesmanlike? They told the farmers the Corn Laws were to be repealed, and then they told their tools of the press to deal out, in their diurnal twaddle, that if the Corn Laws were repealed the farmers would not be able to pay their rents. (Hear, hear.) They thus kept the farmer upon the tenter-hooks of suspense. They alarmed him with all sorts of raw-head-and-bloody-bone stories that free trade would inflict upon them, and yet the premier tells them he was about to repeal the Corn Laws. What was the policy morally? They waited for a period of famine. They waited for the day when Palace Yard should be crowded with famishing thousands. (Cheers.) Was not that teaching the people of the country that moral principle had no influence over their legislation. (Cheers.) They might have a small duty of 8s., and sliding off a shilling every year. What effect had that upon the farmers? The farmer was told by the agent or the landlord that they had passed a law for a fixed duty of 8s., and that they would see how that operated. The farmer goes on, rent day comes on; he goes to pay his rent, and is then told to wait another year; and when the duty comes down to 3s., the foreigners are told that the door will be opened wide for the importation of foreign corn, and the farmer is then to be swamped under an inundation of foreign corn under the sliding scale. When were they to have total and immediate repeal? Why, he said now. (Cheers.) What was there to be afraid of in the total and immediate repeal? They were told there was a large quantity of grain hoarded up abroad, ready to be poured into this country. Mr. Cobden again referred to a leader in the *Times* on this subject. He said of it, that it was profound philosophy invested with all the charms of poetical language. (Cheers.) Let them, however, take the language of experience. In 1839, 1840, and 1841, the average price of wheat was 67s. a quarter. The world was ransacked for corn to supply this country during those years. In one year every region on the face of the globe was searched for corn. In 1839, 2,945,605 quarters of corn were brought to this country; in 1840, 2,432,765; and in 1841, 2,713,602 quarters; making a total of 8,091,972 quarters in three years. That corn was all brought here under the conviction that it would be allowed to come in at the 1s. duty. Now, that corn was brought to this country when the price was 67s., and now it is rather more than 40s., and little foreign corn is imported. There was no such thing as a store of corn abroad, kept there waiting for a contingency that might arise. (Hear, hear.) It was their opponents who wished to produce an unnatural inundation on the market, by waiting for a time of scarcity and starvation. (Cheers.) Their opponents were not contented with spreading fallacies at home, but they were trying to spread delusions on the Ukraine and in the valley of the Mississippi. (Cheers.) That was the question as regarded the farmer. The agitation had not been sustained because the bill was an error in political economy, but because it intended to put the nation upon short commons (cheers); and he opposed it in the name of the people at large (cheers); and its total and immediate repeal was therefore pressed for. They had never heard it argued that this law was passed for the benefit of the whole nation. They had heard it said that it was for the benefit of the farmers and landlords. If it was not for the benefit of the great body, why on earth should they now come forward and say that it should not be repealed? Sir Robert Peel came forward and talked about the interests that had arisen under this law; he (Mr. Cobden) pleaded for the great interests that had been crushed to the earth by it, and, to prove what it had done, he would bring their Home Secretary and his Prison Report into the witness box. He pleaded for the total and immediate repeal for the great body of the working men. The government was going to repeal these laws at a season of distress, at a time like the years 1839, 1840, and 1841. In those years scarcely any corn could be got from abroad, and yet these countries were to be depended on for a supply of corn, should Divine Providence think fit to punish us with a bad harvest. Where was the supply to come from? The government ought to be called upon to answer that question. It ought to be thrust upon them. (Cheers.) Let the whole of the responsibility be thrown upon them. That was his case, as the lawyers said, for the total and immediate repeal."

He concluded by urging on all present to attend to the registration of themselves and their neighbours. Mr. Bright and Mr. W. J. Fox followed, in eloquent and spirit-stirring speeches, which excited great enthusiasm in the meeting.

A brief discussion took place in the House of Commons on July 22nd, on a motion by Mr. Ewart for a committee on the Customs Act, with a view to his proposing an alteration of the duties on butter and cheese. He was of opinion that these duties should be totally repealed: in the first place, because they placed well nigh a prohibition on the consumption, by the poorer classes, of articles of the greatest importance to them ; in the second place, because they operated as a great restriction upon our trade and commerce ; in the third place, because their repeal, so far from injuring the revenue, would increase it ; and, in the fourth place, because, when they were imposed originally, it was with no intention of their being permanent, the object of their being imposed, at the close of the war, being to give an impulse to the sale of Irish produce. As to the poorer classes, these duties had the effect of doubling for them the price of these essential articles. As to our trade, their repeal would infallibly extend our commerce with Holland 50 per cent., and that with the United States from 75 to 100 per cent. ; this extension, moreover, especially applying to those states with which our relations required to be established on a greater and more friendly footing. Experience had fully shown, in the case of coffee, tea, and other articles, that a reduction of duty was sure to produce more than an equal amount of revenue, from the greater consumption of the articles, while in every other respect the results were clearly most beneficial. His proposition, doubtless, would be resisted by agricultural members ; yet their constituents were deeply interested in the repeal of these duties, so large a proportion of what butter and cheese they did manage to get being of foreign produce, and the price of this being, as he had said, doubled to them in consequence of the tariff. He would not trouble the House farther at present, but simply move that the House go into committee. The Chancellor of the Exchequer said he would be as brief as the honourable member. He felt it to be his *imperative duty* to resist the honourable gentleman's proposition. The financial views of the government had long since been fully laid before the House and the country, and their financial arrangements for the year completed. Those arrangements involved reductions in various articles for the benefit of trade, so extensive that, on a calculation of the revenue and expenditure for the year, they found there would be a surplus of revenue over the expenditure of not more than £100,000. The duties which the honourable member now proposed to repeal produced to the revenue the sum of £347,000, and it was, therefore, obviously impossible to adopt the honourable gentleman's views without involving the imminent risk, nay, the certainty, of a very large deficiency, instead of the small surplus he had stated. Mr. Milner Gibson said he was glad to find the right honourable gentleman justifying the duty on these articles solely on fiscal grounds, and without making any reference to the obsolete pretence of protection to agriculture. The entire amount of the revenue raised from this most impolitic and mischievous source was, it was admitted, only £347,000—a sum which would most assuredly be increased, rather than diminished, by reducing the duty on articles which this country itself could not supply to half the extent of the wants of the population, more especially now that in every quarter pasture land was being converted into arable. Mr. Hume supported the motion. Mr. P. Howard said, that, after the great concessions made by government this year in favour of trade, it was hardly fair to call upon them to make more at present, however deserving the duties in question might be of the attention of the government and of the House next session. Mr. Newdegate expressed a hope that, though the agricultural members might be silent on the present occasion, the House would not suppose them to be indifferent to the subject under consideration. Mr. Cobden said that, though the honourable members for Derbyshire, and some other counties, might find it to be for the interest of their constituents to support the duties on butter and cheese, he could not see why the members for Norfolk and Suffolk, for instance, should adopt the same course. If the right honourable baronet would take the trouble of making inquiries on the subject, he would find that there were six or eight counties taxing the rest of the country, as well as all Ireland and Scotland, in order that they might receive a high price for their cheese. Mr. Tatton Egerton did not, he said, reproach the manufacturers for making large fortunes; but he would ask, why were not the landed proprietors to have also a return for their capital? Dr. Bowring said that the manufacturers had repeatedly declared that they required no protection, and they even showed that those manufacturers which had been most protected had progressed least. Sir Robert Peel asked, how was it to be expected that Her Majesty's government could seriously consider a reduction of £350,000 in the revenue at the present period of the session? Did the House think it right to annihilate the small sum that would remain in the hands of the government, and to run the risk of having a deficiency of £200,000 or £300,000 at the end of the present year? He, therefore, hoped that the House would give no countenance to the motion of the honourable member, but that they would leave the subject to be considered with the financial policy of the government in the ensuing session. Mr. M. J. O'Connell said his constituents depended more on the sale of butter than even on corn; but still he thought one rule should be applied to all agricultural produce. The House then divided—

> For the motion........................... 38
> Against it 136

Majority against the motion... 98

The parliamentary session was drawing to a close, while the weather continued to be unsettled. The state of trade fluctuated with the rise and fall of the barometer. When the sun shone out goods were in demand and prices were reported " firm;" and in cloudy and rainy days there was a report of depression in the goods, and of firmness and advance in the corn market. As yet there were hopes of a fair harvest—if there could but be a month of dry weather. That single month of dry weather would get rid of the repeal of the corn laws for one year at least, and then there was the *possibility* of a good harvest in 1846 still farther to protract the evil day, and carry ministers through their eighteen-forty-one-elected parliament. The session of 1845, however, was not permitted to terminate without some more discussion on the Corn Laws. In the usual " Review-of-the-Session" debate on the 5th August, Lord John Russell showed that ministers had gained office under false pretences. With regard to the Corn Law, they had made admissions totally at variance with their previous doctrines as to protection :—

"But let us look at the foundation on which that law now rests. Can anybody have heard of what has been passing within the last ten days, without feeling the misery of an uncertain law with respect to corn? Can anybody feel that there is a doubt whether the next fortnight will bring us a harvest tolerably good or miserably deficient, and not wish that the labouring classes of this country should be provided with food from all quarters where it can be obtained? *I maintain that it is the duty of this House to provide for such a contingency.* As the matter at present stands, there being uncertainty in the seasons, there being the uncertainty of a foreign supply, you, by your legislative wisdom, add *a new and artificial uncertainty ;* you add the uncertainty whether six or ten weeks hence the duty shall be 20s. or 1s. ; you thereby double the amount of speculation ; you double the hazard to which the people of this country are exposed ; and *you double the gambling in this necessary article of subsistence for human life.* Why, sir, is it wise to continue such a system? Only the other day we had a gentleman who has always been a constant supporter not only of the present ministry, but especially of their policy with regard to the Corn Law and the sliding-scale,—we had that gentleman, I say, avowing publicly that he did not think that law would last; and that two years, probably, would see the end of it. Well, then, I say if it is to be abandoned, *do not leave us in this miserable uncertainty.* While you have done much in the way of making an approach to free trade with those main articles of supply—timber, sugar, and above all, corn, you are keeping up restrictions which are contrary to every sound principle, and to which it is impossible, if your own theories are sound, you can mean to adhere

At this very moment, with respect to corn, *the stock of supply in this
country is unusually small;* and I shall move, therefore, *for an account
of the quantity that is now in bond. It is unusually small in consequence
of your own law;* and let it not be forgotten, when gentlemen refer, as
I have sometimes seen them do with great satisfaction, to the failure of
speculations in the foreign corn trade, that the consequences of the
failure of these speculations are very often injurious, not only to those
immediately engaged in them but to the whole country—manufacturing,
commercial, and agricultural; that the indisposition to get together a
supply, to make a store of corn on which this country can rely in case
of a sudden failure in the harvest, is a national misfortune, and therefore, everything which tends to make this trade *gambling and uncertain* is
a loss to the agricultural interests as well as to all others, and that no
law based upon such principles can be for the permanent advantage of
the country."

No other than the *tu-quoque* argument in reply to this
could be expected. Sir James Graham durst not deny
the evil of speculation and gambling, at a period of great
uncertainty and danger; but when charged with being
indifferent to the welfare of millions the answer to be
expected was, "Why, so were you when you were in office";
and such was the reply, not with the blush of shame, but
with the effrontery of triumph. He said :

" There are at the present moment in bond of foreign corn, wheat,
and barley, no less than 450,000 quarters. In the year 1839, when the
noble lord was responsible for the conduct of affairs, what was the
position of the country in this respect? was it similar to the present
position of affairs, which the noble lord says is unexampled ! Allow me
to remind the noble lord, that on the 6th of August, 1839, there was in
bond in this country, only 51,000 quarters of foreign corn, whereas, we
have 450,000 quarters in bond now, and that further, on the same 6th
of August, 1839, there was in the Bank of England, only £2,450,000
in specie, whereas, at this moment there are £16,000,000 of specie, in
the coffers of the Bank of England. Did the noble lord in 1839, at the
end of the session, such being the position of the country, come forward
and propose any alteration of the corn laws? Did he come forward to
do so at the end of the session of 1840 ? Did he at the end of the session of 1841 ? As a member of the government, and as a responsible
minister of the crown, feeling deeply the situation of the country,
with only 51,000 quarters of foreign corn in bond, and only £2,450,000

of specie, in the coffers of the Bank of England, did he come forward and propose a remedy by means of an alteration in the Corn Laws? No, neither then nor in the immediately succeeding sessions did he propose any such thing."

And thus, because in 1839, when the stock of corn was so low, Lord John Russell did not propose to relax a law which hindered importation, Sir James Graham would not, in 1845, when the continuance of prosperity, which had been mainly the result of two good harvests, depended upon a month's uninterrupted sunshine, so improbable at that time of the year. But Sir James had another reason for excluding foreign corn—high prices of food would teach the people frugality in its use! "I am not one of those" he said, "who think that it is an evil, that at a time when there are serious apprehensions of a deficient harvest, there is imposed upon the consumer the necessity of caution and frugality; that was the operation of the existing Corn Law." Who were those on whom frugality was thus imposed? Not those who had bread enough and to spare, for they would not lessen their consumption by a single ounce. It would be imposed on those who already had not enough, and on those who had barely enough. And parliament was to separate with the assurance that if the Corn Law effected no other beneficial purpose, it was an efficient teacher of frugality in the use of food!

In this debate, Mr. T. M. Gibson and Mr. Villiers eloquently and indignantly protested against the continuance of the landlords' monopoly, but the prospects of the harvest were not yet so bad as to remove the impression from the minds of ministers that they might yet weather another session, and warnings went unheeded. On the 9th August parliament was prorogued.

The following were the imperial averages of wheat for the weeks ending

June 28 .... 47s. 11d.
July 5 .... 47s. 11d.

July 12 .... 48s. 10d.

„ 19 .... 50s.

„ 26 .... 51s. 7d.

August 2 .... 53s. 3d.

Making the aggregate average of the six weeks 49s. 11d. so that by Peel's bill of 1842, which, according to its author, had not yet had a sufficient trial, there could not be imported a single quarter of wheat, without the payment of a duty of twenty shillings. I subjoin his scale to show by what a slow process the duty would be reduced until it ceased when a famine price should be reached, and place beside it Wellington's scale of 1828 :—

Market price in shillings per quarter.	Wellington's scale, 1828.	Peel's scale, 1842.
73s.	1s. 0d.	1s.
72s.	2s. 8d.	2s.
71s.	4s. 8d.	3s.
70s.	10s. 8d.	4s.
69s.	13s. 8d.	5s.
68s.	16s. 8d.	5s.
67s.	18s. 8d.	5s.
66s.	20s. 8d.	6s.
65s.	21s. 8d.	7s.
64s.	22s. 8d.	8s.
63s.	23s. 8d.	9s.
62s.	24s. 8d.	10s.
61s,	25s. 8d.	11s.
60s.	26s. 8d.	12s.
59s.	27s. 8d.	13s.
58s.	28s. 8d.	14s.
57s.	29s. 8d.	15s.
56s.	30s. 8d.	16s.
55s.	31s. 8d.	17s.
54s.	32s. 8d.	17s.
53s.	33s. 8d.	17s.
52s.	33s. 8d.	18s.
51s.	33s. 8d.	19s.
All under	33s. 8d.	20s.

When parliament was prorogued Peel was in effect saying: "You can now under my act import wheat at a duty of twenty shillings—under Wellington's act of 1828, you could not have imported it under a duty of thirty-three shillings and eightpence—give my bill, therefore, a fair trial. When the price rises from 49s. 11d. to 73s. you may then import it at a shilling duty, instead of the six shillings duty Lord John Russell asks for at that advanced price."

In August, the cause of free trade lost a zealous and influential friend by the death of Mr. Thomas Ashton, of Hyde. The following is from the *League* of the 30th of that month :—

" With sincere sorrow we have to notice the death of Thomas Ashton, Esq. of Hyde, widely known and respected as a merchant and manufacturer; warmly admired and fondly loved by a wide circle of acquaintance, for his amiable disposition, his energetic talent, and his untiring beneficence. In him, the cotton trade has lost one of its brightest ornaments—the League one of its best friends—and the general cause of humanity, one whose personal exertions and pecuniary contributions were ever ready to support the exertions made for the benefit of the community. Mr. Ashton possessed, in a remarkable degree, those qualities of mind which characterize the inhabitants of Lancashire : his head was clear and his heart was warm. By the force of native talent, industry and integrity, he raised himself from a comparatively humble position to the possession of great wealth : by his enlightened philanthropy and judicious management, he rendered this wealth a source of comfort and happiness to all around him. The comforts of the operatives he employed were as dear to him as his own : he successfully laboured to train his workpeople in habits of order, industry, and strict morality; and he rendered Hyde a model of comfort, of neatness, and of social happiness. He lived with his people like one of the ancient patriarchs : they revered him as a father, and confided in him as a friend. In the manufacturing circles, Mr. Ashton was regarded as one of the greatest authorities on all matters connected with the cotton-trade : his opinions were known to be the result of strong common sense, never biassed by self-interest. His name was well-known on the Continent, for no intelligent traveller ever visited Lancashire who did not seek to profit by his practical intelligence. To all inquirers his house and heart were open; and no one ever left his door who did not carry away an affectionate remembrance of the generous hospitality he had received, and a reverence for the character of one whose whole life was a continued scene of enlightened benevolence displayed in action. Fortunately for the district which owes so much to Thomas Ashton, the inheritors of his name and fortune are also worthy repre-sentatives of his virtues: his spirit will still direct the establishment at Hyde; his name be upheld as a bright example in the manufacturing districts, and his memory have a living monument in the continuation of his noble principles, developed in equally noble practice."

In Herbert's painting of the Council of the League, now in the musem of the Peel Park, Salford, the portraits of Sir Thomas Potter and Mr. Ashton are represented as adorning the walls of the Council Room, where they had so often given their aid to the movement.

Miss Martineau, referring to the debates on the Corn Law, in her "History of the Thirty Years' Peace," says :— "Meantime, it had begun to rain. It began to rain, after a cold and late spring, at the beginning of the summer; and it seemed as if it was never going to leave off again. In some parts of the country, the sun was scarcely seen from the month of May till the next spring. Those who first marked the soft perseverance of the soft falling rain, thought of the budding and blossoming promised in scrip-ture, where the snow and rain are shown forth as illustra-tions of the fertilizing influences of Providence; and thus far there was nothing but hope of good. Then, as the fall went on with less softness and more chill, and fewer inter-missions, men began to fear for the harvest, and to calcu-late that much dry foreign wheat would be necessary to mix with our own damp and unripened grain. Then arose the fear that our own inferior grain would not keep, so thoroughly ready for sprouting would some of it appear to be; and, in the midst of this, it became clear that through-out Europe, with a few local exceptions, the harvest would prove a deficient one; so that, unless there was unusual abundance in America, the prospect was a fearful one. Still the most sagacious and the most timid were far from conceiving what the rain was doing by its persevering continual soaking into the ground. First a market gar-

dener here and there, a farmer, an Irish cottier, saw a
brown spot appear on the margin of the potatoe, and did
not remember to have seen such a thing before. The
brown spot grew black, and spread and covered the stalk,
till a whole potatoe field looked as if a scorching wind had
passed over it. Yet, perhaps, the roots might appear to be
in a good state ; and one man would let the plants alone,
while another would move off the tops and wait to see
what happened. The stealthy rain, by some means yet as
mysterious as ever, generated some minute plague—of
what nature nobody yet knows, if indeed it is certain that
the rain was the instrument ; a plague so minute that no
microscope has yet convicted it, yet so powerful that it was
soon to overthrow governments, and derange commerce,
and affect for all time to come the political fate of England,
and settle the question of the regeneration or the destruction of Ireland. The minute plague spread and spread,
till it blackened thousands of acres and destroyed the food
of millions of men. In some wholesome regions, the last
to be affected, the inhabitants would hardly believe what
they read. The newspapers were exaggerating shamefully
for some political object ; the League was trading on the
rain and frightening the public, private correspondents
were credulous and too fond of excitement ; their own
potatoes, and those of their neighbours', looked very well ;
and the clergy were again ready with rebuke for anxiety
and doubt, saying that there had always been talk about
bad weather, but that, somehow or other, there was always
a harvest. When, in such a favoured region, two or three
benevolent gentry stored up their own sound potatoes for
the use of the sick and aged in case of need, and laid in
rice and macaroni, and other substitutes, for winter use at
their own tables, their neighbours for a time laughed at the
precaution, and said that potatoes were abundant and
excessively cheap in the markets. But soon the change
appeared even in these healthiest district. A man might

exhibit his green and flourishing crop to a stranger, and
say that he should take it up on Monday. On that night
would come a thunderstorm, and the next morning, if the
owner stirred the soil of his blackened field with a pitch-
fork, up came such a steaming stench as showed him that
his field was turned putrid. And then it became known
why potatoes were abundant and cheap in the markets.
Everybody was eager to sell before his potatoes had time
to rot. What was to become of the poor Irish if this went
on was now the most anxious question of the time."

The weather was not so constantly gloomy as Miss Martineau has represented it to have been. Until near the end of
September there was enough of sunshine to keep alive the
hope that the harvest, though late, would not be very much
deficient. In the middle of August, the price of wheat
had risen to 57s. but by the middle of September it had
receded to 54s. It was not until the beginning of October
that a great failure of the wheat crop, both as regarded
quantity and quality, was acknowledged; and even then,
I see that I looked more at the contingent effect of a bad
harvest in 1846 than on that of 1845. The potato rot, not
only throughout Ireland but all over England and Scotland,
was not apprehended. Men hoped for a good harvest,
knowing the misery that would follow a bad one, and the
hope influenced the judgment. In my paper of the 4th
October, I said : " If the harvest of 1846 be bad, or even if
it should be such as the one which has now been gathered
into the barn-yard, the country will be again plunged into
the distress from which it has so recently emerged. Should
we fold our arms and wait patiently for the result, or
should we demand, and *instantly* demand, the right of
supplying the deficiency of our own harvest, by importing,
without duty, the surplus produce of other lands ? The
League has not been idle. The result of the registrations
in certain selected counties, and the rousing in others of a
spirit which was supposed to be dead, has thrown conster-

nation into the rank of the monopolists. What has been done shows what may be done. Another year's labour in the same direction will repeal the corn-laws; but it must be labour REDOUBLED. He who gave an hour's work to the good cause must now give two. He who gave a pound in money must now give more than two. We must not talk of a hundred thousand pounds' fund for the next campaign, but one of a *Quarter of a Million.* There is a great reward in prospect—the continuance and the increase of the now-enjoyed prosperity. There is a great punishment in prospect if there be any remission of work for the emancipation of commerce—ruin to the employer and starvation to the employed. Every merchant, every spinner, every manufacturer, every holder of railway shares, every man who earns his daily bread by his daily labour, must now come to the rescue, determined to have an instant and total repeal of an enactment disgraceful to humanity, and to the profession of that Christianity which is said to be part and parcel of the law of the land."

By the middle of October, the almost total failure of the potato crop was too obvious to admit of dispute, and even the monopolist papers, seeing the possibility of *millions* of people being exposed to utter starvation, earnestly recommended liberal *subscriptions* to avert the dire calamity. The free traders feeling quite as acutely the necessity of some immediate movement to meet the approaching danger, and quite as willing to relieve the coming distress by liberal contributions, thought that much of its intensity might be averted by opening the ports to the admission of foreign provisions; and the cry of "open the ports" rung throughout the kingdom, startling, in their retreats, the ministers who had prorogued parliament without preparation to meet any such emergency. In the universal outcry and alarm, some of the supporters of monopoly, whether from fear or from humanity, began to exhibit symptoms of yielding. Lord Ashley, in addressing his constituents of

Dorsetshire, declared his opinion, that " the destiny of the
Corn Laws was fixed,"and that it would be wise to consider
how best to " break the force of an inevitable blow ;" and a
rumour arose that ministers would issue an Order in
Council, to admit for home consumption, at a low duty,
the grain and flour then in bond, amounting to about a
million of quarters. A Cabinet Council was held on
Friday, October 31st, but there was no announcement of
any intention of action. The *Times* asserted that the open
ing of ports would be adopted, and said : " Henceforth the
League may cease to exist ; it may be dissolved into its
constitutional elements ; it may lay aside its professional
acrimony and vituperation. The ' great fact' is hastening
to become a '*fait accompli*.' It may expire bodily, because
its spirit has already been transfused into its antagonists."
The League would never have become a *fait accompli* had
it rested from its work under this assurance. Ministers
were looking to what the League would do ; the whole
country were looking to what the League would do ; and
the League knew how it was feared on the one hand, and
how much was hoped from it on the other, and went on
with its great work.

CHAPTER XXII.

FREE TRADE HALL MEETING.

A meeting of the members of the League was held in the Free Trade Hall on Tuesday, October 28. The attendance from the neighbouring towns was very numerous, arrangements having been made with the railway companies for trains to return after the proceedings were closed. The audience mustered more than eight thousand, and hundreds went away without obtaining admittance. On the platform were the representatives of an amount of wealth and capital such as had never before been collected in the north of England. Mr. Wilson having taken the chair, introduced Mr. Cobden, who started at once into the object of the meeting, which was to point out the remedy for the famine which threatened our own island, and to avert the misery, starvation, and death of millions in Ireland. The natural and obvious remedy was to open the ports. Russia, Turkey, Germany, and Holland had done so, and why should not our government follow the example? Peel might apply it if he would. He would have the support of Lancashire, the West Riding of Yorkshire, and the vast multitudes of the people, and if with such support he shrunk from the task he would be a criminal and a poltroon. Mr. Cobden then referred to the rumours of a new Corn Law being intended, and said that some delusive modification would be made unless the country declared against the acceptance of either a fixed duty or a reduced sliding scale. Alluding to the changes made in many of the counties and boroughs by attention to the registrations, he said there was every reason to be hopeful, and concluded an eloquent speech by saying : " We must not relax in our labours ; on the contrary, we must be more zealous, more energetic, more laborious, than we ever yet have been. When the enemy is wavering, then is the time to press upon him. I call, then, on all who have any sympathy in our cause, who have any promptings of humanity, or who feel any interest in the well being of their fellow-men, all who have apprehensions of scarcity and privations, to come forward to avert this horrible destiny, this dreadfully impending visitation." The prolonged cheers that followed promised the increased activity that had been so earnestly recommended.

Mr. Henry Ashworth, of Turton, followed, and dwelt with much effect on the duty which the free traders owed to their country in the continuance, with redoubled vigour, of the instructions which they had already so widely spread. Their whole moral force must now be exerted to consummate what they had begun. If other seven years' labour was required it must be given. " I know," he said, " that there are around me those whose cheeks are furrowed with the exercise of the last seven years ; but I fully believe they will endure another seven years' labour, if such were needful, in the same cause, and to spend quarter-of-a-million of money in the contest, confident that it would be the wisest expenditure they ever made."

Mr. Bright followed Mr. Ashworth, and dashed at once into the question. "At this moment," he said, "all around us is strengthening the conviction of former years ; all around us is telling us, in a voice louder than ever, that every word of reproach, that every harsh saying, which we have uttered against the Corn Law, has not by any means conveyed its true character as it is now exhibited before us. The present state of feeling throughout

the country is one which we must all understand—
one of distrust and alarm. And why ? Is it not because
the price of provisions are rising, and that there is an
apprehended scarcity before us ? It has been said that
the Corn Law was a law to secure plenty, and to secure it
from our own soil. If that be true, then in this hour of
apprehended scarcity, of distrust and alarm, what is there
to which we should so readily turn, in the hope of relief,
as to this very Corn Law, which has been pronounced to
be the height of legislative wisdom." Mr. Bright proceeded
to show that Peel's pet law was now working precisely as
its supporters wished it to work. " It was," he said, " to
prevent the trade in corn—to make you and your fellow-
men—the twenty-seven millions—work and work, and
scramble and scramble, and starve it may be, in order that
out of the produce of your industry—out of the scanty
wages of the many, something may be taken by law, and
handed over to the rich and to the great by whom the law
was made." He went on to compare the present condition
of the country under the Corn Law with what it would be
under no Corn Law, and then referred to the improved
state of the registrations, and the increased number of
freeholds, as ground of encouragement to increased energy,
and concluded by saying : "How dreadful the abandonment
of duty, how awful the crime, not less than that of those who
made the Corn Law, if we step back from our place, if we
fail in the work we have set ourselves, which is to abolish
the law that restricts the bounty of Providence, and to
establish the original and heaven-given law, which will
give plenty to all the earth."

Cabinet councils were held on the Friday after this meeting, on Saturday the 1st, on Monday the 3rd, and on
Thursday the 5th of November. It was said that the
ministers were deliberating upon the alarming accounts
which had reached them from Ireland, and that Peel had
been unable to bring his colleagues to consent that parlia-

ment should be called together, or that the ports should be opened by an order in council.　On Friday, the 7th, the *Standard*, which had previously declared that those councils had been held expressly to devise the means of preventing " any one of Her Majesty's subjects perishing from famine," thus announced the result of the deliberations :—
" We are, we trust, in a condition to congratulate the Leaguers upon the certainty that the *ports will not be opened*, inasmuch as the stock of provisions in Great Britain is *amply sufficient !*"

I do not recollect a period in which there was so eager a desire to see the London papers as during the week in which these cabinet deliberations were held.　Every morning and every evening witnessed the deep disappointment of thousands upon thousands who had been hopeful enough to believe that what was right to be done would be done. In the prospect of starvation to one half of Ireland, and great distress in England, there were as yet no indications of the ministerial policy.　Cabinet meetings had followed cabinet meetings, and yet there was no sign of relief.　The corn markets throughout the kingdom were in a state of confusion ; merchants and manufacturers were waiting in deep anxiety, not knowing what they might safely do ; and millions of working men, who were now convinced that full employment and good wages could never be had while there was a scarcity of food, were almost breathlessly looking to the result of all these deliberations ; and yet nothing was done, and no hope was given that anything would be done.　The Lord Lieutenant of Ireland, in reply to a deputation from the citizens of Dublin, had indeed said that ministers were inquiring how far scarcity might be permitted to prevail without the risk of tumult—inquiring whether one-fourth or one-half of the potato was rotten— inquiring whether the people could be made to believe that, because the price of wheat was not high, in consequence of the general inferiority of its quality, good bread was not,

and would not be dear—inquiring, in short, how infinitis-
simally small the homœopathic dose of relief might be
made!

A public dinner to Mr. Villiers, in the Town Hall,
Birmingham, attended by upwards of six hundred gentlemen, the Earl of Ducie of the number, and presided over
by the mayor, came in good time to excite the country to
renewed exertion against the starvation-creating monopoly.
The speeches of the Mayor, Mr. Villiers, Earl Ducie, Mr.
Cobden, Mr. Bright, Mr. W. J. Fox, Colonel Thompson,
and Mr. W. Brown, of Liverpool, all breathing a spirit of
determination and hope,—reported in full in the *League*,
and in nearly all the newspapers of the kingdom which
had any influence,—gave a tone to public opinion every
where. Remonstrances began to flow in upon the ministry
from every quarter. The freeholders of the county of
Lanark, presided over by the Duke of Hamilton, agreed to
a declaration that the potatoes in that county would not
amount to half a crop, and that the disease continued to
be progressive. The town council of Perth passed a resolution in favour of opening the ports. Crayford, in Kent,
memorialised Sir Robert Peel to the same effect. The
parish of St. Paul, Covent Garden; the Gateshead town
conncil: Lord Cloncurry, on behalf of an influential meeting in Dublin; a meeting of the working classes in Kendal;
a public meeting in the Town Hall, Manchester, the
mayor, Mr. W. B. Watkins, in the chair; the town council
of Manchester; the town council of Salford; the town
council of Sheffield; the town council of Nottingham;
the town council of Stockport; the inhabitants of Oldham;
the Newcastle Chamber of Commerce; the town councils
of Ayr and Montrose; the town council of Gateshead;
and many other places and public bodies, memorialised
the government instantly to open the ports.

In the midst of this excitement appeared a letter,
addressed to the electors of London, from Lord John

Russell, dated Edinburgh, November 22nd. His lordship, after stating his expectations that ministers would have called parliament together, and showing the evils attendant on the exclusion of foreign corn at this crisis, said :—

"I confess that, on the general subject, my views have, in the course of twenty years, undergone a great alteration. I used to be of opinion that corn was an exception to the general rules of political economy; but observation and experience have convinced me that we ought to abstain from all interference with the supply of food. Neither a government nor a legislature can ever regulate the corn markets with the beneficial effects which the entire freedom of sale and purchase are sure of themselves to produce.

"I have for several years endeavoured to obtain a compromise on this subject. In 1839 I voted for a committee of the whole house, with the view of supporting the substitution of a moderate fixed duty for the sliding-scale. In 1841 I announced the intention of the then government of proposing a fixed duty of 8s. a quarter. In the past session I proposed the imposition of some lower duty. These propositions were successively rejected. The present First Lord of the Treasury met them in 1839, 1840, and 1841, by eloquent panegyrics of the existing system—the plenty it had caused, the rural happiness it had diffused. He met the propositions for diminished protection in the same way in which he had met the offer of securities for protestant interests in 1817 and 1825—in the same way in which he met the proposal to allow Manchester, Leeds, and Birmingham to send members to parliament in 1830.

"The result of resistance to qualified concession must be the same in the present instance as in those I have mentioned. *It is no longer worth while to contend for a fixed duty.* In 1841 the free-trade party would have agreed to a duty of 8s. a quarter on wheat, and after a lapse of years this duty might have been further reduced, and ultimately abolished. But the imposition of any duty, at present, without a provision for its extension within a short period, would but prolong a contest already sufficiently fruitful of animosity and discontent. The struggle to make bread scarce and dear, when it is clear that part, at least, of the additional price goes to increase rent, is a struggle deeply injurious to an aristocracy which (this quarrel once removed) is strong in property, strong in the construction of our legislature, strong in opinion, strong in ancient associations, and the memory of immortal services.

"Let us, then, unite to put an end to a system which has been proved to be the blight of commerce, the bane of agriculture, the source of bitter divisions among classes, the cause of penury, fever, mortality, and crime among the people.

" But if this end is to be achieved, it must be gained by the unequi-vocal expression of the public voice. It is not to be denied that many elections for cities and towns in 1841, and some in 1845, appear to favour the assertion that free trade is not popular with the great mass of the community. The government appear to be waiting for some excuse to give up the present Corn Law. Let the people, by petition, by address, by remonstrance, afford them the excuse they seek. Let the ministry propose such a revision of the taxes as, in their opinion, may render the public burdens more just and more equal; let them add any other provisions which caution and even scrupulous forbearance may suggest; but let the removal of restrictions on the admission of the main articles of food and clothing used by the mass of the people be required, in plain terms, as useful to all great interests, and indispensable to the progress of the nation."

In 1841, the free-trade party would not have agreed to a duty of 8s There were a few persons, here and there, whose greater affection for whiggism than for free trade would have led them to accept Lord John Russell's pro-posed compromise, but their opinions never found utterance at any of the meetings of the League. There might have been a few to utter such disposition in Lord John's ears, or in private conversation, but not one ever dared to utter it at any public meeting. The League could not consent, if, instead of being steadfastly opposed to his lordship's proposition, it had listened to it with favour, for it had been constituted for the entire repeal of the Corn Law.

It was much to have Lord John Russell's declaration, that it was no longer worth while to contend for a fixed duty; but the country generally thought that his lordship had been a great deal too long in contending for that which was not worth while. Many there were whose reply to his advice was, that they had been doing all they could in that direction, while he was opposing them with his obsolete shibboleth; and some there were who uncharitably regarded his lordship's appearance in the field at the eleventh hour as a bid for office. The following letter from Lord Mor-peth was received with much more favour and gratitude, as quite in accordance with his character and the public expectation :—

"Castle Howard, Nov. 24, 1845.

"My dear Mr. Baines,—I perceive that you are about to have a meeting at Leeds to promote the qualification of electors, with a view to further the objects of the Anti-Corn-Law League.

"You will probably remember being present upon an occasion when, amidst very strong surrounding inducement, I forebore from pledging myself to the entire extent of those objects. All that has since intervened, all especially that is now occurring, a fellow feeling with my old friends in the riding (although I less than ever anticipate any probable renewal of a political connection between us), and a sense of what has been effected by the Anti-Corn-Law League to advance their great end, alike combine to put an end to all further doubt or reserve on my own part, and I write this without concert or consultation with any one else. The contribution I enclose for your immediate purposes is of very trifling amount; it would not be easy to foresee what calls may not be made upon any of us in the course of the ensuing year; but I wish to record in the most emphatic way I can my conviction that the time is come for a final repeal of the Corn Laws, and my protest against the continued inaction of the state in the present emergency.—Believe me, dear Mr. Baines, yours very faithfully, "MORPETH.

"Edward Baines, jun. Esq."

With the certainty now that, if ever a whig administration came into power, it must come with an unequivocal adoption of free-trade principles, much speculation arose whether Peel, either with the desire of retaining office, or with the more statesmanlike desire to rescue his country from, not an impending, but an already inflicted calamity, would have the courage to do that which his political opponents were promising to do; and the continuance of Cabinet councils led to the belief that he was struggling with his refractory colleagues for that purpose. "It was in the midst of the second series of consultations," says Miss Martineau, "that an incident occurred which startled the whole kingdom, and gave the newspapers plenty to say :

"On the 4th of December the *Times* announced that it was the intention of government to repeal the Corn Laws, and to call parliament together in January for that purpose. Some ministerial papers doubted, and then indignantly denied this. Some journals said that it could not be known to the *Times*, because the fact could transpire only through the breach of the Cabinet oath. Others said that it might fairly be a matter of

inference from the general policy being understood; but to this there
was the objection that the *Times* asserted that its news was not a matter
of inference, but of fact; and the ordinary Government papers persevered in denying the truth of the news altogether. The *Times* was
scolded, insulted, jeered at, lectured; and everybody was warned not
to mind the *Times;* but everybody did mind it; and the *Times* persevered
day after day, week after week, in haughtily asserting that its intelligence would be found correct within an assigned period. Meantime,
the general conviction was complete, that the *Times* had some peculiar
means of information. One report was that the Duke of Wellington
had come down to the Horse Guards in great wrath, swearing, as he
threw himself from his horse, at the pass things had come to when the
Corn Laws were to be given up; but, besides that such a freak was not
very like the shrewd and loyal Duke of Wellington, there was no reason
here why the *Times* should be exclusively in possession of the information. There are some, of course, who know, and many more who
believe they know, how the thing happened; but it is not fitting to
record, in a permanent form, the chit-chat of London, about any but
the historical bearings of an incident like this. The *Times* had true
information—and that is all that is important to the narrative. As we
have said, the announcement was made on the 4th of December. On
the 5th, the *Standard* exhibited a conspicuous title to a counter-state-
ment: 'Atrocious fabrication by the *Times*;' but, meanwhile, 'the
effect of the announcement by the *Times*, at the Corn Exchange, was
immense surprise, not so much displeasure as might have been expected,
and an instant downward tendency in the price of grain.' So said other
papers. 'We adhere to our original announcement,' said the *Times* of
December 6th, ' that Parliament will meet early in January, and that a
repeal of the Corn Laws will be proposed in one House by Sir R. Peel,
and in the other by the Duke of Wellington.' The Free Traders so
far gave weight to the assertion, as to announce everywhere, with
diligence, that they would accept of ' nothing short of total repeal; not
a shilling, nor a farthing, of duty should be imposed without sound
reason shown.' "

The free traders did not need the assertion for *their*
announcement, for " nothing short of total repeal" had
been their demand during the whole seven years of their
agitation. It was as much their cry in 1841 as it was in
1845; as much their cry when they asked for a fund of
£100,000 as now, when they were about to ask for one of
£250,000. The prospect of famine, not the accession of

whig auxiliaries, had stimulated them to increased exertion. Applications for freeholds had been made to the League from all parts of the kingdom previous to that accession. Cobden and Bright had received as many invitations to attend meetings at large towns, as would have occupied them for every night until February. On Monday, November 23rd, they were at Sheffield; on Tuesday, at Leeds, where they first heard of Lord Morpeth's letter; at Wakefield, on Thursday; and at Bradford, on Friday, where they were received by numerous and enthusiastic meetings. On the following week, according to appointments made before the whig accessions, they attended similarly enthusiastic meetings at Gloucester and Stroud, where Earl Ducie was in the chair; Bath and Bristol; and on the week following that, at Nottingham, Derby, and Stockport, also on invitations given before the whig accessions. During that tour, meetings were held at Ashton, Bury, Lees, Newton, and Failsworth, in Lancashire; and the movement received an additional impulse from great meetings held in London, Leicester, Edinburgh, Glasgow, Huddersfield, and numerous other large towns, where the demand was, as it had been for seven years, for total and immediate repeal. There was no throwing up of caps as if the work had been done. There was a deep conviction that it must be finished by those who had begun it, and the stern determination was to have no juggle to stave off the final settlement by any temporary expedient. The people had no faith in either whig or tory movement. They saw their way to victory through redoubled zeal and activity, and they braced themselves up to the work.

On Sunday, the 7th of December, it was rumoured that the Duke of Wellington had reluctantly yielded; on Tuesday, it was asserted that he had withdrawn his assent. On Thursday, it was known that ministers had resigned: that the " STRONG GOVERNMENT" had fallen to pieces before the shadow of coming events. It appeared that the startling announcement of the *Times* was substantially true. The cabinet had, on Wednesday, assented to Sir Robert Peel's proposal, that the ports should be opened, and that new financial arrangements, including a repeal of the present Corn Law, should be laid before parliament at its opening. The Duke of Wellington, it was said, had become alarmed at the consequences of the contemplated liberality to which he had given his assent, and he returned to his old obstructive position with a dogged obstinacy that was not to be reasoned with, and some of his colleagues, who were willing to permit a greater degree of commercial liberty, manifested their dislike to be made the instruments of carrying that which they had always opposed. Hence the defeat of Sir Robert Peel, and hence the denunciation in Friday's *Standard* of the *Times*' announcement, as an " atrocious fabrication." It was understood that, when the premier discovered his inability to move his cabinet onward, he immediately made his position known to Lord John Russell, then in Scotland, who consequently proceeded to London, where he arrived at the time when ministers had departed to Osborne House to tender their resignation to the Queen. On the following day his lordship proceeded to Osborne House, and received instructions from Her Majesty to form a new administration.

The free traders believed that had Sir Robert Peel possessed the courage to choose for himself colleagues to carry out his intended measures, the contest for free trade would be neither so protracted nor so difficult as it would be under ministers who had so many dislikings to overcome ; that, had he remained in office and shown an honest determination to effect the repeal of the Corn Law, he would have had the earnest support of all the free-traders in the House and throughout the country ; that the whigs, in common consistency, would have given their aid to the principles which they had then adopted ; that the moderate conservatives would have followed Peel ; that although they might not have formed a majority in the present parliament, an appeal to the country would have given them power, not only to carry the repeal of the Corn Law triumphantly through the House of Commons, but to compel the Lords to yield to the demand for justice; that there were many conservatives who would have followed Peel IN OFFICE who would not follow him when OUT OF OFFICE, when that following would place them under the direction of Lord John Russell and the members of a former administration whom they had been in the habit of regarding as their political enemies; and that they would have been led or driven by Peel, but would neither be led on nor driven by Russell. It was foreseen, therefore, that an arduous struggle was to ensue — triumphant, no doubt, and triumphant sooner than anyone could have anticipated a few weeks before, but much more protracted and much more beset with formidable difficulties than it would have been, had Peel possessed the statesman-like courage to throw himself upon the country for support, and to treat with contempt the obstructive faction headed by the Duke of Wellington, the Duke of Buccleuch, and Lord Stanley.

While Lord John Russell, who had been brought hurriedly from Scotland, was endeavouring to form an administration, there was much speculation as to his power of carrying the object to which he had now given his adhesion. Although it was understood that Sir Robert Peel would give his assistance to the removal of the Corn Law, and that the Duke of Wellington would not be found amongst the obstructives of that great commercial and social reform, it required no extraordinary degree of foresight to be convinced that it was not to be obtained without a severe struggle, and probably not without the dissolution of a parliament pledged at its election to the principles of protection. The League was ready for the emergency—ready for a five year's energetic struggle, if it should be necessary. On Saturday, December 13th, upwards of seventy of the principal subscribers to its funds in Manchester and its neighbourhood met at the League Rooms, and resolved unanimously that an appeal to the public should be made for a fund of £250,000, and that a meeting should be held in the Town Hall on Tuesday, the 23rd, for that purpose.

Before that time Lord John Russell had relinquished his attempt to form a ministry. The following narrative of the negociations is from Miss Martineau's " History" :—

" Lord J. Russell was at Edinburgh. The royal summons reached him at night on the 8th of December. As there was then no railway to London, it was the 10th before he arrived in town; and the 11th before he appeared in the Queen's presence at Osborne, in the Isle of Wight. He had made up his mind, that if asked to undertake the formation of a ministry, he must decline, because his party was in a minority in the Commons of from 90 to 100. This was his answer when the Queen made the expected request: but Sir Robert Peel had left with the Queen a paper, in which, after declaring the reasons of his resignation, he avowed his readiness, 'in his private capacity, to aid and give every support to the new ministry whom Her Majesty might select to effect a settlement of the question of the Corn Laws.' This wholly changed the state and prospect of the case. Lord J. Russell returned to consult such of his friends as were within reach. Through J. Graham, Lord J. Russell was put in possession of all the information on which the late ministers had proceeded; but not of the details of their proposed measures. It was no time for a general election. None but a rash minister would dream of requiring it while the country was in strong excitement, and under the visible doom of a great calamity. Instead of this, the thing to be done was to frame such a measure of Corn-Law repeal as would secure the support of Sir R. Peel and the colleagues who had adhered to him. After a good deal of correspondence, through the Queen, of difficult transactions by statesmen so delicately placed with regard to each other, Lord J. Russell conceived himself justified in attempting to form an administration; and he communicated with the sovereign to that effect on the 18th of December. But next morning an insuperable difficulty arose. One of the friends on whom he had confidently rested as a coadjutor, declined to enter the Cabinet. This was Lord Grey. Highly as Lord J. Russell valued him, he would at any other time have endeavoured to form a Cabinet without him, at his own desire; but the position of the whigs was now too critical—or at least their leaders thought so—to admit the risk of such speculation as would be excited at the exclusion of Lord Grey. On the 20th, therefore, the Queen was finally informed that Lord John Russell found it impossible to form an administration.

" Among the newspaper reports of the public talk during this interval, we find a few words in italics about the popular surprise at there being no mention of Lord Grey ' in the list of whig conferences :' and close beside this, we meet with notice of the ' alarm' excited by the consideration that Lord Palmerston must have some office, and most probably the foreign department. Our foreign relations were now in a critical state, as our history of the French and American questions will have shown : and there were many who stood in fear of Lord Palmerston's ' talent of keeping perpetually open all vital questions and dangerous controversies.' It was well understood that Lord Grey thought it unsafe to make Lord Palmerston foreign minister at such a juncture ; and that he declined to act inconsistently with his long avowed principles of peace, by sitting in the Cabinet with a minister who had done more than any other man to foster the war-spirit in 1840 and 1841. The disappointed whig party bitterly complained that Lord Grey had done it all ; but with the country at large Lord Grey lost nothing by this difficult act of self-exclusion, or by his honourable silence in the midst of the censure which was abundantly poured out upon him.

"On Friday the 19th, the Queen intimated to Sir R. Peel, that as their political relation was to terminate, she wished to see him next day to bid him farewell. Before he went to Windsor on the Saturday, he was informed by Lord John Russell of the failure of his enterprize, and when he entered the Queen's presence, he was told that, so far from taking leave, he must prepare for the resumption of office. He returned to town as minister of the crown, and found no difficulty in reconstructing his Cabinet. Lord Stanley, of course, retired. All the others resumed—all but one, who had died suddenly from the anxiety of the crisis. Lord Wharncliffe had been suffering from gout, but no danger was apprehended. He was, however, in no state to bear the turmoil of the time; and he suddenly sank on the 19th of December, in the 70th year of his age. As president of the council, he had proved himself a zealous and effective minister; and his earnestness in fulfilling to the utmost such provisions for education as had been obtained, secured him much gratitude from society. It was an untoward time for a West Riding election ; but this elevation of Mr. Stuart Wortley to the peerage rendered it necessary ; and Lord Morpeth was returned to his old seat in parliament. Mr. Gladstone became colonial secretary, instead of Lord Stanley; and the Duke of Buccleuch succeeded Lord Wharncliffe, as president of the council."

The return of Sir Robert Peel to office, with much

greater power to effect the reform than the whigs possessed, did not lessen the determination of the free traders to put forth all their energy, for it was seen that a desperate struggle was still to be endured. The announced meeting in the Manchester Town Hall was held on the 23rd December, and was attended by almost every merchant and manufacturer of eminence in the town and neighbourhood. Robert Hyde Greg, Esq. was called to the chair, and in a short and pithy speech, characteristic of the man, called upon the meeting to cash the cheque which the League had drawn upon them. He alluded to the sacrifice of time, health, and comfort which the leaders of the movement had made; the unwearying perseverance, consummate skill, and brilliant talents they had displayed; and said they called for the deepest gratitude and the most earnest support. What, he asked, was money compared to these? If they showed in that crisis the same determination which they had shown on so many former occasions, there could be no doubt that, the next time they met, it would be to celebrate their triumph. The Chairman then introduced to the meeting Mr. George Wilson, who rendered an account, on behalf of the treasurer, of the receipts and expenditure; by which it appeared that the total amount raised by the last subscription was £123,508, of which £59,333 was expended in 1844 and £51,141 in 1845, leaving a balance in hand of £12,033. The meeting received the statement with a burst of cheers; and Mr. W. R. Callender immediately rose and moved their approval, observing that, from his own knowledge of the manner in which the accounts were kept, there was no private establishment more exact and punctual. The motion was seconded by Mr. Lawrence Heyworth, of Liverpool, and carried unanimously. The second resolution, pledging the meeting not to relax in their exertions until the Corn Laws were entirely abolished, was moved by Mr. Alderman Nield, seconded by Mr. Robert Ashton, of Hyde, and carried. unanimously.

The third resolution was, "That this meeting hereby expresses its high sense of the invaluable services which the National Anti Corn Law League has rendered to the cause of free trade ; and in order to enable the Council to make renewed and increased exertions for the repeal of the Corn and Provision Laws, a subscription, in aid of the great fund of £250,000, be now commenced." The resolution was moved by Mr. Henry Ashworth, of Bolton, seconded by Mr. Alderman Kershaw, and carrried unanimously and with great cheering.

The Chairman then called upon the assemblage practically to back their words by their deeds, and becomingly set the example, on behalf of himself and partner, by giving a thousand pounds. The meeting hailed this spirited commencement with loud cheers, which were renewed with great vehemence when another thousand from Mr. James Chadwick, the gentleman who complained that, in the raising of the £100,000 fund, he had been allowed to subscribe only £500 instead of £1,000. From this time, for an hour and-a-half, cards were placed in the Chairman's hands nearly as fast as he could read them, from or on behalf of individuals subscribing their thousands, seven, five, four, three, two, and one hundreds, and smaller amounts. Twenty-three persons and firms gave in their names for £1000 each ; twenty-five for £500 ; fifty-one for sums of from £200 to £400; sixty-one for sums between £100 and £150; and about fifty for sums of £50 each. The first pause in the proceedings was taken advantage of by the Chairman to call upon Mr. Cobden, who was received with almost overwhelming cheers. He said he was glad to witness the tone of the meeting, for there had not been the slightest reference to changes that had occurred at government head-quarters, like the shiftings of a pantomime. "We have not lost time," he said, "by speculation on what this or that administration is going to do, but we have resorted to the much safer mode of depending only

upon ourselves. This meeting will afford to any administration the best possible support in carrying out its principles. If Sir Robert Peel will go on in an intelligible and
straightforward course—if he will promulgate plainly and
candidly that he purposes fully to carry out the principles
of free trade, he will see that there is strength enough in
the country to support him; and I should not be speaking
the sentiments of the meeting if I did not say, that if he
takes the straightforward, honest course, he shall have the
support of the League and the country as fully and cordially as any other prime minister."

The subscriptions again poured in: Mr. Bright, Mr.
James Heywood, Mr. Brotherton, and Mr. Wylie, of Liverpool, filling up the intervals with brief addresses. Mr.
Bright was hailed with great cheering. He said he could
not command words to express the delight he felt in the
proceedings. He was surrounded by gentlemen, some of
whom had attended meetings in Manchester for thirty or
forty years, but they had never seen in all their experience
any to compare with that they had been witnesses to now.
No man, even amongst their enemies, could now say that
there was anything unsubstantial, anything insincere in the
character of the great movement. The past meetings had
demonstrated that the supporters of the League were in
earnest, and this meeting, if any confirmation were
required, furnished that confirmation; and he was convinced that it would have a powerful effect on public
opinion. At the close of the meeting, the Chairman
announced that the amount subscribed was Fifty-nine
thousand, one hundred and sixty-five pounds. Before the
day closed, the amount had increased to Sixty thousand
pounds! The following is a list of some of the subscriptions:—

£1000 each.—S. Greg and Sons; James Chadwick; T. Thomasson
Bolton; Kershaw, Leese, and Co.; T. Hoyle and Sons; John Brooks;
Robert Ashton, Hyde; W. Bailey and Brothers, Stalybridge; Robert
Platt, Stalybridge; Robert Lees and Son, Dukinfield; J. Whitaker and

Sons, Hurst; J. Bright and Brothers, Rochdale; Thomas Ashton and Sons, Hyde; James King and Sons, Rochdale; T. Booth, and J. T. and James Hoyle, Rochdale; S. Ashton and James Ashton and Bros., Pole Bank; P. Dixon, sen. Carlisle; Josh. Eccles, Blackburn; Eccles, Shorrocks, and Co. Darwen; H. and E. Ashworth, Bolton; Pilkington and Brothers, Blackburn; A. and S. Henry and Co.; A. and F. Reyner; J. and N. Philips and Co.

£700.—Family of the Mathers, Liverpool.

£500 each.—James Buckley and Brothers Ashton; N. Buckley and Sons, Saddleworth; John Buckley and Brothers, Mossley; Laurence Heyworth, Liverpool; John Ben. Smith; John Cheetham, Stalybridge; Richard Matley; Gardner and Bazley; John Ashton, Hyde; Callender, Bickham, and Co.; James Heywood; John Fenton, late M.P. for Rochdale; M'Connell and Co.; John and Thomas Potter; Henry Bannerman and Son; Richard Cobden; Elkanah Armitage and Son; a Friend, by John Bright; Sam. Fletcher, Son, and Co.; George Foster, Sabden; William Ross; Thomas Whitehead and Brothers, Rawtenstall; Robert Johnston; Shunck, Suchay, and Co.

The subscription of £60,000 in an hour-and-a-half, threw the monopolists into a state of great consternation. They could not deny the fact, but they could depreciate the motive. The *Standard* said: " It is not uncharitable to pronounce it a selfish, sordid object, for, on looking over the names of the subscribers, we cannot find a single name connected with any pious, generous, or humane enterprise. They are not the men to build churches, or schools, or hospitals, or alms-houses, or who contribute to any plans of benevolence unconnected with the advancement of their trade." Persons who knew the individuals better than the *Standard* did; knew that they were the men who were the most distinguished for their plans of benevolence totally unconnected with their trade interests. If a church, chapel Sunday school, day school, infants' school, or mechanics' institution, was to be erected, these were the men who were first applied to; if a local charitable institution was needed or land was required for places of recreation for the pent-up multitudes, these were the men to whom the first application was made. Nor was their benevolence confined to the promotion of the physical and moral advancement of their fellow-men. I could name twenty or thirty of them who had each built a church, or school for the religious instruction of their workpeople and workpeople's children, and individually bore its annual expenses. These were the men who, according to the *Standard*, were actuated only by sordid and selfish motives !

With £60,000 of fresh subscriptions ; with full faith that the whole £250,000 fund would be realized ; with hope excited by the declared conversion of the most distinguished leaders of the whig and tory parties in parliament; with determined resolution to accept of nothing short of justice ; and with renewed spirit for action during the great parliamentary struggle which was sure to ensue, the members of the League looked forwards, from their advanced post at this end of 1845, to the accomplishment of their object within the approaching year ; but fully prepared, and with ample means, to carry on their work of instruction, and their operation upon the constituencies, for *five years more if necessary.* The prompt subscription of that Quarter-of-a-Million fund made many converts.

CHAPTER XXIII.

THE NEW MEASURES.

The meetings at the Free Trade Hall had always been crowded, but so great was the desire for admittance on the 15th January, 1845, that the seats had to be taken out of the body of the hall, to increase the number admitted to 9,000, instead of the usual 8,000. Mr. Wilson stated that since the day when the sum of £60,000 had been subscribed, the subscription had increased to £75,600 ; that at a meeting at Liverpool, on the previous Friday, £12,000 had been subscribed, of which £1,000 was from Mr. William Brown ; that at a meeting at Leeds, addressed by Mr. Cobden, Mr. Bright, and Col. Thompson, £34,000 had been subscribed ; that at Dundee, where the five Messrs. Baxter had put down £150 each, the amount subscribed was more than £2,000 ; that at Stroud, without any deputation, the amount was £1,300 ; and that the total amount was then £128,800. Before the meeting of parliament, Edinburgh had followed with a subscription of £2,000 ; Glasgow with one of £10,000 ; and Preston one of £2,500 ; the Liverpool subscription had risen to £17,000 ; and all were to be considerably increased. In one month £150,000 of the quarter of a million fund, had been subscribed, and a considerable proportion of the twenty per cent. instalment had been paid.

On the 19th January, the Queen's speech, read by Her Majesty in person, lamented the failure of the potato crop, especially in Ireland, and expressed satisfaction in the

results of the repeal of the Customs' duties, as far as they
had yet gone, and recommended to parliament the consideration whether the repeal of restrictions might not
be carried yet further; whether there might not still be
a remission " of the existing duties upon many articles
the produce or manufacture of other countries." In the
House of Lords much bitterness was manifested by the
protectionists at the prospects before them, many bitter
denunciations of the League; and the Duke of Richmond,
in his spleen, asked why ministers did not make Mr.
Cobden a peer, and place him on the Treasury bench in
the House of Lords?

In the Commons the scene was exceedingly animated,
and the House was crowded in expectation of hearing
Sir Robert Peel's explanations. Lord Francis Egerton
in moving the address, declared that his own opinions on
the Corn Laws, had undergone an entire alteration, and
he implored the house to bring about " a full, satisfactory,
and final settlement of the question." Mr. Beckett
Denison, as seconder, said, that experience had " driven"
him to the same conclusion. Sir Robert Peel then rose,
and the full gaze and attention of the House were rivetted
upon him. He acknowledged that the prospects of famine
in Ireland had been the subject of the frequent Cabinet
consultations; but he said it would be unfair to make that
cause occupy the prominent place. The laws which
regulated the IMPORTATION *of* FOOD, were the primary, the
grand subject of the deliberations of a reluctant Cabinet.
On the question of the CORN LAW, *his opinion had undergone
a complete* CHANGE! This announcement was received
with triumphant cheering from the opposition benches,
with profound silence from the ministerial. Then the
prime minister proceeded, with great ability, to show
that all the grounds on which " protection to native
industry" was advocated, had been proved to be *wholly
untenable.* Very deliberately adopting the speeches of

Mr. VILLIERS as his model, he went on as if he were
about to conclude with a motion for the immediate and total
abolition of the Corn Law. Protection, he said, was not
a labourer's question; for during the last three years, prices
had been low and food abundant; and during that period,
the working classes had been better off than during the
preceding three years. High prices did not produce high
wages, nor *vice versa*. In the last three years, with low
prices and abundance of food, wages were comparatively
high, and labour was in demand; in the three years preceding, with high prices and scarcity, wages were low and
employment was scarce. Experience thus proved that
wages were ruled by abundance of capital and demand for
labour, and did not vary with the price of provisions.
Again, increased freedom of trade was favourable to the
prosperity of our commerce. In three scarce and dear
years, namely, from 1839 to 1841, our foreign exports fell
off from fifty-three millions in value to forty-seven millions.
But in three years of reduction of duties and low prices,
namely, from 1842 to 1844, the value of our exports rose
from forty-seven millions to fifty-eight millions.   Even
deducting the amount of the China trade, a similar result
was shown.   Nor was the reduction in the Customs' duties
unfavourable to the revenue.   In 1842, there was an
estimated loss of a million-and-a half; in 1843, a smaller
one of £273,000; but in 1845, there was a reduction, at
an estimated loss to the revenue of no less than two
millions and a-half.   The total amount of the various
reductions effected in three years exceeded four millions
sterling; and many of the duties were totally abolished;
the loss, therefore, not being compensated by any increased
consumption.   Had four millions been lost to the revenue?
He believed that on the 5th of April next, the revenue
would be found to be more buoyant than ever.   Sir Robert
Peel referred to other proofs of prosperity resulting from
reduced import duties, and then adverted to his own

position, and declared that " he would not hold office on a servile tenure."

Notice had been given, that on the evening of Tuesday, January 27, Sir Robert Peel would state what measures he had to propose. The house was crowded both by members and strangers, and Prince Albert and the Duke of Cambridge were amongst the visitants. Sir Robert spoke for three hours and a-half, and proposed the reduction of the duty on Russian tallow from 3s. 2d. to 1s. 6d.; the abolition of duty on the coarser fabrics of linen, cotton, and woollen, and the reduction on the finer from 20 to 10 per cent.; on French brandy and Geneva, a reduction from 22s. 10d. to 15s.; on foreign free-grown Muscovada sugar, a reduction from 9s. 4d. to 5s. 10d.; and on clayed, from 11s. 10d. to 8s.; the admission of Indian corn and buckwheat, duty free; on butter, the duty to be reduced from 20s. to 10s. and on cheese, from 10s. to 5s.; the duty on live animals, and fresh and salted meats, pork, and vegetables, to be abolished. As to Corn, in lieu of the then sliding scale, he proposed, that when the average price of wheat was 48s. the duty should be 10s.—the duty falling by 1s. with every shilling of rise in price, till on reaching 53s. the duty should be a fixed one of 4s.; that this mitigated scale should last for *three years*, and, by a positive enactment, to disappear on the 1st of February, 1849, leaving for the future only a nominal rate of duty; that all British colonial wheat and flour should be forthwith admitted at a nominal rate of duty : that as a compensation, or rather alleviation, for this great change, some local burdens should be revised, with a view to their economical collection and application ;—that the highway rates, which were then under the control of 16,000 local functionaries, should be placed, by union of parishes, &c. under the management of 600, and their applicants more effectually supervised ; that the law of settlement should be altered, so as to give every resident of five years in towns a status, and thus save rural districts from a flood of pauperism, thrown upon them in times of commercial and manufacturing revulsion; that various other charges should be taken off county rates, and placed on the consolidated fund, as expenses of convicted prisoners, of prosecutions, &c. which were to be wholly or partly borne by the state; that the state should encourage agriculture by lending money, at a moderate rate of interest, on adequate security, for the drainage and other improvement of estates, and that the newly-constituted board for the enclosure of commons, and the Exchequer bill commissioners should be the machinery for this purpose.

It was agreed that the debate on Sir Robert Peel's propositions should be postponed till Monday, 9th February, but the more violent of the protectionists, amongst whom were Mr. Liddell, the Earl of March, Colonel Sibthorp, and Sir John Tyrrell, poured forth bitter denunciations of the " Potato Peel Government," as one of them designated the ministers, accusing them, at the same time, of compromising not with the agriculturists but with the League.

A numerously attended meeting of the Council of the League was held at Manchester, on January 29th, Mr. Wilson in the chair, at which the proposed measures of Sir Robert Peel were discussed at some length. Congratulations were exchanged at the progress which the great question had made in the minds of the most distinguished statesmen of all parties. With respect to the measure itself, several parts of it elicited expressions of satisfaction; but the feeling of regret at the re-enactment of the sliding scale was universal. The meeting was addressed, among others, by Messrs. R. H. Greg, Alderman Kershaw, J. B. Smith, A. Prentice, James Heywood, H. Rawson, J. Whitaker, W. Bickham, T. Woolley, &c. All were of opinion that the League and its friends should stand firm to the principle of immediate and total repeal; and the following resolution, recommending universal

petitioning, was unanimously passed : Resolved,—" That
the announcement of a new Corn Law renders it desirable
that the friends of free trade throughout the kingdom
should originate petitions for the total and immediate
abolition of all laws imposing duties on foreign corn and
provisions."

The country was ready to respond to this invitation. It
gave the assurance that the League would seek no compromise ; that Sir Robert Peel's measure was not the
League's measure ; and that, if the members of the League
could throw it out, and replace it with their own, they
unquestionably would. There was no fear of " embar-
rassing Sir R. Peel." The conviction was that, looking at
the bitterness of his opponents, he would be more embarrassed if the free traders departed one iota from their just
demand. Amidst that universally reiterated demand, the
triumphant return of Lord Morpeth for the West Riding
of Yorkshire, gave additional energy to the agitation, as a
demonstration from the constituency which most fully and
fairly represented public opinion in England.

On Monday, February 9th, when the order of the day
was moved that the House should resolve itself into committee on the propositions of the Government, Mr. Philip
Miles moved, as an amendment, that the House should go
into committee " that day six months." The amendment
was seconded by Sir W. Heathcote. The Hon. Mr. Las-
celles supported ministers ; Lord Norreys expressed his
dismay at their sweeping propositions. Mr. A. B. Cochrane ridiculed the idea that members were never to change
their minds. Mr. Deedes, of Kent, took the protective
side. Sir John Walsh prognosticated utter ruin to the
farmer and farm labourer. Mr. A. G. Beresford Hope denounced Peel as an apostate. Lord Sandon spoke strongly
against the propositions, and yet said he would vote for
them. Lord John Russell would support the propositions,
if in committee the right hon. baronet would substitute

immediate for prospective repeal.   Sir R. Inglis thought
the protective system gave the best security for a regular
supply of food.   Mr. Fitzmaurice thought the farmers
might as well die by the manly open thrust of Mr. Cobden
as by the mince-meat, ladylike interference of Sir R. Peel.
Mr Sidney Herbert, in an able speech, supported the ministerial propositions, and then the debate was adjourned
till next day.

On Tuesday, the motion was opposed by Mr. Stafford
O'Brien, supported by Mr. Sharman Crawford and Mr. H.
Baillie, opposed by Mr. Lefroy, supported by Lord Cle-
mens, opposed by the Marquis of Granby, supported by
Mr. Gregory and Lord Brooke, supported by Lord Worsley, and by Sir James Graham, who said that, on his conscience, he believed the measures would save a great and
powerful nation from anarchy, misery, and ruin.   Lord
Clive opposed the motion.   The debate was again adjourned.

On Thursday, the debate was resumed by Mr. Colquhoun, who opposed the motion, denying that public opinion was in its favour.   Mr. C. W. Martin would support
the propositions, although at variance with his former
opinions.   Lord Morpeth, in a speech which made a great
impression on the House, spoke in favour of immediate
adjustment.   Mr. Gaskell saw no reason to change his
opinions which were in favour of protection.   Mr. Roebuck
expressed a hope that the measures would pass.   Mr.
Hinde was not heard in the impatience of the house, and
again the debate was adjourned.

The Friday night's debate would have been unbearably
tedious but for a telling and pithy speech by Mr. Ward.
Mr. Miles read an unwieldy and undigested mass of docu-
ments in favour of protection, exceedingly provocative of
yawning, and threatened the country with an inundation
of wheat from Tamboff.   Mr. Francis Scott compared Sir
Robert Peel to a lawyer, who, after taking a fee for advocat-

ing one side, took the other when the case came into court.
Sir Robert Peel quietly asked—"Whose counsel are you
now?" Sir Howard Douglas also bestowed his tediousness
on the House. A little scene ensued between Lord Northland and Ferrand the coarse, which somewhat enlivened the
dulness of the debate; Lord Northland avowed his intention to support Sir Robert Peel, because he had more confidence in him than in Lord John Russell. A story had
been told of his lordship that at the time of the passing
of the Maynooth Act he was caught in the house as it was
going to a division, and, being unwilling to vote either for
or against the bill, he hid himself in a small recess, which
had been formerly used as a coal-hole, and some mischievous "friend" having observed it, told the Sergeant-at-
Arms, and Lord Northland was compelled to come out and
vote. Mr. B. Ferrand recalled this circumstance to the
recollection of the noble lord, amidst uproarious laughter.
"What confidence," he bellowed, "had you in the right
honourable baronet when you were dragged out of the
coal-hole to vote for him?" The debate was again adjourned.

The fifth night's debate on the following Monday was
opened by Lord March, eldest son of the Duke of Richmond, and about as sensible a protectionist. The House
was relieved by the rising of Mr. Milner Gibson, whose
easy, fluent, and agreeable style, secured him the attention
of the House, notwithstanding the home truths which he
uttered, to the utter discomfiture, so far as argument went,
of the protectionist orators. Sir William Clay discussed
several points at issue clearly and well. Lord Alfred
Churchill, sent from Woodstock, was, of course, in favour
of protection. Mr. James supported the motion, and so
did Lord Harry Vane, brother to the monopolist Duke of
Cleveland. Sir John Tyrell amused the House—it was
as much as he could do for protection.

Sir Robert Peel rose about ten o'clock and spoke for

nearly three hours. He seemed to feel as one emancipated from a long and hated thraldom, and spoke with great earnestness and power, vindicating his measures with consummate ability; and, confident of the favour of the house, indulging himself in a sarcastic pleasantry, upon some of the absurdities of his opponents, which excited bursts of laughter. He was luxuriating in his newly acquired liberty—a man renovated by the touch of truth—a statesman, not longer a led leader. After exhausting the field of argument and ridicule, he appealed to the justice and the humanity of the house :

"The memory of the winters of 1841 and 1842 never can be effaced from my recollection. Recollect the course we pursued. Then, on every occasion on which the sovereign met her parliament, there was the expression of the deepest sympathy with privation and suffering, but an expression, also, of the warmest admiration of the patience and fortitude with which they were borne. (Hear.) This time may recur. The years of plenteousness may intermit, and years of dearth may succeed. And if they do come, and if it be our duty again to express sympathy with sufferings, and again to exhort fortitude in their endurance, I do ask every man who hears me, to commune with his own heart, and to ask himself that question—If these calamitous times do come, if we must express sympathy with distress, if we must again proffer exhortations to fortitude, will it not be a consolation to reflect, that we have relieved ourselves from the heavy responsibility of regulating the supply of human food? (Great cheering.) Will not our expressions of sympathy seem more sincere ; will not our exhortations to fortitude be more impressive, if we can, at the same time say, and with pride, that in a time of comparative plenty, urged by no necessity, yielding to no clamour, we anticipated all those difficulties, and removed every impediment to the free circulation of the bounty of the Creator? (Loud cheers.) Will it not be a long and lasting consolation to us to be enabled to say to a suffering people, these calamities are the chastenings of an all-wise and beneficent Providence, inflicted for some great and humane purpose—perhaps to abate our pride, possibly to convince us of our nothingness, and awaken to a sense of our dependence; they are to be borne without repining at the dipensations of Providence, for they have not been aggravated by human institutions restricting the supply of food."

The resumption of the debate on Tuesday night was

retarded a short time by a motion brought on by Mr.
O'Connell, on the impending famine and disease in
Ireland. He appeared to be labouring under great debility,
and his splendid, full-toned voice, was subdued almost to
a whisper. The broken-spirited man being assured by
Sir James Graham that means would be used to mitigate
the calamity of his country, withdrew his motion. Lord
John Manners resumed the debate, and said that the time
was come for a settlement of the question, but that a
dissolution of parliament ought to be taken first to test the
opinion of the constituencies. Captain Layard, member
for Carlow, made a spirited speech, in favour of free trade,
and Mr. Robert Palmer, a prosy one against it. Mr. Shaw,
the Recorder of Dublin, previously a humble follower of
Sir Robert Peel, now charged him with treason, faithless-
ness, instability, cowardice, and trickery. Sir Charles
Napier, in his bluff sailor-like style, denied that agriculture
benefited by monopoly. Mr. Bright followed in a powerful
speech, the more powerful in effect that it followed so
much inanity. " The singularity of his position," says a
writer in the *Sun*, " as he rose to address the ministerialists
and oppositionists, seemed to animate him to an unwonted
pitch of rhetorical excellence ; his periods were, as usual,
adroitly and elegantly turned ; but in addition to this, they
alternately glittered with satire, and burnt and thrilled
with a tone even pathetic." He was generously eloquent
in defence of his former antagonist. " I watched the right
honourable baronet go home last night," he said, " and I
confess I envied him the ennobling feelings which must
have filled his breast after delivering that speech—a speech,
I venture to say, more powerful and more to be admired
than any speech ever heard in this house, within the
memory of any man in it ;" and in allusion to the bitter
denunciations which were poured on the minister by his
former supporters, he said : " When the right honourable
baronet resigned, he was no longer your minister ; he

came back to office as the minister of the sovereign, as
the minister of the people, and not again as the minister
of a class who made him such for their own selfish
objects." It was observed by those who sat near Sir
Robert, that the tears started into his eyes at this unexpected generosity. Mr. Bright was followed by Mr.
Hudson, a coarse man, who was at that time celebrated for
his railway successes, and had been returned by Sunderland, in preference to Colonel Thompson, because the
constituency expected him to build some docks there.
His defence of monopoly was such as might have been
expected from such a person. The debate was again
adjourned.

On Thursday, the debate was resumed by Lord Duncan,
who was followed by Alderman Thomson; Sir William
Molesworth, who made an excellent speech; Mr. Benet,
who said that a mortal blow was aimed at the agricultural
interest; Mr. Henry Berkeley, for the motion; Mr. John
Tollemache, against it; Mr. Thomas Duncombe, in a tone
of banter directed against both promoters and objectors;
Sir T. D. Acland, who could not very well tell what he
wished to be done; Lord A. Paget, who would rather have
immediate than prospective repeal; and Mr. W. B. Baring,
who said that protection now was unnecessary. Again the
House was adjourned.

There was nothing in the Friday night's debate worth
notice, except a long speech by Mr. Disraeli; noticeable
only for its virulence against Sir Robert Peel. Again there
was an adjournment. Monday night's debate had more
diversity, for Sir George Clerk, vice-president of the board
of trade, emancipated, like his leader, made a good speech.
Another adjournment took place. On Tuesday, Mr.
Goulburn, the chancellor of the exchequer, also emancipated, made a better speech than any one would have
expected of him. Before another adjournment, Mr. Ferrand,
substituting abuse, in which he excelled, for argument, of

which he was incapable, denounced the factory system as having a tendency to produce murder and every atrocity. On Thursday, after Mr. Ferrand's slanders had received prompt and indignant contradiction, the debate was resumed by Mr. Ross, of Belfast, who showed the benefit that would accrue to Ireland from free trade. Mr. Beckett Denison expressed a high opinion of Sir Robert Peel's integrity, but could not follow him in his free-trade policy. Mr. Brotherton made a sensible speech, which told well on the House. Mr. Edward Cardwell, secretary to the treasury, spoke ably, clearly, and logically; and Mr. Villiers closed the night's debate with an excellent and closely reasoned speech, in which the position of the question was pointed out, and the helplessness of the protectionists exposed with great spirit.

The debate was resumed on Friday by Mr. G. Bankes, who expressed his hope that in another place (the Lords) such delay might take place as would allow the constituencies to speak out. Mr. B. Escott supported the motion, and Captain Gladstone opposed it. Mr. Cobden told the monopolists that the majority in that House would be against them; and that it would be increased by an appeal to the constituencies :—

"You want a dissolution in order to ascertain the opinion of the country. Have you ever thought, or considered, or defined what the opinion of the country means? (Hear.) Do you think it means a numerical majority of this House? We shall have that to-night. (Loud cheers.) You are not satisfied with that. (Hear, hear.) You are preaching the democratic doctrine, that this question must be referred to the people. (Hear, and a laugh.) Now, I want to have well defined what you mean by public opinion. You will perhaps say, 'We will abide by the decision of a numerical majority of this House returned at another general election,' and you will consider that the decision of the country. Well, I totally disagree with all those who believe for a moment that you would obtain a numerical majority in this House in the event of a dissolution. (Hear, and cheers.) I ought to know as much about the state of the representation of this country, and of the registration, as any man in the House. (Hear, and cheers.) Probably no one has given so much attention to that question as I have done; and I distinctly deny that you have the slightest probability of gaining a numerical majority in this House, if a dissolution took place to-morrow. Now, I would not have said this three months ago. (Hear.) On the contrary, at a public meeting three months ago, I distinctly recognised the great probability of your having a numerical majority in the event of a dissolution. But your party is since broken up. Though you may still have a firm phalanx in Dorsetshire and Buckinghamshire, what has been the effect of the separation from you of the most authoritative and intelligent of your party upon the boroughs, and among the population of the north? I told you, three years ago, that the Con- servatives of the towns of the north of England were not the followers of the Duke of Richmond. They were, almost to a man, the followers of that section of the government represented by the first lord of the treasury and the right honourable home secre- tary. (Hear, hear.) Every one acquainted with the towns in the north of England will bear me out when I say that those conservatives who follow the right honourable baronet (Sir R. Peel) comprise at least four-fifths of the party, while the remainder may look up to the Duke of Richmond as their leader, and sympathise with the section below the gangway. That large portion of the conservative party in the north of England has ever been in favour of free trade. The language they have used to free-traders like myself has been this: ' Sir Robert will do it at the proper time. (Hear, hear, and cheers.) We have confidence in him; and, when the proper period arrives, he will give us free trade.' (Renewed cheers.) Then I say that, in this state of your party, I wholly deny the possibility of your gaining a majority. But I will assume, for the sake of argument, that, in the event of a dissolution of parliament, you obtained a numerical majority. Let us see of what that majority, and of what the minority opposed to you, would consist. (Hear, hear.) There are 18 representatives in parliament for this metropolis, and there are two members for the metropolitan county. We have the whole 20. (Loud cheers.) They represent 110,000 electors; they represent a population of 2,000,000 of souls—(hear, hear); the most intelligent, the most wealthy, the most orderly, and—notwith- standing my acquaintance with the business habits of those in the north of England—I must add, with respect to business and mechanical life, the hardest working people in England. (Hear, hear.) Do those people express public opinion, think you? Why, this metropolis assumed to itself, centuries ago, the power and privilege of closing its gates in the face of its sovereign,—a power which is still retained, and which is exercised on state occasions. This metropolis is now twenty times as populous, as wealthy, as important in the world's eye, as it was

then; and do you think it will be content that you count it as nothing
in your estimate of public opinion? (Hear, hear, and cheers.) But
turn elsewhere. What says the metropolis of Scotland, Edinburgh?
Do you reckon on having a member for that city to vote in the glorious
majority which you anticipate? (Hear, hear.) Turn to Dublin. Will
you have a representative for that city with you? Go to Glasgow,
Manchester, Leeds, Birmingham, and Liverpool; take every town
containing 20,000 inhabitants, and I defy you to show that you can
reckon on a single representative for any town in the kingdom which
has such a population. I tell you that you have not with you now a
town in Great Briiain containing 20,000 inhabitants. ('Oh, oh!' from
the protectionists; some honourable members mentioning 'Liverpool,'
and 'Bristol.') No, no, no; you have neither Liverpool nor Bristol.
(A laugh.) That shows you have not weighed these matters as you are
bound to weigh them. (Laughter.) Don't be led away by the men
who cheer and hallo there, like the school boy whistling in the church-
yard to keep up his courage. Examine these facts, for those who were
formerly your leaders have weighed them already—(hear, hear, and
cheers),—and there is none among you deserving to be your leaders
unless they have well considered these important matters. I repeat that
you cannot reckon upon any town of 20,000 inhabitants sending up a
representative to vote with the great majority you expect to obtain.
True, you will have your pocket boroughs, and your nomination counties. (Hear, hear.) And I will say a word or two directly as to the
county representation. But I now place before you broadly the situation
in which you will find yourselves after a dissolution. I will assume that
you have a majority, derived from pocket boroughs and nomination
counties, of twenty or thirty members. But on this side you will see
the representatives for London, for South Lancashire, for West Yorkshire, for North Cheshire, for North Lancashire, and the members
for all the large towns of England, Ireland, and Scotland: nay,
not one member will come from any town in Scotland to vote with
you. (Hear.) Now, what would then be your situation? Why, you
shrink aghast from the position in which you would find yourselves.
There would be more defections from your ranks, pledged as you are,—
steeped to the chin in pledges. So much alarmed would you be at your
position that you would cross the floor to join us in larger numbers than
you have ever yet done. (Laughter.) I tell you there would be no
safety for you without it. I say that the members who came up under
such circumstances, to attempt to maintain the Corn Laws, from your
Ripons and Stamfords, Woodstocks and Marlboroughs, would hold those
opinions only till they found it was determined by public opinion to
repeal them. They could not hold them one week longer; for, if the

country found that they would not give way to moral force, they might think it requisite to place them in another Schedule A. (Laughter.)"

Mr. Cobden proceeded to notice the state of the agricultural counties where the protectionists did not dare to call meetings, and reminded them of the progress which was made there in the purchase of forty-shilling freeholds, which would soon neutralize the effects of the Chandos clause; asserted that the farmers and farm-labourers now denied that protection was any benefit to them; invited the House to recognise the principles that the community should not be taxed for the benefit of a class; and concluded by saying: " We have set an example to the world in all ages; we have given them the representative system. Why, the very rules and regulations of this House have been taken as the model for every representative assembly throughout the whole civilized world; and having besides given them the example of a free press, of civil and religious liberty, and of every institution that belongs to freedom and civilisation, we are now about to offer a still greater example; we are going to set the example of making industry free—to set the example of giving the whole world every advantage in every clime, and latitude, and production; relying ourselves on the freedom of our industry. Yes, we are going to teach the world that other lesson. Don't think there is anything selfish in this, or anything at all discordant with Christian principles. I can prove that we advocate nothing but what is agreeable to the highest behests of Christianity. To buy in the cheapest market and sell in the dearest. What is the meaning of the maxim? It means that you take the article which you have in the greatest abundance, and obtain from others that of which they have the most to spare, so giving to mankind the means of enjoying the fullest abundance of every earthly good, and in doing so carrying out to the fullest extent the Christian doctrine of

' Doing unto all men as ye would they should do unto you.' "

Mr. Spooner was proceeding to express the reasons which induced him to support the amendment in preference to the proposition of the government; but the interruptions in the House were so frequent that it was impossible to follow the chain of his arguments. Mr. P. Borthwick followed on the same side amid still greater interruptions. Lord G. Bentinck condemned the proposition of the government as vicious in principle, and likely to be deeply injurious, not only to agriculture, but to all the great interests of the country. He contended that the rate of wages would fall with the price of corn, and that the working classes would be better off with undiminished wages and wheat at 70s. per quarter, than with corn at 45s. and reduced means of procuring it. The apprehension of famine was altogether a mistake. The crop was more than an average one in some parts of the country; in Scotland particularly, there was a positive repletion, and the potato murrain was by no means so extensive as it had been represented!

The House divided at twenty minutes to three o'clock. The numbers were for the motion—

Ayes 337
Noes 240
                                              ____
            Majority against it 97

The House then resolved itself *pro forma* into committee. The chairman was ordered to report progress, and to ask leave to sit again on Monday.

CHAPTER XXIV.

TERMINATION OF THE CONTEST.

A majority of ninety-seven in so large a House, when the question was only whether it should go into committee or not, offered no very strong gaurantee that the measures would pass unmutilated through the committee. Of the whole county members, 149 had voted against the motion, and 67 for it. Of the tories, 231 had voted against, and 112 for it. There might be a secession from the majority, in favour either of a higher scale of duties for the three years, or against the abolition of that scale after the three years; and if that secession amounted to 40 or 50, the measure either would be defeated, or carried by so very small a majority, as to encourage the Lords to throw it out. The division, however, gave an encouraging view of the state of opinion out of doors, for while the borough members, who voted in the majority, represented 286,373 electors, those who voted in the minority, represented only 31,268. The apprehension, on one view of the subject, and the hope inspired by the other, gave additional vigour to the Anti-Corn-Law agitation, which, throughout the country, had been uninterrupted by the declarations of the the ministers and the long-protracted debate.

Sir Robert Peel must have felt, that those who demanded that repeal should not be prospective but immediate, were his best supporters, and had availed himself of the first opportunity to remove from their minds the hostility which had been engendered by his hasty accusation of

Mr. Cobden.   Mr. Ferrand, in the last night of the debate
had unconsciously presented that opportunity. After a
torrent of abuse of the League, Mr. Bright reminded him
how he had shrunk from maintaining, in a court of justice,
his base allegation that Mr. George Wilson and Mr.
William Rawson were present at a public meeting, where
the idea of assassinating the prime minister was started.
This point was taken up by Mr. Disraeli in a speech, in
which he criticized the League, praised the purity of his
own motives, and censured, "with a bitterness amounting
to cold ferocity," the manners and conduct of Mr. Roebuck, who had said that the minister should retract his
accusâtion.   This brought up both Sir Robert and Mr.
Cobden :

" Sir R. Peel said, 'I did not mean to take part in this discussion,
and should not have done so but for some observations that have fallen
from the hon. member for Shrewsbury, in which he recalled to recollection something that occurred, I think three years ago, in the course of a
debate at that time, in which I put an erroneous construction on some
remarks of the hon. member for Stockport. (Hear, hear). That hon.
gentleman made an explanation of the meaning of the expressions he
then used; I followed the hon. gentleman in the course of the debate,
and my intention, after that explanation was distinctly to relieve him
him from the imputation I had cast on him under my erroneous apprehension of the remarks he had made. (Hear, hear.) If any one who was
present at that debate had hinted to me that my reparation was not
complete, and that my acceptation of the disavowal was less unequivocal
than it should have been, I should have taken the earliest opportunity
of stating what I meant to convey. This was my intention, and I think
a reference to the record of the debate will show that this must have
been my intention. I am sorry, Sir, that the hon. member for Shrewsbury has thought fit to revive the subject; at least I should be sorry that
he has done so, if it did not give me an opportunity of stating what my
intention was, and of entirely withdrawing the imputation I threw out
under what was at the time an erroneous impression. (Hear, hear).'

" Mr. Cobden (who spoke from the lower part of the house) said—' I
feel happy that the right hon. baronet has had an opportunity of correct-
ing what fell from each other on a former occasion. At the time the
occurrence took place I did feel, and I think the country felt, that the
right hon. baronet's language did not convey that distinct disavowal

which it might have done, and which was due to me. (Hear, hear.) Still, the matter itself was so extraordinary, and so incapable of bearing the interpretation which many on that side of the House put upon it, that I did not see how I could return to it. I take the present statement, however, as a full and entire disavowal of the imputation made by the right hon. baronet, and I am glad it has been made, since it gives me the opportunity—quite as pleasant to my feelings as to those of the right hon. baronet; of expressing my regret that whilst the remembrance of what had passed in this House was rankling in my mind, I have alluded to the right hon. gentleman in terms which I lament having adopted. After the explanation that has been given, I hope no one will feel justified in ever alluding to the matter.' "

The free traders in the Commons, while they gave their cordial support to the minister in his arduous struggle against a selfish and an unreasoning obstruction, held firmly to the principle of immediate repeal. On Monday, March 1st, when the House went into committee, Mr. Villiers moved, by way of amendment on the first resolution, " That all duties on imported corn do now eease and determine." He supported his motion in a speech of brief duration, but full of unanswerable argument, urged with great force. Sir John Tyrrell and Colonel Sibthorp first amused and then tired the House with their objurgations. Mr. Goring revived the old " whine" about incumbrances, which led to a reply from Mr. Bright, that the agriculturists thought their complaints were more pitiable than the appeal in Dickens' to " vote for Scroggins and eleven small children." Mr. Gibson made a spirited speech, showing the absurdity of delay. Sir R. Peel defended his measure mainly on the ground that it would allow importation at a reasonable duty. Lord John Russell wished the settlement of the question to be then, instead of being delayed for three years. After much clamour, the debate was adjourned· It was resumed next evening, when Mr. Cobden warned the obstructives against a protracted resistance, which would compel the Anti-Corn-Law League to maintain its agitation, and concentrate its energies. The House then divided, and the numbers were :—

For Mr. Villiers' Amendment 78

Against it 267

The following are the names of the spirited men who, true to their free-trade principles, voted in the minority for the amendment :—

MINORITY—NOES.

Bannerman, A	Evans, Sir De Lacy	Parker, J
Berkeley, C	Ewart, W	Pattison, J
Berkeley, Hon Captain	Fielden, J	Pechell, Captain
Berkeley, Hon H. F	Ferguson, Colonel	Philips, M
Blewitt, R. J	Fitzroy, Lord C.	Plumridge, Captain
Bouverie, Hon E. P	Fox, C. R	Protheroe, E
Bowring, Dr	Gibson, T. M	Ross, D. R
Brotherton, J	Hall, Sir B	Russell, Lord E
Busfield, W	Hastie, A	Stansfield, W. R. C
Chapman, B	Hindley, C	Staunton, Sir G. T
Christie, W. D	Holland, R	Stuart, Lord J
Cobden, R	Langston, J. H	Strutt, E
Colborne, Hon W. N. R	Layard, Captain	Tancred, H. W
Collett, J	M'Carthy, A	Thornely, T
Crawford, W. S	M'Taggart, Sir J	Trelawny, J. S
Currie, R	Marjoribanks, S	Troubridge, Sir E. T
Dalmeny, Lord	Marshall, W	Walker, R
Dalrymple, Captain	Martin, J	Warburton, H
Dennistoun, J	Mitcalf, H	Ward, H. G
Duncan, Viscount	Mitchell, T. A	Wawn, J. T
Duncan, G	Moffatt, G	White, S
Dundas, Admiral	Morpeth, Viscount	Williams, W
Ebrington, Viscount	Morris, D	Wood, C
Ellice, E	O'Connell, D	Yorke, H. R
Elphinstone, H	O'Connell, M. J	Tellers.
Escott, B	O'Connell, J	Villiers, C
Etwall, R	Oswald, J	Bright, J.

The history of the League draws to a close. Its members in the House of Commons had done their duty to its principles. Thereafter they were merged amongst the body which supported the minister in his really noble struggle with the stubborn obstructionists. Inch by inch the ground was gained, and it was not until the 27th March, after probably the most statesmanlike speech that Sir

Robert Peel ever delivered, that the second reading was carried, the numbers being :

For the second reading 302
Against it 214

Notwithstanding this very decided majority, and, notwithstanding the almost universal expression of feeling in the country, in favour of free trade, the protectionists fought most stubbornly against any innovation on their "vested right" to tax the community for their own especial benefit, and it was not until four o'clock in the morning of Saturday, May 16th, that the third reading was carried. Near the conclusion of the debate, Sir Robert Peel delivered a speech of great eloquence and power, from which the following are a few passages :

"You have a right, I admit, to taunt me with my change of opinion on the corn laws; but when you say by my adoption of the principles of free trade, I have acted in contradiction to those principles which I have always avowed during my whole life, that charge, at least, I say is destitute of foundation. Sir, I will not enter at this late hour into the discussion of any other topic; I foresaw the consequences that have resulted from the measures which I thought it my duty to propose. We were charged with the heavy responsibility of taking security against a great calamity in Ireland. We did not act lightly. We did not form our opinion upon merely local information—the information of local authorities likely to be inflamed by an undue alarm. Before I, and those who agreed with me, came to that conclusion, we had adopted every means—by local inquiry, and by sending perfectly disinterested persons of authority to Ireland to form a just and correct opinion. Whether we were mistaken or not—I believe we were not mistaken, but even if we were mistaken, a generous construction should be put upon the motives and conduct of those who are charged with the responsibility of *protecting millions of subjects of the Queen from the consequences of scarcity and famine.* * * * * My earnest wish has been, during my tenure of power, to impress the people of this country with a belief that the legislature was animated by a sincere desire to frame its legislation upon the principles of equity and justice. I have a strong belief that the greatest object which we or any other government can contemplate should be to elevate the social condition of that class of the people with whom we are brought into no direct relation by the exercise of elective franchise. I wish to convince them that our object has been so to apportion taxation that we shall relieve industry and labour from any undue burden, and transfer it, so far as it is consistent with the public good, to those who are better enabled to bear it. I look to the present peace of this country; I look to the absence of all disturbance—to the non-existence of any commitment for a seditious offence; I look to the calm that prevails in the public mind; I look to the absence of all disaffection; I look to the increased and growing public confidence on account of the course you have taken in relieving trade from restrictions, and industry from unjust burdens; and where there was disatisfaction, I see contentment; and where there was turbulence, I see there is peace; where there was disloyalty, I see there is loyalty. I see a disposition to confide in you, and not to agitate questions that are at the foundations of your institutions."

On the division, the members were :

    For the third reading 327

    Against it 229

                                  ———

      Majority............................. 98

In the House of Lords there was less delay than was anticipated. For the second reading, there was a majority of 47. On the 22d May the bill was passed, and became law on the 26th.

From May, 1815, to May 1846, a period nearly equal to the life time of an entire generation, the nation had suffered grievous wrong. During all that long period, comfort and prosperity had been only exceptions to the rule of wide-spread misery. The law was mitigated now : in three years more it was to cease. The man who had long supported the heavy infliction, at last yielding to the calls of justice and humanity, and breaking through all the ties and trammels of party, and earning, by his last and best act, the gratitude of his country and a deathless fame, soon after lost the official position for which he was now so well qualified. In the last speech he made before quitting office, he said :—

"I must say, with reference to hon. gentlemen opposite, as I say with reference to ourselves, neither of us is the party which is justly entitled to the credit of those measures. There has been a combination of parties, and that combination, and the influence of government, have led to their ultimate success; but the name which ought to be, and will be associated with the success of those measures, is the name of the man who, acting, I believe, from pure and disinterested motives, has, with untiring energy, by appeals to reason, enforced their necessity with an eloquence the more to be admired because it was unaffected and unadorned—the name which ought to be associated with the success of those measures, is the name of RICHARD COBDEN. Sir, I now close the address which it has been my duty to make to the House, thanking them sincerely for the favour with which they have listened to me in performing the last act of my official career. Within a few hours, probably, that favour which I have held for the period of five years will be surrendered into the hands of another—without repining—I can say without complaint—with a more lively recollection of the support and confidence I have received than of the opposition which, during a recent period, I have met with. I shall leave office, with a name, severely censured, I fear, by many who, on public grounds, deeply regret the severance of party ties—deeply regret that severance, not from interested or personal motives, but from the firm conviction that fidelity to party engagements—the existence and maintenance of a great party—constitutes a powerful instrument of government. I shall surrender power severely censured also by others who, from no interested motives, adhere to the principle of protection, considering the maintenance of it to be essential to the welfare and interests of the country. I shall leave a name execrated by every monopolist who, from less honourable motives, clamours for protection because it conduces to his own individual benefit; but IT MAY BE THAT I SHALL LEAVE A NAME SOMETIMES REMEMBERED WITH EXPRESSIONS OF GOOD-WILL IN THE ABODES OF THOSE WHOSE LOT IT IS TO LABOUR, AND TO EARN THEIR DAILY BREAD BY THE SWEAT OF THEIR BROW, WHEN THEY SHALL RECRUIT THEIR EXHAUSTED STRENGTH WITH ABUNDANT AND UNTAXED FOOD, THE SWEETER BECAUSE IT IS NO LONGER LEAVENED BY THE SENSE OF INJUSTICE."

These latter emphatic words are engraved on the pedestal of one of the statues erected to the memory of the statesman; and the thought will arise in the minds of multitudes who peruse them, that a still deeper debt of gratitude is due to those whose long continued and energetic efforts led to the recognition of an enlightened commercial policy, which has set an example to all the nations of the earth.

On the 2nd July, a meeting was held in the Manchester Town Hall of the Council of the League, attended not only by the resident executive body, but of members from all parts of the kingdom.   Mr. G. Wilson, the chairman, gave a sketch of the operations of the League from its first formation to its triumph. Mr. Cobden then addressed the meeting, congratulating them not only on the success achieved, but on the instruction conveyed to the people, which would render it impossible ever again to impose the Corn Laws. Of the premier, he said: "If he has lost office, he has gained a country. For my part, I would rather descend into private life with that last measure of his, which led to his discomfiture, in my hand, than mount to the highest pinnacle of human power."   He acknowledged with gratitude Lord John Russell's latter services, and the services of such men as Mr. Deacon Hume, Mr. M'Gregor, and Mr. Porter, for their statistics, arguments, and facts ; and in reference to his own labours and those of his colleagues, said : " Many people will think that we have our reward in the applause and *eclat* of public meetings; but I declare that it is not so with me, for the inherent reluctance I have to address public meetings is so great that I do not even get up to present a petition to the House of Commons without reluctance.   I, therefore, hope I may be believed when I say that, if this agitation terminates now, it will be very acceptable to my feelings; but if there should be the same necessity, the same feeling which impelled me to take the part I have taken, will impel me to a new agitation—ay, and with tenfold more vigour, after having had a little time to recruit my health."   He moved : " That an act of parliament having been passed, providing for the abolition of the Corn Laws in February, 1849, it is deemed expedient to suspend the active operation of the Anti-Corn-Law League; and the executive council in Manchester is hereby requested to take the necessary steps for making up and closing the affairs of the League with as little delay as possible."   Mr. Bright, in an eloquent speech, seconded the resolution, which was carried unanimously.   Mr. R. H. Greg moved, and Mr. Henry

Ashworth seconded the next resolution : " That after the payment of the first instalment (20 per cent.) the subscribers of the £250,000 League Fund be released from all further liabilities." It was carried unanimously. Mr. Edward Baines, jun., of Leeds, then moved : " That the Council of the League, whilst discontinuing its own operations, cannot be insensible to the intimation given in both houses of parliament, of a determination to contest the ensuing general election with a view to obtain the repeal of the corn importation bill ; and under these circumstances, the Council offer their earnest recommendation to the free traders in the parliamentary constituencies to continue their vigilant attention to the registration, so as to be able to return a decided free-trade majority to the next House of Commons." Mr. P. A. Taylor, of London, seconded the resolution, which was carried unanimously. Mr. William Brown, of Liverpool, and Mr. John Cheetham, of Stalybridge, both of them afterwards members for South Lancashire, moved and seconded a motion : " That in case any serious attempts were made by the protectionist party to induce the legislation to retrace its steps, or prevent the final extinction of the Corn Law in 1849, the gentlemen who have hitherto so ably fulfilled the duties of the executive council, be hereby authorized to call the League into renewed existence." Mr. F. R. Atkinson counselled free traders to keep a sharp look out, and " keep their powder dry," as he feared there would be some treachery. Mr. George Thomas, of Bristol, thought the resolution was the safety valve. It was then put and carried unanimously.

Mr. John Whitaker, of Hurst, then moved : " That Mr. Wilson should leave the chair, and Mr. Robert Hyde Greg should take his place." Mr. Greg having taken the chair, Mr. Cobden, adverting to the labours of the executive council, stated that Mr. Wilson had attended meetings, at which resolutions had been passed, 1,361 times ; Mr. Prentice, 1,117 times ; Mr. S. Lees, 863 times ; Mr. W. Rawson, 601 times ;

Mr. T. Woolley, 485 times; Mr. W. Bickham, 474 times; Mr. W. Evans, 444 times ; and Mr. Henry Rawson, 258 times. In an early part of the agitation, Mr. Wilson, who gave almost his entire time to its business, had been pressed to accept a salary of £500 a-year, which he declined. He had afterwards been urged to accept £1000 a-year, which he also declined, and never received a farthing of remuneration for his unceasing labours. He concluded by moving that Mr. Wilson be requested to accept a sum of not less than £10,000 for his invaluable services. The motion was seconded by Mr. Smith, and supported by Mr. Brotherton, M.P., Mr. Biggs, of Leicester, now M.P., and myself, and carried by acclamation.

Mr. Rathbone of Liverpool, seconded by Mr. Biggs, moved ; " That the members of the Executive Council of the League are entitled to the warmest gratitude of the League and of the country, for their high-principled, laborious, and most successful labours during the seven years of our constitutional agitation ; and that a committee be appointed, consisting of Joseph Brotherton, M.P., and such gentlemen as he may associate with himself to determine on some suitable testimonial to those gentlemen out of the funds of the League." The resolution was carried unanimously. (The testimonial took the shape of a tea and coffee silver service, of 240 ounces, to each of the gentlemen whose names had been read by Mr. Cobden after Mr. Wilson's.) The chairman then said: " As no other gentleman has anything to address to this meeting, it is now my duty to say that the Anti-Corn-Law League stands conditionally dissolved."

An air of grave solemnity had spread over the meeting, as it drew to a close. There were five hundred gentlemen who had often met together during the great contest, and, notwithstanding their exultation over a victory achieved, the feeling stole over their minds that they were never to meet again. Mr. Cobden reminded them that they were under obligations to the Queen who was said to have favoured their cause as one of humanity and justice, and three hearty cheers in her honour loyally closed the proceedings.

The cessation of active operations by the League was followed by a spontaneous act of justice and gratitude to its acknowledged leader. In a very short period the sum of £75,000 was presented to Mr. Cobden by the free traders of the kingdom. By a similar spontaneous movement, Mr. Bright, his friend and closest coadjutor in the great struggle, was presented with a splendid library.

The advice of Mr. Atkinson to "keep their powder dry," was not neglected by the free-traders. The registrations were strictly attended to, and before there was any seeming danger to the existence of free trade, Mr. Cobden was a member for the West Riding of Yorkshire; Mr. Bright for Manchester; Mr. Brown, and Mr. John Cheetham, for South Lancashire; Mr. James Heywood for North Lancashire; and the people's strength in the Commons had been considerably increased, when, six years after the conditional dissolution of the League, the usurpation of office by the Derby-Disraeli ministry threatened the safety of free trade measures. The League was revived, a £50,000 fund was asked for, and in a great proportion subscribed, and active operations were commenced and continued until the danger was over. Not one of the ruinous results prophecied, have occurred from the repeal of the Corn Laws; and those who laboured for the destruction of those poverty-creating enactments, can now look with deep satisfaction on the improved condition of the great mass of the people, emancipated from a cruel subjection to class interests.

Manchester, 30th September, 1853.